Brief Contents

iii

Extended Contents

Guided Tour

Part overviews

At the start of each part is an outline of the common themes shared by the chapters in the part, as well as an introduction to the key arguments of each individual chapter.

Chapter overviews

Each chapter begins with short summary of the chapter to aid navigation.

Key terms

A list of terms at the start of each chapter helps to identify the important concepts covered in the chapter.

Issues questions

Questions at the start of each chapter help to foster a questioning and reflective approach by outlining some of the broad questions the chapter raises.

Activities

Throughout the book, activities test students' understanding of the topics and make links from theory to practice.

Glossary definitions

At the points in the text that they need to be understood, the key terms and concepts are defined. The definitions are also collected in a glossary at the end of the book.

Think about it questions

These questions pinpoint the significant topics and encourage a questioning and reflective approach to the issues raised.

Chapter summaries

A concise summary at the end of each chapter helps students to identify the most important issues covered in the chapter.

Tutorial questions

Questions at the end of each chapter encourage discussion and debate.

Recommended reading & websites

Lists of recommended chapter-specific readings and websites allow students to explore different subjects in more detail and provide resources for assignments.

Theory links

Notes in the margins indicate other chapters that include discussion of the same theories.

Part summaries

At the end of each part is a summary of the common themes of the part, with questions to aid understanding and recommended readings to assist further learning.

Contributors

Simon Burton is Associate Professor of Sociology in the School of Sociology and Social Studies at the University of KwaZulu-Natal, South Africa.

Nico Carpentier is a Lecturer at the Communication Studies Departments of the Free University of Brussels (VUB) and the Catholic University of Brussels (KUB).

Jackie Cook is a Lecturer in the School of Communications at the University of South Australia in Adelaide.

Tim Dwyer is a Lecturer in Media Policy and Research in the School of Communication Arts, University of Western Sydney.

Gunn Enli is a Research Fellow in the Department of Media and Communication at the University of Oslo.

Jacqui Ewart is a Senior Lecturer in Journalism with the School of Arts Media and Culture at Griffith University in Brisbane.

Susan Forde is a Senior Lecturer in Journalism with the School of Arts Media and Culture at Griffith University in Brisbane.

Kerrie Foxwell is a Lecturer in Journalism with the School of Arts Media and Culture at Griffith University in Brisbane.

Gerard Goggin is Professor and Deputy Director in the Centre for Social Research in Journalism and Communication at the University of New South Wales.

Anton van der Hoven is a Professor and Head of the Media and Cultural Studies Programme at the University of KwaZulu-Natal, Pietermaritzburg, South Africa.

Ullamaija Kivikuru is Professor of Journalism and Head of Research in the Swedish School of Social Sciences at the University of Helsinki.

Elaine Lally is Senior Research Fellow and Assistant Director of the Centre for Cultural Research at the University of Western Sydney.

Stephen Lax is Lecturer in Communications Technology at the Institute of Communications Studies, University of Leeds.

Celia Lury is Professor and Department Head of the Sociology Department at Goldsmiths College, University of London.

Jim McGuigan is Professor of Cultural Analysis in the Department of Social Sciences at Loughborough University.

Michael Meadows is Associate Professor in Journalism at Griffith University in Brisbane.

Graham Murdock is Reader in the Sociology of Culture at Loughborough University.

Christopher Newell is Associate Professor in the School of Medicine, University of Tasmania.

Virginia Nightingale is Associate Professor in the School of Communication Arts, University of Western Sydney.

Juan Francisco Salazar is Lecturer in Media Studies in the School of Communication Arts, University of Western Sydney.

Trine Syvertsen is Professor in the Department of Media and Communication at the University of Oslo.

Herman Wasserman lectures in Media, Communication and Cultural Studies at the University of Newcastle, UK, and is Associate Professor Extraordinary in the Department of Journalism, University of Stellenbosch, South Africa.

Derek Wilding is Manager, Compliance, Monitoring and Review (Control Section) at the Australian Communications and Media Authority.

Acknowledgments

The production of this book has been supported by strong ties of international collaboration, collegiality and friendship. In their different ways, the contributors have produced a critique of the impact of new media that has exceeded our initial expectations. Their scholarship and commitment to research has added a welcome complexity and depth to the issues the book addresses.

The International Association for Media and Communication Research provided the context for developing collaborative ties with many of the international scholars whose work is included in the book. In this regard it has been a privilege to work with Ullamaija Kivikuru, Nico Carpentier, Trine Syvertsen, Gunn Enli, Simon Burton and Anton van der Hoven, and Herman Wasserman. Their involvement in the project has significantly enriched the book. Beyond IAMCR, and still on the international scene, we are indebted to two contributors we had neither met nor worked with prior to this project, and yet who entrusted their work to our collection. In this regard we particularly acknowledge the work of Celia Lury and Stephen Lax.

Virginia and Tim both wish also to acknowledge the importance, not just for this project but over many years, of their links with the Social Science Department at Loughborough University. While Jim McGuigan and Graham Murdock each provided important chapters for this book, the Social Science Department hosted both Virginia and Tim during their respective periods of academic leave in 2005 and 2006. The collegiality and friendship of Peter Golding and Mike Pickering are noted in this regard.

The Australian contributors to this collection address a cross-section of Australian research of relevance to the social and cultural analysis of the impact of new media and the development of media policy. We count it an honour that Gerard Goggin and Chris Newell, Jackie Cook, Juan Salazar, Elaine Lally, Derek Wilding and the team from Griffith University made time to develop chapters for our collection. These chapters provide a strong statement about the work of Australian researchers in this emerging field.

On a practical note, the School of Communication Arts at the University of Western Sydney has provided the scholarly environment that has produced this book. We have valued the support of this publication project in the form of research time and personal encouragement, particularly from Hart Cohen, Stephen Sheehan and the Head of School, Professor Lynette Sheridan Burns. From UWS, this book includes the work not only of Virginia and Tim, but also of our colleagues Juan Salazar and Elaine Lally from the University's Centre for Cultural Research. The emergence of an environment of collaboration between the School of Communication Arts and the Centre for Cultural Research has enlarged the field of discussion and debate around the social and cultural analysis of new media at the University, and the production of this book provided a context for putting that collaboration into practice.

We also extend our sincere thanks firstly to Debra James of Oxford University Press for recommending the publication of the book, and secondly to Lucy McLoughlin for guiding us through the production process. The support and follow-up from Oxford University Press, from Tim Campbell and Liz Filleul in particular, has been exceptional.

Finally and most importantly, we acknowledge the selfless support and encouragement of our families, Garry and Anna and Susan and Declan, who have witnessed the late nights and long weekends the publication of this book has demanded of us.

Introduction

This book provides an illuminating insight into the ways in which people reconfigure their worlds around the new digital devices of cyber culture, and the role that industries, policy makers and technologies play in the management of users and audiences for new media. In planning it, we have sought to create a space where the social and cultural impact of media technologies could be discussed alongside case studies and contemporary analysis of the realities and diversity of today's media world. We wanted this book to differ in orientation from usual analyses of technoculture by taking an audience-oriented approach, and by highlighting the impact of new technologies and new media on the world experienced by audiences as citizens, consumers and communities.

The researchers and theorists who responded to our call for contributions were invited to either discuss the social, cultural and economic aspects of digitisation, convergence, interactivity and globalisation, or alternatively to report on their research into the reconfiguration of personal, local, regional and national media spaces and audiences. We were delighted that so many high-profile researchers responded to our invitation, and subsequently provided us with the contributions included in this excellent collection of scholarship and research.

New media worlds

We chose the title 'New Media Worlds', knowing that there is currently considerable debate about whether and to what extent there is in fact anything 'new' about the changes associated with digital media—changes such as mobility, connectivity, networks as audience formations, increasing commercialisation, individualisation and privatisation, and dependence of the new media on user-generated content. However, we believe that at the very least the new media accelerate social change, and for this reason it is important that students in the developed world understand that their assumptions and expectations about the range of media services available to them, services they have probably grown up with, are not necessarily universally shared.

The media world we live in today offers individuals vastly different opportunities depending on when, where and to whom they happen to have been be born. The global diffusion of media technologies is uneven and incomplete—even in the developed world. Global connectivity does not guarantee access for all, and the primarily commercial rollout of Internet access increases economic, social and cultural divisions, particularly in the underdeveloped world. The character of this book therefore reflects our attempt to develop a global agenda to contextualise the experiences of those who grow up in a world rich in media services with the realities facing those from less richly endowed media environments. The diverse realities discussed by our contributors, however, look inwards at the unevenness of service in the developed world, as much as outwards at the limited nature of the services available in the developing world, and forward to the unknowable but promising future.

Challenges for convergence

The convergence process is the process whereby new technologies are accommodated by existing media and communication industries and cultures. The fact that the term 'convergence' is used to describe the process is an indication that the confrontation of old and new technologies is a far from simple process.

This book therefore challenges the view that social networking and the privileged position assigned to user-generated content reflects an inherently democratising bias in the emerging media cultures. It argues instead that audience/user access and participation cannot be separated from policy and access issues, many of which are as yet unresolved. The nature and scope of the need to develop an acceptable context for ubiquitous access and participation is becoming clear only as convergence proceeds. The traditional media are transforming themselves to fit a new media environment that challenges their *raison d'être*; the broadcast and print media are moving online. The book argues that unless new media industries and policy makers are able to create a context of ubiquitous access and participation, the emergence of new media worlds will inevitably falter.

Organisation

The book is organized into four sections. Part 1 addresses digitisation and convergence. Part 2 presents case studies and examples of research that constitute various forms of media activism. Part 3 expands the discussion of access and addresses some of the policy concerns it raises. Part 4 presents a series of arguments about the politics of participation in the context of new media.

The book has been organised as a teaching text that provides a useful context for the study of new media technologies. It focuses on the key industry and policy issues associated with the convergence process, and explores the ways users and audiences contribute to this process through their media activism and their demands for access and participation. The book is designed to retain the distinctive character of the original contributions, yet is presented in a pedagogical framework that facilitates individual student research alongside suggestions for classroom discussion and debate. In addition the chapters provide useful reference materials and activities to allow for further research.

Part 1: Digitisation and Convergence

This section begins with a discussion of technological determinism and the social and cultural implications of the increasing privatisation of contemporary life. The theme of digitisation and convergence in traditional media explores the implications of media convergence for everyday media use and for the policy context. It examines the ways convergence is affecting the media experiences of new media audiences and user groups.

Part 2: Activism

The activism section consists of a series of case studies that explore how diverse user communities are going about ensuring they are not denied access to emerging new media worlds. The case studies allow an insight into how the introduction of new media technologies affects Indigenous communities, disability groups, people caught up in global catastrophes, and people who are regionally, economically or culturally disadvantaged. This section shows that while audience activism importantly involves the production of user-generated content, it also seeks to achieve greater political equality in both global and local politics and policy debates. Case studies discuss the media activism of Indigenous communities; people living with disabilities; people confronted by crisis situations; and urban youth groups and local communities.

Part 3: Access

Decisions about how new media will be introduced and which social and cultural groups will benefit foreground the importance of sound policy development. This section provides an overview of the areas where the introduction of new media has created debate about how new media policy should be developed and what form social consultation should take. It includes both theoretical analysis of access issues and case studies on the dynamics of consultation.

Part 4: Participation

The emerging world of new media seems inevitably to involve commercialisation, often of aspects of media use that have previously been free. The transformation of free services into pay-to-use services has shaken the very foundation of media use; for this reason the emphasis in this section is on 'participation' and the ways it is organising the internet and of mobile communications. This section examines the implications of the resulting commodification of information for the way audience formations are structured and operate. It identifies the importance of the online brand, the development of new approaches to search for the future of the Internet, and questions the impact of new media on what we mean and expect when we use the term 'participation'.

★   ★   ★

The contextualised vision we have sought to achieve is a synthesis of critical reflection on current trends. We have intended that it offer an informed understanding of the past in combination with a breadth of vision that recognises that media exist so that people can do the things that people (not machines) like to do. After reading this book we hope that you will think a bit differently about your own media world and any future media world you would consider worth creating; we also hope that you will better understand what is at stake for those who still fight to gain access to digital media technologies.

If we see the 'New Media World' as today's media world, then we are also presupposing a past 'media world' that has historical bearing on the present; of course, we are also assuming the emergence, based on the present, of future media worlds. One of the achievements of the book, then, is the way it demonstrates that at this moment in time, past, present and future exist in a discursive present.

PART ONE

Digitisation and Convergence

The introduction of digital media has brought about profound changes in the nature and organisation of contemporary communication. Its impact has been felt across the board—in interpersonal as much as in mediated communications. Access to new media, and especially to mobile media, means that people are able to organise their everyday contacts and their personal, leisure and work activities while on the move. New media increase the versatility of human action. The application of digital technologies in personal communication devices, like mobile phones, MP3 players and BlackBerrys, has provided the impetus for change in the traditional media industries and revitalised the confidence of Internet industries damaged by the Nasdaq tech crash in 2000. One aspect of the rapid change in the balance of power between 'old' and 'new' media before the crash was the collision of content and communications and the policy issues this brought to the fore.

The first phase of convergence occurred well before the tech crash, when it seemed to many that digital media would totally eclipse the traditional media, and that the new media world would be dominated by one medium— the computer. Today, however, this mono-medium scenario has been replaced by a new ideal. In this scenario, each individual is equipped with multiple media devices all of which talk to each other wirelessly. Coordination of the personal devices is considered to be an aspect of the way an individual customises those devices. Convergence is no longer just a technological process but is involved in, and expressed as, profound and ongoing social, cultural and economic change.

The chapters presented in Part 1 demonstrate the process of convergence at work in a range of environments. In Chapter 1, Jim McGuigan addresses arguments about technological innovation and its social impact. He introduces two key concepts for making sense of such developments: technological determinism and mobile privatisation. 'Technological determinism' assumes that technological innovation is caused exclusively by an autonomous process of scientific research and discovery, the findings of which are applied directly to technical development. The chapter criticises the one-dimensional character of technological determinism. In his analysis of 'Mobile privatisation', McGuigan demonstrates how the pursuit of communicational mobility and privatised living and organisation of life have driven the development of 'cool capitalism'. This chapter contextualises the study of digital media within a long-standing sociological tradition of investigations about society and technology.

In Chapter 2, Virginia Nightingale identifies three challenges confronting the convergence process. The first challenge is the unpreparedness of old media industries for the impact digital media have had on their core business activities. Online activity means people are no longer dependent on the media releasing information when it suits them—people now routinely create, borrow, share and even steal content that has been created by others. These activities have brought the second challenge into focus—the problem of how content might be 'protected', copyrights enforced and how the established media industries might access some of the income they believe they have lost through illegal file sharing. The content problem is central to the understanding of convergence. It is both about protecting copyrighted content and simultaneously about the problem of how to develop new content for the digital environment. Fortunately for the industry, in regard to the creation of new content, users came to the rescue by demonstrating that economic value can be extracted from the content users create for their own enjoyment. User-generated content is both a solution and an additional challenge for the convergence process. User-generated content requires a quite specific environment in which to grow—that environment is usually described by the term 'social networking'. The third challenge for convergence arises because social networking is based on 'sharing' while media industries repurpose shared content for commercial transactions. The disjunctions between social networks, new audience formations of the World Wide

Web, and consumer markets therefore arguably represents the most challenging issue facing the convergence.

In Chapter 3, Tim Dwyer explores the differences between today's media world and its predecessors by focusing on the proliferation of delivery modes and media platforms that characterise the 'new media world'. Dwyer examines the implications and challenges for media policy formation implicit in these changes. Where once it was imagined that convergence meant that all media would be delivered via the personal computer, it is now recognised that the new media reality is a multimedia one. Stories, news, commentary and gossip are packaged for delivery via media as different as domestic television sets and the personal mobile phone (m-TV) screen. These content changes have necessitated changes in the policies developed for media regulation. While in the past it was adequate to treat the regulation of each medium separately (for example, to treat television as a different media industry from radio or the press), the current situation demands that the old media 'silos' be opened. Dwyer advocates policy development based on (delivery) platforms rather than media. In the past the link between the service (such as broadcasting or voice telephony) and the platform over which it was delivered was clear. Now proliferating wireline and wireless network infrastructures (DSL, satellite, cable, 3G mobile, WiFi and WiMAX) are blurring the distinction between the service and the platform. In these circumstances, the flow of formats across different platforms, often repurposed, and different ways of accessing content becomes the focus of both regulatory and scholarly interest.

The case of radio is investigated by Jackie Cook in Chapter 4. Cook provides an important case study of the impact of multi-platform delivery on radio, one of the traditional media. Radio has always been a multi-platform medium, but today its platforms include two-way, broadcasting, Web streaming and, most recently, podcasting. Until the arrival of podcasting, radio was a 'live' medium— always 'on air'. The radio station controlled the delivery of both live-to-air and pre-recorded programs. With podcasting, however, the user decides when to listen to a program, and is able to completely break radio's live broadcasting tradition. This means that the nature of radio's audiences is also changing. Instead of being classified by time slots or day parts—for example, 'drive time', 'breakfast' or 'late night'—the audience for podcasting is able to escape such classification and can integrate radio as a component of their everyday 'social networking'. For this reason, Cook asks us to think about how/whether podcasting qualifies as a radio platform or whether it might suggest that new futures for radio are on the horizon—futures that aggregate audiences in quite different ways.

Technological Determinism and Mobile Privatisation

JIM MCGUIGAN

1

CHAPTER OVERVIEW

This chapter looks at arguments concerning technological innovation and social impact in the field of communications and media. It introduces two key concepts for making sense of such developments: technological determinism and mobile privatisation. 'Technological determinism' refers to mono- or uni-causality in technological innovation. It assumes that technological innovation is caused exclusively by an autonomous process of scientific research and discovery, the findings of which are applied directly to technical development. The chapter criticises this one-dimensional explanation and counterposes to it a multi-causal or multi-dimensional mode of explanation. Further, in considering the sociality of newer information and communication technologies, it is argued that the concept of mobile privatisation suggests that, while communicational mobility is enhanced, privatised living and organisation of life are also accentuated. These general points are illustrated with reference to digitalisation and mobile communication devices.

Key terms

consumer seduction
cool capitalism
mobile privatisation
technological determinism

Issues

- How do new communication and information technologies emerge and develop?
- Is technological innovation self-determining or the result of multiple determinations deriving from economic, political and cultural factors?
- What is the impact of new communications technology on patterns of sociability?

Activity 1.1

- List the communications media that you use.
- What kinds of mobility, if any, do you associate with these media technologies?
- In what ways does your use of such technologies enhance or diminish your communication with significant others?

Technological determinism

The most profound thesis on the social and cultural significance of digital 'new media', published around the turn of the millennium, is Manuel Castells's (2000 [1996], 2004a [1997], 2004b [1998]) three-volume treatise *The Information Age*, in which he declared the emergence of 'network society'. Castells's thesis, though compelling in many respects, is especially vulnerable to the critique of technological determinism, initiated by Raymond Williams (1974; McGuigan, 2006a [1999]). However, in addition to 'the information technology revolution', Castells argues in his defence that the restructuring of capitalism and communism (in effect, its collapse) and the cultural social movements from the 1960s and 1970s (including feminism) are of equal importance in fashioning the world of today. Yet, it is also true that Castells does lavish inordinate attention on the impact of information and communication technologies (ICTs) on developing the network paradigm that has arisen to restructure social and cultural life in many particular ways and, moreover, in general. This reading, quite likely, is how Castells is normally read, as the latest guru of technology's all-consuming power.

Information and communication technologies (ICTs) The range of communications technologies associated with the distribution of information.

There is no doubt that digitalisation and computing have enormous consequences, for instance, with regard to television and telephony: bringing about technological convergence and proliferating communication services and gadgets such as the online mobile phone with televisual features. Nevertheless, the processes by which such technologies come about and are used are much more complicated than the usual hype would suggest. Let us return to what Williams had to say, then, in order to see more clearly the problems associated with overstating the determinacy of technology.

Technological determinism assumes a linear process from scientific research and discovery to technical invention and implementation with consequential social and cultural impact, more or less unfolding smoothly over time. It is not just a simplistic model of socio-technical change but also a dominant ideological assumption, nowadays allied especially to free-market economics and politics.

Alternatively, according to Williams, technologies are developed and implemented in a complex of determinations that are not only scientific and technical but also include economic, political and cultural factors. To assume that technology is the sole cause of cultural and social change with highly predictable results is a deeply flawed assumption, though it is widely believed and to a considerable extent simply taken for granted. To appreciate why technological determinism results in fallacious argumentation, it is necessary to examine how technologies have actually developed historically. Historical knowledge should encourage scepticism about exaggerated claims concerning the magical and all-transforming power of technology.

Think about it

Why do you think it is that people prefer to believe that technology causes change rather than that people or groups, or governments, or corporations like Microsoft and Apple create technologies to change the world so that it suits them better?

Do you think that we would appraise media technologies differently if they were routinely presented as 'the latest bright idea' of big business, rather than as a technological breakthrough?

The classic critique of technological determinism was formulated in Raymond Williams's book, *Television—Technology and Cultural Form*, originally published in 1974. As long ago as that, Williams was aware of most of the potential technological developments in television that have actually occurred since then and with which we are now so familiar. In his ground-breaking book, Williams discussed the multiplication of cable and satellite channels, facilities for recording programs off the television set and rescheduling, interactivity, large-screen receivers and the rest of it.

At the time, Williams posed the question of who would gain the upper hand in controlling these developments, specifically whether they would be commanded by global capital or become a public means for fostering greater democracy and participation. He feared that the interests of big business would win out. In that, he has surely been proven right.

Williams takes the oft-stated claim that 'television has altered our world' and considers what it means. In the television book, he identifies no less than nine ways of stating the cause–effect relation between television and society, stretching from strong to weaker forms of technological determinism to, at the other extreme, what can be called social or cultural determinism.

The strongest forms of technological determinism go like this:

(i) Television was invented as a result of scientific and technical research. Its power as a medium of news and entertainment was then so great that it altered all preceding media of news and entertainment.

(ii) [...]Its power as a medium of social communication was so great that it altered many of our institutions and forms of social relationships.

(iii)[...]Its inherent properties as an electronic medium altered our basic perceptions of reality, and thence our relations with each other and with the world (Williams, 1974, p. 11).

The most extreme form of social or cultural determinism, on the other hand, is stated as follows:

(ix)Television became available as a result of scientific and technical research, and its character and uses both served and exploited the needs of a new kind of large-scale and complex but atomised society (p. 12).

It is not often appreciated that, for Williams, this kind of social and cultural determinism is not much better than technological determinism, though it does have the virtue of seeing television as symptomatic of historical change and not just the cause of it. The trouble with both views is that they see the invention and implementation of television as a sort of accident. Williams summarised his critical attitude to both positions as follows:

In *technological determinism*, research and development have been assumed as self-generating. The new technologies are invented as it were in an independent sphere, and then create new societies or new human conditions. The view of *symptomatic technology*, similarly, assumes that research and development are self-generating, but in a more marginal way. What is discovered in the margins is then taken up and used (pp. 13–14).

Neither of them actually tell you why television was developed at all!

Williams then goes on to outline a third way of accounting for the development of television and its relation to society:

... [I]n the case of television it may be possible to outline a different kind of interpretation, which would allow us to see not only its history but also its uses in a more radical way. Such an interpretation would differ from technological determinism in that it would restore *intention* to the process of research and development. The technology would be seen, that is to say, as being looked for and developed with certain purposes and practices already in mind. At the same time the interpretation would differ from symptomatic technology in that purposes and practices would be seen as *direct*: as known social needs, purposes and practices in which the technology is not marginal but central (p. 14).

The crucial term here is *intention*, making the assumption that television was developed deliberately out of a combination of scientific knowledge produced for various reasons, the exploration of technical feasibility, the identification and creation of social needs, the testing out of possibilities, etc. Inventive developments in electricity, telegraphy, photography, the moving image and radio came together around television.

It is important to note that the earliest uses of what became broadcasting, in the case of radio, during the first couple of decades of the twentieth century, were military and imperial. They were developed in order to aid the conduct of war and colonial administration. It was only subsequently that the possibilities of a *broadcast*—as opposed to a *narrowcast*—medium were explored.

Another important thing about early broadcasting—both radio and television—is that it was not inevitable for it to become a mainly domestic medium of reception. In Germany, for instance, during the 1930s, television was used limitedly as a medium of reception in public spaces, such as shopping centres, instead of the private space of the home. This is a form of television that has been somewhat revived in recent years with the viewing of sport collectively in public settings such as bars.

The development of radio and then television as a domestic medium was pioneered in the USA and Britain in relation to the general formation of mass culture and consumerism during the interwar years. In the USA, wireless set manufacturers were the key players. So were they at first in Britain as well until the state intervened to set up the BBC as a separate company that soon became a publicly owned corporation. Across the Atlantic, on the other hand, radio and television were always exclusively commercial media, set up as vehicles for advertising and sponsorship, a feature of a thoroughgoing commodification of culture in the USA.

Brian Winston (1995 [1990], 1996) has refined Williams's ideas concerning the development of communication technologies into a sophisticated model of 'how media are born'. With evidence from detailed case studies, Winston demonstrates the historical contingencies of 'new media' emergence. He traces the advent of cinema, the racism of colour film chemistry, the marginalisation of 16 mm film as 'amateur' until its eventual deployment in television news, the dead-end of analogue high-definition television and the limbo status of holography.

Editor's comment   Patrice Flichy, a media historian, in his book *Dynamics of Modern Communication: The Shaping and Impact of New Communication Technologies*, quotes the French historian, Ferdinand Braudel, who wrote 'An innovation is conditional upon the social force on which it is based and which necessitates it' (Braudel, 1979, p. 477). For Flichy, the role of these 'social forces' in the invention of communications machines has enjoyed relatively little attention. Yet, he notes, 'numerous historical works on the subject all but ignore the uses to which technologies are put; in fact they implicitly assume that the utilization of machines is the natural result of their technical characteristics. In contrast, certain sociological studies of technology focus solely on the diffusion of a tool and tend to consider it as a 'black box' ... (My) aim is precisely to articulate these two contrasting positions. The history of an invention is that of a series of technological and social developments, together with interactions between the two spheres' (p. 2).

There always has to be a 'supervening social necessity' behind the emergence of a new medium of communication. In the case of cinema, the formation of a mass entertainment market and the sociality of theatre in an urban-industrial society were at least as important determinants, if not more so, than the inventiveness of 'great men', the myth of orthodox cinematic history. As well as supervening social necessities, accelerating the development of a medium at a particular moment in time, there is the brake on development that Winston (1996, p. 9) calls 'the 'law of the suppression of radical potential'. In the case of the denigration of 16 mm film, its use thereby confined to 'amateurs' and 'subversives', classic Hollywood's expensive 35 mm 'standard' was a means of controlling entry to the industry. Winston's historical researches provide considerable substantiation for the critique of technological determinism, though he rather overstates the alternative explanation of what he calls 'cultural determinism' and ignores the criticisms that Williams made of it.

Activity 1.2

Consider how 'accelerators' and 'brakes' have worked in the development of (a) the Internet and (b) the mobile phone.

Mobile privatisation

Ultimately, the development of communication technologies is not as interesting as their use and how they actually operate in relation to ways of life. To make sense of the sociality of television, in the first instance but also of broader significance, Williams formulated the notion of mobile privatisation. For him, this referred to a relatively new patterning of everyday life associated with urban-industrial society in general as much as with the specific use of communication technologies. First, Williams (1974, p. 26) notes 'two apparently paradoxical yet deeply connected tendencies of modern urban industrial living: on the one hand mobility, on the other hand the more apparently self-sufficient family home'. Developments in transport, especially building of the railways and mass migration in steam ships, had increased the mobility of people and peoples. Yet, at the same time the atomisation of modern societies had concentrated life outside paid work in the small family home. There had emerged 'an at once mobile and home-centred way of living: a form of *mobile privatisation*' (p. 26). Broadcasting fitted perfectly into this arrangement, not only with the radio and television replacing the hearth as the site of gathering together in the home, but also in giving access to events occurring at a distance.

The concept of mobile privatisation captures the contradictory role of television as a characteristic feature of modern life. Television facilitates a much expanded albeit imaginary mobility through the vast array of representations available to the ordinary viewer. Here, a distinction might be drawn between physical mobility—facilitated by modern transport—and the virtual mobility that is facilitated by telegraphy and broadcasting from the late-nineteenth through to the mid-twentieth century. Domesticity becomes the focus of expanded consumerism, labour-saving devices and the like, and indeed broadcasting's typical mode of address to the listener and viewer in the domestic setting with all that this entails. To some extent, broadcasting would come to actually schedule activities in the home: day-time programs addressed to 'the housewife', children's programming when the kids get home from school, 'the toddler's truce', 'family viewing', adult viewing after 'the watershed' when children should be in bed. And with the advent of satellite communications from the 1960s, it became possible, from the comfort of the home, to see events actually unfolding simultaneously across the other side of the world.

Returning to the concept of mobile privatisation several years after formulating it, Williams (1985 [1983]), p. 188) remarked, 'It is an ugly phrase for an unprecedented condition'. It was not just that people in urban-industrial societies were living in small family units (the nuclear family replacing the extended family) but that many were comparatively isolated and private individuals while 'at the same time there is a quite unprecedented mobility of such restricted privacies' (p. 188). Williams notes that in his novel *Second Generation*, published in the 1960s, he had commented upon the sociality of motor car traffic:

Looked at from right outside, the traffic flows and their regularities are clearly a social order of a determined kind, yet what is experienced inside them—in the conditioned atmosphere and internal music of the windowed shell—is movement, choice of direction, the pursuit of self-determined private purposes. All the other shells are moving in comparable ways but for their own different private ends. They are not so much other people, in any full sense, but other units which signal and are signalled to, so that private mobilities can proceed safely and relatively unhindered. And if all this is seen from outside as in deep ways determined, or in some sweeping glance as dehumanised, that is not at all how it feels like inside the shell, with people you want to be with, going where you want to go (Williams 1985 [1983], pp. 188–89).

So mobile privatisation is not a social phenomenon confined to broadcasting in general and television in particular. It also includes driving a motor car either by yourself or with a few significant others as passengers, separate from yet coordinated, in some remote sense, with others doing the same thing in their little, shell-like worlds. For Williams, these phenomena—watching television, driving a car—are synecdoche for a larger whole, 'a now dominant level of social relations' (p. 189). He links this larger whole to the market system: 'The international market in every kind of commodity receives its deep assent from this system of mobile-privatised social relations' (p. 189). The shell, to return to our given examples, might be a house or a car, sites of private consumption and mobility.

It is not difficult to conjure up other examples appearing at a later date than Williams's preliminary ruminations on mobile privatisation: desk-top computing online and portable telephonic and music-playing devices being the most obvious ones. An additional point to make, of course, is to do with screening, certainly in the convergence of computing and television, whereby everything is seen, literally, through a screen, mediated and packaged for consumption, sometimes quite active consumption. In the next section we will explore further the technological developments associated with the intensification of what Williams called 'mobile privatisation' in the modern world.

Think about it

- What is distinctively modern about mobile privatisation?
- Did mobile privatisation not exist in any form in pre-modern times?
- Where in the world does mobile privatisation not figure significantly today?

Mobility

Mobility is now such a hot topic that a new school of sociology has even been announced in its name (Urry, 2007). During the 1990s the mobile phone became the coolest 'icon' of the age. In the 2000s its position has looked vulnerable to usurpation by the iPod/MP3 player. The most likely victor, however, is a hybrid of the two: the all-purpose mobile communication device.

The history of the mobile phone is an exemplary one with regard to technological innovation and turnover, changing patterns of sociality and consumer seduction.

Transition from first generation (1G) to second generation (2G) mobile phones —the shift from besuited business users with their large and expensive bricks on display to mass-popular use, particularly as a leisure medium for the young—was dramatic to say the least. Suddenly everyone seemed to have one and was using it incessantly. The transition to third generation (3G) devices (in effect, online access to multiple services) has been much more stuttering, with an endlessly awaited and ever delayed 'tipping point' about to be reached.

Fortunes were made from the mass-marketisation of 2G, which eventually meant that phones themselves could be literally given away by the telecommunications companies in order to sign up more and more customers to contracts. However, with such rapid success the market became saturated. The business dynamic, then, required the introduction of replacement devices and services at much greater cost to consumers (WAP, etc.). In the late 1990s at the height of the dot.com boom, several countries, such as Britain and Germany, sold 3G franchises to the telecoms companies at astronomical figures in the billions whether you count it in dollars, euros or pounds. However, very soon consumer reluctance to move on put revenue and future profits at risk. This can only be explained by the remarkably swift and embedded sociality that was fostered by actual 2G use. People were apparently satisfied with their 2G phones and were not much attracted by the extravagant promises of 3G.

Ethnographic research conducted in the late 1990s and early 2000s goes some way to explaining why this was so (McGuigan, 2005). A great deal of attention is lavished in the trade press upon the practice of early adopters, those readily seduced by advertising claims and most enthusiastic about tooling up with whatever the market has to offer. However, these are not necessarily the most significant users. There are discernible patterns of mass use that are much more significant and, indeed, consequential for the take-up of new communication technologies.

By the mid 1990s, mobile phones had become a striking feature of youth culture, seen as desirable objects in themselves and essential tools for the conduct of everyday social life. In fact, the typically compact design of mobile phones is especially amenable, not accidentally so, to the young with their tiny buttons and quick-finger facilities, including text-messaging, the enormous success of which was never anticipated by the telecommunications companies. For the young, however, it was cheap, easy and, equally important, mysterious to the grown-ups. Older people with failing eye sight and slower sensory-motor skills find it harder to use mobiles.

The mobile may at one time have been a luxury but, for some users, however, it became a necessity. For keeping in touch with a circle of friends, arranging meetings and simply being in society, the mobile was seen widely as a must-have tool by the young, children and, increasingly, older people as well. This was accentuated by the fad of picture-messaging a few years ago.

Research also shows that the mobile phone facilitated the routine conduct of work and domestic management for older groups. For example, working mothers found the mobile invaluable when arranging child care and keeping tabs on the kids. Mundane use of this kind became ubiquitous. The value of more expensive 3G mobile communications was not so obvious to such users.

At the same time, significant developments were occurring in mobile music-listening. The Sony Walkman was the pioneering device of the late 1970s and 1980s. It went through a typical process of diffusion, beginning with the young and eventually capturing the attention of older generations as well. It was designed and marketed deliberately in order to do so (du Gay at al., 1997). This was a miniaturised cassette tape recorder that played back but did not record. Thus, it took a device both of production and consumption and turned into one solely of consumption. Cassettes had to be otherwise recorded or bought already recorded. Notionally, the earplugs only allowed the listener to hear, though others might be rather too well aware of a crackly noise nearby. The Walkman epitomised mobile privatisation in the 1980s. The individual could be cocooned in his or her own private audio-space separate from others in public space. It was objected to on similar grounds to the way the mobile was objected to later. There were health panics and complaints about the breakdown of communication brought about, paradoxically, by a communication device.

The Apple iPod and kindred MP3 devices slot neatly into the space carved out by the Sony Walkman. As market leader in mobile devices for listening to downloaded music from the Internet, the iPod sets the tone. Apple is one of the 'coolest' of business corporations, combining innovation, profitability and a rebellious style. Apple users have been encouraged to see themselves as 'outlaws', somehow distancing themselves from corporate capitalism while simultaneously contributing to the coffers of the same. 'Cool' is actually the dominant tone of capitalism today. Corporations have incorporated counter-cultural traditions and deployed signs of 'resistance' in order to market their wares (see Frank, 1997; McGuigan, 2006b).

This is the era of *cool capitalism*. The original 'spirit of capitalism', often associated with puritanical Protestantism, emphasised deferred gratification and hard work. The 'new spirit of capitalism' (Boltanski and Chiapello, 2006 [1999]) is much more hedonistic and, indeed, 'cool'. Immediate gratification is sought and sold in the sphere of consumption. Consumers are, in effect, seduced by the delights of high-tech and 'cool' commodities, promising to satisfy their every desire, especially if they are 'different' and vaguely rebellious in tone. Great stress is placed on individual autonomy and the more complex notion of 'individualisation' (Beck & Beck-Gernsheim, 2002 [2001]). The individual perpetually on the move, accompanied by a personal soundtrack and in constant touch, is the ideal figure of such a culture (Agar, 2003; Jones, 2005).

In February 2006, the 3GSM World Congress was held in Barcelona (Wray, 2006). This was an industry event, not something to trouble the minds of the ordinary punter. The key problem of the congress, however, was to find ways of encouraging consumers to do more with their mobile communication devices. Executives at the conference will have been supplied with plenty of market research to tell them what consumers could reasonably be encouraged to want. It was still proving easy to sell new ring tones to consumers in large numbers but not much else. Picture-messaging had been a bit of a disaster, partly because of incompatibility between different systems and, also, because it was only a fad anyway. The reluctant customer was the industry's biggest problem. New services—such as email, music downloads, gaming and Internet access—were simply not selling in sufficient volume from the business point of view despite all the hype in the trade press and on the specialist pages of the news press.

By this time, everyone knew what 'the killer application'—in the unfortunate term used by the industry in spite of occasional health scares over the effects of radiation—was, at least in broad terms: the hybrid device, most notably, combining telephony with music. Still, it was thought, but probably with little conviction, that more people could be persuaded to watch television on their mobile phones.

The story has become very familiar over a number of years now. It is the story of successive false starts and re-launches, recurrent declarations that have all been heard before. If it were only about technology, all this would be incomprehensible. But, it is not. It is about sociality, cultural preference and economic contradictions as well.

Conclusion

Raymond Williams was critical of simplistic cause-effect determinism, such as you find in specialist and demotic forms of technological determinism. Instead, he favoured the notion of 'determination', which he said is the setting of limits within which there are variable possibilities. Clearly, there are limits to the determinacy of newer communication technologies but within these limits there are alternatives. The industrial and commercial interests that promote constant change in product manufacture and marketing so as to seduce consumers and enhance profitability are not all powerful. Their schemes do not necessarily come to the fruition they so ardently seek and ordinary people may make all sorts of uses of the gadgets that were hardly imagined possible.

CHAPTER SUMMARY

- This chapter introduces two key concepts for making sense of technological innovation and social impact in the field of communications and media: technological determinism and mobile privatisation.
- The chapter was critical of 'technological determinism', which assumes mono- or uni-causality in technological innovation asserting that it can be directly applied to technical development.
- The chapter counterposes this one-dimensional explanation with a more complex multi-causal or multi-dimensional mode of explanation.
- It was argued that in the context of the sociality of newer information and communication technologies the concept of mobile privatisation assists us in explaining the characteristics of new forms of privatised ways of being.

Tutorial questions

- Why, according to Williams, is the social condition of mobile privatisation so amenable to sales and consumerism?
- In what ways is capitalism 'cool'—is its 'coolness' mostly attributable to what the new technologies can do, or to one-upmanship between the people who use the technologies, or to some other aspect of the new media?
- To what extent would you say you have been seduced by the 'coolness' of capitalism?

Recommended reading

Castells, M., 2000 [1996], *The Rise of the Network Society*, Basil Blackwell, Malden MA and Oxford.

Frank, T., 1997, *The Conquest of Cool—Business Culture, Counterculture, and the Rise of Hip Consumerism*, University of Chicago Press, Chicago.

McGuigan, J., 2006, 'The Politics of Cultural Studies and Cool Capitalism', *Cultural Politics* 2.2, July, pp. 137–58.

Websites

Third Generation: www.en.wikipedia.org/wiki/3G

Museum of Broadcast Communications, Raymond Williams on TV: www.museum. tv/archives/etv/W/htmlW/williamsray/williamsray.htm

Wikipedia: www.en.wikipedia.org/wiki/Technological_determinism

References

Agar, J., 2003, *Constant Touch—A Global History of the Mobile Phone*, Icon, Cambridge.

Beck, U. & Beck-Gernsheim, E., 2002 [2001], *Individualization—Institutionalized Individualism and its Social and Political Consequences*, Sage, London.

Boltanski, L. & Chiapello, E., 2006 [1999], *The New Spirit of Capitalism*, Verso, London.

Braudel, F., 1979, *Civilisation materielle, economie et capitalisme. XVe–XVIIIe siécles*, Vol. 3, Armand Collin, Paris.

Castells, M., 2004a [1997], *The Power of Identity*, Basil Blackwell, Malden MA and Oxford.

Castells, M., 2004b [1998], *End of Millennium*, Basil Blackwell, Malden MA and Oxford.

Castells, M., 2000 [1996], *The Rise of the Network Society*, Basil Blackwell, Malden MA and Oxford.

du Gay, P., Hall, S., Janes, L., Mackay H. &.Negus, K., 1997, *Doing Cultural Studies— The Story of the Sony Walkman*, Sage, London.

Flichy, P., 1995, *Dynamics of Modern Communication: The Shaping and Impact of New Communication Technologies*, Sage, London.

Frank, T., 1997, *The Conquest of Cool—Business Culture, Counterculture, and the Rise of Hip Consumerism*, University of Chicago Press, Chicago.

Jones, D., 2005, *iPod, Therefore I Am—A Personal Journey Through Music*, Wiedenfeld & Nicolson, London.

McGuigan, J., 2006a [1999], *Modernity and Postmodern Culture*, Open University Press, Maidenhead.

McGuigan, J., 2006b, 'The Politics of Cultural Studies and Cool Capitalism', Cultural Politics 2.2, July, pp. 137–58.

McGuigan, J., 2005, 'Towards a Sociology of the Mobile Phone', *Human Technology* 1.1, April, pp. 41–53.

Urry, J., 2000, *Sociology Beyond Societies—Mobilities for the Twenty-First Century*, Routledge, London.

Urry, J., 2007, *Mobilities*, Polity, London.

Williams, R., 1985 [1983], *Towards 2000*, Penguin, London.

Williams, R., 1974, *Television—Technology and Cultural Form*, Fontana, London.

Winston, B., 1996, *Technologies of Seeing—Photography, Cinematography and Television*, British Film Institute, London.

Winston, B., 1995 [1990], 'How are Media Born and Developed?' in Downing, J., Mohammadi, A., & Sreberny-Mohammadi, A. (eds), 1995, *Questioning the Media—A Critical Introduction*, Sage, London.

Wray, R., 2006, 'Mobile Phone World Meets in Search of the Next Big Thing', *Guardian*, 13 February, p. 28.

New Media Worlds? Challenges for Convergence

VIRGINIA NIGHTINGALE

2

CHAPTER OVERVIEW

This chapter discusses **convergence** and its role in the emergence of the social and cultural conditions that characterise a digitised world. Beyond its technological dimensions, convergence both precipitates and is accelerated or slowed by the social, cultural, managerial and structural responses of media industries, media users and media audiences to digitisation. The emphasis in this chapter is firstly on the ways convergence has the capacity to disrupt existing media industries by precipitating deconstruction or disintermediation (Evans and Wurster, 2000). Secondly it explores convergence as a process of **internetisation-mediatisation** (Fortunati, 2005), where the traditional media are trying to accommodate the challenges of digital technologies, and where Internet-based industries are trying to make themselves more media-like. Three arenas where the impact of the convergence process is most keenly felt are identified: in the structural adaptation of traditional media; in the changing character of content; and in the changing character of audience formations. It is argued that the way these challenges are resolved will shape the nature of the emerging digital media worlds.

Key terms

convergence
internetisation
mediatisation
enhanced media
networked individualism
social networking

Issues

- What problems has the convergence process created for traditional media?
- Why does 'content' pose a challenge for both the convergence process and the future of traditional media?
- In what ways are the new audience formations of the Internet affecting the convergence process and the traditional media?

Convergence A word that describes technological, industrial, cultural and social changes in the ways media circulates within our culture. Some common ideas referenced by the term include the flow of content across multiple media platforms, the cooperation between multiple media industries, the search for new structures of media financing that fall at the interstices between old and new media, and the migratory behaviour of media audiences who would go almost anywhere in search of the kind of entertainment experiences they want. Perhaps most broadly, media convergence refers to a situation in which multiple media systems coexist and where media content flows fluidly across them. Convergence is understood here as an ongoing process or series of intersections between different media systems, not a fixed relationship (from Jenkins, 2006, p. 282).

Digitisation and convergence

The things we do by using the internet today are in need of both radical contextualization and radical historicization. They are obviously new in scale and form, but they are less obviously new in kind—and all center on communication. Indeed if there is any kind of truth to the notions of 'convergence' it is not to be found in the packing together of technologies into single devices; rather it is to be found in the ongoing proliferation of communication media and tools (Jones, 2004, p. 326).

As the above quotation from Steve Jones notes, where it was once assumed that digitisation and convergence would result in a mono-media world it is now recognised that digitisation has instead resulted in a dramatic expansion and diversification of media platforms, devices and activities. Digitisation and the media convergence process it produces are changing the shape and contours of contemporary **mediascapes**, but far from the media world becoming simplified as a result, it has become increasingly complex. Rather than concentrating media in one device, the current expression of convergence addresses multiple devices, wireless access and continuous connectivity to individually preferred networks of personal and work contacts, and leisure and entertainment resources. This expansion and diversification has led to:

- a degree of uncertainty about the future of traditional media and how they should be reshaped for a multi-platform digital environment;
- the emergence of new audience formations that challenge the existing orderly system of media distribution;
- a concomitant concern about content and its marketing online.

Theory link

see Dwyer, Chapter 3

Mediascapes 'Mediascapes ... provide ... large and complex repertoires of images, narratives, and ethnoscapes to viewers throughout the world, in which the world of commodities and the worlds of news and politics are profoundly mixed. What this means is that many audiences around the world experience the media themselves as a complicated and interconnected repertoire of print, celluloid, electronic screens, and billboards. The lines between the realistic and the fictional landscapes they see are blurred, so that the farther away these audiences are from the direct experiences of metropolitan life, the more likely they are to construct imagined worlds that are chimerical, aesthetic, even fantastic objects, particularly if assessed by the criteria of some other perspective, some other imagined world' (Appadurai, 1996, p. 35).

GLOSSARY

The future of traditional media

Evans and Wurster (2000) provide an interesting account of the underlying reasons why the impact of digital media has been experienced as disruptive by some business enterprises and corporations and not by others. Firstly they suggest that digitisation is leading to the separation of the information economy from the economy of things, and of the informational chain of value from the physical value chain. This separation releases the value previously suppressed by the 'embedded compromises' businesses are forced to make in defining the scope and scale of their operations (Evans and Wurster, 2000, pp. 20–1). One of the most important compromises firms make, and 'embed' in their management structures, is between information *richness and reach* (see Activity 2.1), where richness is an indication of the quality of the information or service the business offers and reach refers to the numbers of people accessing the information. The separation of informational and physical value opens the way for competitors to take over some of the core functions of the business without having to invest in the levels of infrastructure cost that caused the original business to settle on its 'embedded compromises'. Once these compromises are exposed by digitisation, a business is vulnerable to the disruptive processes they describe as **deconstruction** and/or **disintermediation** (Evans and Wurster, 2000, pp. 39–44).

Activity 2.1

Evans and Wurster (2000, p. 25) provide the following definition of richness and reach.

THE DEFINITIONS OF RICHNESS AND REACH

Reach is easy to understand. It simply means the number of people—at home or at work—exchanging information. The definition of richness of information is a bit more complex. It concerns six aspects of information:

- *Bandwidth,* or the amount of information that can be moved from sender to receiver in a given time: stock quotes are narrowband; a feature film is broadband.
- The *degree to which the information can be customised*: an advertisement is far less customised than a personal sales pitch but reaches many more people.
- *Interactivity*: dialogue is possible for a small group, but to reach millions the message must be monologue.
- *Reliability*: information is reliable when exchanged among a small group of trusted individuals but is not when circulating among a large group of strangers.
- *Security*: managers share highly sensitive business information only in closed-door meetings, but they will disseminate less sensitive information to a wider audience.
- *Currency*: on Wall Street, where seconds count, a few market makers have instantaneous quotes, a larger group of financial institutions receives quotes with a three to fifteen minute delay, and most retail investors receive quotes with at least a fifteen minute delay.

a) Explore the implications of this definition by considering the richness and reach compromises i) you think traditional media have been willing to accept, and ii) that you are willing to accept in regard to the following media:
   - **News**—online versus on television
   - **Music**—downloading a music file versus the release date of the recording; and of the composition.
   - **Film**—downloading a film versus release date of the film.

b) Evans and Wurster developed their definition with business managers in mind, but from a media and entertainment perspective, what refinements would you want to suggest for their definitions?

Evans and Wurster refer to the newspaper industry for their explanation of deconstruction (ibid, pp. 39–44). They point out that newspapers have had to adjust to loss of income central to the industry's cost structure because classified advertising has been attacked by online competition which is more current and better customised. Classified advertising was once the prerogative of print media, but it can be published online more efficiently and at less cost, to a wider audience, and with more information than in the hard copy of the newspaper. As a result, more people are accessing classified advertising online, and the readership for newspapers is dropping. When a key source of income in a bundle of services suddenly becomes uncompetitive like this, the continued viability of the business is called into question. In response, the newspaper industry has restructured some of its services online and expanded its emphasis on other aspects of its information service—the online sale of reprints of news reports and online subscriptions.

Deconstruction   The dismantling and reformulation of traditional business structures (Evans and Wurster, 2000, p. 39).

Disintermediation   Evans and Wurster distinguish between 'two basic forms of disintermediation':

- In its first (traditional) form, disintermediation occurs when a 'new competitor attacks the established intermediary by offering greater reach and less richness' (p. 70). The competitor 'typically offers a lower cost version of the product or service. This is a *different* value proposition and not necessarily a superior one. It does not destroy the established intermediary, but it does re-segment the market' (Evans and Wurster, op.cit., pp. 70–1).

- 'The second and more radical form occurs when technology allows for the richness/reach curve to be displaced, allowing new players to offer greater reach and greater richness simultaneously. This poses a far more direct threat to the established intermediary's business model. It threatens not just a re-segmentation of the business, but a total transformation' (ibid, p. 72).

GLOSSARY

The advertising industry, by contrast, exists to facilitate communication and interaction between manufacturers and the general public, and between manufacturers and the media industries that carry advertising. Its purpose is mediation, acting as a go-between for both industry and media. Its expertise was once mostly limited to the development of mass media advertising campaigns. Mass advertising privileged the quest for reach over richness. However, the Internet permits manufacturers to create, cultivate and manage their own presentation and sales online and many companies decided to explore the possibility that they no longer needed to use traditional mass media. The existence of media advertising was called into question because audiences have become less responsive to mass advertising, better equipped to find the information they need online, and more used to the availability of specific and relevant information—when they want it. Advertising therefore faced and has survived 'disintermediation' in its 'more radical form'. It responded by reinventing itself as *Integrated Marketing Communications or IMC* (e.g. Duncan, 2005), offering advice on all 'four Ps' of marketing—price, packaging, promotion and product qualities—and taking a 'media neutral' approach. Instead of immediately pursuing reach through broadcast television, media agencies now offer their clients 'total media' or 'media neutral' service where the emphasis is on communication with audiences rather than on display and image, and where information is crafted for carefully defined audience segments. In IMC, the role of advertising has been downgraded and other services, like promotion, publicity, campaign strategy, communication design and product design have been upgraded (Duncan, 2005).

Theory link

Lury,
Chapter 18

Editor's comment: A News Report (Geoff Kitney at World Economic Forum, Davos, 2007). WEF prediction for the future of television: 'Within five years, conventional terrestrial television programming will be overtaken in viewer preferences by the explosion of online video content and the merging of PCs and TV sets' (Kitney, 2007, p. 52).

In some cases media industries face a combination of disintermediation and deconstruction. The television industry is a case in point. Television faces increased competition from additional television platforms—Internet TV; subscription TV services; movie download services; and mTV (mobile TV for the third screen, i.e. cell phone). Many of its entertainment and information services now compete for the youth audience with richer (more highly customised) online content providers—like YouTube, MySpace, forums and blogs. The online competition (Internet TV) is continually inventing and reinventing services that offer new levels of interactivity and customisation. In addition, the shift away from their former dependence on TV by advertising and media agencies has resulted in massive increases in spending on Internet advertising and a gradual but inexorable reduction in spending on TV advertising and in the size of the audience for broadcast television (Nightingale, 2007a). Television is facing not just a re-segmentation of its audience but the need for total transformation.

Where Evans and Wurster's analysis points to the need to reimagine and reconstruct the organisation and management of businesses and industries in the wake of digitalisation, Fortunati (2005) has taken a different approach. She describes convergence as a process of **internetisation** and **mediatisation**, where the Internet is mediatising itself, and the traditional media are internetising. For Fortunati, convergence is a process that both unifies media (so that they are all digital in form) and yet promotes diversification. While the traditional media have been slow in responding to the challenge of internetisation, they have at least begun to develop strategies that link their offline activities to online *'enhancements'* (Nightingale and Dwyer, 2006). This is effectively a 'content' response to the challenge of deconstruction—a doomed attempt to hold onto fickle youth audiences. In this sense it is an inadequate reaction to the threats to television inherent in the convergence process, even though the Internet enhancements include a burgeoning array of innovations and interaction: websites, blogs, chat, voting and polling, Internet subscriptions and sales, online auctions, downloads, competitions, and more.

The enhancement trend is best exemplified by the globally franchised *Big Brother* and *Pop Idol* formats (Nightingale and Dwyer, 2006). Enhancing broadcast programs involves providing online or other digital options to encourage more depth to viewer participation with the program and/or its sponsors' products. From a broadcast television perspective, the enhancing of a television program can be seen as simply the continuation of a repertoire of audience participation options, inherited in some cases from radio, which have been used to boost ratings since the earliest days of television. The scope for enhancement expanded quickly and dramatically once the Internet became both widely accessible and an integrated component, in particular, of young people's media activity. Internetisation has expanded the available audience response options for broadcast TV but it has not greatly assisted the security of broadcast TV stations. The digital add-ons to free-to-air broadcast TV demonstrate the limits of what is covered by the concept 'free-to-air' as the costs of digital enhancement have been passed on to the consumer-audience. In effect enhancements are also spin-off services that deliver independent and increasingly substantial revenue streams for both broadcaster and production companies (Nightingale, 2007a; Nightingale and Dwyer, 2006). Yet the underlying structure of the television industry remains unaltered by enhancements and the sums generated by the new income streams, while substantial, are insufficient to significantly compensate for the ongoing loss of viewers and the scale of change predicted for the broadcast television industry.

A more constructive approach to internetisation by television is evident in the strategic investments television companies are committing to online businesses that complement the television business. One example I have used elsewhere (Nightingale, 2007a) is the takeover of Friends Reunited and its associated services by the British television company, ITV. Friends Reunited has an online membership numbering in the millions and its user-generated content is a source of narrative content for both television news and entertainment. This positioning is interesting for recognising the importance of increasing the richness of broadcast content and the relationship between the television station and its audiences. In

see Dwyer, Chapter 3

other cases, television companies have negotiated deals with search companies (in Australia for example, Seven Network has links with Yahoo! and the Nine Network with MSN) in preparation for the introduction of Internet Protocol TV and its associated data service capacity.

Think about it

Reality TV like *Idol* and *Big Brother* is just one form of reality TV. Do-it-yourself programs (e.g. *Better Homes and Gardens*; *Changing Rooms*) and personal make-over programs (e.g. *The Biggest Loser; What Not To Wear*) are also examples.

- Do you think the popularity of reality TV stems from the 'enhancements' offered by programs like *Big Brother* or from the insights they give into the lives of others?
- Is there anything reality TV can do that can't be achieved online at sites like MySpace, Bebo or YouTube?

Content—its use and misuse

The 'content' issues usually associated with the Internet primarily focus on the threats to copyright and privacy posed by peer-to-peer file sharing, stopping the distribution of unwanted SPAM and offensive material, and ensuring that the young do not accidentally (or even purposefully) encounter pornography, gambling or other age inappropriate materials online. While the protection of vulnerable groups from inappropriate forms of content is important, it should also be recognised that the protection of people from certain categories of content, whether on account of their youth, or regard for personal privacy or other personal, religious or moral values, can also function as a way of protecting content and of managing differential access to protected content. In the online environment, the protection of content online is generating burgeoning levels of surveillance and monitoring (Reiter's Camera Phone Report, 2006; Nightingale, 2007b). Unlike content classification and censorship for traditional media, which is managed by state legislatures, online surveillance is managed privately, by site owners and managers. This creates a situation where affected individuals are denied the right to dispute action taken to remove materials they have posted online. The problem with the private management of online surveillance is that the public is denied access to information about where site managers draw the line.

see Murdock, Chapter 19

Paradoxically, privately managed surveillance is increasing in proportion to the recognition that user-generated content is *the* content best able to attract and maintain online networks. An abundance of user-generated content indicates a vibrant and active online site membership. The problem is that Internet users are disinclined to pay for content they can access for free, and that they enjoy repurposing copyright material (Jenkins, 1993, 2006). So the possibility that user-generated content might infringe copyright or censorship law or other national or international content regulation is emerging as an area of concern for those who develop and manage file-sharing sites. There is ongoing tension between traditional (or 'old') media and the emerging entrepreneurial culture of the World Wide Web.

Activity 2.2

In January 2007, 20th Century Fox subpoenaed YouTube because copies of two of its programs, *The Simpsons* and *24*, had been posted on the site prior to being broadcast on TV. The illegal posts included the four-hour premier episode for 2007 of *24* and 12 episodes of *The Simpsons*. 20th Century Fox demanded access to information that would identify the people who posted the content online. In reporting the incident, Dan Glaister commented that, 'The case pits the behemoths of the old and new media against each other, and threatens the free-spirited ethos that underpins file-sharing websites such as YouTube' (Glaister, 27 January 2007). It appears that the materials had been posted on YouTube by another file-sharing site, LiveDigital, which immediately removed the episodes. Glaister comments that this incident mirrors at least two similar incidents during 2006 when an unreleased episode of *Family Guy* and a twelve-minute clip from the feature film *Twin Towers* were posted on YouTube in contravention of copyright laws. Glaister notes that 'the Motion Picture Association estimates that major film studios lost about $US2.3 billion to internet piracy in 2005' (Glaister, 27 January 2007).

Discuss the following

In relation to such cases, individuals have been named and shamed (and occasionally prosecuted) and file-sharing sites have been subject to legal action, yet the ratio of prosecution to lost revenue remains hopelessly disproportionate.

- In what sense do such prosecutions threaten the 'the free-spirited ethos that underpins file-sharing'?
- Is it possible to reconcile the ethos of sharing with the management practices of copyright ownership?

> • In terms of the discussion of richness and reach, deconstruction and disinter-
> mediation, why do you think the attempts to prosecute Internet piracy are
> proving so unsuccessful?

In part the content problem reflects the difference in funding models between the Internet and traditional media. Where the broadcast media organised revenue through the sale of audiences to advertisers, based on a combination of time plus access to audience eyeballs within and between programs (Ross and Nightingale, 2003, Chapter 3), Internet advertising revenue is generated on the basis of an expanded range of measures: the number of times an online ad is seen; the length of time people spend at a site; the number of people who click through to the advertiser's home site; and the volume of sales or sales prospects generated.

The primary objective for Internet entrepreneurs is to keep people active online as this is how advertising revenue will accumulate. By using the Internet people generate information that documents their online activity. They leave traces that, cumulatively, provide commercially useful information. Andy Clark (2003) has explained this as:

> … The simple tactic of allowing consumer activity to lay down cumulative trails thus supports a kind of *automatic pooling of knowledge and expertise.* … One reason why this kind of procedure is so potent is because it allows patterns of consumer action to speak for themselves and to lay down tracks and trails in consumer space as a by-product of the primary activity, which is online shopping (Clark, 2003, p. 146).

Even if a user does not look at the advertising displayed at a site, the activity of visiting it contributes to the likelihood that others will follow the trail and perhaps notice the advertising. So where for broadcast media scheduling high-rating programs played a central role in attracting and holding viewers, content that keeps people active online is what is sought for the Internet.

Content concepts versus texts

Now, audiences still enjoy and value narratives and documentaries—entertainment forms the traditional media are arguably still best at producing. The market for these media commodities has not diminished. In fact convergence has increased the potential reach of media commodities because access is no longer limited to a broadcast schedule or a place-based audience. Programs of all sorts can be scheduled by the viewer to suit their individual viewing preference—whether of place, time or platform. Previously schedules dictated where, when and how media might be consumed, and it is schedules rather than programs that are endangered by convergence. This has repercussions for the way content is imagined and developed for distribution, particularly in a multi-platform environment. For the traditional media, this initially meant repurposing existing media content for the online environment—using a bundle of enhancements to protect the central product. One version of the product package typically included the concept program plus magazine plus online enhancements. In this case the central product remains the 'old media' products—the television program and/or the magazine—while the online enhancements perform a support role to the main media 'act'. This is the case whether the program is *Big Brother,* which uses the online enhancements to differentiate its audience segments, or *Better Homes and Gardens,* where the television program was backed up by a monthly magazine and linked to a website.

An ambitious example of multi-platform content that sought to break the dependence of a story on a single medium (a film, print or television) has been described by Jenkins as '**transmedia storytelling**' (Jenkins, 2006, Chapter 3). Jenkins uses the example of *The Matrix* to show how a 'story' can be dispersed over a range of media platforms, with different aspects of plot and character unfolding in different media. In this case the primary text becomes a projection, a hologram, a chimera. The possibility that any one person will have accessed and mastered every aspect of this distributed text is quite unlikely, so the 'text' any two people are able to discuss will differ even more dramatically than if the differences of interpretation had arisen only from everyday life experience with its inherent ideological biases.

Transmedia storytelling A transmedia story unfolds across multiple media platforms, with each new text making a distinctive and valuable contribution to the whole. In the ideal form of transmedia storytelling each medium does what it does best—so that a story might be introduced in a film, expanded through television, novels, and comics, and its world might be explored through game play or experienced as an amusement park attraction. Each franchise entry needs to be self-contained so you don't need to have seen the film to enjoy the game and vice versa. Any given product is a point of entry into the franchise as a whole. Reading across the media sustains a depth of experience that motivates more consumption. Redundancy burns up fan interest and causes franchises to fail (Jenkins, 2006, p. 96).

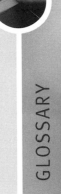

GLOSSARY

Content as brand

Transmedia storytelling provides an interesting example of how media content is increasingly treated as though it were a **brand**. According to Jenkins, *The Matrix* brand includes three films, a program of short animated films, a series of comics and two games (ibid, p. 101). Each *Matrix* product is a separate franchise and each franchise manages separate components of the main story. This arrangement means that the production company leverages more revenue from those who are captivated by the story than would normally be the case. This strategy is far from new. Disney began a similar process with the diversification of Disney across comic books, television, films, animation, theme parks and product licensing in the 1950s (Wasco, 2001). What is different now is the development of the brand around a story concept, as in the case of *The Matrix*, or a celebrity, as in the case of Britney Spears (BritneySpears.com). However, this brand model is complicating the situation confronting the internetisation of broadcast TV. Importantly, both the story concept and the celebrity are 'open-ended and incomplete' texts.

Theory link

see Lury, Chapter 18

GLOSSARY

Brand   Ardvisson (2006) proposes that brand refers to 'A context of consumption constructed by links between material objects, media discourses and life-world environments, and by accumulated consumer affect. This brand-space was furthermore open-ended and incomplete. It constituted a virtual promise or anticipation, to be actualised by the active involvement of consumers themselves. In their ongoing production of a common, consumers create the actual value of the brand: its share in meaningful experiences, its connection to social identities or forms of community: the practices that underpin measurable (and hence valuable) forms of attention' (Ardvisson, 2006, p. 95).

Commercial TV channels mostly broadcast content produced under licence from independent production houses or sporting bodies. Their problem is that their direct involvement as content producers (except in the context of news, sports casting and a very few children's programs) is limited. In addition, television stations do not usually own the copyright on programming, but instead buy broadcasting rights. This means that they don't necessarily own the programs they broadcast and therefore may not be able to use them to create online archives. They have no product to sell online. As a result it's possible for a content producer like Endemol/ Southern Star to make a brand out of a program like *Big Brother* by spinning off online services, while the TV station that broadcast the program is restricted in its ability to do so.

On the other hand, both commercial networks and public broadcasters (like the CBS network in the USA, the BBC in the UK and the ABC in Australia) produce large amounts of content in-house, and are therefore in a position to brand (and potentially to sell) their multi-platform content online. The BBC and the ABC maintain extensive Internet sites where their archives are made available to the public. A slightly different tack has been taken by CBS. Recognising that a lot of YouTube content is derived from television, CBS has created a YouTube channel where a selection of its network shows are available, in the hope that viewers will return to the box (Bogatin, 2006). On the mediatisation front, Google and Live Digital have announced that they intend to pay a proportion of the advertising revenue generated by YouTube and LiveDigital to the creators of high-rating user-generated videos logged at their sites (Sullivan, 2007). While such action recognises (and possibly partially recompenses) the creative work of YouTubers, it also consolidates the brand positioning of Google and LiveDigital, and is likely to privilege commercial over collaborative creative efforts, with a resultant 'regression to the middle' of video content. The content problem challenging convergence therefore reflects the lack of fit between the free-flowing digital environment where users feel free to create, access and recycle amateur content, the tightening of industry control over copyright and professionally produced media content, and the repercussion of the commoditisation of user-generated content. As the mediatisation of the Internet continues, however, it is becoming obvious that traditional media approaches to audience segmentation are creeping into the online environment.

'Networked individuals' and the consumer audience

In 1997, Pierre Lévy (1997, p. 41) proposed that we are living through a technological evolution that will result in diminished dependence on 'molar' technologies (like mass broadcasting or the Hollywood studio system) and in the replacement of that dependence by user/audience participation in 'molecular' communication environments like Internet-based weblogs and email, in mobile phone-based forms like text messaging or picture phoning, or in game-based environments where system users routinely create new communicative forms in the process of engagement. If the masses, as audiences and publics are still imagined to be by most media industries, shift to the 'engaged' forms of audience Lévy anticipated, the consequences for the control of production and distribution of media content and for the management of myth, legend and story in global culture would be exciting, but extremely unreliable and unpredictable. A media world where audiences themselves decide what stories will be made and how they will be told increases the possibility that stories that question established interests may gain currency and result in destabilising social or political action, regardless of whether those stories are true or not. But equally such a world could be a place where the truth claims of established interests are unchallengeable regardless of their reliability.

Social networking is a powerful addition to the media options available to marginal and vulnerable audiences. The popularity of social networking among the young in particular testifies to the importance they attach to the options the Internet provides for content creation, for meeting and 'socialising' with people beyond their local environments, and for the satisfaction of their curiosity about global issues. Their online explorations provide evidence of their determination to discover what lies behind the barriers posed by classification and censorship (UWS and ABA, 2000). Social networking is also the means by which other social formations (for example indigenous communities, the disabled, victims of crime, etc.) are able to coordinate and collaborate to ensure that the type of content they value, and that expresses their visions and experiences of the world, is created and distributed to a potentially global audience. The result is that audience activism is enacted in the pursuit of communication rights and pursued through the production of content, in order to bring about changes in their conditions of life.

However, as Castells (2001, p. 129) importantly suggests, digital media amplify and deepen the West's pre-existing socio-cultural shift from place-based affiliation to 'networked individualism'. If information and content are predominantly privately owned and controlled, access to public spaces where truth claims can be openly and accountably contested will become scarce, and the scope for political action through social networking will be correspondingly limited. In such situations, established interests hold a much more powerful position than the humble consumer or the marginal group. For this reason it is important to supplement the enthusiastic rhetoric about social networking with a realistic assessment of the dynamic forces acting to limit social networking.

In regard to audiences, what changes irrevocably with the impact of digital media is the increasingly commercial nature of voluntary affiliation, and the role brands and branding play in its coordination. Online transactions are increasingly brand-based, with almost every online transaction demanding 'voluntary' affiliation to a branded site or source. The option of not registering for site membership or not agreeing to the terms and conditions of use is exclusion. So the audience formations of the Internet are increasingly predominantly consumer formations, and the future for online publics seems limited to the burgeoning array of online forums (see www.big-boards.com) and blogs where topic categories work to segment the huge membership lists into manageable and knowable communities of users.

Theory link

see Part 2,
Activism

Think about it

Based on the Internet sites you have joined, the Internet purchases you have made, and the Web-surfing you have done, are you able to identify ways you may have been 'shaped' as a consumer by these activities?

see Lax,
Chapter 12

Theory link

The 'consumer shaping' of social networking is a major plank in the mediatisation of the Internet. This has been usefully demonstrated by the customisation of Microsoft's Vista operating system for the Australian market (Davidson, 2007). Vista incorporates digital rights management (DMR) technology that forces users to maintain subscription to its download services in order to exert and maintain use rights over products. This technology is designed to prevent sharing of files, even with family and friends. Vista is also linked to online ordering of photo prints and to a movie download service, all operating at premium prices. This customer shaping process is a direct attack on social networking and existing unregulated file-sharing activities, and seems destined either to ensure the expansion of illegal file sharing, and/or to shore up the position of existing media copyright holders by removing their online competition. It is also likely to segment the online audience into two discreet groups, social networkers versus online shoppers; content creators versus content users. Not everyone is suited to be a content producer and as Sinnreich (2007) has commented, the demand for content creation inherent in social networking 'Raises the bar for participation, potentially widening the gap between information haves and have-nots, the media literate and illiterate' (Sinnreich, 2007, p. 45). Since, as Carpentier (Chapter 13) has argued, the loss of the political connotations of the concept, participation, has facilitated the displacement of the public sphere from cyber-culture, the avenues for social networking appear likely to be considerably narrower in scope in the future.

see Part 3,
Access

Theory link

Conclusion

This chapter has argued that the convergence process is challenged by core differences between the traditional media and the Internet. The Internet has raised expectations for increased richness and reach of information by users and audiences (Evans and Wurster, 2000). This has resulted in the embedded compromises of media industries being revealed and opened up to competition from Internet businesses. The threat from the Internet has in turn caused the traditional media to redefine their activities in order to be able to compete for Internet audiences and to protect their content rights. As a result, convergence has become a push-me-pull-you process of internetisation and mediatisation (Fortunati, 2005). The mediatisation of the Internet is currently transforming cyberspace into a highly commercialised environment where the consumer rights formerly associated with ownership of commodities are being transformed into use-only rights, conditional on subscription to services. The distinction between professional and user-generated content is amplified by these developments that promise to increase the gap between the information rich and the information poor, and to make the quest for equality in access and participation more difficult.

CHAPTER SUMMARY

- This chapter introduced the concept of convergence, and examined its role in the emergence of the social and cultural conditions that characterise a digitised world. It was argued that beyond technological dimensions, convergence both precipitates and is accelerated or slowed by the social, cultural, managerial and structural responses of media industries, media users and media audiences to digitisation.
- It was argued that convergence has the capacity to disrupt existing media industries by precipitating deconstruction or disintermediation (Evans and Wurster, 2000). Following on from this it explored convergence as a process of internetisation–mediatisation, where the traditional media are trying to accommodate the challenges of digital technologies, and where Internet-based industries are trying to make themselves more media-like.
- Three arenas where the impact of the convergence process is most keenly felt were identified: in the structural adaptation of traditional media; in the changing character of content across platforms; and in the changing character of audience formations. It was argued that the way these challenges are resolved will shape the nature of the emerging digital media worlds.

Tutorial questions

- What 'core differences' between the traditional media and the Internet are discussed in this chapter?
- In what ways is the Internet changing the television-viewing experience?
- Who is winning the tug-of-war between mediatisation and internetisation, and why?

Recommended reading

Ardvisson, A., 2006, *Brands: Meaning and Value in Media Culture*, Chapter 5, Routledge, London and New York.

Evans, P. & Wurster, T.E., 2000, *Blown To Bits: How the New Economics of Information Transforms Strategy,* Chapters 2–5, Harvard Business School Press, Boston, Massachusetts.

Fortunati, L., 2005, 'Mediatization of the Net and Internetization of the Mass Media', in *Gazette: The International Journal for Communication Studies*, vol 67 (1), pp. 27–44, Sage Publications, London, Thousand Oaks and New Delhi.

Jenkins, H., 2006, *Convergence Culture: Where Old and New Media Collide,* Chapter 3, New York University Press, New York and London.

Websites

Big Boards: www.bigboards.com

Britney Spears: www.BritneySpears.com

Reiter's Camera Phone Report: www.cameraphonereport.com

The Red Herring, Business Technology: www.redherring.com

Zdnet: www.zdnet.com

References

Appadurai, A., 1996, *Modernity at Large: Cultural Dimensions of Globalization,* University of Minnesota Press, Minneapolis.

Ardvisson, A., 2006, *Brands: Meaning and Value in Media Culture,* Chapter 5, Routledge, London and New York.

Bogatin, D., 2006, Google's Fuzzy YouTube Logic, *Zdnet.com*, 24 November 2006: http://blogs.zdnet.com/micro-markets/?p=695

Castells, M., 2001, *The Internet Galaxy: Reflections on the Internet, Business and Society*, Oxford University Press, Oxford and New York.

Clark, A., 2003, *Natural-Born Cyborgs: Minds, Technologies, and the Future of Human Intelligence,* Oxford University Press, Oxford.

Davidson, J., 2007, 'Vista Opens on Photo, Music Services', *Australian Financial Review*, Information, Wednesday 31 January 2007, p. 50.

Duncan, T., 2005 [2002], *Principles of Advertising and IMC,* 2e, McGraw Hill/Irwin, New York.

Evans, P. & Wurster, T.E., 2000, *Blown To Bits: How the New Economics of Information Transforms Strategy,* Harvard Business School Press, Boston, Massachusetts.

Fortunati, L., 2005, 'Mediatization of the Net and Internetization of the Mass Media', in *Gazette: the International Journal for Communication Studies*, vol. 67 (1), pp. 27–44, Sage Publications, London, Thousand Oaks and New Delhi.

Glaister, D., 2007, 'YouTube v Fox Pits Net Against Network', Accessed 29 January 2007, *The Hindu*, News Update Service, Saturday 27 January, 2007: 0940 hrs. Section: Science and Technology, Dan Glaister, Los Angeles, Guardian News Service: http://www.hindu.com/thehindu/holnus/008200701270922.htm

Jenkins, H., 2006, *Convergence Culture: Where Old and New Media Collide,* New York University Press, New York and London.

Jenkins, H., 1993, *Textual Poachers: Television Fans and Participatory Culture,* Methuen, London and New York.

Jones, S., 2004, 'Conclusion: Contexting the Network', in Howard, P.N. & Jones, S., *Society Online: The Internet in Context,* Sage Publications, London, Thousand Oaks and New Delhi.

Kitney, G., 2007, 'Climate change in Davos', *Australian Financial Review*, Features, Monday 29 January 2007, p. 52.

Lévy, P., 1997, *Collective Intelligence: Mankind's Emerging World in Cyberspace,* pp. 13–19, (trans.) R. Bonnono, Perseus Books. Cambridge, Mass.

Nightingale, V., 2007a, 'Lost in Space: Television's Missing Publics', in Butsch, R. (ed.), *Media and Public Spheres,* pp. 185–97, Palgrave, London.

Nightingale, V., 2007b, 'The Cameraphone and Online Image Sharing', in Goggin, G. (ed.), *Continuum,* (forthcoming).

Nightingale V. & Dwyer, T., 2006, 'The Audience Politics of "Enhanced" Television Formats', *International Journal of Media and Cultural Politics*, Vol. 2, No. 1, pp. 25–42.

Reiter's Camera Phone Report: http://www.cameraphonereport.com/, 17 May 2006.

Ross, K, & Nightingale, V., 2003, *Media and Audiences: New Perspectives,* Open University Press, McGraw Hill, Maidenhead, Berkshire.

Sinnreich, A., 2007, 'Come Together Right Now: We Know Something's Happening But We Don't Know What It Is', *International Journal of Communication* 1 (2007), pp. 45–47.

Sullivan, L., 2007, 'YouTube and LiveDigital to Share Ad Profits: Video creators will be able to choose ads to insert in and around online videos', *REDHerring: The Business of Technology*, 29 January: www.redherring.com/PrintArticle.aspx?a=2099 3&sector=Briefings

University of Western Sydney and Australian Broadcasting Authority, 2000, *Children's Views About Media Harm,* Monograph 10, Australian Broadcasting Authority, Sydney.

UWS and ABA, *see* University of Western Sydney and Australian Broadcasting Authority.

Wasco, J., 2001, *Understanding Disney: The Manufacture of Fantasy*, Polity Press, Cambridge.

New Media:
The Policy Agenda

TIM DWYER

3

CHAPTER OVERVIEW

This chapter considers the converging media industries and high-lights some key policy challenges that arise from proliferating delivery modes. The chapter considers changes occurring in the way media are produced and delivered to audiences over critical ICT infrastructures. These infrastructures, including the Internet, wireless access devices, and the new digital media products and services they make available, have been referred to as 'the new manufacturing' sector driving global 'knowledge economies'. It's argued that new media ICTs are 'socially shaped', and will require ongoing public policy interventions in the interest of sustaining our democracies.

Key terms

Convergence
IPTV
content-on-demand
Next Generation Networks
ICTs
silo structures
Internet governance
Universal Service Obligations

Issues

- How are the communications media industries transforming?
- How are networked Information and Communication Technologies (or 'ICT') developments affecting new media production, distribution and consumption practices?
- Will media policy makers need to respond to these changes in the public interest?

Introduction

A short mockumentary zapping around the Internet in 2005 prophesied the future of media. The eight-minute, flash-generated, animation video entitled 'Epic 2015' was produced by Robin Sloan and Matt Thompson for a time-shifted, virtual 'Museum of Media History'.

Editor's comment Watch 'EPIC 2015' at the *New Media Worlds* website: ‹http://www.oup.com.au/orc/resources/New_Media_Worlds›. The 'Museum of Media History' is a virtual museum invented for 'EPIC 2015': it does not actually exist. However, this short film is useful in an heuristic sense. It helps us to think about the implications and consequences of changes in new media industries.

Its 'voice of God' narrator describes a convergent future mediascape through a lens of actual, and speculative, developments in media industry alliances and consolidation. These kinds of alliances occur incessantly, as cashed-up media businesses devise new strategies, depending on the perceived attraction within and between particular industry sectors.

But perhaps of equal significance, this short animation video was an example of a 'viral video'—a new media form that became an increasingly widespread practice on the Internet. It was symbolic of wider DIY trends too: to make your own content and to 'distribute-it-yourself', which became popular for various genres of movies and television programming using peer-to-peer (P2P) sharing software.

In downloading and viewing this short video, people separated by geography, social and cultural differences were linked into a social network; thus a community of interest was created or augmented by the video itself. In this sense, such video distribution practices were a harbinger of the rich media possibilities some researchers have called **'Web 2.0'**.

Theory link

see Nightingale, Chapter 17

While communications media are constantly undergoing significant transformations, in an era of deregulation and the Internet it is important to recognise that the fundamental debates involving communication and society both change and stay the same. This underscores what Niels Finnemann refers to as the 'co-evolution' of old and new media (Finnemann, 2006). An important implication of this observation is that traditional media of television, radio and the press are evolving along with the rising popularity of new media forms. Accordingly, some policies and laws that have been developed in the context of existing media may also be relevant to new media such as the Internet. These enduring concerns include issues such as the media and democracy; the representation of race, ethnic and other

'Web 2.0' This should exhibit some basic characteristics. These include: 'Network as platform'—delivering (and allowing users to use) applications entirely through a Web browser; users own the data on the site and can exert control over the data; an architecture of participation and democracy that encourages users to add value to the application as they use it; a rich, interactive, user-friendly interface; and, some social networking aspects. Source: Wikipedia (Wikipedia is itself an example of Web 2.0. Although the online encyclopedia is criticised for inaccurate information, at the same time, as in this case, it can also provide the most up-to-date definitions based on 'collaborative' or 'collective intelligence').

diversities; media concentration and ownership; news and coverage of elections; the availability of a range of programming genres; protection of the child audience; and the provision of services for less-able audiences. Clearly traditional policy concerns don't just disappear because of new media delivery modes. We can safely predict that new modes will change *social and cultural uses* as a result of innovation in provision; for example, developments in the way people are using media while in transit based on their specific locations, accessing content that originates almost anywhere in the world, the ease of falsifying identity, or the content itself, through software that enables such modification.

Transformations in communications media industries are requiring governments and their regulatory agencies to respond to these changing mediascapes.

Table 3.1 Media policy evolution and ICT connectivities

Delivery Infrastructures	1. Analogue/Legacy	2. Digital IP
Wired (copper, HFC, optical)	Content • cultural maintenance/ localism • accuracy & fairness • classification	Access • speed/mobility/privacy • network interconnection • consumer price
	Ownership & control	Diversity & genre choice
Spectrum/Wireless (broadcast, cellular, WiFi, WiMAX)	Licensing	Origination
	Codes of practice	Authentication
	USOs	Intellectual property rights
Satellite (GPS)	Price controls	Network architecture

This table models the evolving concerns of media policy makers in the transition from analogue (or legacy) systems to digital Internet Protocol-based new media worlds. The model assumes that the issues applying in 1 may also apply in 2.

Key transformations in communications media industries

There are significant global industry trends indicating some profound shifts in the way audiences increasingly receive their daily media (Croteau and Hoynes, 2006). In particular, changing patterns of distribution are underpinned by the complex processes we refer to in convenient shorthand as convergence, to account for the evolution of communications media in society. Since the 1990s the term 'convergence' has been applied most commonly to the development of digital technology, the integration of text, numbers, images and sound (Briggs and Bourke, 2002, p. 267).

Yet, as Jenkins notes, convergence was used as early as 1983 by Ithiel de Sola Pool (in *Technologies of Freedom*) to describe a force of change in media industries: 'A process called the "convergence of modes" is blurring the lines between media, even between point-to-point communications, such as the post, telephone and telegraph, and mass communications, such as the press, radio, and television. A single physical means—be it wires, cables or airwaves—may carry services that in the past were provided in separate ways. Conversely, a service that in the past was provided by any one medium—be it broadcasting, the press, or telephony—can now be provided in several different physical ways. So the one-to-one relationship that used to exist between a medium and its use is eroding' (Pool, 1983, p. 23 in Jenkins, 2006, p. 10).

In effect, the earlier **silo structures** of broadcasting, telecommunications, publishing, and information technology industries in the twentieth century have been shaken by more flexible industrial dynamics and technological changes in advanced capitalist societies (Harvey, 1990 and 2001).

The implications of these developments will require significant rethinking by governments, policy makers and industry regulators. And as the lines blur between industry sectors there is a gradual converging of the functions of governance bodies and responsibilities: it no longer makes sense to have totally separate governance systems for telecommunications, the Internet and broadcasting.

Jenkins sees the importance of the 'cultural logic of media convergence'; involving matters beyond simply 'commercially produced materials and services traveling along well-regulated and predictable circuits'. Rather, convergence means 'entertainment content isn't the only thing that flows across multiple platforms'. For him, 'our lives, relationships, memories, fantasies, desires also flow across media channels' (2006, p. 17). In other words his definition of convergence is a deeper cultural one, covering a great deal more than just 'content' flowing through various utility 'infrastructures' like water, gas or electricity.

In these new networked media worlds existing laws and policies for content, ownership and control will need to be supplemented with a broader set of access policies focusing on network delivery speed (for both downloads and uploads), mobility, privacy, network interconnection, and diversity in genre and origin of content (see Table 3.1). The shift from a predominantly wireline telecommunications network environment to a competitive telecommunications data market and **Next Generation Networks** (NGNs), requires a fundamental rethinking about coverage, funding and other arrangements concerning universal service. In this process, a core issue is whether broadband should be part of **Universal Service Obligations** (USOs). In the event that governments use broadband to deliver certain education, health and other public services, it can be seen that these might become as essential for households as emergency services over a telephone are today (OECD, 2006).

Silo structures   This term refers to the separate broadcasting, telecommunications, publishing, and information technology industries that can be described as 'pre-convergence' and bound up with the previous industrial mass production organisations of the 'Fordist' period.

Next Generation Networks (NGNs)   NGN is partly a marketing term but it is also a concept used to describe the replacement of 'legacy' fixed copper wire distribution networks with a more diverse range of higher speed and capacity, mobile and 'nomadic', fibre, wireless and satellite networks. At the heart of the concept is the integration of existing separate voice and data networks into a simpler more flexible network using packet switch and Internet protocols. This will enable voice, text and visual messages to be carried on the same network and for each type of message to be responded to in any of these formats on that network.

Universal Service Obligation (USO)   USO arrangements refer to the fundamental access and service provision regimes offered by networks that have traditionally been regulated by governments in developed countries. USO arrangements vary from country to country, but, in general, the current understanding of the term is that all users regardless of location can access quality voice service at an affordable price.

GLOSSARY

Theory link

see Dwyer,
Chapter 15

A clear implication of such industry change is that powerful corporations will continue to lobby and apply pressure to liberalise public interest protections to suit their own particular interests. Bagdikian has argued that only five corporations, 'The Big Five', absorb the lion's share of the 37,000 different media outlets (daily newspapers, magazines, radio and television stations, book publishers and movie companies) in the United States (2004). These corporations are Time Warner (AOL), Disney, Viacom, Vivendi-Universal and the Bertelsmann group. Bagdikian's core argument is that concentrated ownership of the media means that the public is only exposed to the viewpoints and opinions of five corporations whose interests are quite similar. Messages that do not fit within the attitudes, values or revenue goals of these corporations get little, if any, exposure. Democracy is the poorer for this reduced *diversity* in available media messages.

Industry convergence is a multidimensional process involving various combinations of the earlier silo structures. One of the most fundamental has been the coming together of the Internet and telecommunications industries: this is also seen to be essential to the 'shift from voice to data' infrastructure. Telecommunications corporations are being re-engineered as *Internet Protocol* (IP) businesses where voice is now just one category in an array of data services. The complexity of these transformations is underpinned by the fact that different content services (voice, video, music, radio) are capable of being delivered by a diversity of suppliers or 'platforms' (including telecommunications, digital terrestrial broadcast, cable and Internet corporations). Moreover, all content, sometimes made originally for a particular platform (e.g. Television or 3G mobile telephony) can now be repurposed and delivered over the Internet.

These transformations have also facilitated the reconfiguring of traditional businesses. For example, IT search businesses have streamlined traditional media advertising. Google has become a powerhouse in advertising largely by selling short text advertising on highly targeted topics people are searching for, or reading about, on the Internet (Vise, 2005, p. 3). Google now competes with television advertising by placing short video ads on many of the websites where it sells advertising. And the prospect of bringing audiovisual material and targeted advertising together with social networking is undoubtedly an area to be developed by Google and other corporations. Further evidence of this trend can be seen in the announcement of a billion dollar alliance between News Corporation and Google in 2006. The deal was an agreement making Google the exclusive provider of search and keyword targeted advertising for New's Fox Interactive Media Group, the entity responsible for managing News Corporation's growing stable of online sites (Shultz, 2006).

As a consequence of the rise of 'search' businesses like Google, eBay, MSN, Yahoo! and Amazon, the advertising industry has been forced to respond to these altered practices by more strategically matching fragmenting audience consumers to goods and services through specific media providers (see Spurgeon, 2006).

Existing computer giants such as Microsoft, Intel, IBM, Cisco and Apple are an important part of the mosaic of change too. Their vast investment strategies have an impact on the direction and shape of new media developments as social shaping of technology theorists have argued (Winston, 1998; Sørensen and Williams, 2002).

In other words, there's sound evidence that structural transformations are occurring in the mass media, suggesting that they are no longer dominated by the traditional broadcasting industries. The consequences of these transformations resonate through our everyday lives: socially, culturally, economically, politically and technologically. Yet, in many ways, the development of the commercial Internet is a similar story to that of the telegraph and radio: that is, a story about the consolidation of information-based entertainment and e-commerce markets (Williams, 2001).

In relation to all new media technologies, their introduction is shaped by competing interests, with governments being involved to varying extents, and they are always underpinned by prevailing ideologies, or ways of imagining their utility (Winston, 1998; Hesmondhalgh, 2006). Some commentators suggest the ideological framing in the development of media in this early period of the twenty-first century can be summed up in the word 'marketisation'. Graham Murdock has criticised the process the term describes, noting that it involves an erosion of the public interest. The rhetoric of marketisation promises an opening up of markets, ensuring free and fair competition and promoting the interests of consumers. But, as Murdock notes, in this formulation the actual requirements of full citizenship, though at times ritually evoked, trail some way behind (Murdock, 2004). For him, full citizenship in democracies with pluralist media entails access to a range of ICT resources to allow audiences to exercise their rights.

New media ICT developments and practices

There are many examples of how the Internet is changing the way media are distributed and consumed. Yet we need to bear in mind that unlike traditional broadcast media the Internet is *both* a *point-to-point* and *point-to-multipoint* (or mass) medium: it connects individuals but it also speaks to vast numbers of people simultaneously. Some of the new media practices that have emerged in the last decade include:

- music and videos being downloadable from the Internet to portable players;
- digital media replacing analogue products and services with interactive and convergent ones;

- broadcast TV and other news and entertainment content distributed over broad-band telecommunication networks;
- audio and audiovisual telephony over the Internet (known as **voice over Internet Protocol** or 'VoIP');
- Internet access and audiovisual packet communication by mobile telephony;
- proliferating of 'intelligent' wireless networks, products and services such as location-based devices.

This restructuring of media networks and the content and applications they make available is occurring at a number of levels and sites. The engineering term of 'network layers' is a useful way to understand infrastructure and content provision. Networks are divided into three layers: the infrastructure, logical and content. The 'physical infrastructure' layer is the conduit through which information travels, a 'logical' or software 'code' layer controls the infrastructure and a 'content' layer contains the actual information that travels through the network (Kapur, 2005).

The division of issues and actors into layers, each of which corresponds to a different facet of the network, can assist our understanding of a complex range of issues and actors that take place in 'the' Internet. For example, it can help us to understand the commercial battles that are being waged over the continuing availability of a diverse range of 'premium', independent and not-for-profit content on the Internet, as we discuss later in this chapter.

The provision of fast, 'always-on' broadband Internet is becoming more widely available throughout the developed world. Yet access to information and entertainment by broadband Internet is occurring at varying national levels of access to the home (OECD, 2005). In parallel with this trend, Internet over PSTN infrastructure is rapidly declining in high broadband usage nations, according to recent telecommunications indicators (ACMA, 2005). While broadband Internet is a key distribution technology, other access technologies (often with wireless Internet connectivity), such as digital TV and 3G telephony, are also being used extensively for entertainment and information products; including for news and information delivery.

Content-on-demand

The long offered promise of 'video-on-demand' has made its way to the audiences in several forms: from 'pay-per-view' events on digital television (cable and satellite) which has been commonplace for many years; to short and longer form audiovisual content from telecommunications corporations and the websites of media corporations; to in airline travel; through P2P software sharing and websites; and now, to various categories of Internet content, including '**Internet Protocol Television**' (or IPTV).

There are many different versions of IPTV or similar video-based services on offer around the world. Examples include NowbroadbandTV.com in Hong Kong, or CurrentTV.com and YouTube.com (on which reportedly 100 million video clips were viewed each day in 2006) in the USA. These are offered variously by former telecommunications monopolies, Internet Service Providers (ISPs), cable corporations and new media start-ups. Some sites are in the user-generated category; while others have retained elements of traditional scheduled TV offerings or, like CurrentTV, rely on a combination of these approaches.

The shift to a new media world of 'content-on-demand' is impacting on regulatory arrangements, as well as distribution and consumption. Not surprisingly, the take-up of services that rely on wired and wireless infrastructures varies enormously and depends on numerous factors. Public policies to subsidise or encourage wider usage play an important role. High among these are policies that assist or promote the roll-out of high-speed broadband networks capable of supporting rich media content, and the availability of sufficient quantities of specific categories of content that are attractive to audiences. This involves owning the relevant **intellectual property rights (IPRs)**, being a party to strategic alliances to share movie and sports event rights, or having rights to use television series and archival content. Other factors influencing the take-up include pricing, the availability of competitor offerings, including content provided on mobile phones; and any restrictions placed on services by regulatory agencies.

Voice over Internet Protocol or **VoIP**   This works by converting your voice into a digital signal (using Internet Protocol packets) that travels over the Internet via a broadband connection. Using specific software, VoIP converts the voice signal from the caller's telephone into a digital signal then converts it back at the other end to enable voice communication with anyone with a phone number. Typically, callers use the software on their computer, a handset connected to their broadband modem, or certain kinds of mobile (cell) handsets, to send and receive calls. VoIP offers several benefits including cost savings and nomadicity or the ability to use the service in different locations.

IPTV   The distribution of video services over Internet Protocol networks (Ofcom, 2005–06).

Intellectual property rights (IPRs)   Rights that arise from copyright laws that protect owners from the unauthorised use of their creative or 'intellectual property' works, for example, audiovisual content or other kinds of cultural products.

GLOSSARY

Think about it

What might be some of the main advantages and disadvantages of IPTV for audiences, regulators or IPTV providers, compared with conventional TV?

New business models

In the transition to digital broadcasting and Internet delivery, new regulatory policy debates have emerged linking issues of content provision, distribution and access to digital television and broadband networks (Flew, 2005; Butt, 2006; Stein and Sinha, 2006). From an economic perspective, these issues are premised on a different cluster of assumptions than have prevailed in traditional media delivery contexts.

For example, when audiovisual content can be supplied on an on-demand basis in multi-platformed format versions, business models developed for the scheduled provision of programming may no longer apply. As Stephen Carter, the first CEO of Ofcom (the UK's convergent regulator set up in 2003) has argued: 'Broadcasting is high fixed cost (transmission and production infrastructures), virtually zero marginal cost (being a public good it costs the same whether it is sent to one or to many). Broadband is stepped, fixed and marginal cost (based on incremental speed increases). Mobile is (under current auction rules) high entry cost and fixed cost but also high marginal cost … in the on-demand world marginal costs rise with the volume of users' (Carter, 2005). This means that different cost structures for the operators of these media businesses will have particular impacts on the genres of content, and how services will be priced, packaged and delivered to audiences.

Peer-to-Peer (P2P) has reconfigured the distribution of audiovisual content as it has already done for music distribution. For example, BitTorrent, a software equivalent of Limewire or Kazaa for movies and TV programming, has greatly facilitated the sharing of copyrighted audiovisual materials over the Internet. Copyright owners (e.g. major Hollywood studios and TV networks) are constantly trying to head these developments off, often with specific digital 'technological protection measures'. This has had a dramatic impact on existing IPR protections. Some commentators have argued that it's probably too late for them to attempt to control these industry transformations (Lessig, 2004).

In 2005 Apple began offering downloads of TV shows and movies (after a content deal with Disney/ABC networks) that followed their already highly successfully iTunes music download service. In 2006 MTV, the cable television music channel owned by Viacom, teamed with Microsoft to launch their own digital music download service called 'Urge', targeting non-Apple iPod users. Unlike Apple, the MTV service uses a monthly subscription business model as well as single downloads (for the same US 99 cents as iTunes). But the ultimate direction of how portable music players are taken up and used in global markets depends on the results of legal and regulatory battles fought in relation to copyright, including patent, standards and trade practices. For example, Creative Technology, the Singapore-based consumer electronics group filed patent complaints (in the US District Court and with the US International Trade Commission) against its main rival Apple Computers, seeking to stop the sale of hugely successful iPods in the US. The matter was eventually settled in 2006 with Apple paying Creative Technology $US100 million in compensation and, as part of the agreement, Apple agreed to pay for a license to use Creative's patent (Noguchi, 2006).

User-generated content

Arguably a significant moment in the so-called user-generated content trend occurred when those caught up in the bomb attacks on the London Underground on 7 July 2005 took still and video shots of these events. Immediately after it happened this content was uploaded to moblog sites and emailed directly to the BBC. Within the first few hours of those bombings the BBC had received 20,000 email messages, 1000 images and twenty packages of video, all recorded by people on their mobile phones (Gowing, 2006).

The BBC has announced a six-year plan to implement its 'Creative Futures' strategy, and reinvent itself as a public broadcaster for the 'on-demand world' (BBC, 2006). This plan is to extend practices already seen at BBC Online, of encouraging and facilitating its audiences to create and upload their own commentaries, images and video, and to modify BBC-originated content. But the BBC is going well beyond its trialled podcasting service to include downloads of archived TV and radio shows for people to watch online. The BBC commenced the trial of its integrated Media Player (iMP) in 2005. It allows users to download TV and radio programs from the BBC website to their computer. Google has announced similar services, albeit under entirely different logics: their model is based on attracting large audiences to drive advertising revenue. The BBC remains committed to a Public Service Broadcasting (PSB) or, as it is increasingly referred to as, its 'public service communications' remit. These developments point to new ways of using what we have called until now, 'television', redefining it as a 'technology and cultural form' (Williams, 1974). In new media worlds user-generated and other independent audiovisual entertainments made available via websites such as the

see
Murdock,
Chapter 19

BBC's, or YouTube or CurrentTV, the 'flow' experienced by audiences is a different experience to mass broadcast television, being neither completely shaped by traditional institutional nor advertiser logics.

In following this strategy the BBC was also consolidating and extending existing practices involving 'social networks' such as those seen in MySpace, popular among, mostly, younger audiences (the under 25s). Commentators have argued that participation in online social networks is a key feature of Web 2.0 mentioned above. Yet some argue that it is difficult to know exactly how popular the facilitation of these practices will become for traditional media organisations, given they are 'inherently bottom-up rather than top-down, and where constant innovation quickly sweeps away yesterday's products' (Willman, 2006). But the colonisation of the online space by traditional media corporations is now a clear trend, with one of the largest acquisitions being the purchase of MySpace by News Corporation for US $576 million in 2005. News Corporation has signalled that it will use MySpace to deliver on-demand their own branded TV and movie programming.

Recycling genres

see Wilding,
Chapter 16

Throughout the history of the regulation of traditional broadcast media, governments have intervened to control the *content* of media production (Hitchens, 2006). These regulations and policies have been established to intervene at different points of the production-distribution-consumption supply chain. Typically this has meant that parliaments have legislated to set up particular industry licensing structures as well as specific rules governing the presentation of content. Usually these are aimed at a combination of market and non-market media outlets. Broadcasters have then been required to make specified quantities of kinds of programming (e.g. news and current affairs, drama, children's) and directed how they should make programming in terms of particular normative proscriptions (e.g. in relation to news conventions, depictions of sex and violence); and also in relation to how it can be distinguished from advertising.

In the past the major priorities for nation-state regulation of media content has tended to fall into two broad clusters: those relating to fictional genres (notably television drama for maintaining regional or national cultures); and those concerning 'factual' genres (mainly news and current affairs and, to a lesser extent, documentaries and sport). In recent times another enormously popular 'factual' genre, so-called 'reality' programming, has complicated such a convenient division, tending as it does, to hybridise such neat categorisation. Despite this, in broad terms, the traditional concerns of policy (e.g. 'moral panics' in sexual and violent depictions, or the political objectives associated with pluralism of voices in a democracy, and accuracy and fairness in news and current affairs programming) are bound up with these genre distinctions. In other words, traditional content issues in the governance of new media continue to relate to existing representational conventions.

Yet the Internet *has* problematised these broadcasting-like approaches to regulation because of its structure as a decentralised 'network of networks'. In short, its origins as a decentralised structure for military and then scientific research purposes has had a long-term impact on the capacity of governments to regulate it. Whereas in broadcasting regulation liberal democracies can potentially require the holders of licences to return them if certain practices were considered to contravene legal requirements, in an Internet context the lines of accountability are far less clear cut. In practice, this has meant that the entities controlling the 'pipes' are not usually or necessarily related to the entities (or individuals) providing content.

News and information

Behind these new developments in delivering audiovisual content to audiences over the Internet are important questions in relation to the availability of diverse, meaningful sources of information, which remain critical in a healthy democracy.

Even though the technological characteristics of media provision and consumption are changing, few would dispute that news and information genres are important, and that they remain the responsibility of our parliaments, corporations and civil society groups.

A fundamental question for twenty-first century citizenship is whether new ICTs are leading to a splintering of civic discourse, or revitalising public sphere communication by providing new forms of information provision. Many websites use **RSS feeds** to alert us to news from our favourite websites. It is in this context of changing business models and methods of delivery that matching regulatory frameworks and content-provision structures with audience-needs will become most challenging. Arguably this issue is even more acute in rural, regional and remote communities, who traditionally have less service options than metropolitan areas (Dwyer et al., 2006).

RSS (or Really Simple Syndication) feeds An easy way to be alerted when content that interests you appears on your favourite websites. Instead of visiting a particular website to browse for new articles and features, RSS automatically tells you when something new is posted online.

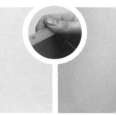

New mass delivery systems and civic discourses

While some commentators suggest that Internet diversity constitutes an alternative to existing media power, others argue that claims about the diversity of opinion in new media are greatly overstated. In fact, a number of studies have shown that most news content on the Internet is repurposed or supplied by traditional media sources (Doyle, 2002; Sparks, 2004; Downie and Macintosh, 2006). Clearly this should be a matter of concern for governments and civil society groups wishing to promote the diversity of opinions and viewpoints in new media.

Indeed, debates over the implications of P2P online news formats is dividing expert commentators: Turner argues that online journalism remains an elite, individualistic pursuit, lacking sufficient audience reach, sustainable business models, or the pro-social objectives of public service broadcasting (2005, pp. 135–47). By contrast, Dennis argues that 'the Internet has greatly benefited journalism by allowing for the development of new media, whether websites, cable outlets, or so-called web TV alongside traditional media that have cautiously used it as a platform' (Dennis and Merrill, 2006, p. 165).

If it is the case that younger audiences' media consumption is shifting dramatically then this is a major concern for all democracies (Carnegie Foundation, 2005). In particular, it raises concerns about the power and influence of new online media and the functioning of modern plural nation states. As Clark quite rightly asks: 'Where will young people be kept informed about a range of political, social, health, education and international news in an increasingly fragmented media landscape, where recognised benchmarks for fairness and accuracy are regarded as vestigial organs of a past era' (Clark, 2005, pp. 103–15)?

Over the longer term we need to track how changing media delivery modes will affect the important policy settings of universality, equitable access and service provision to diverse publics. Traditionally, the model of professional news interpreters/makers (journalists) has dominated both commercial and public service news media provision. Now, hybrid forms delivered over P2P broadband Internet networks that mix those earlier forms with netizen/blogger modes of practice are creating new **audience taste publics.** The implications of these developments for the provision of news and information content in democracies are potentially far-reaching.

Audience taste publics   A term that derives from Bourdieu's classic work *Distinction: A Social Critique of the Judgement of Taste*. Bennett et al., (1999), Ross and Nightingale,

(2003) and McGuigan (2004) all variously apply the term to correlate 'taste' choices of cultural products and social and cultural capital, or hierarchies, which audiences bring to their media consumption.

Activity 3.1

Consider the different kinds of news formats and services on the Internet: online news (run by both traditional media outlets and 'new' media owners); web radio news; expert organisation websites; expert and opinion blogs; audio and video podcasts; SMS news alerts; and, RSS feeds. In the public sphere the provision of 'trustworthy' news has historically been an important issue for regulators.

Questions

- Will regulation be able to apply this notion to these different Internet formats and technologies?
- What important roles do news and information formats have in this public sphere space?

Responses by media policy makers in the public interest

It is not clear at this stage in their evolution the extent to which on-demand, interactive video or IPTV will be regulated. Clearly, many industry players hope that there will be little or no regulation for local, nationally based production quotas, or controls over the way certain products are advertised in traditional media environments. Proposed changes in Europe to the **Television Without Frontiers (TVWF)** policy directive, championed by EC Commissioner for the Information Society and Media, Viviane Reding, to extend the regulation of 'linear' (conventionally scheduled television broadcasts) to 'non-linear' new media services (on-demand, interactive video or IPTV provision) met with strong opposition from a neoliberal alliance of old and new media groups including Cisco Systems, ITV, Vodafone, Yahoo!, Intellect, the UK trade association for the Information Technology Industry, and a UK Government advisory group, the Broadband Stakeholder Group. The alliance's preference was that the definition of 'linear' services needed to be amended so that it would include 'services that are identical in nature to traditional scheduled broadcast services, but delivered over different platforms', and that 'non-linear' services be subject to self-regulation (Edgecliffe-Johnson, 2006).

Television Without Frontiers (TVWF) directive: For the full text, historical context, recent debates and amendments see http://www.euractiv.com/en/infosociety/twf-television-frontiers/article-117550

In spite of this opposition, the European Parliament has amended key provisions in the TVWF directive so that existing content rules that previously applied only to traditional TV will now apply to certain Internet-based services. It is now called the Audiovisual Without Frontiers (AVWF) Directive. Commissioner Reding has argued that these changes will provide a roadmap for convergence (EEC, 2006; Euractiv.com, 2007). The irony of such *reregulation* of new digital media services, at a time of neoliberal *deregulation* through bilateral and multilateral free trade agreements driven by US negotiators, has been interpreted as a proactive step on the part of European policy makers to protect cultural content (Chakravartty and Sarikakis, 2006, pp. 105).

Internet governance: Access, use and coordination

As the Internet has evolved over the past two decades, so too has the debate over the best way to regulate it in the interests of its audience users. There has always been government involvement in regulating the Internet. That involvement, however, changes depending on the circumstance; from being a creator and participant, through to moral guardian, business facilitator and services provider. And while the early culture of the Internet was dominated by an ethic of libertarianism, and the discussion on how best to run the Internet was a matter for network engineers requiring detailed technical knowledge, today the domain name industry is worth hundreds of millions of dollars and an international forum on Internet Governance has been established by the Secretary-General of the United Nations (Butt, 2005).

Think about it

Why might the networked structure of the Internet present difficulties from a regulatory and governance perspective?

The UN's 'Working Group on Internet Governance' (WGIG) represents a range of stakeholders including nation states, powerful IT corporations and a range of civil society groups. The WGIG was established by the Secretary-General of the United Nations after the first phase of the World Summit on the Information Society (WSIS) in Geneva, Switzerland, in 2003, to explore the public policy dimensions of **Internet governance**.

Internet governance The development and application by governments, the private sector and civil society, in their respective roles, of shared principles, norms, rules, decision-making procedures and programs that shape the evolution and use of the Internet (Butt, 2005).

The WGIG is comparable to other fields of international regulatory tension (e.g. International Telecommunications Union or ITU) where the task is often to search for a sustainable model for cooperation between vested interest groups. In this regard, Internet governance reflects long-held geopolitical differences in culture and power. Their 2005 report found Internet governance falls into several key public policy categories including:

- issues of access to infrastructure and management of key Internet resources (e.g. domain names like .com and .org and Internet Protocol, or IP, technical standards);
- issues relating to use of the Internet (e.g. Spam, network security and cybercrime, protection of minors);
- issues relating to developmental aspects of the Internet (e.g. resources for capacity building in developing countries to ensure participation in global governance) (Butt, 2005).

These set of public policy concerns, then, constitute a broad overview of contemporary Internet governance issues.

'Net neutrality' debates

As an increasingly important social and economic infrastructure, the issue of how, and in whose interests, governments regulate the Internet is an ongoing power struggle. Not only is the Internet at the core of the economic success of national and international commerce and trade, but it has also become a key social and cultural infrastructure. The universal ability to access and effectively use the Internet in our everyday lives has emerged in the first decade of the twenty-first century as a matter of fundamental social equity for policy makers (Burgelman, 1997; Castells, 2001; Castells and Himanen 2002; OECD, 2006).

In 2004–05 major US telecommunications and cable companies, who together control the telecommunications networks over which Internet data flows, put forward the idea of creating the electronic equivalent of a paid 'fast lane'. In other words, the suggestion is that some content or services would be given priority over others. The **net neutrality** debate was a response to these proposals by companies like AT&T and Verizon, who spend millions lobbying Congress to have their way.

Network neutrality   The proposal by a coalition of private sector and public interest groups that no website's traffic should be privileged over any other site.

Proponents of net neutrality argued that whether a user searches for recipes using Google, reads an article online, visits a not-for-profit or community site, or looks at a friend's MySpace profile, all of that data ought to be treated equally and delivered from the originating website to the user's Web browser with the same priority, and at the same speed. The alternative, it was argued, was a tiered Internet where access became a matter of affiliation to particular corporate groups who control preferential content delivery. A movement championing net neutrality, and warning of the inherent risks of the proposals, called 'Save the Internet' had some limited success, even if only at a public awareness raising level (SavetheInternet. com, 2007).

In this worst-case scenario a few major corporations and their commercial affiliates alone would benefit. On the other hand, large telecommunications corporations argue that the ability to charge for services such as high-quality video from websites ranging from Google to eBay is crucial to being able to afford the multibillion-dollar price tag of upgrading its network-to-fibre links. Their argument is that in order to roll out bandwidth-hungry audiovisual services they need to charge heavy users to make it more economically viable, and for them to compete. It is worth noting, however, that the European Union has warned telecommunications corporations that they will not tolerate discriminatory access regimes (Foroohar, 2006). Future governance debates will require legislators and policy makers to move beyond these current impasses, and equitably balance commerce, culture and connectivity.

Conclusion

There are many changes taking place in the way ICT products and services are delivered to audiences over multiple communications media platforms. The Internet, and in particular broadband delivery infrastructures, is driving these industry transformations. The social and cultural implications of these developments will require significant rethinking by governments, policy makers and industry regulators.

It has been argued in this chapter that traditional media of television, radio and newspapers are evolving along with the rising popularity of new media forms.

An important consequence of this co-evolution is that policies, laws and regulation developed for existing media will often also be relevant to new media such as the Internet. After all, the values and principles that guide and sustain our democracies remain significant, despite rapid industry change.

CHAPTER SUMMARY

- We have considered some of the key transformations occurring in the communications media industries.
- Traditional silo structures communications media are morphing into convergent multi-platform products and services.
- This chapter gave an account of some of the new media ICT developments affecting production, distribution and consumption practices.
- We discussed how new media policies will need to respond to these changes to promote public interest priorities.
- In these networked new media worlds, existing laws and policies for content, ownership and control will need to be supplemented with a broader set of access policies focusing on network delivery speed (for both downloads and uploads), mobility, network interconnection, privacy, and diversity in genre and origin of content.

Tutorial questions

- How have new media production, distribution and consumption practices changed in recent years?
- Which major public policy issues will affect how we use the Internet in the future?

Recommended reading

Castells, M., 2001, *The Internet Galaxy: Reflections on the Internet, Business and Society*, Oxford University Press, Oxford and New York.

Castells, M. & Himanen, P., 2002, *The Information Society and the Welfare State—The Finnish Model*, Oxford University Press, Oxford.

Jenkins, H., 2006, *Convergence Culture. Where Old and New Media Collide*, New York University Press, NY and London.

OECD (Xavier, P.), 2006, 'Rethinking universal service for a next generation network environment' Working Party on Telecommunication and Information Services Policies, Directorate for Science, Technology and Industry, Committee for Information, Computer and Communications Policy. DSTI/ICCP/TISP (2005) 5/FINAL. OECD, Brussels.

Websites

Australian Communications and Media Authority: www.acma.gov.au

Benton Foundation: www.benton.org

British Broadcasting Corporation: www.bbc.co.uk

Centre for Digital Democracy: www.democraticmedia.org

Commission of the European Communities: www.euractiv.com/en/infosociety/

CurrentTV: www.currentTV.com

Federal Communications Commission: www.fcc.gov

Media Access: www.mediaaccess.org

MySpace: www.myspace.com

New Media Worlds: www.oup.com.au/orc/resources/New_Media_Worlds

Now Broadband TV: www.nowbroadbandTV.com

Office of Communications: www.ofcom.gov.uk

Public Knowledge: www.PublicKnowledge.org

Save the Internet: www.savetheinternet.com

YouTube: www.youtube.com

References

ACMA, 2005, *Digital Media in Australian Homes*, Monograph 1, *Telecommunications Performance Report, 2004–2005*. (See www.acma.gov.au).

BBC 'Creative Futures' strategy. (See Media Release at www.bbc.co.uk/pressoffice/pressreleases/stories/2006/04_april/25/)

Bagdikian, B., 2004, *The New Media Monopoly*, Beacon Press, Boston, Massachusetts.

Bennett, T., Emmison, M. & Frow, J., 1999, *Accounting for Tastes: Australian Everyday Cultures,* Cambridge University Press, Cambridge.

Briggs, A. & Bourke, P., 2002, *A Social History of the Media: From Gutenberg to the Internet,* Polity, Cambridge, UK.

Burgelman, J.C., 1997, 'Communication, Citizenship and Social Policy: Rethinking the Limits of the Welfare State', 12th EURICOM (European Institute for Communication and Culture) symposium, University of Colorado, Boulder, USA.

Butt, D. (2006) 'Net Neutrality: No easy answers', *Media International Australia, incorporating Culture and Policy*, No. 120.

Butt, D. (ed.), 2005, *Internet Governance: Asia-Pacific Perspectives*, UNDP-APDIP, Elsevier, New Delhi.

Carnegie Foundation, 2005, *Abandoning the News*, Carnegie Reporter, Vol. 3, No. 2, Spring, New York.

Carter, S., 2005, Conference paper at 'Digital Britain: FT Broadcasting and New Media', Ofcom conference, 9 March.

Castells, M., 2001, *The Internet Galaxy: Reflections on the Internet, Business and Society*, Oxford University Press, Oxford and New York, pp. 125–33.

Castells, M. & Himanen, P., 2002, *The Information Society and the Welfare State—The Finnish Model,* Oxford University Press, Oxford.

Chakravartty, P. & Sarikakis, K, 2006, *Media Policy and Globalization,* Edinburgh University Press, Edinburgh.

Clark, A., 2005, 'Scaling the Icy Peaks of the New Media', in Mills, J. (ed.) 2005, *Barrons to Bloggers: Confronting Media Power,* The Miegunyah Press/MUP, Melbourne.

Commission of the European Communities, 2006, 'Proposal for a Directive of the European Parliament and the Council Amending Council Directive, 89/552/EEC', Brussels, 13/12/05, COM (2005) 646 Final, 2005/0260 (COD): http://www.euractiv.com/en/infosociety/twf-television-frontiers/article-117550, accessed, January 2007.

Croteau, D. & Hoynes, W., 2006, *The Business of Media: Corporate Media and the Public Interest* (2nd edn), Pine Forge Press/Sage Publications, London, Thousand Oaks, CA, New Delhi.

Dennis, E.E. & Merrill, J.C., (eds) 2006, *Media Debates: Great Issues for the Digital Age* (4th edn), Thomson Wadsworth, Toronto, Canada.

Doyle, G., 2002, *Media Ownership: The economics and politics of convergence and concentration in the UK and European Media,* Sage Publications, London, Thousand Oaks, CA, New Delhi.

Downie, C. & Macintosh, A., 2006, 'New media or more of the same?: The cross-media ownership debate', The Australia Institute, Canberra.

Dwyer, T., Wilding, D., Wilson, H. & Curtis, S., 2006, *Content, Consolidation and Clout: How will regional Australia be affected by media ownership changes?*, Communications Law Centre, Melbourne.

Edgecliffe-Johnson, A., 2006, 'Media groups blast Brussels over directive', *Financial Times*, 18 April.

Finnemann N., 2006, 'Co-evolution of Old and New Media', in Leandros, N. (Ed) *The Impact of Internet on the Mass Media in Europe*, COST A2O International Conference, Abramis, Suffolk, UK.

Flew, T., 2005, *New Media: An Introduction* (2nd edn), Oxford University Press, Melbourne.

Foroohar, R., 2006, 'The Internet Splits Up', *Newsweek*, 16 May.

Gowing, N., 2006, ABC Radio, *The Media Report*, transcript 18 May 2006.

Harvey, D., 2001, *Spaces of Capital: Towards a Critical Geography*, Edinburgh University Press, Edinburgh.

Harvey, D., 1990, *The Condition of Postmodernity: An Enquiry into the Origins of Cultural Change*, Blackwell, Oxford.

Hesmondhalgh, D., 2006, (2nd Edn), *The Cultural Industries*, Sage, London, Thousand Oaks, New Delhi.

Hitchens, L., 2006, *Broadcasting Pluralism and Diversity: A Comparative Study of Policy and Regulation*, Hart Publishing, Portland, USA and Oxford, UK.

Jenkins, H., 2006, *Convergence Culture: Where Old and New Media Collide*, New York University Press, New York and London.

Kapur, A., 2005, *Internet Governance: A Primer*, Elsevier, UN Development Programme Asia-Pacific Development Information Programme (UNDP-APDIP).

Lessig, L., 2004, *Free Culture: How Big Media Uses Technology and The Law to Lock Down Culture and Control Creativity*, Penguin Press, USA.

McGuigan, J., 2004, *Rethinking Cultural Policy*, Open University Press, Maidenhead, Berkshire, UK.

Murdock, G., 2004, 'Building the Digital Commons: Public Broadcasting in the Age of the Internet', Spry Lecture, Vancouver, 18 November 2004, Montreal, 22 November 2004.

Noguchi, Y., 2006, 'IPod Patent Dispute Settled', *Washington Post*, 24 August.

OECD (Xavier, P.), 2006, 'Rethinking universal service for a next generation network environment' Working Party on Telecommunication and Information Services Policies, Directorate for Science, Technology and Industry, Committee for Information, Computer and Communications Policy. DSTI/ICCP/TISP (2005) 5/FINAL. OECD, Brussels.

OECD, 2005, *Communications Outlook*, Secretary General, OECD Publishing, Paris, France.

Ofcom, 2005–6, *The Communications Market Report*, Office of Communications, London, UK.

Ofcom, 2006, 'BBC iPlayer Market Impact Assessment', August–October.

Pool, I. de Sola., 1983, *Technologies of Freedom,* Harvard University Press, Cambridge, MA.

Ross, K. & Nightingale, V., 2003, *Media and Audiences: New Perspectives,* Open University Press, McGraw Hill, Buckinghamshire.

Save the Internet (2007) see SavetheInternet.com

Secretary-General of the United Nations, 2005, *Report of the Working Group on Internet Governance,* June, Chateau de Bossey.

Shultz, J., 2006, 'Google ads cash to News', *The Australian,* 9 August.

Sørensen, K.H. & Williams, R. (eds), 2002, *Shaping Technology, Guiding Policy: Concepts, Spaces and Tools,* Edward Elgar, Cheltenham, UK.

Sparks, C., 2004, 'The Impact of the Internet on the Existing Media', in Calabrese, A. & Sparks, C. (eds), *Toward a Political Economy of Culture: Capitalism and Communications in the 21st Century,* Roman & Littlefield, Maryland, USA.

Spurgeon, C., 2006, 'Advertising and the New Search Media', *Media International Australia, Incorporating Culture and Policy,* No. 119, Centre for Critical and Cultural Studies, University of Queensland.

Stein, L. & Sinha, N., 2006, 'New Global Media and the Role of the State', in Lievrouw, A. & Livingstone, S. (eds), *The Handbook of New Media: Social Shaping and Social Consequences of ICTs,* Student Edition, Sage Publications, London, Thousand Oaks, CA, New Delhi.

Turner, G., 2005, *Ending the Affair: The Decline of Television Current Affairs in Australia,* UNSW Press, Sydney.

Vise, D., 2005, *The Google Story,* Delecourt Press (Random House), New York.

Willman, J., 2006, 'Old media confront a new world that puts users in charge', *Financial Times,* 29/30 April 2006, p. 11.

Williams, G., 2001, 'Selling Off Cyberspace', In Lax, S. (ed.) *Access Denied in the Information Age,* Palgrave MacMillan, Basingstoke, Hampshire, UK and New York.

Williams, R., 1974, *Television: Technology and Cultural Form,* Fontana, London.

Winston, B., 1998, *Media, Technology and Society: A History from the Telegraph to the Internet,* Routledge, London and New York.

JACKIE COOK

4

The Contrary 'Pulls' of Digital Media: Radio Listener Networks in the Era of Mobile Communications Media

Key terms

radio
technology
technology application
social uses of radio
Web streaming

Issues

- Can radio survive the current round of two-way, interactive talk and music streaming?
- Are radio 'audiences' today the same as in previous generations—and why might any of this matter?

CHAPTER OVERVIEW

Radio as we know it—an established set of industries in daily contact with huge audiences—has a complex history of adaptive change to evolving technologies. Witness the rivalry of television; the shift from AM to FM transmission, and now the move to digital content on multiple platforms, from Internet to mobile phone. The new streams of audio talk and music made possible by digitised media have released radio from its old apparatus of broadcast studio, transmission tower and home receiver set—but also problematised the concept of a radio audience. This chapter considers whether we should think of applications such as podcasting as seeking to link into radio industries; as servicing audiences 'massed' in new ways for financial return; or as something altogether different—perhaps remaining a medium of self-expression, like the telephone.

Think about it

Consider the following scenarios:

1   I am driving to work in South Australia, listening to ABC Classic FM on the car radio. A Singaporean woman has emailed the station from Massachusetts in the USA, where she is studying for a Harvard University business degree, to report that this Australian public radio 'fine music' service, streamed internationally through the Internet, 'keeps her sane' as she studies at her computer, long into the night. She requests that they play The Scottish Symphony, just for her. Italian composer. Dutch conductor. Japanese orchestra. The presenter jokes about the size of the world as he programs her CD ...

2   At work I download student assignments from Malaysia, where I teach a course called New Communications and Media Technologies. Aziz has based his analysis of contemporary patterns of 'user-pull' communications innovation on his experiences as a Scottish League soccer fan who has never visited Scotland: a serious follower of Glasgow Rangers. But Malaysian television broadcasts only the English League fixtures. Unless Rangers qualify for one of the European tournaments, Aziz can never watch them play. Instead he sits glued to his PC, scanning the online merchandising and team website, while he listens to an audio webcast of their matches ...

These two experiences represent the unravelling of 'radio' as it is usually explained in textbooks, and its rapidly growing experimentation with new, digital streams of audio-service.

Introduction

There once were vast, massed groups of the listening public, stable, and relatively predictable in tastes and listening habits. Radio presenters addressed them as 'all of you out there, in Radio Land'. Industry professionals referred to 'the rusted-on audience'—those whose radio dials were rarely if ever changed. But in recent years this secure radio audience has shifted ground—not just literally and geographically, as my mobile international examples suggest, but in terms of how it can be thought about, addressed by program presenters, and organised into coherent groups or 'demographics', on a scale large enough to warrant audio-file production and transmission. For audiences are more than casually gathering networks of listeners, selecting programming at random. The daily miracle of their continuing to link into networks of common interest makes economic demands on very expensive technologies, infrastructure, professional and technical training, and content-production creativity. Even for today's home podcaster, producing more for fun than for profit, someone has to fund the digital recorder, the microphone, the PC and the ISP. And in an era of profitability as the decisive factor 'mediating' or bridging private and public lives and spaces, we must consider the economics of sending and receiving radio signal. Certain financial flows of production and transmission funding came to dominate twentieth-century radio as an industry, and for all our current enthusiasm over experimental and free digital-audio flows, funding questions still challenge the limits of digital audio-communication potential and creativity in the twenty-first century.

There are three key issues to consider when examining what radio 'is', and 'could be':

- radio as a technology
- radio as a technology-application, and so as a media industry
- the social uses we make—and could make—of radio.

Activity 4.1

Create your own audio profile—a 'map' of your regular audio listening habits and preferences—and add your own observations of new, or newly revealed, forms of radio use. Ask yourself the following:

- Am I listening to radio in unpredicted ways: perhaps downloading a friend's recommendation of a comedy talk—PODcast to iPod—then I laugh out loud as I listen on the bus ...
- Do I send audiofiles of music to friends, via email?
- Have newsclips 'viralled' their way to me on my personal networks?

Maybe, like Singapore's Ngee-Ann Polytech, students known only as 'Mr Brown', you are already a digital media star, Web streaming your own take on the world, with the aid of a digi-recorder and Internet connection.

Radio as an audio-communications technology

'Radio' as we use the term in daily life, is not itself a technology, but only an application of a technology. It is, in computing terms, a piece of software—but one which, like the software that drives email or MP3 downloads, became invisible to its users; absorbed into the devices that ran it. We think of the service, or the functioning, as what is meant by the term 'radio'. For ordinary members of the listening public, 'the radio' was the receiver set in our homes, cars, or pockets—absorbing even the transmission work of the radio station, which we mostly never witnessed. We were, after all, usually told by radio staff that we had 'invited them into our homes'; that all of the programs, news, music, and advertising messages were 'for us.'

Radio as an industry is oddly schizoid in audio-streaming its content to us. On the one hand, it is ultra-personalised, sending endless, 24/7, back-to-back messages and emotionally laden music (how many songs per hour are NOT, at core, love songs?) linked together with the friendly tones of chat and banter from presenters, and interrupted only by advertisements—which themselves use the same talk-tones and music themes, to sell us products for personal and home use. On the other hand, for all the effort deployed in producing a 'you and I together' inter-personal relation, radio wants not the 'audience of one' it constantly addresses, but thousands of like-minded, taste-tribe-member consumers, able to indicate the success and popularity of the programming formula—and so keep the broadcasts funded and on air.

There is, however, nothing inherent in radio as a technology that meant it had to evolve as a medium for this personalised, individually-addressed stream of audio-content. Radio as a technology was, is, could have been, and still could be, so much more than music-and-talk broadcast services, as the twentieth century configured it.

Invented as a means of extending the nineteenth-century telegraph's 'dot and dash' Morse-code signals to ships at sea, 'wirelessly', the technology of radio simply streamed electrically generated impulses through the air, without cables—impulses that could be picked up and decoded by a 'receiver'. Once Italian scientist Guglielmo Marconi had achieved this breakthrough, patent-seeking Canadians and Americans worked to strengthen, or 'amplify', those signals, until they could carry sound, and so music and voice.

Consider the potential of that amplified transmission of sound, and you confront exactly the dilemma of the early twentieth-century 'wireless' fanatic. What can you make wireless audio transmission *do?* The IT specialists of their era, early radio pioneers were looking for that 'killer application': the good idea that would make radio popular—perhaps a household necessity; a major business tool; saleable in as many ways as possible. Just as with early computing, the challenge to find applications was passing from scientists and technologists to businesses.

Here we reach the second central issue for understanding radio. Once the technology is in place, which applications will emerge and succeed? For digital radio, the possible applications are once again wide open.

Finding successful applications for radio's wireless transmission

So how was radio technology applied in its first period of development in the 1920s? Early proponents urged its use in many services that were subsequently suppressed, ignored or delayed. Amateur or backyard 'ham' operators arose, just as they are doing now with podcasting—and were dealt many of the same criticisms as today's experimenters: dull content; self-obsession … even 'moral panic' over who might be listening to them, and imagining intimate relationships with these 'voices on air' (Hilmes, 1997).

In Australia some especially inventive early uses were proposed for radio. On-air 'announcers' discovered that the telephone placed in front of the microphone would transmit fully-audible 'phone-in' talk—thus producing a form of radio talkback programming, fifty years before it became a central part of radio practice. It was disallowed by the postmaster general, who claimed a monopoly over the telephone cables, threatened by radio transmission. Still in Australia, labour trades unions wanted to use radio to transmit union meetings through what is called 'point-to-point' transmission, linking union offices across a city or state, in a form of early telephone conference-call. And town halls installed radio sets for less affluent citizens, who would congregate there at weekends to listen together to football matches and stay on to dance to live band-music transmissions (Johnson, 1988).

Each imaginable as a use for radio, these were eclipsed by the emergence of two powerful models of 'broadcasting'—a system in which one radio transmitter sends wireless signal to thousands, potentially millions, of 'receiver sets,' owned by families in private homes. Drawn from the agricultural metaphor of sowing seed by scattering it about in a fan-shaped arc, 'broad-casting' served the needs of both producers and private citizens, at a moment of increasing social pressure on public communications of all forms.

Technology historian Brian Winston (1998) reminds us that many technologies are born, but few achieve full development. Good ideas are cheap. What counts is the 'fit' that a given technology has, first with its application, and then, even more importantly, with the social and economic moment in which the public, its users, find themselves. The specific circumstances of this social and economic moment set up what Winston calls 'a supervening social necessity'. Whether by good research or sheer good luck, a new technology and its application have to line up with some new and urgent social need.

Radio's moments:
The social and economic forces driving
its development as an industry

Radio's first communicative 'necessity' developed during 1920s economic growth, alongside a modernised transport infrastructure (Thompson, 1995). In cities, industrial and commercial workforces could move to newly expanding suburbs, following the tramway or bus systems, or using their new mass-produced personal automobiles or bicycles, 'commuting' into the city centre, for work, leisure or shopping. But this exodus stranded women in the family home, far from shops, entertainment or friends, exerting a 'pull' effect on both retailing and advertising. Door-to-door salesmen and delivery-vans flourished, to sell goods to housewives at home—and so did their new-technology information and entertainment equivalents: the telephone, colour-print-photo magazines—and radio, with its daytime programming of cheerful chat and popular music.

As a communications technology application radio had found a social use—but curiously, it had found more than one. To re-contact a 'private' audience in suburban households, it addressed listeners as 'at home' individuals, yet simultaneously 'massed' them into networks of shared popular taste and consensual thinking. Larger than any audiences ever before assembled, even in the high-circulation hey-day of print media, the networks of citizens who comprised radio audiences were valuable assets to the major power blocs of society: business, and government. Not only did each move quickly to form a suitable broadcasting model to harness the new information flows to citizen networks—and so harvest the revenues that flowed back—but in doing so they produced two major radio sectors, dominant to this day.

American commercial radio networks

In America, David Sarnoff, beginning as a telegraph delivery boy for the Marconi cablegram company, came to control RCA: the Radio Corporation of America. As the dominant company in a new industry, it was the Microsoft of its day. Sarnoff himself is credited with the one central great idea for radio as a technology application, suggesting in a memo to his CEO in 1916 that it could become 'an electrical musical box in every home' (Lewis, 1991). RCA marketed radio sets and recorded music discs, as well as broadcasting radio programs, profiting from two sorts of music-entertainment—and incidentally promoting its own products. Sales of music 'records' hugely increased once a disc was played 'on the air'. The highly successful US model of commercial broadcasting was launched. There remained only the discovery of radio's huge powers of persuasiveness: the semi-accidental experiences of on-air presenters that when they chatted in front of the microphone about a product or event, demand mounted to the thousands. Radio, it seemed, had enormous potential for marketing. But why?

To answer that is to understand the role of talk in radio, and how it is both part and not part of everyday conversation. Radio talk constitutes the third of the radio industry's great innovations, marking it as a specific media form, and allowing it to meet the 'social necessities' of its day. Radio's dominant sound-flows, talk and music, addressed 'audience of one' individualised listeners who were able to feel personally drawn into the powerful core of a network of like-minded, dynamic, up-to-the-minute 'radio-land' inhabitants. The BBC in particular worked to evolve a new form of audience 'address', one which approximated a more personal, everyday talk relation. At the core of its famed formality lay this rather more casual mode of broadcast talk.

Early innovations from UK national radio networks

Part of the concept of broadcasting that had seen it triumph over narrow-channelled applications—such as the Australian trades unions' 'point-to-point' or office to office suggestion—was its capacity to 'bind' huge audiences into one, creating a massed experience on an unprecedented scale. Think of how historical movies or TV dramas show listeners in 1939, sitting around the radio as the Second World War is announced... Entire nations could be focused around a single event and its central message. Nation states controlling vast expanses of territory, such as the USA, Canada or Australia, India and China; or maintaining political and economic empires, such as Great Britain, could standardise information from a single, central point, and so provide a sense of union, common purpose and identity. Even in a small and highly urbanised state such as Singapore, a centralising system called 're-diffusion' radio (transmission received in a single set in a large apartment block, and flowed on via cables to an audio-speaker in each apartment) saw the state maintain a controlled flow of information and entertainment to its less-affluent citizens, long after it had been abandoned in most other developed economies.

For the British, radio became a tool of state, not in the sense of direct government control of programming (for the BBC always had control over its own programming), but in terms of its remit or 'charter', which required it to provide public information, serious talks and quality music to help maintain and further develop British cultural life. In an Imperial moment, with Britain controlling major parts of the world, that 'cultural life' had come to seem a justification of British global dominance. The nation that delivered Shakespeare, Dickens, the British Museum, pre-eminence in science and engineering, kept its colonial populations in touch via 'the Home Service', broadcasting global news, drama productions, documentaries, instructive talks, and classical music concerts. It was making claims as a global cultural power. And while ultimately this high-minded BBC cultural formula was forced by sheer weight of popular taste into compromise with a more commercial radio format, a national radio broadcasting network is still part of the cultural life of many countries, as they assert their identity and views through a nationwide state-funded broadcasting system.

Radio learns to speak to its audience-of-one

The BBC model meant public funding through taxpayer support and compulsory 'radio licence' fees to own and use a radio receiver. Programming was for 'the national good', and audiences thought of as united around a common message. The 'tone' of broadcasting was serious and restrained, so much so that in early years on-air presenters had to be retrained to be stopped from speaking as if making a speech in a public hall.

Early talk producer Hilda Matheson was among the first to realise that the technology of the microphone, best when a speaker works within a few inches of the sound-capture, means that on-air talk must be like interpersonal conversation. Radio presenters are not projecting their voices across twenty metres of space to the back rows of a crowded hall, but speaking as they would for the ears of a listener sitting very near to them at just ten centimetres distance. If you are that close to someone in real life, then they know or trust you—so that friendliness and intimacy were being conveyed by the ways radio came to 'mike' its on-air speakers. For radio professionals, this new, intimate, microphone performance was a learned art form. But for listeners, the radio talk that the microphone produced appeared continuous with everyday conversation, and that had consequences for how 'audience' was conceived.

In the US commercial model, 'the consumer' whose attention was being on-sold to marketers and commodity producers, was spoken to as an individual: an at-home 'you' who could be persuaded into purchasing. In the UK model, while the 'massing' of the audience remained central, and the relay of the chimes of the

Westminster clock 'Big Ben' introduced news services to remind nation and Empire of the supremacy of events at its core, the capacity to present individual speakers and to access important national figures 'in their own voice' altered many of the ways in which information and entertainment were presented. The on-air 'interview' for instance—a way of talking to an expert that drew out their information in an ordered conversation—was not widely used in print media or news services until radio saw the need for experienced on-air staff to put guest-experts at their ease by controlling their flow of talk.

More and more non-specialist broadcasters began to appear on radio. Presidents in the USA and royalty in the UK began to broadcast—even though the Archbishop of Canterbury, advising on whether the coronation of King George VI should be broadcast, showed his incapacity to understand the new medium when he feared that men might listen in pubs, without removing their hats. But if archbishops failed to understand the new merging of public and private, radio audiences adapted very well. New music performers understood the 'intimacy' of the radio microphone, adapting their singing style to a more nuanced and subtle presentation, popular with audiences (Scannell, 1996). Bing Crosby's 'crooning' style, an adaptation of Irish lyrical singing, worked perfectly on microphones, while the vocalisation of the operatic or music hall entertainer sounded shrill and overblown. UK wartime singer Vera Lynn achieved the same sound; a mellow tone with very clear diction, 'read' by listeners as sincerity. For audiences sitting in their own living rooms, personalised performances appealed.

Today's radio is personalised and networked as never before into the tastes and concerns of its audiences. The immediacy of contact and responsiveness—the sense of an ever-present, ever-accessible communicative space, its focus co-extensive with our own experiences and interests—has pre-established for us the sorts of postmodern digitised streams of hypertexted information that flow online in 'new' media, accessing our most private spaces. Radio long ago went mobile. It has accompanied individuals pretty well everywhere since transistorisation and talkback delivered portability and interactivity in the 1960s. So powerful has it become, that the cheaper, multimedia-enhanced, personalised 'pull' systems of webcasting, DABcasting and podcasting must each prove able to supply something even more desirable and useful before they can fully overturn broadcast radio.

So far, problems abound with new media. Digital radio multiplies audio-streams—but does it multiply, or split, the audience? How might an audio-based production culture form around the individualised, downloading, time-deferring, 'pull' user of the early twenty-first century, who has access to so many other on-demand sources of information and entertainment? Are such services valuable, to the extent of warranting funding, either by user-pays, fee-for-service subscription, corporate sponsorship, or public or community levy—whether through taxes, arts grants, or fundraising? Are there as-yet-undiscovered economic models that might pay production costs to content creators?

This means looking not to digital technology *per se,* but to its technologisation of the relation between presenter and listener—all that is left to digital radio of the concept of 'audience'. What is under construction in the many different zones of contemporary radio practice?

Singapore goes DABcasting: Digital Audio Broadcasting as a solution for radio industries

The Singapore Broadcasting Service's Digital Audio Broadcasting model (DAB) allows us to question how broadcasting might or might not be keeping pace in a multi-channelled world of personalised 'pull' servicing, especially when the economics of its full potential programming have not yet developed.

In two books outlining how the SBS set out to reformat radio programming for the new digital systems, Oei (2002, 2005) shows how a fully digitised system—producing, transmitting and receiving radio signal as a flexible digital stream—has not yet fully evolved. DAB may in fact have been seriously derailed by the unexpected emergence of the mobile phone as a platform for experimentation with two-way digital information flows (telephony, text messaging, news and finance updates, photography, email, MP3 music—plus pod files and radio itself).

Oei, working in Singapore to develop the first programming strategies and trained technicians and presenters for DAB, understood in detail how far digital radio could deepen and enhance 'rich information' flows. Improved efficiencies of digital transmission—its capacity to flow signal further and more cheaply—'bundled' into multi-channels, allow digital radio to handle at an acceptable price the split-service, specialised or 'narrowcast' programming that 'taste tribes' of today demand. DAB receivers, every bit as 'smart' as the technologies behind production, let audiences auto-select their preferred programming, pre-setting their tuners to deliver the blend of cross-station, cross-channel news, music and talk that they prefer. Just as on the World Wide Web, where search engines can deliver relevant text, sound or graphic files at the entry of a single search-term, audiofile-sensing i-Bots (intelligent 'robotic' information software) can track and deliver at pre-nominated times the radio programming you or I want.

Or it could, if DAB had developed to the stage predicted a decade ago (i.e. had it been built into new cars; appeared on the shelves of electronic stores at reasonable prices; developed the new advertising flows through inner-city local transponders that promised the localisation of sponsorship funding). As you drive, DAB has the capacity for local advertising messages to intersect your chosen programming with something like this:

I see you are on the corner of Main Street and First Avenue!

There are car-park spaces available now in the Parking Station at the next intersection.

Take one of these spaces, and your ticket will entitle you to 15% off the cost of a Pizza from Dino's-on-Main, sponsors of this message ...

But for these sorts of micro-application of digital audio to occur, entire communities have to be brought to see a need. Further, that need has to *not* be met by existing systems, to drive behavioural change in audiences, and system change in industries.

Was DABcasting too specialised? Too early? Hijacked by other communications technologies? Or wrongly oriented, in terms of audience understandings of how information and entertainment flows ought to operate?

Two other digital radio flows help in understanding what is still possible and might be on the way.

Web streaming: Radio from *anywhere* to *everywhere*

Think about it

In the 1990s an Australian Community Radio station began to Web stream its programming, only to receive an angry email from a man in Virginia, in the USA. He liked listening to their Web Radio service as he worked away on his computer. He enjoyed the vagaries of the Australian accent; liked the strangeness of the music selections, and even the opportunity to hear news services from another nation. But the previous night's program from Student Radio had personally insulted *him*! How did they even know he was a listener? What had he done to deserve the barrage of jokes?

The email was signed 'Jeff Kennett'. Unknown to this distant American web-listener, his name was shared by a prominent Australian politician—a target far too tempting for that night's Student Radio presenters.

Web streaming can access radio signal from around the globe. But it also illustrates the perils of audience dis/location: the degree to which radio's address of a common culture, arising through its establishment of a colloquial talk-register to bind in its audience, can also lock out any '*un*common' audience members.

Welcomed by global travellers, international students and diasporic communities cut off from their particular 'common culture', Web streaming preserves up-to-date information flows and binds the self to 'home'. It provides a link to talk, news and music that you can fully understand because it is spoken and selected by those who think and feel and speak just as you do.

But beyond the capacity to reconnect the geographically dispersed, Web streaming can create new audiences, aggregating the often very small special interest groups within a local audience into global clusters of sufficient size to exert production influence. The World Music movement for instance, with content once reliant on expert, and adventurous, music ethnographers who identified and recorded remote indigenous music *in situ,* now has world audiences large enough to dictate its own category in music stores, and to pull huge live audiences to major annual tours by key performers.

Such groups have built a new and very complex form of social connection. It works through what is called 'irrealis', the 'unreal', imagined sharing of feelings and meanings developed partly through the emotional charge of popular music, and partly through the personal and 'intimate' talk of regular radio presenters. Web streamed radio's sense of 'connection' doubles that of other online or 'virtual' communities, where a 'secure' relationship is mediated by technologies that make reciprocated self-revelation and intimacy seem 'safe'. Together in time but apart in space, users of radio, like those using online chat, can develop a sense of social self, without having to commit to any real or physical engagement.

Radio produced a 'quasi de-sequestration' of individual listeners, as music radio and its DJ hosts bridged the dream-lives of young audiences into the adult world of sex, romance and dating (Thompson, 1995). This imagined connectedness remains central to Web streaming; extending the dreamworld further across space, into the exotic. But has Web streaming actually delivered the selectiveness and interactivity it promises?

WEBradio, as Geert Lovink pointed out when it began (Lovink, 2001), is so far mostly streaming existing radio signal through the World Wide Web. It is a secondary function of broadcasting; an experiential and relatively uncreative form, able to unlock a new audience formation globally, but not itself reformatted to access and use the creativity which those 'audiences' may be producing in response. Lovinck called for radio to challenge itself, producing first for its webcasts; then editing back to analogue format and transmitting through its old broadcast networks. Only then, he suggested, would radio producers understand the potential of the digital format, recognising the constitution of new 'active' audiences and their 'flow back' of self-produced content.

As in DABcasting, the march of technology, combined with the relative inertia of still-profitable existing broadcast systems, and the lack of focus from populations busily confronting technological change in all other media formats, blocked the creative responses that true webcasting would require.

Waiting, as Sarnoff had done in the 1920s for broadcast radio, until a (fully legal) recorded music-marketing system emerged, plus ways of streaming and contracting advertising revenues to support content providers, webcasting is only now seeing a successful 'application' evolve.

Podcasting: Radio that waits

Podcasting, an asynchronous or user-selected system of audio-file selection, operates according to a concept of 'vertical streaming,' as outlined by Canadian Podcast guru Todd Maffin. Radio is 'horizontal' in its broadcast stream, flowing past potential listeners in a number of possible channels, and available whether an individual listener tunes in or not. Podcasts, 'Playable On Demand' sound files posted to a website for voluntary download by listeners, are 'vertical'. Soundfiles are indexed into website lists, from which listeners, or their i-Bot agents, can select.

The key element of difference between traditional radio and post-digital audio services is the relation between transmission and reception, the broadcaster and the audience. This is now a relation in which the power of content selection, and even production, can reverse.

Because of the massively increased technical efficiencies of digital streaming, digital 'radio' can enhance or enrich programming, as within DAB and Web streaming. But it has also had to confront a more problematic erosion of its once-exclusive 'listener' base by new rival services. Radio in the digital era has both won and lost.

Consider the gradual reduction of cost in transmission and reception of radio signal over broadcast radio's 90-year history. Radio initially needed expensive recording and sound-amplification systems; purpose-built studios; specially designed electricity-guzzling transmission towers, mostly in inaccessible locations such as hilltops, to provide signal range; and finally expensive reception sets, often designed as highly decorated pieces of furniture, to signify the fashion sense and status of their owners.

By the 1970s, as transistorisation delivered cheap, mobile 'pocket' radios and began to split the mass audiences of major radio networks into smaller, more specialised 'narrowcast' taste-streams, costs for radio production and transmission lowered. 'Public' or Community Radio stations became possible, with volunteer broadcasters programming from cheap cassette recorders, and gaining shared transmission access on radio towers.

With digitisation, however, radio confronted a dilemma. Cheap digital recorders can easily interface with the various signal-streaming devices that most of us already have, such as a PC and Internet connection. But how and where do we each choose to 'interface' on the system, to upload and download signal? Do we want the trouble of locating, selecting and downloading our own radio programming— especially when we can already for instance download MP3 music files onto iPods or MUVO devices? Will we really upload our own music or talk signals on a regular basis, and who might be interested in listening to them if we did?

Once again the issue is audience, finding listeners to engage with these digital systems, 'commissioning' their own download flows, day by day, and finding persistently active programmers who want to command an audience by regularly uploading their own product.

This time radio confronts in real terms the problem of the audience-of-one. In the past it found ways to 'mass' that audience, as numbers for the advertising dollar or as 'style tribe' specialist music or talk taste cultures for 'narrowcast' channels. Now it confronts a lone and as yet unconnected 'user' who has access to many other channels, asserts totally personal tastes, and is very likely to have the technical capacity to stream signal back.

This new interactive user of the digital era is problematic. They can and do 'pull' whatever they want so need 'asynchronous' flows, accessed in their own time. To maintain a rich supply at least some of them need the drive to recombine the product they access into their own personalised or 'tailored' flows, reordering their own compilations of music tracks, or 'value-adding' to a product by attaching data files about artistes, photo files of images, 'slash fiction' self-authored scripts, to deliver Podcasts of new information. Within the online streams of audio-connectivity such activities establish new, if virtual, communities of taste and interest. But where is the social necessity? What motivates this hyperactive auto-production, which at the moment at least, is still unrewarded, and certainly, except for a celebrated few, unpaid.

Podcasting occupies and activates the 'back channels' of the system, the spaces of production and reception where experts lurked selecting music and so, in their way, dictating music taste; contacting interviewees, and so building celebrity; screening phone-in callers, and so talent-spotting 'acceptable' on-air contributions; running ratings measurements to quality-control program content and formats to optimise audiences.

Now, these functions are superseded by RSS, an audio keyword search-system that locates and delivers audiofiles and sends their URLs to a potential listener's computer, 'on request'. What matters now is not *access*, which we all have equally, but *activation*, the motivation to select, produce and 'post' new product. But with statistics showing that in 2006 over 85% of young Americans were involved in some form of content creation for digital media, the 'e-habitus' or development of communication behaviours around content creation and shared self-expressiveness seem assured.

Continuity, or a new beginning?

Should we think of applications such as Podcasting as seeking to link into radio industries, to service audiences which are 'massed' in new ways for financial return, or as something altogether different, perhaps remaining a medium of self-expression like the telephone?

Each of the new digital audio systems to date has been, in its own way, economically active, returning value and income at the level of technology purchase (hardware) and application use (software). Each has developed ways of involving users, not as we once thought, as passive end-consumers, but as increasingly active 're-combiners' and 'on-users' of products, applying them to countless social and cultural tasks in everyday life.

This recombinant role has become a form of content creation, one that enthusiasts hope may be the space for development of new sorts of industry. Communications technology theorists such as Castells (1996, 1997) consider these content aggregation and re-use spaces as new 'nodes' on the digital 'networks', new concentrations of creative potential and activity around which audiences, and so industries, might settle. Certainly Todd Maffin sees these online spaces as Podcasting's future, as successful amateurs congregate to pool content, meeting the web-based POD streams of established broadcasting industries, somewhere in a future that will combine horizontal broadcast streams with vertical, self-selected Podcasts.

Conclusion

To date, however, there are few indications of what might emerge as radio's future. DAB casting, Web streaming and Podcasting have each so far been unable to deliver the downloading-and-purchasing audiences upon which an industry version is predicated, with advertising sponsorship, credit-card auto-purchase and ratings-tracking apparatus attached. The shake-down of technological potential, through the right sorts of applications, workable financing structures, connecting with the necessary social networks, is what builds real industries, and the enduring cultural patterns of use that guarantee audiences. So far, digital formats have found only parts of the needed solutions.

There is, however, one final and intriguing model. As the work of futures-populist Richard Florida (2004, 2005) has enticed governments in various developed and digitised economies into a vision of how 'creative content providers' need to be aggregated within populations—clustered together to innovate through hybridised and culturally active productivity—there is the possibility of adding to 'the creative city' what Castells reminds us is now a 'real virtuality' of creative congress. Rather than seeking to replicate a 'Left Bank' bohemianism in the unlikely remnants of abandoned outer-metropolitan industrial zones, or the over-regulated urban white-collar ghettoes of 'office tower' CBDs, why not recognise the same pooling and inspirational impact within the interactive flows of Web streams, DAB channels and POD exchanges? 'Interactivity' develops in the comparative freedom of online networks as so much more than a mere provider–consumer relation. It may prove to be these locations, the electronic 'creative commons', rather than their real life 'Boho-Soho' equivalents, which become the 'creative cultures' and 'smart technopoles' of the future.

- This chapter has discussed whether the new developments in radio, particularly its transformation into a digital medium, constitute the beginning of a new era in radio.
- The new developments have been contextualised by an in-depth analysis of the history of radio in different parts of the world that reveal radio as a versatile medium, particularly in its capacity to mould itself to very different everyday life contexts—home, work, commuting or leisure.
- The future of radio in a digital world remains uncertain. Neither webcasting nor Podcasting have yet been able to deliver sufficiently large audiences to prove commercially viable.
- This indeterminate point in the history of radio presents itself as a time of opportunity to explore new futures and new options for this medium.

CHAPTER SUMMARY

Tutorial questions

This chapter makes three fundamental distinctions. It points out that radio is:
- a technology;
- an application of a technology—an application that is administered by the radio industry;

- a response to the 'communicative necessities' experienced within the socio-cultural context where it is deployed and where the word 'radio' is used to refer to the nature, form, content and variety of the programming-to-audiences mix radio can deliver.
  1. What is a 'communicative necessity' and to what 'communicative necessities' has radio responded in the past?
  2. To what contemporary 'communicative necessities' is Podcasting a response?
  3. Is Podcasting a technological response to an industry necessity or and industry response to a socio-cultural necessity?

Recommended reading

Oei, R., 2002, *Borderless Bandwidth: DNA of Digital Radio*, Eastern University Press, Washington.

Scannell, P., 1996, *Radio, Television and Modern Life: A Phenomenological Approach*, Blackwell, Oxford.

Winston, B., 1998, *Media Technology and Society: A History, From the Telegraph to the Internet*, Routledge, London.

Websites

Australian Broadcasting Corporation: www.abc.net.au/services/podcasting/
BBC podcasting: www.bbc.co.uk/radio/downloadtrial/
Podcast network: www.podcast.net/
Wikipedia: en.wikipedia.org/wiki/Podcasting

References

Castells, M., 1997, *The Information Age: Economy, Society and Culture, Vol. 2: The Power of Identity*, Blackwell, Oxford.

Castells, M., 1996, *The Information Age: Economy, Society and Culture, Vol. 1: The Rise of the Network Society*, Blackwell, Oxford.

Florida, R., 2005, *Cities and the Creative Class*, Routledge, New York.

Florida, R., 2004, *Rise of the Creative Class, and How it's Transforming Work, Leisure, Community and Everyday Life*, Basic Books, New York.

Hilmes, M., 1997, *Radio Voices: American Broadcasting, 1922–1952*, University of Minnesota Press, Minneapolis.

Johnson, L., 1988, *The Unseen Voice: A Cultural Study of Early Australian Radio*, Routledge, London.

Lewis, T., 1991, *Empire of the Air: The Men Who Made Radio*, Harper Collins, New York.

Lovink, G., 2001, Address to Fibreculture: Network of Critical Internet Research and Culture in Australasia, Inaugural Meeting, Melbourne, December.

Maffin, T., http://todmaffin.com/

Oei, R., 2005, *Riding the Bandwidth: producing for Digital Radio*, Springer, New York,

Oei, R., 2002, *Borderless Bandwidth: DNA of Digital Radio*, Eastern University Press, Washington.

Scannell, P., 1996, *Radio, Television and Modern Life: A Phenomenological Approach*, Blackwell, Oxford.

Thompson, J.B., 1995, *The Media and Modernity: A Social Theory of the Media*, Polity Press, Oxford.

Winston, B., 1998, *Media Technology and Society: A History, From the Telegraph to the Internet*, Routledge, London.

Part One Summary

The chapters presented here have explored the character of a sociological perspective on new media, digitisation and convergence. In particular the shift to privatised modes of consumption and living is identified as an important driver of the technological changes we see expressed in fashionable new media devices. The 'coolness' of capitalism has captivated the young in particular and led to unprecedented investment in technological innovation. The shift to a mobile communications environment has clarified three key challenges for convergence: the problem of industry preparedness to deal with the implications of the changes; the challenge of protecting copyrighted materials while simultaneously encouraging the production of user-generated content; and the difficulty of creating environments where the new audience formations of the Internet voluntarily keep busy (and therefore productive) online.

The convergence of communication and content has rendered many of the policy contexts responsible for media regulation in need of an overhaul. The sluggishness of response to the new media by industry has in many respects been amplified by the fact that the national bureaucracies responsible for regulation of the media industries were established to assist individual media (for example, television or radio), rather to regulate a multimedia and multi-platform digital communications environment. This means that almost every aspect of media regulation and its social and cultural impact has to be reconsidered from a policy perspective. As the case study of radio shows, even for a frequently changing medium like radio, which has successfully redefined itself from two-way to one-way, and withstood the introduction of television, digitisation poses some extremely difficult challenges. In particular, the break with scheduling and the shift from local and national to global and international audience formation and from mass broadcasting to social networking poses challenges that have yet to be resolved.

- Why does the assumption that technologies cause change make it difficult to develop a rounded view of the changes associated with digitisation and convergence?
- What is the link between the perceived coolness of capitalism and the success of mobile technologies?
- What are the three key challenges facing convergence?
- Why is a multimedia and multi-platform approach to media regulation so important?
- What are the main transformations which radio has survived in the past, and what challenges are now presented for it by podcasting?

Recommended reading

Beck, Ulrich & Elisabeth Beck-Gernsheim, 2002 [2001], *Individualization—Institutionalized Individualism and its Social and Political Consequences*, Sage, London.

Calabrese, A. & Sparks, C. (eds), 2004, *Toward a Political Economy of Culture: Capitalism and Communications in the 21st Century*, Roman & Littlefield, Maryland.

Fortunati, Leopoldina, 2005, 'Mediatization of the Net and Internetization of the Mass Media', in *Gazette: the International Journal for Communication Studies*, Vol. 67 (1), pp. 27–44, Sage Publications, London, Thousand Oaks and New Delhi.

Hitchens, L., 2006, *Broadcasting Pluralism and Diversity: A Comparative Study of Policy and Regulation*, Hart Publishing, Portland, USA and Oxford, UK,.

Jenkins, H., 2006, *Convergence Culture: Where Old and New Media Collide*, New York University Press, New York and London.

Oei, R., 2002, *Borderless Bandwidth: DNA of Digital Radio*, Eastern University Press, Washington.

Urry, J., 2000, *Sociology Beyond Societies—Mobilities for the Twenty-First Century*, Routledge, London.

Activism

Communication rights are routinely associated with political power, yet the experience of communication rights is far from equally distributed, whether within or between nations. This section will address the importance of community media for indigenous, diaspora and other marginalised communities and for citizenship and participation in a media-driven world. It is recognised that the experience of communication rights is very different for citizens (and non-citizens) of first and third world nations. One of the main advantages offered by digital media is the opportunity for ordinary people to engage in the creative process and to publish their work online or in traditional media.

In this section the spotlight is trained on media activism and the ways that marginalised communities and other groups with interests and needs in common engage in collaborative action to change their life circumstances. Media activism can be directed at many different points in the media system, and it can aim to bring change about in many different ways. This section looks at two expressions of media activism: activism aimed at changing the media to make the world a better place; and activism that uses the media more directly to change society and make the world a better place. It also draws our attention to the dependence of diverse local communities on access to traditional media for training and development of the capacity to give expression to local cultural interests and concerns.

- What do you believe are your 'communication rights' and how important are they to you?
- Why do some groups need to agitate to have their communication rights recognised?
- Why is play an important component of new media participation and what does an understanding of its importance contribute to the communication rights debates?

ACTIVISM TO REFORM THE MEDIA

Juan Francisco Salazar (Chapter 5) questions the scope of UNESCO definitions of 'communication rights', drawing attention to the fact that basic understandings of authorship, ownership and content need to be reconsidered if indigenous peoples are to be in a position to exercise their communication rights. He draws attention to the interventions indigenous and Aboriginal communities throughout the world have initiated, often in the face of indifference or hostility from their national governments, to secure their communication rights under the United Nations charters. The key objectives are to gain recognition and assistance to protect cultural rights, cultural knowledge, cultural heritage and artefacts from expropriation so that they will be available for future generations. Digital media have assisted the Aboriginal and indigenous peoples of the world to work together to pursue their very different agendas in a global environment.

Gerard Goggin and Christopher Newell (Chapter 6) draw attention to the ways new media overlook the needs and interests of the disability sector. They argue that this neglect extends from the materialities of communication (the design and organisation of keyboards, monitors and the screen layout, etc.) to the nature of new media forms (like podcasts; weblogs; audiovisual archives). In a wealthy country like Australia, the disability lobby faces a strong barrier to change because of the inertia and the unwillingness of policy makers and media industries alike to look at the special needs of this group. In fact Goggin and Newell argue that the Internet creates rather than assists disability because it adds to the social and cultural arenas from which the sector is excluded. This chapter draws attention to the ways new media are designed around a biased and discriminatory understanding of the human and the human body.

In a case study from Finland, Ullamaija Kivikuru (Chapter 7) describes how people who are normally part of the social mainstream can suddenly find themselves to be a group apart, with needs and interests that are of little interest to most of their fellow citizens. This study explores the impact of the Asian Boxing Day Tsunami on relatives of Finnish nationals holidaying in the disaster area, and on the holidaymakers themselves, stranded in a disaster zone. As with other emergency situations, most notably Cyclone Katrina in the USA, the authorities and the media were unprepared for the scale of assistance their citizens might need. The Finns with relatives affected at a distance by the tsunami situation responded by improvising—establishing makeshift websites to share information, stories and problems and by using SMS (text messaging) to relay what was happening to people in the affected area who were cut off from normal communications. This study points to a series of shortcomings in the response strategies of governments and national media that need to be improved.

ACTIVISM TO CHANGE SOCIETY

The second approach to media activism sees it as a way of using the media for development—whether of communities or nations. Media activism in this sense involves using the media to achieve social and cultural ends that may or may not be media-related. The communications infrastructure provides opportunities for and places limitations on how people are able to use media to achieve personal, social and cultural goals. For example, the situation facing activists in South Africa, where a majority of the population do not have access to digital media is compared here with two different accounts of the media in Australia— where the richness of provision available in the cities compares poorly with the provision of communication infrastructure in rural, regional and remote areas. The particular conditions people face make a difference to exactly what media they use to bring about change and also to the tactics they adopt to achieve their ends. The strategies detailed here all include the use of media—media as they enter into the lived realities of daily life and media as a means of making life meaningful.

In Chapter 8, Herman Wasserman documents how community activist groups use new media to profile their causes and to bring about social change in the face of hostility from political elites and to counteract their lack of mainstream media presence. This study is extremely useful in reiterating the importance of entry-level new media skills like email newsgroups and dedicated websites when trying to bring about social change. Wasserman contrasts an activist group working among South Africa's poor to alleviate the difficulties faced by HIV sufferers, with a group of poor and middle-class South Africans seeking to reform the health insurance system. The two groups used diametrically opposed methods to communicate with their members. The first relied mostly on its website to influence the influencers—echoing Katz and Lazarsfeld's two-step flow approach to communication (see Ross and Nightingale, 2003, pp. 16–28). The website was used as a noticeboard for the dispersed members of the group. The second group preferred email distribution lists for communication within its core membership. The first approach was adopted to have maximum effect in a situation where most group members had little or no private access to ICTs, so the website was designed for maximum effect and used to complement word of mouth, telephone and other informal communication among committed members. The second group was better equipped in terms of access to computers and the Internet. Many of its members were middle class, and while they made extensive use of email to create a cohesive team, they did not use it for communication with people outside the group. Both groups used their websites to archive press releases and information about their activities, thus contributing to a sense of group history and achievement. This chapter shows how effective new media can be allowing people who are geographically dispersed to work together to bring about social change.

Worlds apart, in the northern hemisphere, Gunn Enli and Trine Syvertsen (Chapter 9) report on their research into the importance of play and socialising as components of television viewing. They investigated which enhanced options viewers used most. Their work reiterates the fact that not only rhetoric, but also opportunities, are needed to ensure people actually enjoy using new media technologies. While the politics of participation is important, the role of play and sociality must not be overlooked. This research demonstrates another dimension of access. Even if access is used 'only' for play and making friends, these activities are the essential precursors for future productive engagement with new media. Their chapter reminds us that we may need to play and have fun with new technologies before we are able to fully appreciate how they might best be used productively.

The city of Sydney is situated on the east coast of the continent. Sydney's western suburbs have been the focus of new land developments and expanding communities that are frequently under-resourced in terms of communications infrastructure, especially for the young. Elaine Lally (Chapter 10) looks at how new media have been used to improve community infrastructure in outer metropolitan Sydney. Here the communications infrastructure may be richer than in remote and rural areas, but the urban landscape can appear inhospitable to a culturally diverse population. Poor transport provision makes it difficult for the area's youth to engage in artistic or creative activities outside the school situation. Lally therefore examines how new media can offer opportunities for creative collaborations that result in changes to people in terms of their sense of identity and the setting of achievable life goals, and in changes to the social and cultural environment of a major global city. These changes come about as much as a result of the sometimes difficult interpersonal intercultural interaction required in creative collaborations as because of the achievement in completed projects and the learning of new skills.

The limits of existing communications infrastructures are discussed by Jacqui Ewart, Susan Forde, Kerrie Foxwell and Michael Meadows (Chapter 11) in their discussion of community radio. In Australia community radio is booming—both in the cities and in rural and remote areas. While metropolitan areas are rich in media provision they offer less in terms of opportunities for participation. Rural and remote communities, by contrast, often lack access to any media, let alone new media prepared to provide current local information and to work at a grass-roots level. This is why community radio is most valued. It is personally and communally relevant to the management of everyday life and is a key focus for community building.

The development agenda explored in these chapters shows that geographic dispersal of groups with common interests can be manifest in very different ways, and connection established using the most readily available media. The chapters also show how very important connectivity is in terms of identity and social and cultural equality.

Indigenous People and the Communication Rights Agenda: A Global Perspective

JUAN FRANCISCO SALAZAR

5

CHAPTER OVERVIEW

The chapter discusses indigenous people's involvement in current debates on communication rights and the use of information and communication technologies for development (ICT4D). In the context of a so-called information society the chapter argues that communication rights are to be regarded as a new frontier for indigenous people's civil rights struggle in a global knowledge society, particularly when looking at the political and cultural complexities between indigenous and non-indigenous ways of conceiving the protection and dissemination of tangible and intangible cultural material.

The analysis is grounded in the emergence of indigenous movements across the world in the last decade, which arise simultaneously along many other social movements appropriating new technologies and socio-technical systems of communication, participation and collaboration. The chapter draws on current international literature to examine the role of ICTs in development and community participation. It points out the need for culturally appropriate legal frameworks to support the full incorporation of indigenous cultural producers into the new national and transnational creative economies where the conditions for a different regime that identifies and protects particular forms of indigenous copyright and intellectual property based on traditional knowledge and collective ownership are considered.

Key terms

Communication rights
ICT for development
traditional knowledge system
cultural diversity
collective intellectual property
information society

Issues

- How might governments ensure that indigenous peoples are able to participate as equals in the information society?
- What are the economic, social and cultural costs of denying indigenous peoples access to new media technologies as a human right?
- What special contributions might indigenous people bring to ways of thinking about new media cultures?
- Why is an appropriate understanding of cultural diversity necessary to the provision of suitable Internet access?

Introduction

When discussing indigenous and tribal peoples' involvement in the information society and the possibilities for participating in public domains as citizens of their indigenous nations, it seems important to take into account an increased politicisation of indigenous affairs in recent decades. The global indigenous social movement that emerged strongly in North America in the late 1960s, Australia in the 1970s and since 1992 in Latin America has become an important site of power in this era of increased globalisation. In this context it is interesting to note how the growing importance of traditional knowledge systems and global environmental concerns have meant that the possession of such knowledge becomes a valuable political instrument.

On another level, the notion of indigenous peoples itself is often taken for granted, and we tend to dismiss the idea of an ideologically constructed concept that reproduces a form of cultural domination affecting native and indigenous communities that share a common historical experience of colonialism. Moreover, this conceptualisation has also allowed for the organised and institutionalised management of indigenous issues through state and international policies. But the question of politicisation also draws on the strategic responses by indigenous cultural formations to the nature of sovereign power of the states in which they have been in most cases forcefully inserted. As Maori researcher Linda Tuhiwai Smith (1999) suggests,

> the term [Indigenous peoples] has enabled the collective voices of colonized people to be expressed strategically in the international arena. It has also been an umbrella enabling communities and peoples to come together, transcending their own colonized contexts and experiences, in order to learn, share, plan, organize and struggle collectively for self-determination on the global and local stages (Smith, 1999, p. 7).

Indigenous people around the world are incredibly heterogeneous and diverse. Different sources, such as the World Bank for example, estimate the existence of around 400 million indigenous, aboriginal and tribal people in the world. In Latin America, for example, there are today around 50 million indigenous persons who form part of around 400 culturally diverse nations, groups or tribes inhabiting the big metropolises of the continent, as well as some of the most varied, rich and remote ecosystems in the planet. This is a pattern that can be recognised all over the world. Many are peasants, and many live in ways they have lived for centuries. Many others are today world citizens, professionals in many disciplines and international experts in different fields.

In order to look specifically at indigenous peoples' communication and media rights we must also distinguish between what occurs at the local, national and international level. In most parts of the world, indigenous cultural production happens at the local level as a system of social relations and networking aimed at reaffirming communal social solidarities and cultural identity. In this sense, indigenous media is often thought to be a product of struggle and opposition; the outcome of a struggle for cultural survival and self-determination.

In the following sections it is argued that communication rights are rapidly becoming a critical new battleground for indigenous peoples in their ongoing struggle for cultural self-determination worldwide. The indigenous movements across the globe are today demanding new intellectual property policies that better address the specificities of indigenous cultures. New forms of global governance regarding intellectual property are required mainly because the new international regulatory frameworks introduced during the last decade have been incapable of preventing the illicit use and appropriation of the cultural and biological heritage of indigenous people. Since much of the current wave of international intellectual property regulations is driven mostly by only two organisations, the World Trade Organization (WTO) and the World Intellectual Property Organization (WIPO), what is needed is an appropriate project on intellectual property policy that includes indigenous leaders at the decision-making level who may be able to counter the often negative impact that international communications standards have on local and traditional culture and knowledge. The main problem here is the imposing of international or general standards over the cultural specificity and difference of local contexts.

In this regard, communication, its practices and technologies, must always be a central aspect of culture since it provides the means for the expression, dissemination and exchange of cultural meanings and artefacts across time and space. It is therefore important to acknowledge from the outset that customary and traditional indigenous laws, as well as the intellectual property needs of indigenous knowledge holders, is enormously varied among indigenous and tribal communities throughout the world.

From a Western perspective, intangible culture, such as songs or stories for example, are protected by legal frameworks that guarantee property rights to either individuals or private corporations. These frameworks, such as copyright, patent and trademark, provide the legal system through which cultural materials (tangible or intangible) are formally registered in public domains and are protected against other individuals or corporations that infringe on the property rights held by another person or institution.

What is absent from this equation is the notion of community, and a better understanding of how, in indigenous legal systems, culture belongs to a community, which is ultimately the organic unit that holds the collective 'ownership' of these materials. Therefore given the vast array of indigenous cultures worldwide and the immense variety of traditional knowledge systems, it becomes very problematic to impose a legal regime which does not regard traditional legal frameworks for protecting cultural materials. Perhaps the main issue with indigenous intellectual property rights is that most of the time these are informal and unwritten, consensual, even implicit communal agreements. Therefore, they are often open to speculation and are easy targets for people or institutions such as large transnational corporations to illegally appropriate, ignoring and therefore violating traditional legal systems.

Activity 5.1

1 The increase in the use of the images of indigenous and aboriginal communities is a highly visible fact in contemporary Western societies such as the USA, Canada, Australia, New Zealand, India and many Latin American countries. Think for a minute of the number of images of indigenous peoples that appear in books, films, TV advertising and tourism campaigns. Who do you think has control and 'ownership' of those images?

2 Think of the Aboriginal name Billabong in Australia, which in traditional Wiradjuri language means 'lifeless creek'. The name Billabong has since the 1980s been adopted as the brand name for a popular brand of Australian surfing wear that today is sold to millions around the world by Billabong International in the USA. Who do you think has control and 'ownership' of this name?

Brief history of the communication rights agenda

With the purpose of understanding the origins and frameworks that govern the principles of the current international communication rights program, we could divide this history into three distinctive, though somewhat overlapping phases; the *human* rights charter, the *civil* rights charter, and more recently, the *cultural* rights program. Therefore in order to contextualise the discussion around the notion of communication rights in the information society, it might be good to start a few decades back, somewhere around the late 1940s.

When much of the world was still recovering from the huge cost of a six-year-long World War, the League of Nations (created in France in 1919) was replaced by what today we know as the United Nations. In 1945, a United Nations Conference on International Organization was convened to set up the United Nations Charter, which was signed on 26 June of the same year by representatives of fifty countries. On 24 October 1945, the United Nations came into existence and within the first few years one of the main milestones of this new system of international cooperation was the adoption of the Universal Declaration of Human Rights, on 10 December 1948. Of critical importance within this declaration were, for example, several direct references to the right to freedom of expression (article 19), privacy (article 12), inclusiveness (articles 19, 21 and 28) and participation (articles 21 and 27)[1]. The Declaration of Human Rights established for the first time, even if rather vaguely, that the right to communicate is a fundamental and universal right of all people.

The second phase in the progress towards a communication rights agenda may be located in the 1960s with the emergence of strong civil rights movements across the world, including the Afro-American struggle in the United States, and the indigenous movements in the USA, Canada, Australia and many parts of Latin America. In this regard, one of the landmarks of this period was the UN's International Covenant on Civil and Political Rights of 1966, which was ratified and enacted a decade later, and which put the emphasis on the right to political, social and cultural freedom.

The third and current phase is exemplified by a series of regulatory frameworks such as *Convention 169 on Indigenous Peoples of the International Labour Organization* (ILO) from 1989, the *United Nations Draft Declaration on the Rights of Indigenous People* (1993), the *Universal Declaration on Cultural Diversity* (2001), or the *UNESCO Convention on the Protection and Promotion of the Diversity of Cultural Expressions* (2003). All these normative instruments in the form of conventions, declarations or recommendations promote, directly or indirectly, cultural diversity and the right to communicate as part of the promotion of cultural diversity.

By tracing the development of different international legal instruments, we can better understand the advancement of the notion of human rights in its broadest sense. From the protection of those basic rights that are considered by most societies to belong to everyone, such as freedom, justice, and equality in the 1940s, through the civil rights movements of the 1960s promoting access and equality under the law of all citizens of any given country, to the 1990s with its emphasis on cultural diversity, cultural rights and the protection of indigenous and local knowledge in the context of an information society. The United Nations Human Rights Council's adoption on 29 June 2006, of the UN Draft Declaration on the Rights of Indigenous Peoples is perhaps the best example of this new emphasis on cultural diversity and cultural rights. It is also important to note that this decision comes as a direct result of more than two decades of work by indigenous leaders and the United Nations system.

Activity 5.2

In late 1993, and following a recommendation by the World Conference on Human Rights, the General Assembly of the UN proclaimed the International Decade of the World's Indigenous People (1995–2004) with the theme 'Indigenous People: Partnership in Action'. The goal of the Decade was to foster international cooperation to help solve problems faced by indigenous peoples in such areas as human rights, culture, the environment, development, education and health.

What do you think has been achieved? Think of it in terms of the situation in your own country.

Communication rights and indigenous peoples in the 'information society'

Some scholars have proposed in recent years (Castells, 1996; Van Dijk, 1999) that contemporary global societies may be defined as information or network societies. In general terms what this means is that networks constitute the main form of cultural, political, economic and social organisation in contemporary societies, therefore changing the ways we communicate, work and ultimately live. So information networks play an increasingly important role in linking individuals, groups, organisations and communities, and it is the logic of networks that define new relations of power and participation in this realm. The new global knowledge societies made possible by digital ICTs are not constrained by geographic proximity, but are based on knowledge as the most important cultural capital. Perhaps the key contradiction of this so-called *information society* is that it makes information easily reproducible and widely accessible, giving way to a series of freedom/control issues and problems concerning intellectual property.

What is critically important but often missing from current debates on communication rights and participation by indigenous peoples in an information society, is a multifarious conceptualisation of the notions of traditional knowledge, cultural diversity and intellectual property. Cultural diversity is not only about acknowledging the existence of diverse cultural and ethnic groups. It should be the core concept from which citizens of different nations are invited to participate in the public domain.

Today there are literally hundreds of indigenous media organisations worldwide who have acknowledged the strategic value of digital media in the struggle for cultural autonomy and communication rights. However, in only a handful of

Theory link

see Lax, Chapter 12; Burton and Van der Hoven, Chapter 14

countries, this local production has been able to be structured at a national level and transcend into international media environments. One key example may well be Bolivia, through the non-governmental National Plan for Indigenous Audiovisual Communication begun as early as 1996. It's not easy for indigenous organisations to make their mark in international media environments, therefore cooperation and facilitation from government authorities, non-governmental organisations and international cooperation agencies often makes the difference between a presence and non presence in an international milieu.

Activity 5.3

One of the most successful indigenous media organisations is Isuma Productions, based in Igloolik, the capital of the Inuit Nation in the Canadian Arctic. Visit the website www.isuma.ca and watch the feature film *Atanarjuat: The Fast Runner* directed by Inuit filmmaker, Zacharias Kunuk, set in the Eastern Arctic at the dawn of the first millennium A.D.

In what ways do you think this film has transcended cultural barriers and become an important indigenous cultural presence in world cinema?

Governments have an important role to play in providing more adequate legal and policy frameworks for developing and promoting indigenous cultural and media production, particularly in countries where the indigenous population is significant in terms of total population and political influence. Again, the case of Bolivia is significant as more than 60% of the population claims to belong to one or more indigenous nation. Most important, however, is the political responsibility governments have in ensuring the right of indigenous people to autonomous communication by allowing control, ownership and self-management of broadcasting and other media outlets. Because this commitment so often has not been forthcoming, indigenous media organisations have had to turn to international contexts where they are better protected by international law and where there is often more chance of obtaining funds, but where the possibility that their work will make a material difference to the quality of life of their members at the local level is perhaps reduced.

The past two decades have seen the emergence of a wide range of international communication NGOs and online networks, which have been instrumental in supporting community and civil society communication initiatives, both in terms of opening access to communication and information at the community level, as well as questioning the positions taken by national governments in relation to cultural trade, appropriation and use of ICTs or broadcasting legislation.

These projects are a tremendous step forward in the struggle to unlock the opportunities for civil society to participate in global communication and information structures, including of course the design, implementation, evaluation and revision of communication policy relating to and by indigenous media producers.

The work carried out by these and other organisations also demonstrates the importance of current calls for a new global regime of cultural and media diversity that better understands, protects and promotes the production and flow of cultural materials and ideas. In some cases, these new transnational social networks of academics, activists, advocates and policy makers have reacted with disappointment to the inability of international agencies to effectively protect the available spaces for democratic participation in national and transnational public domains. One example is the UN's World Intellectual Property Organization (WIPO), which, despite efforts to attend to this matter, has been largely ineffective in terms of counteracting the usurpation and 'cultural confiscation' of traditional indigenous knowledges by companies and academic institutions, particularly those in fields such as the environment and biodiversity[2].

In recognising cultural complexity as a condition of diversity, current discussions on intellectual property must consider the fact that material and immaterial forms of culture may coexist; that an object created several hundred years ago may have a spiritual value today, and not just a commercial one; that the collective ownership of traditional resources, and not just copyright by an individual author, should be possible to be legally regulated.

So in summary, an open regime of intellectual property that attempts to be at the service of cultural diversity must ensure that:

- Intellectual property is held by a collective community of people.
- Cultural heritage is understood according to traditional knowledge systems.
- Moral issues are handled and managed according to traditional or customary law.
- Benefits of any kind, economic or otherwise, are shared with traditional custodians or 'owners'.

For Australian scholar Christine Morris (2003), the solution lies in looking back to the traditional processes that determine ownership of cultural products as they have been dealt with for generations. As Morris points out, 'many communities still use this framework as a way of determining ownership of knowledge'. In the new communication environment, this has to be extended to include all cultural products, including media (Morris, 2003). In this specific sense, it should also be acknowledged that different forms of privacy have to be considered, in order to include indigenous understandings of secrecy and sacredness of cultural material, knowledge and beliefs as an integral aspect of managing traditional resources. On a similar note, Von Lewinski suggests that as a starting point towards mutual understanding and a common basis for communication between Western-style industries and indigenous communities, Indigenous Heritage and Intellectual Property be considered as 'immeasurable value' (Von Lewinski, 2003).

Looking in this direction, many non-governmental and civil society groups have started to raise awareness of the importance of communication rights, understanding communication as the key matrix from which it is possible to contest current forms of digital exclusion and social discrimination and to promote democratic and open access to the new technologies of information and communication. Discrimination often refers not only to unfair treatment of one person or group, usually because of prejudice about race, but also in terms of age and gender.

Communication, and not just the imparting of information, is the locus from which various elements of human rights may be shared and promoted. The right to communicate has to do not only with the right to be informed, but also with the entitlement to participate, from a decision-making position, in a plural and democratic public sphere. The access to the new digital information technologies is a right from which a communication platform can be built, from whence it is possible to develop adequate policies and appropriate mechanisms to present the arguments for cultural and biological diversity, cultural autonomy, self-determination, freedom of expression, and effective incorporation of indigenous peoples into the information society.

It is therefore extremely important to innovate by promoting indigenous knowledge related to biological, cultural and media diversity by adopting grounded —and special if required—legal mechanisms that impede the inappropriate commercial use of these knowledges, resources and materials without the free, informed and autonomous consent of indigenous authorities.

Activity 5.4

For indigenous cultures, property is often an unfamiliar concept. Yet market-driven interests of the developed world rarely hesitate to exploit indigenous resources, from songs to medicinal herbs, justifying their actions through existing intellectual property laws that, for the most part, allow industries to use indigenous knowledge and resources without asking for consent and without sharing the benefits of such exploitation with the indigenous people themselves.

Search the Internet for examples of *bioprospecting* and biopiracy and analyse any examples you can find.

In addition, public sector transparency and accountability, together with appropriate legislation, are key elements in, for example, the assurance that Article 29 of the United Nations Draft Declaration on the Rights of Indigenous People is enforced. A core element of international law, this article asserts that

> Indigenous People are entitled to the recognition of the full ownership, control and protection of their cultural and intellectual property. They have the right to special measures to control, develop and protect their sciences, technologies and cultural manifestations, including human and other genetic resources, seeds, medicines, knowledge of the properties of fauna and flora, oral traditions, literatures, designs and visual and performing arts.

An unambiguous example of just such a collective voice, expressed strategically within international structures of power, may be seen in the document released in July 1999 by the UN's Working Group on Indigenous Populations (WGIP) where indigenous groups meeting in Geneva strongly opposed a controversial article of the Trade-Related Aspects of Intellectual Property Rights (TRIPs) agreement proposed by the World Trade Organization (WTO). The document titled 'No to Patenting of Life!' was a critical response to the increased politicisation of indigenous knowledge whereby international policy systems constantly manage and regulate indigenous peoples' wisdom and resources, often favouring the interest of large corporations or governments. In this particular case, the WGIP was opposing to the possibility of patent copyright over living organisms, such as plants or animals.

It is clear that contemporary intellectual and cultural property regulations have increasingly assumed a tendency towards global uniformity, to the detriment of diversity, which explains the partial failure of international agencies like WIPO to adequately protect indigenous knowledge or to promote and support traditional or customary laws governing rights over indigenous knowledge.

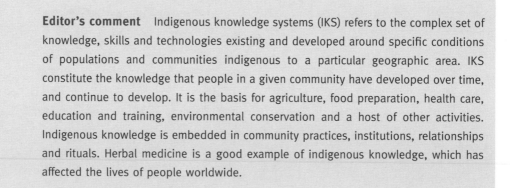

Editor's comment Indigenous knowledge systems (IKS) refers to the complex set of knowledge, skills and technologies existing and developed around specific conditions of populations and communities indigenous to a particular geographic area. IKS constitute the knowledge that people in a given community have developed over time, and continue to develop. It is the basis for agriculture, food preparation, health care, education and training, environmental conservation and a host of other activities. Indigenous knowledge is embedded in community practices, institutions, relationships and rituals. Herbal medicine is a good example of indigenous knowledge, which has affected the lives of people worldwide.

WIPO has in most cases granted monopoly control of a wide range of traditional knowledges and wisdoms to powerful transnational companies by pushing through international treaties for more and more intellectual property protection irrespective of what is benefiting the public domain, artistic practice or traditional knowledge. Yet what hasn't become clear enough is that the answer to the question of appropriate intellectual property regulations does not rest necessarily in more protection and restrictions, but in a more appropriate understanding of cultural diversity.

Activity 5.5

You can check how WIPO defines and regulates the protection of trad-itional knowledge and folklore at http://www.wipo.int/tk/en/.

The site also contains the 1998, 1999 and 2001 WIPO *Roundtables on Intellectual Property & Traditional Knowledge* and includes the draft report of the WIPO Fact Finding Mission on Traditional Knowledge, Innovations & Culture.

What do you think are the main problems with this report?

The lack of an appropriate understanding of cultural diversity also explains the reasons why many organisations are today calling for new forms of global governance, such as a redesign of the goals and mechanisms of the copyright and patent negotiations, or a revision of the UNESCO's declaration of cultural diversity and its impact on media diversity. The main challenge of this revision to the declaration is how to reconcile individual freedoms with collective civil rights. As Steve Buckley points out:

> The relationship between the draft [UNESCO] convention and existing international instruments on intellectual property should be a focus of attention in order to achieve a better equilibrium between the rights of authors and artists, the treatment of Indigenous knowledge and culture and the benefits of access in the public domain to knowledge and information (Buckley, 2004).

One other factor that may explain the inefficacy of legal frameworks at the national or international level to protect intellectual, moral and cultural property rights for indigenous peoples—besides the fact that often they are not strong enough to counter the forces of commercial enterprises—is our lack of understanding of the fact that indigenous people do not usually regard intellectual (individual) and cultural (collective) property as separate components.

In many instances for example, the process—sometimes spiritual—of creative production is not necessarily a separate instance to the final object produced. Clearly, current forms of copyright law—which are mostly concerned with balancing the rights of creators, owners and users—focus almost exclusively on the protection of economic rights associated with individual creators. However, they fail to consider that in many cases traditional indigenous law is more concerned with cultural survival and maintenance of culture; with collective, rather than individual rights; with both material and immaterial aspects of cultural and artistic production. In other words, current forms of intellectual property laws are intended to benefit society through the granting of exclusive rights to 'natural' and 'juridical' persons or 'creative individuals' and not to collective entities such as 'indigenous communities'.

The risk arising from not being able to reconcile individual and collective rights in cultural terms is that we may end up with an inadequate and monolithic definition of cultural diversity that assumes that indigenous knowledge and law are the same way in every indigenous nation worldwide. As has already been said, a sense of cultural diversity, besides recognising the vast diversity of cultural expressions grouped under the notion of indigenous, must therefore acknowledge that a democratic public sphere is a space where citizenship must be enacted. Cultural participation in a democratic and multicultural society must therefore accommodate a series of new actors, like the pledge of indigenous peoples worldwide who reclaim their right to ethnic citizenship as the basis for their struggle for self-determination.

Yet another key matter that arises in terms of finding adequate ways for governance of indigenous knowledge production and dissemination, is how to conceive the commercial value of indigenous cultural and intellectual property. In some countries, like Australia or New Zealand for example, indigenous cultural production contributes substantially to the national economy in a wide range of industries, from arts and crafts (film, music, television, new media, painting, sculpture, photography) to tourism and biotechnology. As Meadows (1998) points out, the Indigenous media sector in Australia– incorporating radio, television, film, print, and multimedia technologies—is not only an influential cultural resource but the fastest growing media sector in the country (Meadows, 1998, p. 69). Also important are the commercial uses of Indigenous cultural heritage and knowledge for academic research.

New forms of governance mean we need to look at decolonising our policy and research methodologies to fully understand what really is involved in the commercialisation of indigenous cultural material, biodiversity, heritage and knowledge, and what's at stake for traditional 'owners' of this 'property'. A decolonisation of intellectual property regimes, or what Morris and Meadows (2000) call the 'indigenising of intellectual property' should push us to find alternatives to the dominant conceptions of creative industries, which are mostly defined on the basis of cultural consumption—primarily entertainment—and the maximising of profit from the ownership of content produced by an individual 'creator'. A problem arises in this sense when we look at the nature of indigenous knowledge. It is transgenerational; orally transmitted through complex lineage groups; communally shared; and often transmitted by ancestors, spirits of nature, or ancestral cosmologies. Indigenous people worldwide therefore have usually been denied proper copyright protection as such knowledge is usually judged to fall under the category of 'public domain' and hence is unprotectable. As a result, the question of collective copyright has started to be debated in several circles as attempts made to register indigenous works with IP institutions are always blocked by the problem of collective authorship.

This is another important element in the matrix of indigenous communication rights, which hasn't been properly discussed in international forums on communications. In this regard, the proposition that restrictions on knowledge sharing through copyright and intellectual property are necessary to protect cultural production and trade may be as limited as those promoting an end to restrictions and the free access to knowledge and flow of information of all kinds. Neither approach considers the importance of indigenous secret/sacred material or practices, which often are essential for the cultural maintenance of a particular traditional system of knowledge.

Conclusion

This chapter has drawn attention to the fact that today indigenous nations worldwide face a double challenge in participating in the information society. On one hand, the vibrant re-emergence of pan-indigenous movements across the region has exposed the importance of revaluing ethnic identities and citizenships in the endeavour of pluri-cultural and democratic states. On the other hand, indigenous nations must also fight against the lack of institutional and constitutional recognition and ultimately against the indifference and neglect of the nation states onto which they find themselves—often forcibly—grafted.

To incorporate indigenous peoples into the information society we must ensure that the appropriate procedures are in place to allow indigenous actors to take part in decision-making aspects of the global information society as subjects–producers of content and not merely as objects–receivers of information.

Consequently, the responsibility of states to guarantee indigenous communication rights for their citizens resides in transparency and accountability, while gaining public access to government procedures becomes an important step for indigenous people who have been marginalised in their countries.

Disinformation, or lack of accurate, relevant and appropriate information, is the key element that needs to be countered. Therefore communication rights are an integral aspect of the indigenous movements for cultural recognition and political autonomy. As has been argued in this chapter, communication must always be conceptualised and put into practice as a central aspect of culture. It is therefore important to acknowledge and also to expand the definitions of key terms and concepts in Intellectual Property and Communication Rights debates to ensure that the expanded range of ideas, values and practices indigenous peoples bring to the media practices are covered by international policy outcomes. This includes the critical importance of promoting and recognising indigenous forms of customary or traditional law; and may reflect on special considerations that appropriately consider cultural diversity and the specificity of intellectual property needs of indigenous knowledge holders.

CHAPTER SUMMARY

This chapter has presented two main arguments about indigenous peoples and the communication rights agenda:

- What is needed and often lacking in current debates on communication rights and participation by indigenous peoples in an information society is a different conceptualisation of the notions of cultural diversity and intellectual property rights.
- Cultural diversity is not only about acknowledging the existence of diverse cultural and ethnic groups. It should be the core concept from which citizens of different nations are invited to participate in the public domain.

Tutorial questions

- How have some indigenous media organisations strategically used digital media in the struggle for cultural autonomy and communication rights?
- What should an expanded definition of Intellectual Property and Communication Rights for indigenous peoples include?

Recommended reading

Araújo, A.V., 2000, 'Copyrights and Image Copyrights: Indigenous peoples in Brazil':
www.socioambiental.org/pib/english/rights/copyrights.shtm

Smith, L.T., 1999, *Decolonising Methodologies: Research and Indigenous Peoples,* University
of Otago Press, Dunedin, New Zealand.

Thomas, P., 2004, 'Contemporary "Denial of Access": Knowledge, IPR and the Public
Good'. *Media Development* 2004/4.

Websites

Isuma productions: http://www.isuma.ca

Statement on communications rights: http://www.communicationrights.org/
statement_en.html Universal Declaration on Cultural Diversity

World Intellectual Property Organisation (WIPO): http://www.wipo.int/treaties/en

Notes

1   For more detailed information refer to Statement on Communication Rights by Cees Hammelink,
World Forum on Communication Rights, Geneva 2003: www.communicationrights.org/statement_
en.html

2   You can check the text of the WIPO copyright treaties online athttp://www.wipo.int/treaties/en

References

Buckley S., 2004, 'Cultural Diversity and Communication Rights', unpublished
manuscript.

Castells, M., 1996, *The Rise of the Network Society, The Information Age: Economy, Society
and Culture,* Vol. I, Blackwell, Cambridge, MA and Oxford, UK.

Kuhlen, R., 2004, 'Why are Communication Rights So Controversial?' *Media
Development* 2004/3, Special issue: Communication Rights: an Unfinished Agenda.

Meadows, M. and Morris, C. 1998, 'Into the New Millenium: The Role of Indigenous
Media in Australia', *Media International Australia Incorporating Culture and Policy*,
No. 88 pp. 67–78.

Morris, C., 2003, 'Intellectual Property and Indigenous Law', in *Media Development*
2003/1, Special issue: Intellectual Property Rights and Communication.

Morris, C. & Meadows, M., 2000, 'Indigenising Intellectual Property', *Griffith Law
Review* 9:2, pp. 212–26.

Seton, K., 1999, 'Fourth World Nations in the Era of Globalization: An introduction
to contemporary theorising posed by Indigenous Nations' Fourth World Journal
4:1. Center for World Indigenous Studies.

Smith, L.T., 1999, *Decolonising Methodologies: Research and Indigenous Peoples,* University of Otago Press, Dunedin, New Zealand.

Van Dijk, J., 1999, *The Network Society: Social Aspects of New Media,* Sage, London.

Von Lewinski, S., 2003, *Indigenous Heritage and Intellectual Property: Genetic Resources, Traditional Knowledge and Folklore,* Aspen Publishers, London.

GERARD GOGGIN AND CHRISTOPHER NEWELL

Disability and Online Culture

6

CHAPTER OVERVIEW

In this chapter, we present a burgeoning, vibrant, diverse and important area of new media worlds—that of disability online. One of the dominant myths is that technology is inherently beneficial to people with disability (such as the idea that the Internet removes one's disability).[1] We suggest a more complex and troubling reality: new media technologies, more often than not, are implicated in the creation of disability. Yet disabled people are users intimately engaged in the domestication and appropriation of new media, and so are actively involved in the shaping of their digital worlds.

To explore this topic, in this chapter we sketch a brief history of disability, new media technology, and the politics of access, focusing on computers, email and the World Wide Web. Then we look at three case studies of disability and online culture: web culture, blogging and uses of mobile phones and wireless technologies among people with disabilities.

Key terms

accessibility

disability

impairment

medical model

social model

Issues

- What does it mean to take a social or cultural approach to disability?
- How have people with disabilities created distinctive online cultures and uses of new media?
- What are some of these new media worlds of people with disabilities?
- What are the implications of disability for understanding new media technologies, cultures and institutions?

Accessibility   The potential for a technology to be used by a wide range of users (ideally even *all* users), without barriers being placed in their way through discriminatory or exclusionary design or norms.

Disability   What society and culture makes of impairment; disability is shaped by power relations (like other categories such as gender, race, sex, class).

Impairment   An injury, illness or condition that is held to cause or held likely to cause a long-term effect or limitation on appearance or function within the individual that differs from the norm.

Medical model   The position that sees disability as a defect, handicap or health problem located in an individual.

Social model   The position that sees disability as socially created through structures of oppression and exclusion; social model theorists draw a distinction between impairment (the bedrock biological or bodily condition) and disability (regarded as the social construction of impairment).

It's not natural!: Technology and disability

In this book we are concerned with new media technologies and the worlds that are created through and out of them. One of the most interesting, paradoxical and rich collections of these worlds relate to **disability**. To understand disability and online cultures, however, and also the important lessons they teach us about new media worlds in general, we need to reconsider at least two taken-for-granted concepts in most societies: technology and disability.

When we think about disability and technology, the associated ideas and images are often about how technology can help, or even fix, people with disabilities. We are all familiar with mainstream media narration of biomedical research, genetics, and information and communication technology. In particular such narration promises to bring great transformations in the lives of the disabled. Better still, so the mythology says, this is how technology can stop that great social fear— disability—from happening (by avoiding disabled babies), or by providing a cure for disability—or even how you can 'lose your disability on the Internet'. Rarely do we conceptualise disability as a positive attribute.

Christopher, one of the authors of this chapter, identifies as living with disability. While he doesn't advocate rushing out and getting a disability, for him it has been a very important, if difficult, part of shaping who he is and what he has to offer to society. He even thinks he's a better academic because of his disability! Such thinking is of course deeply disturbing, given our cultural assumptions. After all, disability has been present in all societies since before written or recorded history (Stiker, 1999). Yet often when we think of technology and disability we think of the latest technical fix, as if disability has just arisen as a problem. However, to take but one example, since the beginning of warfare, humankind has needed to attend to acquired **impairment** and the management of the disabled body. Since the inception of birth(!), we have needed to recognise the realities of congenital impairment, ascribing meanings to those conditions in their human diversity.

Indeed, our norms and narration of technology and disability revolve around deeply entrenched myths, one central function of which is ideological. That is, such stereotypes speak to a set of power relations and structures in which disability is seen as the 'other', and in which people with disabilities are systematically marginalised, oppressed, discriminated against and impoverished—a thoroughgoing, organised, exclusion we have called a kind of apartheid (Goggin and Newell, 2005).

So, how can we rethink these ancient myths of technology and disability? Let's start with technology. In keeping with science and technology studies, especially what has been called social studies of science and technology, we regard technology as socially and culturally shaped (MacKenzie and Wajcman, 1999) or even constructed. Influenced by the feminist theorist of technology Judy Wajcman (2004), and the important work by scholars such as Janet Abbate's *Inventing the Internet* (1999), we are interested in how even the most apparently neutral (technical or technicised) arrangements bear the marks of their social and cultural shaping. Such work has been extended by actor-network theorists (Latour, 2005), who argue that in principle it is actually very difficult, if not impossible, to tell apart society and technology because these two things mutually coexist and are created together. By these lights, technology cannot straightforwardly *determine*, or cause, other things, such as society; nor can it remedy or do away with disability.

For its part, disability can also be regarded not as fixed, static or given, but as socially, culturally and politically constructed. To illustrate this account of disability, we often have recourse to the famous thought-experiment offered by British disability activist and theorist Vic Finkelstein (1981): imagine a village where all its inhabitants are people of small stature, and where as a result all houses, furniture, fittings, and appliances are designed with them in mind. When taller people come into the village—such as people we would consider as having 'normal' height— they find it difficult to walk into houses without bumping their heads, and so require 'special' equipment and 'modifications' in order to be able to gain access to society.

Finkelstein is one of the pioneers of what is termed the **'social' model** of disability. Instead of disability being something that is about a defective, diseased, crippled, injured or maimed body that needs a cure, medication, or rehabilitation, proponents of the social model contend that disability is created by society (Barnes and Mercer, 2004; Oliver, 1996). Whereas a person might be regarded as having an impairment (such as loss of sensory function or bodily capacity), his or her disability is the meaning, role, and systems of organisation that society attaches to that impairment.

For our part we draw selectively on work in the social model of disability tradition, but also its critiques (see for example, Corker and Thomas, 2000) as we are not convinced by cleaving to a strict binary distinction between 'disability' and 'impairment'. We also draw from other traditions in disability theory, activism, and practice, not least Australian (Fulcher, 1989), New Zealand (O'Brien and Sullivan, 2005) and North American (Mitchell and Snyder, 2000) work, and so characterise our approach as one that sees disability as socio-political space, and that explores alternative accounts of disability's social, cultural and ethical relations (Goggin and Newell, 2003 and 2005).

Think about it

It is very disconcerting to consider disability as more than deviance contained within the individual. How do you respond to this?

Drawing on these two intersecting critiques and alternative theories of technology and disability, we turn to new media technology. The Internet has often been seen as a space of limitless potential, giving effect to new practices and dimensions of freedom. Yet people with disabilities have had a prolonged and difficult battle to gain access to and use the Internet, and to be represented, and to express themselves in online digital cultures. Perhaps an even more disturbing hypothesis is that the Internet has actually created disability, for all the well-intentioned rhetoric of access and inclusion.

Shaping disability in computers, software and their networks

Early computers with punch-cards featured in the advent of commercial computing after the Second World War, requiring manual dexterity associated with card readers and other inputting devices. Herman Hollerith, who devised punch cards for processing and tabulating data, used in the 1890 US census, is said to have had great problems learning spelling, something which might be regarded today as a learning disability. In 1896, Hollerith founded the Tabulating Machine Company, which later became International Business Machines (IBM).

In the early 1970s, the invention of the microprocessor displaced both mainframe and mini-computers, and led to the personal computer in 1974–75. The PC's development saw the increasing role of IT in everyday lives. The basic PC unit was built around particular norms of design, code and input and output, requiring people to conform to those norms. The PC needs of people with disabilities saw a set of contests regarding three key technologies: hardware, operating systems and applications.

Specialised assistive technology, hardware and software, emerged for people with disabilities. This showed the potential range of input and output devices that could be used in conjunction with computers, such as braille embossers to provide documents readable by blind people, as well as hardware and software for speech synthesis (such as the 1976 Kurzweil Reaching Machine). Yet such developments also posed the political and practical question of whether disability demands special or mainstream solutions. The consumer and disability movements took an early lead, for example, in the formation in Illinois in 1981 of the Committee of Personal Computers and the Handicapped.

Breakthroughs in **accessibility** of mainstream computing proved elusive. Apple introduced the Macintosh computer in 1984. While its graphic-user interface was acclaimed as user-friendly by many, greatly influencing the development of its now ubiquitous Windows counterpart, for some people with disabilities, such as blind users, it was not ideal. However, Macintosh took an early lead in incorporating accessibility into its operating system.

In contrast to the graphical interface, the MS-DOS operating system was a text-based platform, and worked in conjunction with text-based programs such as early versions of Word or WordPerfect. Computer users who were blind or vision impaired could use a screen reader to speak text.

Microsoft's relatively late introduction of a graphical-user interface with Windows (especially its successful 1990 Windows version 3) was hailed as a breakthrough by many, but seen as a grave threat by blind and vision-impaired users. The move from text-oriented DOS-based to graphical Windows-based computer operating systems resulted in serious losses in access and jobs for persons using speech or Braille for communication.

Corporate initiative alone was not sufficient, and other strategies, such as legislative protections were utilised. One of these was the *Americans with Disability Act*. Also critical was section 508 of the 1973 *Rehabilitation Act*. Section 508 requires that information technology procured, developed, maintained and used by federal agencies must be accessible to people with disabilities, unless such requirement imposes an undue burden. Effectively US federal and state governments could use their purchasing power to encourage companies to make IT accessible. Activists in the state of Massachusetts took the lead, lobbying their government to use section 508 to require accessible computers.

The IT industry took several years to develop adequate accessibility strategies for Windows software, with little interest among mainstream software developers. In the early 1990s Microsoft had only one person working on accessibility issues. Even as late as 1998 it shipped Internet Explorer 4.0 with fewer accessibility features than the previous version. Pitched battles fought by the disability movement with Microsoft were required before accessibility was incorporated in operating systems and programs.

Networking of computers via telecommunications to share resources, exchange data, and facilitate communications developed from the 1960s. In the 1980s, with the growth of bulletin boards, private networks such as America Online (AOL) and Compuserve, and the spread of the Internet, people with disabilities started to communicate and share computer files online. Blind people, and other people with disabilities, were among early Internet pioneers.

Disability accessibility has been a key issue for networked IT. One important test case involved blind people invoking the *Americans with Disability Act* to force AOL to adopt accessibility measures. After some years requesting accessible Internet services, the National Federation of the Blind filed suit against AOL in November 1999. Negotiations commenced between AOL and the NFB, and the suit was suspended in July 2000 with AOL agreeing to make its software accessible by April 2001.

Disability was an integral feature of the design and deployment of the World Wide Web with the launch of the World Wide Web Accessibility Initiative (WAI) in April 1997. The WAI has raised the level of awareness of disability accessibility issues within the Internet community, especially those designing and implementing web pages. W3C is a consortium of organisations working consensually and issuing recommendations. However, it is left to others to implement those recommendations and many organisations do not. Hence access to the Internet for people with disabilities remains quite precarious (as is illustrated in the *Sydney Olympics Organising Committee v. Maguire* case; see Goggin and Newell, 2003). Yet largely unasked in all of these cases and technologies is why it is that we need special solutions and pleading, even legal action, given the myth of an egalitarian and inclusive online community (Goggin and Newell, 2007; Stienstra, Annable and Goggin, 2007).

Activity 6.1

Identify a new media technology you might investigate in terms of its histories and cultures, and also a critical investigation of the way it builds in or addresses disability.

When blogging meets disability

Weblogs (blogs) emerged in 1998–99, with thousands of blogs evident by 2000 (Blood, 2000) and a fully fledged parallel universe of blogging—the blogosphere— soon thereafter being recognised as an integral part of new media cultures, if not mainstream media itself (Bruns and Jacobs, 2006). Blogs are a set of software, applications, code, and interfaces that drawn upon the Internet, but, especially with the sorts of linking, listing, interactions, diary and journal entries, comments, blogrolls, and other features, became a genre as well as technology in their own right.

Disability had already become a significant feature of Web culture, with many websites devoted to disability-related topics or to the representation and cultivation of disability identities. Blogging offered new ways for disability and online culture to intersect—with disability featuring prominently among the labelling and creation of blogs, and also in the self-representation of bloggers themselves.

To make some provisional sense of the disabled blogosphere, we would point to the existence of a number of particular types of blogs in which disability figures (drawing here on the work of Goggin and Noonan, 2006). Firstly, there are blogs written from an explicitly critical disability studies or movement perspective, such as Gimp Parade: a 'thirtysomething disabled feminist. Overeducated, underemployed': 'A website with personal reviews of books and movies from a disability culture perspective.' Secondly, the hugely popular LiveJournal blogging site and community features a number of disability blogs. Thirdly, there are activist and information blogs, often with a focus on a particular perspective or topic.[2] Fourthly, as Goggin and Noonan note:

> By far the largest category of self-identified blogging by people with disabilities is of a diaristic or journal nature. There are many blogs the prime purpose of which is to share someone's experience of life, and so—as a part of that person's life—thoughts and recountings of impairment and disability, and to share this with whatever large or, more realistically, small (or micro) audience might be interested (Goggin and Noonan, 2006).[3]

Fifthly, there are audio blogs that feature resources and files on Podcasting or Internet radio. These are especially for blind people, for most of whom Podcasting has been by far the more exciting development: 'many blogs of blind people either incorporate links to audio ramblings, hard hitting journalistic inquiry or sharing of technology barriers and solutions of interest to people with disability' (Goggin and Noonan, 2006). Such blogs include *The Mosen Explosion, Blindspot: Marlaina by Ear*, and *Blindchance: David Faucheux's Audio Web Log*. Sixthly, there is the emergence of disability blogs in mainstream media, such as the blog established by the BBC's disability lifestyle Ouch! website.

There is a great deal more to be explored and debated about these developments, but it is worth thinking about what disability has to teach us about blogging. Not least how disability is co-created alongside technology in this volatile new sphere of micro- as well as larger publics, user-generated information and communication, and new architectures of broadcasting, distributing, receiving and responding to information. A representative view of blogging, perhaps even characteristic of a certain ideology of blogging, can be found in pioneer blogger Rebecca Blood's short history of the form:

> We are being pummeled by a deluge of data and unless we create time and spaces in which to reflect, we will be left with only our reactions. I strongly believe in the power of weblogs to transform both writers and readers from 'audience' to 'public' and from 'consumer' to 'creator.' Weblogs are no panacea for the crippling effects of a media-saturated culture, but I believe they are one antidote (Blood, 2000).

Punning on the metaphor of 'crippling' here, we see disability and blogging as adding a distinctive form of active audience to online cultures.

Mobile disabilities[4]

Mobile cellular phones were commercially introduced around the world from the late 1970s, commencing with in-car phones. This system was based on analogue technology, which we now call first-generation mobile technology. When handheld mobiles became available these were very bulky, and even the lighter, more portable models were cheerfully referred to as a 'brick'. Obviously at this stage, the mobile phone was difficult for many people with disabilities to hold and use. With advances in miniaturisation, computerisation and manufacturing, mobiles were made smaller and lighter. This made them easier to use for some consumers, but more difficult for others because of the dexterity and nimbleness demanded by tiny buttons and interfaces. Many people with disabilities did use mobiles for a range of purposes, including safety, security, and mobility assistance.

Second-generation mobiles were introduced around the world from the early 1990s onwards, promising better voice quality, data transfer rates, more efficient use of scarce radio spectrum, and security from interception of calls. The innovative features of second-generation mobiles opened up new possibilities but also created new forms of exclusion:

> Blind people cannot use text-based information on the screen at all [including phonebook maintenance and use], while those who are partially-sighted have great difficulty with very small displays. Voice outputs are of no use to deaf people and may be difficult for those who are simply hard of hearing (Shipley and Gill, 2000).

Here mobiles illustrate the general proposition that when technology is reshaped it is because of other sorts of imagined users and markets than people with disabilities (Shipley and Gill, 2000).

For people with disabilities there were also significant difficulties with second-generation mobiles, overlapping other sites of conflict over the technology (such as fears that electromagnetic emission from phones or towers might cause cancer). Not long after the new digital mobile system had been developed and was starting to be introduced commercially in a number of countries in the early 1990s, it was revealed that this technology emitted a high level of electromagnetic interference. Such interference had the potential to cause a buzzing sound in people's hearing aids, as well as actually making the phones difficult to use for people with hearing aids. Phone companies internationally, governments, and regulators put much effort into managing the public outcry. In doing so, they appeared to be motivated by a concern that this new, expensive technology might not be adopted by consumers, despite widespread support from governments.

What was intriguing here was that for quite some time *hearing aids* rather than mobiles were conceptualised as the principal problem by providers of mobile telephony. Attention was directed to the need for hearing aids to cope with higher levels of electromagnetic emission, something that was seen as important given the wide range of technologies emitting such signals—not just mobile phones. A European standard was introduced in 1990 requiring hearing aids to be immune to emissions from mobile phones. Research was also conducted on removing the source of emission further away from the hearing aid, and eventually 'handsfree kits' were designed for hearing aid users as a solution. Even this solution did not provide assistance for many, and other tactics were required on the part of the disability movement (Goggin and Newell, 2003 and 2006). However, the problem remains and is only partially solved in some countries with the availability of an alternative digital mobile technology.

A related and further illustrative aspect of the construction of disability in the new media worlds of mobile telecommunications lay at the intersection of a newer technological system and an older one with their overlapping yet distinctive cultural practices. Deaf people in a number of Western countries, especially the USA, had developed a rich repertoire of communications and cultural practices using an early form of text communications. Devised in the early to mid 1960s, this technology was variously called in different countries the Telecommunications Device for the Deaf (TDD), teletypewriter (TTY), deaf telephones, or just text telephone. TTY communication involves two keyboard devices being connected to the telecommunications network, which are then capable of sending and receiving text messages. Many deaf people own their own text phones, and, to meet the requirements of legislation such as the 1990 *Americans with Disabilities Act*, TTY payphones may be found in public places such as airports.

Like modems, TTYs functioned compatibly (within limits) over the telecommunications work. TTYs also worked satisfactorily with first-generation analogue mobiles. However, the much vaunted second generation digital mobiles threatened this interworking or knitting together of technologies. The consequence of second generation cell phones for the deaf community was quite significant. Internationally, it took concerted pressure from the deaf community and their supporters, with alliances of users, scientists and technologists, academics, and interested industry across national, regional and international settings, and also the invocation of general disability discrimination legislation in various countries, before the mobile phone manufacturers and telecommunications carriers took this problem seriously.

Ironically, while the TTY media worlds of deaf people are not so well known, what has gained widespread attention is another form of text communication—mobile text messaging. Just like the rise of text messaging in general, once mainstream mobile phone companies noticed the deaf community's avid use of text messaging, they were keen to market to deaf consumers, and also publicise this use for wider, public consumption. Specific reworking of the technology in light of such use has been much slower in coming. Problems include SMS not offering asynchronous rather than real-time interaction, as it is a store-and-forward technology resembling email in this respect—despite the often very fast communication it can often afford; textual messages need to be written in hearing languages such as English rather than native sign language; and the high cost of the frequent text messaging required by deaf users. Deaf users have also avidly taken up devices such as text-messaging pagers and portable digital assistants, with the T-Mobile Sidekick becoming a cult object among some communities of US users.

The implications of these new networkings of deaf culture are still being registered and debated. Like wider debates on mobiles, there are those who praise the utility, function, freedoms, intimacies and sociability such technology brings to deaf people and others who lament the threat to and facing of older social forms. For example, face-to-face contact and gatherings have been much prized by deaf communities, not least as a way to communicate via the visual and tactile medium of native sign language. These fears have been more generally raised regarding mobiles, and have a long history in the reception of new media (Marvin, 1988; Winston, 1998)

From the celebrated deaf use of SMS, we would briefly note a contrasting case where a disability culture and its desires and needs regarding a technology have not been reflected in values, design, or narratives of use—the blind community.[5] As with people with disabilities in general, and deaf users in particular, we propose the thesis that for blind users the mobile phone has gone hand-in-hand with new personal and collective possibilities. Yet, to propose an antithesis, the technology has not been imagined or designed with blind users in mind.

As mobile phone manufacturers and mobile service providers did not collectively envisage and design mobile technological systems with affordances and capabilities for blind users, it has been largely left to specialist disability technology providers to design purpose-built workarounds. This was only possible, however, when it became possible for third parties to add software programs and applications to mobile phones. The implications of such an impasse in technology are far-reaching. SMS is now extensively used around the world, especially by young people, and is often pivotal to cultural participation and social membership. Such emergent norms mean that blind people's lack of access to SMS, and neglect in the design and shaping of mobile technologies more broadly, can lead to significant social exclusion. In of all of this, we would point to the way that disability and technology, too, is constituted in social and cultural relations—and that this is an important part of understanding online cultures.

Conclusion

So what does the future for disability in new media worlds hold? In many respects we need to be wary of accounts of technological and economic determinism as well as be aware of the problems of accounts that suggest that the solution to disability is just around the corner with the latest technological advance. Rather, we suggest, the future of disability to a significant extent will depend on you, the reader, as you enter into professional and personal endeavours and engage with daily situations where you can make decisions as to whether we will build in and create disability, or enhance functionality; whether we will plan with impairment in mind, or whether we will unknowingly or knowingly create disability. In terms of dominant culture, we know that disability is contained within the deviant individual. Yet in this chapter we have sought to show how disability is created and replicated in the technologies we often view as either value-neutral or indeed inherently good for people we know as 'disabled'. We dream of a world where such discourse as 'special needs', 'inclusion', and 'special accommodations' are not needed, because the lives of people with impairments are so valued that we guard against the need for special solutions to the troubling problem of the disabled body.

There is a great deal of empirical work that remains to be undertaken to establish, firstly, the histories of disability and technology touched upon here, and, secondly, to debate and theorise these. It is our view that this is an important agenda, not only as a matter of human rights and justice but also because these narratives unsettle our taken-for-grant theories of new media technologies and worlds.

As people with disabilities, we are mostly overlooked as users, consumers and audiences. So we suggest people with disabilities be credited as do-it-yourself consumer-producers of new media, and that their narratives be taken seriously and their uses appropriately studied and analysed.

Think about it

Can you think about how you would design a future technology that built in the needs, desires and cultural preferences of people with disabilities?

CHAPTER SUMMARY

- In this chapter we have told a different story about new media worlds, approaching them from the perspective of disability. We have introduced the new, critical ways of thinking about disability as a social, cultural and political phenomenon, and suggested that such an approach can dovetail productively with approaches from social studies of science and technology that also offer a counter to technological determinism.
- Our case studies of computers, email, the Internet, blogging and mobile cultures illustrate the rich, dense, diverse, overlapping yet relatively self-contained nature of disability and new media worlds.
- We have argued that to explore disability and new media technologies not only teaches us much about the hundreds of millions of people worldwide who identify

as people with disability, it also teaches us much about the constitution and transformation of media, culture and technology—and the new forms of embodiment and mediation we inhabit.

Tutorial questions

- Why has it been possible in this chapter to take a social or cultural approach to the analysis of both technology and disability?
- Describe some of the new media worlds of people with disabilities?
- What specific concerns have emerged to date for people with disabilities using new mobile media technologies?

see McGuigan, Chapter 1; Lax, Chapter 12; Burton and Van der Hoven, Chapter 14

Theory link

Recommended reading

Barnes, C. & Mercer, G. (eds), 2004, *Implementing the Social Model of Disability: Theory and Research*, The Disability Press, Leeds.

Goggin, G. & Newell, C., 2005, *Disability in Australia: Exposing a Social Apartheid*, University of NSW Press, Sydney.

Goggin, G. & Newell, C., 2003, *Digital Disability: The Social Construction of Disability in New Media*, Rowman & Littlefield, Lanham MA.

Websites

A Gimp's Life: http://journals.aol.com/brucer5150/AGimpsLife/

Blind Chance: David Faucheux's Audio Web Log: http://www.teleread.org/blind/

Marlaina by Ear: http://www.blindcast.com/podcast/2005/09/marlaina-by-ear-catch-up-and-listen-to.html

Katja Stokley's *Brokenclay: The Art of Intermittent Disability:* http://brokenclay.org/journal/

Lisy Babe's Blog http://lisybabe.blogspot.com

Ouch!: http://www.bbc.co.uk/ouch/

Scott Laurent's *Disability is an Art* blog: http://www.disabilityisanart.blogspot.com/

Trace Research & Development Centre, University of Wisconsin-Madison: http://www.trace.wisc.edu/

World Wide Web Consortium (W3C) Web Accessibility Initiative: http://www.w3c.org/WAI/

Notes

1   In the United Kingdom, the terminology commonly used is 'disabled people', with the emphasis being on society that disables people with impairments. In Australia and the USA, the 'people with' terminology is favoured due to an emphasis on the personhood being more important than the disability. The conversations have been similar, yet the outcomes in terminology differ a little. As we write within the Australian context, we adopt the appropriate terminology.

2   Frequently read and cited blogs include: Scott *Rains' Rolling Rains Report: Precipitating Dialogue on Travel, Disability, and Universal Design* (http://www.rollingrains.com/); J. Kevin Morton's *Disability Law Blog* (http://jkm.typepad.com/); Disability Law (http://disabilitylaw.blogspot.com/); biotechnology activist Gregor Wolbring's *My Thoughts on Social and Scientific Issues* (http://wolbring.blogspot.com/). Also there are blogs by people with disabilities in other fields, for whom disability is an important part of their professional as well as personal identity, such as disabled writer and performer Greg Walloch's blog (http://gregwallochblog.blogspot.com/).

3   Scott Laurent's Disability is an Art blog (http://www.disabilityisanart.blogspot.com/); Katja Stokley's *Brokenclay: The Art of Intermittent Disability* (http://brokenclay.org/journal/); *Becky's Journal: The Ordinary Life of a Not-So Ordinary Girl* (http://www.dalqe.com/); *Crazy Deaf Joe Blog* (http://www.crazydeafjoe. com/); Schizophrenia Blog: *My Life's Adventure* (http://www.schizophrenia.com/journey/); A Gimp's Life (http://journals.aol.com/brucer5150/AGimpsLife/); *Lisy Babe's Blog* (http://lisybabe.blogspot.com).

4   For an extended discussion of disability and mobiles see Goggin and Newell, 2003 and 2006.

5   We would note the problematic, dynamic, yet intensely invested categories of 'Deaf' and 'Blind', and the entire vexed taxonomic enterprise of knowing the truth of a person via an impairment label (for a discussion of this see the opening chapter of Goggin and Newell, 2005).

References

Abbate, J., 1999, *Inventing the Internet*, MIT Press, Cambridge, MA.

Barnes, C. & Mercer, G. (eds), 2004, *Implementing the Social Model of Disability: Theory and Research*, The Disability Press, Leeds.

Blood, R., 2000 'Weblogs: A History and Perspective', *Rebecca's Pocket*, 07 September 2000: <http://www.rebeccablood.net/essays/weblog_history.html>, retrieved 30 May, 2006.

Bruns, A. & Jacobs, J. (eds), 2006, *The Uses of Blogs*, Peter Lang, New York.

Corker, M. & Thomas, C., 2000, 'A Journey around the Social Model', in Corker, M. & Shakespeare, T. (eds) *Disability/Postmodernity: Embodying Disability Theory*, Coninuums, London and New York.

Finkelstein, V., 1981, 'To Deny or Not to Deny Disability', in Brechin, A., Liddiard, P. & Swain, J. (eds) *Handicap in a Social World*, pp. 34–36, Hodder and Stoughton, Kent.

Fulcher, G., 1989, *Disabling Policies?: A Comparative Approach to Education, Policy and Disability*, Falmer Press, London.

Goggin, G. & Newell, C., 2007, 'The Business of Digital Disability', forthcoming.

Goggin, G. & Newell, C., 2006, 'Disabling Cell Phones: Mobilizing and Regulating the Body', in Kavoori, A.P. & Arceneaux, N. (eds), *Cultural Dialectics and the Cell Phone,* Peter Lang, New York.

Goggin, G. & Newell, C., 2005, *Disability in Australia: Exposing a Social Apartheid*, University of NSW Press, Sydney.

Goggin, G. & Newell, C., 2003, *Digital Disability: The Social Construction of Disability in New Media*, Rowman & Littlefield, Lanham, MD.

Goggin, G. & Noonan, T., 2006, 'Blogging Disability: The Interface Between New Cultural Movements and Internet Technology', in Bruns, A. & Jacobs, J. (eds), *The Uses of Blogs,* Peter Lang, New York.

Latour, B., 2005, *Reassembling the Social: An Introduction to Actor-Network-Theory*, Oxford University Press, Oxford.

MacKenzie, D. & Wajcman, J. (eds), 1999, *The Social Shaping of Technology* (2nd edn), Open University Press, Buckingham, England and Philadelphia, PA.

Marvin, C., 1988,. *When Old Technologies Were New: Thinking about Electric Communication in the Late Nineteenth Century,* Oxford University Press, New York.

Mitchell, D. & Snyder, S., 2000, *Narrative Prosthesis: Disability and the Dependencies of Discourse*, University of Michigan Press, Ann Arbor, MI.

O'Brien, P. & Sullivan, M. (eds), 2005, *Allies in Emancipation: Shifting from Providing Service to Being of Support*, Thomson/Dunmore Press, South Melbourne.

Oliver, M., 1996, *Understanding Disability: From Theory to Practice*, St. Martin's Press, New York.

Shipley, T. & Gill, J., 2000, *Call Barred?: Inclusive Design of Wireless Systems,* Royal National Institute of the Blind, London: <http://www.tiresias.org/phoneability/wireless.htm>.

Stienstra, D., Annable, G. & Goggin, G. (eds), 2007, special issue of *The Information Society* on disability, accessibility and information technologies.

Stiker, H. J., 1999, *A History of Disability*, trans. W. Sayers, University of Michigan Press, Ann Arbor.

Wajcman, J., 2004, *Technofeminism*, Polity, Cambridge.

White, M., 2006, 'Where Do You Want to Sit Today?: Computer Programmers' Static Bodies and Disability', *Information, Communication & Society*, 9.1 (2006).

Winston, B.,1998, *Media Technology and Society, A History: From the Telegraph to the Internet*, Routledge, London.

ULLAMAIJA
KIVIKURU

7 Crisis and Internet Networks

Key terms

crisis communication
state information management
citizen rights

Issues

- What happens to people's use of information when something unexpected happens?
- What happens when a crisis hits citizens of an 'information society' with a multitude of web-based networks?
- In web-based communication, two-way traffic of communication is possible. But is it possible in a crisis situation?
- Is the Internet able to shorten distances and thus to 'globalise' loyalties and accountability in crisis situations?

CHAPTER OVERVIEW

This chapter explores how people use the media when confronted by a crisis. It reports on a case study of the communication problems surrounding the impact of the Asian Boxing Day Tsunami (2004) on the citizens of Finland. It considers how crises are reported and the implications of that reporting for the people who are personally involved in the crisis. It also explores the expectations that people bring to their search for information about relatives and friends who are unaccounted for in the disaster regions. The use of text messages, the setting up of makeshift websites, and the desire for personally relevant information all play a role in the crisis information scenario. Of particular interest is the finding that text messaging was an important way that people in the affected area were able to remain informed about the situations they encountered on the ground.

Introduction

There is a multitude of research evidence about people's media behaviour on dramatic events such as wars, coups, deaths of leaders and big accidents (e.g. Anker, 2005; Bennett and Paletz, 1994; Demers, 2002; Reimer, 1994; Sood et al., 1987). Such studies mostly focus on reception and diffusion of information, and argue that in crisis situations the information needs of those affected are found to increase immediately by roughly one-third. This is quite understandable as people want to know what has happened and whether/how the new development relates to them. This growth in information need depends on the size, nature and closeness of the incident. In this respect, quite crude, even cynical values are present. Ten deaths in a neighbouring town are found to generate much more interest than tens of thousands of lives lost in a far-away country. If only measured by loss of life and destroyed infrastructure, the World Trade Center drama in New York on September 11, 2001 was actually a far smaller event than the annual floods in Bangladesh. Still, the news value of the two cases was of a totally different scale.

Certain types of accidents can be relied on to arouse people's interest. Aeroplane accidents always generate front-page headlines, although far more people die in car accidents. And all over the world, a man's struggle with nature seems to be a theme that arouses affections even if the case does not directly touch the people concerned. Floods and hurricanes fill this criterion. Crises are thus, to a certain extent, not only sudden but man-made and culture-bound. It is also typical that unexpected events gather more attention and create more anxiety than long, oppressing and complicated political processes. Open conflicts and wars belong naturally to such crises that always collect considerable attention and increase the need for information. Governments and other official institutions have to express themselves immediately. Especially in industrialised or post-industrial societies people are used to having access to a continuous flow of information. Rumour spreading is an alternative they do not want to play with, and passivity in action gives an impression that the officials do not care.

In such circumstances people don't need just any kind of information. In the case of crisis, the credibility and experienced truthfulness of information is highly valued, since rumours can be spread very easily if relevant and reliable information is delayed or is shown to be biased. In the case of major accidents, the requirement to gather and distribute reliable information in the midst of chaos is quite a demanding task for the prominent actors in the dilemma, and often the volume or details of the crisis are not even totally clear to those responsible for the activity. The criticism around Cyclone Katrina could be given as an example here. It has been shown that the US administration underestimated the severity of its impact on the local populations. After a year, the various grassroots organisations, established to defend Katrina victims, were still appalled by the negligence shown by the US administration.[1] It is interesting to note that in the case of the WTC disaster, the excess of websites is—finally, years after the disaster—considerably more formal and less grassroots-oriented. There are websites covering crisis counselling and financial support, but the majority of the web-based information available in fact focuses on what is going to happen for the place in the future. This is not the case with the Katrina websites, which are still strongly oriented to what happened in 2005 and what happens to the victims today.

Think about it

It is worth wondering whether we now are at the gate to a new phase: has the Web overtaken television as the dominant medium in crisis situations. Does the Web now offer a faster and far more complex framework for both public and participatory elements in crisis situations?

In a post-industrial society, the increasing use of the Internet has challenged the centrality of radio and television as bearers of bad tidings. The Internet now is part of the everyday routines of a large proportion of the population. The public has become used to the availability of continuously updated information when they want it, although not everybody uses this access regularly. For example in the Nordic countries, some 80 per cent of the population uses the Internet at work on a daily basis, while the use of the Web for personal needs is somewhat lower (Nordic Media Trends, 2003). However, quite often the border line between workplace use and private use is blurred. With increasing expansion of Internet use, it can be safely assumed that in the coming years, a 'new' and more demanding public will emerge. Above all, future web users will obviously demand more two-way traffic in mass communication than has traditionally been the case, and more personalised information (Heinonen, 1999).

The spontaneous emergence of a multiplicity of critical grassroots websites around Katrina indicate the new Internet-based phase, and the importance attached to the Internet as a source of crisis information was already demonstrated in the reporting of the Boxing Day Tsunami of 2004. This event caused widespread distress in the Nordic countries because the area around the Bay of Bengal, which was at the centre of the destruction, is one of the most popular holiday destinations for Nordics. Thus concern about the tsunami catastrophe spread rapidly even in the remote Scandinavian countries. For example, of the roughly 40,000 Nordics spending Christmas in the affected area, forty-seven Danes, eighty-four

Norwegians, 179 Finns and 544 Swedes were killed and several thousands were injured. For the peaceful Nordic countries, the tsunami catastrophe caused more deaths than any other event in peacetime.

In all the Nordic countries, people are heavy media users—the Norwegians lead the global statistics, while the Finns and the Swedes are placed as the third and the fourth. It is normal practice in these countries that a person reads two to three newspapers on a daily basis. Television viewing remains at about 110–115 minutes per workday and somewhat higher during the weekends. Television is considered an 'all round' medium for information, entertainment and education. Practically all big media have had websites for over ten to fifteen years, and government and municipal organisations have established home pages. However, these websites are maintained mostly as one-way channels of information. Some sites provide discussion columns, but these are meant for questions and answers, for general feedback rather than for genuine debate. In this sense it can be argued that the Web has been used in a very restricted way, not utilising its full potential.

Immediately after the tsunami, each of the four Nordic countries set up official investigations and all four commissions reported heavy criticism of public officials and especially the foreign ministries. All reports indicated that the Nordic welfare states were not prepared to respond adequately to this 'new' kind of threat and to their citizens' demands for information, especially during the Christmas season when most officials are on holidays. The Swedish report even demanded that the top political leadership be brought to court for mismanagement (*Sverige och Tsunamin–granskning och förslag,* 2005, Andersson Odén et al., 2005), and in 2006, the political debate on the tsunami continued. The minister of foreign affairs was forced to quit her job. On the other hand, these reports also indicate—mainly with carefully phrased, politically correct formulations—that Nordic citizens perhaps have unrealistic expectations for the efficiency of the state and its capacity to act on behalf of citizens in foreign countries. Many citizens seemed to expect that the

Activity 7.1

In relation to a disaster that has confronted large numbers of people in your own country, list whatever you can remember about the media coverage. Consider how the people personally involved in the crisis acted and discuss how you would react if friends or relatives were involved in a major catastrophe far from home. What information would you want and where would you expect to get it? Discuss how the media should report such issues and the role governments should play in managing such situations.

state is able to protect them even when they travel to far-off countries without reporting their proposed destinations to anyone other than their families. The commissions therefore argued that nation states cannot be held responsible for all kinds of present-day vacation nomadism.

Reporting the tsunami

Initially, the volume of media reporting on the tsunami was enormous, but it decreased quite quickly. In Finland, as many as 20,000 news dispatches and reports were filed in the first month. Nine out of ten stories covering the tsunami followed a news format. Compared with routine news coverage, the tsunami coverage focused on 'ordinary citizens'—Finnish tourists in Asia and their concerned relatives and friends at home—who were given far more space in the media than usual. While the normal proportion of media coverage devoted to this type of coverage rarely exceeds 10 per cent, at this time it increased to 25–35 per cent. In the first two days, the media reports mainly described the phenomenon itself and the destruction it had caused. After the first month, the Finnish media changed its focus almost entirely to what had happened to the Finns in the area. All the Nordic media seem to have behaved in a similar manner. The fact that more than 150,000 Indonesians and thousands of other people from the Bay of Bengal area lost their lives disappeared from the Nordic public arena. The Nordic media attention was totally on what happened to the citizens of their own country only. At least in Finland and in Norway, this kind of 'selfishness' of orientation later created discussion among media critics. Another sign of this kind of narrow orientation was the fact that the news coverage reduced dramatically after all rescued and injured Finns/Norwegians were brought home.

As in the case of Katrina, the Nordic experience seems to suggest that web-based citizen activity is at its strongest when it deals with a concrete, dramatic case with a clear domestic or local focus—it was naïve to interpret that the Internet activity in both cases would be an indication of global or even national solidarity.

In Finland, several detailed studies of the media coverage and people's reactions to news of the tsunami were undertaken (Mörä, 2005; Huhtala et al., 2005; Jääsaari, 2005; Orava, 2005; von Frenckell, 2005; Kivikuru, 2006a, 2006b). In these studies, people criticised the state, especially their ministry of foreign affairs, but they also indicated their unhappiness about the behaviour of the media during the crisis. They criticised the media for ignoring the wishes of interviewees suffering from shock, for exploiting injured and lost children, and in general for not letting the people's voices be heard. It also became clear that the audience was, in fact, divided into two groups, Although many Finns felt that 'I could have been there', the majority remained more dispassionate observers. But a group of 80,000–100,000 individuals experienced the tsunami very personally indeed. Their relatives were among those killed, injured or missing, or they had visited the region quite recently. Understandably, they were those most vocal and critical of government inaction. All were shocked first, because the crisis was 'unprecedented'—it showed Finns in great difficulties in a far-away place, previously considered a safe holiday destination. While the majority of the population seemed to calm down and to lose interest in the issue quite quickly, those whom the crisis had hit personally remained in distress for a much longer period of time.

However, the most shocking criticism emerged from audience statistics. The 'new' media had played a far stronger role in the chaotic period immediately after the tsunami than ever before. Partly, people were forced to access information from new media because radio and television did not have as many bulletins on Boxing Day as usual. People listened first to the radio, then turned to the text-TV in order to get more information, and finally they started phoning. Those most concerned telephoned the ministry for foreign affairs, others telephoned their friends and relatives. At the ministry, again due to Boxing Day, the personnel on duty was minimal, and only three telephone lines were available for crisis work. During the month of January, almost 60,000 phone calls were recorded at the ministry, though a majority never got through. In a country calling itself an 'information society', such a problem decreased the credibility of the whole state apparatus.

Although the media first presented the Asian tsunami as a terrible but distant event, many Finns knew that their loved ones were in the region. Uncertainty pushed people to seek new routes and channels, and new sources of information. People started phoning, sending and receiving text messages with their mobile phones. This was reflected in the telephone statistics. For example, the number of mobile phone calls from Finland to and from Thailand rose by 260 per cent and the number of text messages sent to Thailand by 370 per cent (*Aasian luonnonkatastrofi, 2004*, pp. 116–17). The mobile phone was the only medium available for contacts between Finland and the holiday resorts in Thailand, and text messages became a crucial source of information because the SMS traffic operated smoothly throughout the crisis, while telephone connections were quite fragile. The most crucial information between Finnish tourists in the tsunami region and their families at home were delivered in 160-digit messages. Afterwards, the Nordic tourists in the affected regions stated that they were probably the ones most in need of more information about the event since the destruction of communications infrastructure in the Asian resorts meant they only occasionally ran into a functioning television set at hotels, hospitals or airports. They knew less about the total situation than their relatives at home even though thousands of news dispatches circled around them.

There also was a contradiction embedded in the situation. The Finns at home wanted tailored, specific information about their relatives and friends and felt that too much was said about the whole tsunami process, although quantitatively speaking this was not true because the media in fact focused strongly on Finns. The Finns in the tsunami region wanted more general information about the situation, since the information available to them hardly reached beyond the hotel where they were staying. This is an interesting contradiction and difficult to resolve. Later all the Nordic countries considered whether or not the assistance organisations should have sent information officers to the region. Doctors and nurses did not have time to brief the injured about the total situation, although that could have assisted in calming them down.

In addition to individual mobile phone use, the Finnish Ministry of Traffic and Communications sent a mass text message to 6000 mobile phones on December 29, informing people about evacuation places in Thailand and Sri Lanka. The message was not successful. It came too late and caused additional confusion. Arrangements had been changed because the Communications Regulatory Authority tried to solve the technical and legal problems involved in such an exercise. However, this type of mass messaging is apparently here to stay, since a new Act was passed by the Parliament recently, enabling the Communications Regulatory Authority to more easily send this kind of message to Finns in crisis in the future. Other forms of early warning systems for ordinary people are also in the pipeline. For researchers interested in more theoretical considerations, these messages provide an interesting challenge—should they be defined as interpersonal communication or part of mass communication with fixed messages? By mass communication, it is usually meant information relayed to a large, unidentified mass of people in 'packaged' form and repeated at regular intervals. In this particular situation, the audience is large but not anonymous, the messages are standardised but not regularly repeated. However, the new technology obviously provides potential for a grey zone between the mass communication and interpersonal communication, although official SMS messages, with a volume of 160 digits, are forced to operate on the same lines as conventional mass communication.

During the crisis, the use of conventional media thus rose. In addition people visited official websites, but the most dramatic rise was experienced in the use of amateur-run websites that offered people a forum for debate and also comfort and consolation. The information offered on the websites run by Finnish divers in Thailand or by various friendship associations did not depart much from the conventional media output, and they gave access also to rumours and non-credible information. This clumsy 'mixed grill' approach was able to create a community feeling among mourners and concerned individuals. That was something that the conventional media obviously could not achieve with their packaged and professional output. Conventional media prioritised credibility while the websites prioritised affections. The result was that the websites, usually visited by a few hundred people per day, counted both roughly 300,000 visits per day for a month after the tsunami. In February 2005, the figures started declining and reached the normal volume quite fast.

Perhaps the most interesting outcome was the fact that although 300,000 people visited these websites, only a few hundred actually participated in the discussions. The rest remained as observers, only checking what was going on. In a way, it can be said that the Web behaviour of these people hardly differed much from that of receivers for conventional media since most did not personally participate. However, it should also be noted that the message exchange that they observed at the websites was somewhat more two-way and tailored according to receiver needs than conventional mass communication due to the discussion option. The layout and style of reporting on these Finnish websites have remained quite the same, while in the case of Katrina websites a move towards more organised and professional, newspaper-like style is noticeable, and sender emphasis has grown. It would be interesting to carry out research on the mass communication legacy in web-based communication, but for the time being such longitudinal research is impossible to find.

One could perhaps propose that in these dramatic events, the state and the conventional media, for the first time on a larger scale, met a public that carried the characteristics linked with the 'information age' in slogans: these people were not content to be audienced and served with non-tailored, impersonal messages. They wanted special services, they wanted to have the choice to participate even if not everybody used it. During the first days after the tsunami, neither the state nor the media could meet this challenge. In fact, they used a kind of 'turtle defence', turned conservative and conventional in whatever they did.

On the other hand, the behaviour of the citizens in the tsunami case at least can hardly be called logical and consequent, either. People seemed to be quite confused about their own roles. On the one hand, they wanted the state to take responsibility and secure their and their loved ones' lives; they wanted to be offered services as a right. On the other hand they wanted individual solutions and tailored information services. The requirements set on the public and the private sphere were mixed and diffuse, and this fact became perhaps more striking in the contradictory demands set on information and communication needs than other, more concrete social actions.

Global communities?

While it has often been claimed that new technology assists in the creation of a global village, we have also been warned about global standardisation of cultures. It has been assumed that because of the potential embedded in new technology, people learn to know more about people and events far from them, and subsequently they develop a kind of global community. However, the recent Finnish—and in general, Nordic, because very similar results have been collected at least from Sweden (Nord, 2006) and from Norway (Eide, 2005)—experiences suggest that this is not automatically so. At least in a crisis situation people easily become selfish, egocentric and parochial. They are almost entirely interested only in their own concerns, in people in similar situations as they themselves, or perhaps in the experiences of their countrymen and people from nearby countries. In fact, the new technology seems to increase this selfishness of attitude by offering them a channel for more personally tailored information and debate than has been available via the conventional media. These people are in need of forming a community to compensate for their own feelings of insecurity, but the sense of community does not expand because of the options available through the Internet. Quite the opposite, their sense of community appears to shrink. Another issue concerns the reality of such a community. Several researchers have claimed that the Internet tends to privatise the political public sphere, since individuals can only tap its potential in isolation. Even when conversations in the interactive zones of Internet communications include many people, they still have the air of exchanges between private persons, not action groups. The individual lacks the opportunity to emerge from the private sphere into a public space. True participation and the potential for empowerment are missing.

One can contradict this conclusion by saying that the solidarity shown by the global community can be counted in euros and dollars; the voluntary financial assistance to the tsunami victims all over the world reached enormous sums. It is no doubt true that the Internet enabled people to know and be alerted to the destruction caused by the tsunami. However, the motives of those donating money have not been analysed. They might be far more complicated than it has been assumed. For example in the Nordic countries, several journalistic stories have indicated that many people thought that the funds would be used for their countrymen suffering from the losses caused by the tsunami. In the same way, people have also been irritated about the fact that so little improvement has taken place in the tsunami-affected countries although so much money was donated. Westerners are anxious and suspicious that their money has been wasted, and they have not been motivated to collect more information about the target countries or international donors mediating the funds. The tsunami remained as a news event, and the framing of this event was carried out by the conventional media, although the people used the Web for recovering from the event.

It is problematic that very little is known about how people actually connect media or the Web to their lives as citizens. Within political communication there is a great deal of research (e.g. Bennett and Paletz, 1994) concentrating on questions of transmission; how politicians get their message across or what do people learn about campaign issues from the news-media or the Web arena, but there has been very little research into how people make sense of events and opinions mediated to them on their own terms. As a political being, the citizen is most often treated as an abstract, disconnected bearer of rights, privileges and immunities instead of one of persons whose existence is located in a particular place and draws its sustenance from circumscribed relationships: family, friends, workplace, community etc. Such relationships are the sources from which political beings draw power—symbolic, material and psychological—and they enable them to act together. Our limited knowledge about the linkage between mediated information and citizen interpretation might bring us such surprises as the tsunami aftermath in Finland. Citizen behaviour sounded irrational and contradictory—people did not accept information packaged for them according to professional standards. Instead, they preferred amateurish websites lacking credibility.

Internationally, the perhaps most significant political role that the Internet has played is in promoting links between community groups and political activists from different parts of the world (e.g. Rodriguez, 2001; Cammaerts and van Audenhove, 2005). On the other hand, there is also contradictory information available. Some researchers (e.g. Mayer and Hinchman, 2002; Dahlgren, 2005) claim that the Internet's capacity for social organisation and empowerment is limited, because it tends to privatise the political public sphere. Individuals can only tap its potential in isolation. Even when conversations in the interactive zones of Internet communications include many people, they still have the air of exchanges between private persons, not action groups. However, the Internet is assumed to have positive consequences in extending and pluralising the public sphere. Obviously in crisis situations such as the tsunami, the Internet's capacity for creating a combination of the private and the public pleases and comforts people, at least giving an illusion of audience power.

Conclusion

The news about the tsunami flew all over the world through the conventional media and the Web, and in most countries web discussions on the item started within a few hours. However, although the news item as such was international, it was in a way 'split' into localised pieces in the Web discussions that focussed on national or regional aspects of the catastrophe. A certain amount of loyalty was no doubt shown by the huge sum of money collected for repairing the tsunami casualties all over the world—according to Reuters, the flood of funding amounted to over US $9 billion. It is still hardly probable that a global wave of loyalty would develop in similar situations online only towards those hit by a crisis—in any case, not more so than during the old days with only access to conventional mass media. In 'imagined communities' (Anderson, 1983), the solidarity tends to be quite thin, and without social structures, it dies out soon, as in the case of the 'Live Aid' campaign in 1985 (e.g. Harrison and Palmer, 1986), established to fight the famine in Ethiopia. Sustainable international solidarity requires organisation and structures. In this respect, the growing use of the Web does not seem to have made any change. The transmission of information is perhaps faster, and the volume of discussions on the Web are vivid, but they still focus mainly on localised items. For example, the Finns communicating about the tsunami via the divers' and friendship associations' websites directed their criticism towards domestic institutions and media, not any global ones. They felt themselves strongly localised, although the crisis itself happened far away.

In a way, it can be claimed that production processes lag behind technical development, and when a crisis breaks the normal routines, it can slow down as production staff seek to sort through and authenticate the vast quantities of information accumulating. So while a 'new', more interactive audience is emerging, it is still at an initiation stage. This has become especially clear in crisis situations, when a large proportion of the audience escape to amateurish websites that allow more social networking than the conventional media or public institutions. However, this does not necessarily mean that everybody wants to participate in such discussions. Many remain quiet observers, but they still favour channels that are based on two-way communication. In a conventional media system, receivers have supported their security feelings by credible information from reliable sources. In these more recent cases, people seem to reach the same result by getting confirmative communication from other people in the same situation as they themselves are.

CHAPTER SUMMARY

- In this chapter the use of information in crisis situations has been discussed. In principle, the existence of new technology has not changed the traditional media hierarchy.
- In a crisis situation, the need for information grows, but conventional media are not always able to provide the audience with immediately updated information, either via their traditional formats nor via their web versions.

→

- In the same way, public information providers (ministries, policy makers, health services) play it safe and become conservative in their information activity despite their fine policy documents meant to promote democracy via information.
- In a crisis, people make do with top-down information flows and seem unaware of what to do when citizens demand information and specific action.

Tutorial questions

- Describe what happens to people's use of traditional media and web-based information networks in a crisis situation.
- What kinds of effects does the Internet have on national and global audiences in crisis situations?

Recommended reading

Meyer, T & Hinchman, L., 2002, *Media Democracy: How the Media Colonize Politics*, Polity Press, Cambridge.

Miller, T., 2005, 'Financialization, Emotionalization, and Other Ugly Concepts', in Nohrstedt, S-A & R. Ottosen (eds), *Global War—Local Viewers: Media Images of the Iraq War*, pp. 263–76, Nordicom, Kungälv.

Rodriguez, C., 2001, *Fissures in the Mediascape: An International Study of Citizen's Media*, Hampton Press, Cresskill, NJ.

Websites

Finnish Communications Regulatory Authority: http://www.ficora.fi/en/index.html

Katrina Information Network: www.katrinaaction.org

Finnish Ministry for Foreign Affairs, Asian Tsunami Disaster: Interim Report: http://www.finland.it/netcomm/news/showarticle.asp?intNWSAID=32544

New Orleans Network: www.neworleansnetwork.org

People's Hurricane Relief Fund & Oversight Coalition: www.communitylaborunited.net

Note

1   Such organisations are multiple. See e.g. Katrina Information Network (http://www.katrinaaction.org), the New Orleans Network (http://www.neworleansnetwork.org), the People's Hurricane Relief Fund & Oversight Coalition (http://www.communitylaborunited.net). The sites were strongly discussion-

based immediately after the catastrophe. Now small pieces of relevant information, e.g. about how to apply for extra funding, dominate the sites. However, the focus is still strongly citizen-oriented and the texts indicate suspicions about government actions.

References

Aasian luonnonkatastrofi 26.12.2004, Tutkintaselostus/The natural disaster in Asia on 26 December, 2004, Investigation report, Accident Investigation Board Report A2/2004 Y, Finland.

Anderson, B., 1983, *Imagined Communities: Reflections on the Origin and Spread of Nationalism,* Verso, London.

Andersson, O., Tomas, M., Wallin, G. & U., 2005, Tsunamis genomslag: En studie av svenska mediers bevakning (The strike of tsunami: A study on the coverage by Swedish media), Västerås: KBM:s temaserie 2005:13.

Anker, E., 2005, 'Villains, Victims and Heroes: Melodrama, Media, and September 11', *Journal of Communication,* 55:1, pp. 22–37.

Bennett, W.L. & Paletz, D.L. (eds), 1994, *Taken by Storm: The Media, Public Opinion and the U.S. Foreign Policy in the Gulf War,* University of Chicago Press, London.

Cammaerts, B. & van Audenhove. L., 2005, 'Online political debate, unbounded citizenship and the problematic nature of a trannational public sphere', *Political Communication* 22:2, pp. 179–96.

Dahlgren, P., 2005, 'The Internet, Public Sphere, and Political Communication: Dispersion and Deliberation', *Political Communication* 22:2, pp. 147–62.

Demers, D., 2002, *Global Media: Menace or Messiah?,* Hampton Press, Cresskill, NJ.

Eide, E., 2005, 'Tsunamin, menniskerne og medierne' (Tsunami, men and media), Norsk Medietidskrift 12:1, pp. 48–61.

Evaluering af den samlede danske håndtering af flodbölgekatastrofen i Asien. Udenrigsministeriet, den 24. maj 2005, No 87-7667-172-0, Digital ISBN 87-7667-173-9, www.netpublikationer.dk

Harrison, P., & Palmer, R.,1986, *News Out of Africa: Biafra to Band Aid,* Hilary Shipman, London.

Heinonen, A., 1999, *Journalism in the Age of the Net: Changing Society, Changing Profession,* University of Tampere, Tampere.

Huhtala, H., Hakala, S., Laakso, A. & Falck, A., 2005, Tiedonkulku ja viestintä Aasian hyökyaaltokatastrofissa (Information transmission and communication in the Asian tsunami catastrophe), Report Series 7/2005, Government Office for Information.

Ignatieff, M., 1998, *The Warrior's Honor: Ethnic War and the Modern Conscience,* Henry Holt Books, New York.

Jääsaari, J., 2005, Sivustakatsojan tarina, Suomalaisten näkemyksiä Aasian hyökyaaltokatastrofin käsittelystä mediassa, Finnish Broadcasting Company: Receiver Research.

Katz, E., & Dayan, D., 1991, *Media Events: The Live Broadcasting of History*, Holt, Rinehart and Winston, New York, Chicago and San Francisco.

Kivikuru, U., 2006a, 'Tsunami Communication in Finland Top/Down, Homespun Framing about a Global Phenomenon', in Fuller, L. (ed.), *Tsunami 2004: Communication Perspectives*, Hampton Press, Cresskill, NJ.

Kivikuru, U., 2006b, 'Tsunami communication in Finland: A coverage that revealed tension in sender/receiver relationship', *European Journal of Communication*, Vol. 21:4.

Mayer, T. & Hinchman, L., 2002, *Media Democracy: How the Media Colonize Politics*, Polity Press, Cambridge.

Mörä, T., 2005, Tsunami suomalaisessa mediassa (Tsunami in the Finnish Media), Communication Research Centre, University of Helsinki.

Nord, L., 2006, 'When a natural disaster becomes a political crisis: A study of the 2004 tsunami and Swedish political communication', paper presented at the ICA Conference, Dresden, June.

Nordic Media Trends 2003, Kungälv: Nordicom.

Orava, H., 2005, Rapportering om tsunamikatastrofen i finlandssvensk radio och TV (Reporting on the tsunami in the Swedish-language radio and TV in Finland), Notat serie No 4/2005, Swedish School of Social Science.

Reimers, B., 1994, *The Most Common of Practices: On Mass Media Use in Late Modernity*, Almqvist & Wiksell International, Stockholm.

Rodriguez, C., 2001, *Fissures in the Mediascape: An International Study of Citizen's Media*, Hampton Press, Cresskill, NJ.

Sood, R., Stockdale, G. & Rogers, E., 1987, 'How the News Media Operate in National Disasters', *Journal of Communication* 37:3.

Sverige och Tsunamin—granskning och förslag, extrarapporter från 2005 års katastrofkommission, Stockholm: SOU 2005:104.

Tveiten, O., 2002, 'TV Wars, the Audience and the Public', in Kempf, W. & Heikki Luostarinen (eds) *Journalism and the New World Order: Studying War and the Media*, pp. 73–86. Nordicom, Kungälv.

von Frenckell, J., 2005, Tsunamins framfart i fem finlandssvenska dagstidningar (The presentation of the tsunami in Swedish newspapers in Finland), Swedish School of Social Science Notat serie No 5/2005.

HERMAN
WASSERMAN

8

Surfing Against the Tide: The Use of New Media Technologies for Social Activism in South Africa

Key terms

new media
social movements
media activism
the digital divide

Issues

- What are the main advantages of new media for social movements?
- Are the opportunities created by new media technologies, and the ways in which they are used, the same the world over?
- How effective are these technologies in contexts where connectivity rates are low and where there exist other limitations such as illiteracy and poverty?
- Is there a difference in the way that different social movements use new media technologies and, if so, what are the reasons for these differences?

CHAPTER OVERVIEW

This chapter will provide you with an overview of the potential of new media technologies, especially the Internet and email, for the promotion of social activism. By comparing examples of the successful use of new media by social movements globally with South African examples, the chapter will explain what advantages new media can bring to activists working in a development context. The two South African movements in question are the Treatment Action Campaign (TAC), a movement that works for greater access to anti-retroviral drugs for people living with HIV/AIDS in South Africa, and the Anti-Privatisation Forum (APF), an activist movement opposing the privatisation of public resources, especially basic services like housing, electricity and water. The aim of this comparison is:

- to establish whether the use of new media for social activism in South Africa shows parallels with its use in other international settings;
- to understand how such movements integrate new media into their activities;
- to identify factors that play a role in the ways different types of social movements use new media.

GLOSSARY

Social movements   These can be described in this context as groups of people representing the marginalised in society, such as the poor or the homeless, and who challenge state authority and the dominant socio- economic and political order by insisting on social change around specific issues. These groups aim to effect social transformation outside of formal political means. Social movements seek to change the current social or political order, rather than just attempting to improve conditions through short-term changes like the replacement of a political leader (Van de Donk et al., 2004, p. 3).

New media   The definition of what should be included under this term is often debated. In the context of this chapter, this term will refer mostly to the Internet, email and mobile (or cell) phones.

Think about it

Have you come across news or information online that you have not seen in the mainstream media (commercial newspapers, television etc.)?
Why do you think this news or information failed to make the headlines elsewhere?
   Can you think of examples where the use of new media technologies have been instrumental for the staging of protests or to connect people with similar social concerns?

Introduction: Using new media for social activism

It is often argued that digital media technologies have provided new tools for activists who work for social change. It is argued that these technologies make it possible for grassroots **social movements** to mobilise support on a global level, to spread information about their activities outside the mainstream commercial media and to discuss issues on a wider platform. Still, questions about the effectivity of these media for social action remain. The advent of email and the Internet gave rise to widespread optimism that these media would create new ways for groups that are excluded from mainstream media coverage to make their voices heard (Kellner, 2002, p. 182). **New media** technologies led to expectations that additional avenues for participatory communication, for development and for the networking of local communities would eventuate (Lie, 2005, p. 121). Social movement activists operate outside formal political systems, and would typically not receive extensive coverage in the mainstream commercial media. So potentially new media promise to reduce dependence on mainstream media (Van de Donk et al., 2004, p. 19; Chadwick, 2005). New social movements also 'tend to embrace concepts such as diversity, decentralization, informality and grassroots democracy, rather than unity, centralization, formality and strong leadership' (Van de Donk et al., 2004, p. 4), which makes the architecture and application of new media technologies attractive to them on a practical and ideological level. Although the constantly changing nature of social movements make it difficult to study their use of new media technologies (Van de Donk et al., 2004, p. 3), there have been many documented cases of how new media technologies have assisted social movements worldwide ((Kellner 2002, p. 184). One of the main advantages noted is that they make it possible to spread information on a global scale at relatively low cost (Papacharissi, 1999). Other advantages include: increased speed of communication; possible integration and convergence of different media forms; and the possibility of interactivity, especially the consultation of information stored on the Internet (Lie, 2005, p. 122).

The belief that new media technologies would make it possible for citizens to rise up against state power, to challenge economic systems and work towards a new global social order have often taken utopian proportions. Words like 'network armies', 'netwars' and 'smart mobs' (Bennett, 2003) expressed the revolutionary potential some consider these technologies to possess. This optimism is overstated, and in recent years the 'heroic rhetoric from cyber utopians' (Van de Donk et al., 2004, p. 24) has become tempered. Nevertheless, there are many examples of how social activists have succeeded in using new media technologies to their benefit (see, for instance, McCaughey and Ayers, 2003). The protests against the Multilateral Agreement on Investment (MAI) in 1998 (Bray, 1998; Deibert, 2000, p. 261), the well-known 'Battle for Seattle' during the World Trade Organization meeting in December 1999 (Kellner, 2002, pp. 185–7) the protests by the Tiananmen Square democracy movement (Kellner, 2002, pp. 184–5) and the Zapatista uprising in the province of Chiapas, Mexico (Ferdinand, 2000, pp. 13–15) are all well-known examples of how new media such as the Internet and email assisted activist movements in their mobilisation.

The question, however, is whether social movements would achieve the same success when relying on new media in a context where access to these technologies is much less common? In spite of the optimistic views of new media's democratic potential, it remains important to remember that these media are marked by severe inequalities, even in technologically advanced societies like Europe and the USA. These inequalities are sometimes referred to as the **Digital Divide**. Comparing the situation in Africa with that in richer countries, the Digital Divide looms large. Although the development of new media technologies is often considered crucial for the attainment of developmental goals in Africa (Gillwald, 2005, p. 8), the communications infrastructure on the continent is severely lacking. For example, Nyamnjoh (1999, pp. 42–3) has estimated that there are more telephone lines in Manhattan than in the whole of sub-Saharan Africa. While the number of lines are steadily increasing (Etta and Parvyn-Wamahiu, 2003, p. 20), the lack of fixed lines might account for the important role that mobile phones play in many African countries, and the fact that there are only 150,000 dial-up Internet accounts per 750 million people in Africa (excluding South Africa), mostly concentrated in urban centres (Lesame, 2005a, p. 8). The gaps between access to new media in Africa, in developed countries and even in emerging countries continues to grow (Gillwald, 2005, p. 8). The vast majority of the African population remains without access to new media, and lacks the training and literacy required to use them (Lesame, 2005a, p.3, Wasserman and De Beer, 2004).

Digital Divide   The severe inequalities that mark access to new media technologies, and that often correlates with other societal divisions and reinforces them. The divide between those that are 'connected' and those that are 'disconnected' exists within countries, for instance between ethnic groups, classes or genders, but also on a global scale, between rich and poor countries. In the context of this chapter, for instance, there is a Digital Divide between countries in Africa and those in the 'developed' world (Europe, the USA, Japan), but also internally in South Africa between rich and poor citizens. (See Gillwald, 2005, p. 8; Lesame, 2005a, p. 3).

GLOSSARY

Although South Africa leads the rest of the continent in the development of information and communication technologies (Etta and Parvyn-Wamahiu, 2003, p. 115), connectivity is distributed very unequally among the South African population, and is concentrated in urban centres among the educated elite. Policy initiatives have attempted to bridge this digital divide through the establishment of telecentre services (Lesame, 2005b, p. 20), but severe challenges remain.

Faced with such limitations, can new media technologies be of any use to social movements in South Africa, especially if their constituency is largely the poor and marginalised for whom a computer and an Internet connection would, in most cases, be an inconceivable luxury? To answer this question, we have to be alert to the interesting and creative ways people appropriate new media to fit their lived reality. As Lie (2005, p. 122) points out, considering just the figures

see McGuigan, Chapter 1; Goggin and Newell, Chapter 6; Lax, Chapter 12; Burton and Van der Hoven, Chapter 14

Theory link

denoting levels of connectivity and hardware availability can easily lead to a **technological determinist** view in which the end-users are 'reduced to figures' (Lie, 2005, p. 122), and insufficient attention is paid to the ways in which technologies are used differently in varying contexts. Lie (2005, p. 132) goes on to point out that new media are often used in conjunction with more traditional media. In African countries, this might be even more the case than in more 'developed' contexts, since access to new media is so restricted.

Technological Determinism   The belief that media technologies possess certain inherent qualities that determine their influence in society. A more culturalistic perspective on the use of new media technologies would be to see them as part of social development and part of social and cultural practices (c.f. Lie, 2005, p. 123).

see McGuigan, Chapter 1; Goggin and Newell, Chapter 6; Lax, Chapter 12; Burton and Van der Hoven, Chapter 14

Theory link

Furthermore, the theory of 'amplification' (Agre, 2002; Brants, 2002) posits that the introduction of new media technologies into a setting does not so much create completely new political and social effects, but rather amplifies, strengthens and broadens structures and forces already in place. This means that to understand the role that new media play in social movements, attention has to be paid to the existing communication structures within the movement, as well as to the broader political, social and economic power relations within which they operate. To imagine that new media technologies will have a predictable impact on the organisation and operation of new social movements should therefore be avoided. New technologies, of necessity, interact with existing infrastructures (Van de Donk et al., 2004, p. 6). To illustrate this, let us compare two South African social movements that have come into existence in the post-apartheid era to see how they use new media technologies.

Case study[1]

Two South African social movements and their use of new media

With the end of **apartheid** in South Africa a range of social movements came into being, aiming to eradicate the many socio-economic inequalities that had been inherited from apartheid. Dissatisfied with the slow pace of social reform by the post-apartheid government, these movements wish to see stronger intervention by

→

the state to counter the perpetuation of the inequalities caused by free-market economic policies. Among the issues on their agendas are the provision of basic municipal service, land reform, and the improvement of public health services for the majority that do not have access to private health care.

These movements have not been welcomed by the ANC government, and they have been accused of being 'ultra-left' and unpatriotic (Robins, 2004; McKinley, 2004). With the possible exception of the Treatment Action Campaign, these movements have been largely ignored by the mainstream commercial media, or received negative coverage (Jacobs, 2004, pp. 207, 231). Consequently, they have had to find alternative ways, outside of the mainstream media, to publicise their activities and to mobilise and build networks of support. They did this in a variety of ways, for instance through publishing their own media in the form of newsletters, community media inserts or even printing T-shirts, as well as relying on more traditional forms of communication such as door-to-door visits, public meetings or telephone calls. These strategies may serve to counteract the possible negative consequences of an over-reliance on new media technologies, such as the undermining of more traditional forms of networking (c.f. Wright, 2004, pp. 81–2, 90).

It is interesting to use Lie's (2005, p. 122) set of advantages that new media offer local communities (in our case, social movements)—i.e. speed of communication, decreased costs, integration of media forms, and interactivity—to compare two of these movements, the Anti-Privatisation Forum (APF) and the Treatment Action Campaign (TAC). What is important to note in comparing the two movements' use of

$\longrightarrow$

Apartheid The formalised system of racial discrimination in South Africa put into place when the National Party came to power in 1948. South African society was segregated according to imposed racial categories. Only the minority 'white' section of the population was allowed to vote. The black majority was denied basic rights, and their economic exploitation by the white minority led to the crippling inequalities that continue today. Attempts to resist apartheid or overthrow the regime were met with violence, and many members of the liberation movements such as the African National Congress (ANC) or the Pan-Africanist Congress (PAC) were harassed, tortured or incarcerated. Many leaders of these organisations, including Nelson Mandela (who later became the first president of democratic South Africa), were sent to the infamous Robben Island prison off the coast of Cape Town. A process of negotiations set in motion in 1990 led to the first democratic elections in 1994, when the ANC won control over the government.

GLOSSARY

new media is the difference in constituency and audience. The APF's constituency is the poorest of the poor, who mostly live in informal settlements (i.e. shanty towns) and cannot afford basic services like water and electricity. By contrast, the TAC, although it also works on behalf of the poor (that cannot afford private healthcare and needs to be provided with anti-retrovirals through the public health service), also has considerable middle-class support, locally as well as globally. Its constituents therefore, generally speaking, have better access to new media technologies. As will become clear in the discussion, this difference in constituency also has implications on the differing ways in which the APF and TAC use new media.

The speed of communication

The APF: According to their spokesperson, Dale McKinley, the APF uses new media such as the Internet and email 'mainly for information purposes' (Rolls and October, 2004). This information can be spread instantaneously via email, or posted on the website. This way the APF can make sure that information is made available to a global audience (although limited to those with Internet access), even if mainstream commercial media do not carry it. Its website contains a list of press releases (APF, 2004) where information regarding protest action, reasons for such action, as well as the movement's position on certain developments is published. The press releases on the website serve as a source of alternative information to that found in the mainstream media, but may also provide a source of information for journalists from the mainstream media reporting on events in which the APF is involved. While this alternative information can be spread much faster than would be the case in traditional media such as print, it is subject to infrastructural limitations, which we will return to shortly. Email is also a fast and affordable way for the APF to organise its internal affairs by linking various APF affiliates throughout the country. Roger Wilcox, a member of the APF steering committee, points out that 'the use of email has become essential' for the movement (Rolls & October, 2004). As Themba Mbhele, general secretary of the APF puts it (Rolls & October, 2004): 'Internet and email play a vital role in bringing social movements into the same room, locally and internationally'. Speed and reach combined therefore present advantages to the APF that more traditional media cannot. As will be seen in the next section, however, this use of new media is largely restricted to internal communication in the APF structure, and is not used to mobilise its members, due to infrastructural limitations.

TAC: Although TAC has received much more favourable coverage than any of the other social movements (see Jacobs, 2004, p. 30), it also uses new media for speedy dissemination of information and as a means of communication with supporters and members. Regular news releases are sent to subscribers on its email list and its website serves as an archive, where newsletters going back to 2000 can be downloaded. TAC's website also contains information on a variety of issues related to HIV/AIDS, including medicine, treatment literacy, court cases, speeches, pamphlets etc. Through its website and mailing lists, TAC has built up considerable networks with other African as well as global organisations. One of its mailing lists, africa@tac.org.za, is devoted to the Pan African HIV/AIDS Treatment Access Movement (PHATAM) and according to TAC's national manager Nathan Geffen it has approximately 1000 members. Another list, internat@tac.org.za, is dedicated to activists in and outside South Africa, and has a membership of about 150 (Ahmed and Swart, 2003). TAC's newsletter (news@tac.org.za) is sent out approximately once every two weeks. Through these email lists, information can be sent to a global audience immediately it becomes available, and TAC also sends out alerts in response to news events. By using email, TAC is able to spread news and information at a speed and with a reach that is impossible for traditional media.

Decreased costs for the end-user

The APF: While new media can eventually provide a relatively cheap means of communication, it requires an initial investment in hardware, software and connectivity. This investment is, however, outside the reach of the majority of members of a social movement such as the APF. Because many of their members do not have access to computers or the Internet, the APF mainly uses mobile phones for internal communication, and then mostly for text messaging rather than (the more expensive) voice calls. Because many members cannot even afford to buy airtime, members wanting to communicate with movement leadership would usually send a (free) text message (referred to as a 'please call me') asking someone in the office to call them back. McKinley admits that because of the costs involved, reply calls are limited, and attempts are made to get information across by word of mouth (Rolls & October, 2004):

> We are relying on the Internet and email but we are also restricted by it. We target the poorest of the poor. These people usually do not have the means to ensure basic things like access to decent sanitation. In that regard cell phone or Internet communication does not work. The volunteers on the ground end up going to people's houses, spreading information through word of mouth. This ensures a more hands-on approach which brings the organisation closer to the people. That I think is very important. Things like Internet and cell phones

make our mission easier but in the end it is these old methods that are more appropriate in the set up we are working in.

TAC: TAC uses new media mostly for reaching 'organisations and middle-class people'. TAC's national manager, Nathan Geffen points to website visits peaking just before and during the time that TAC embarked on a civil disobedience campaign in 2003 (Ahmed and Swart, 2003). Significantly, Geffen acknowledges that those site visitors are not necessarily 'the same people who come and march', but considers them as influential in terms of the social positions they occupy because they may have power to influence policy. New media provide a low-cost way for TAC to inform these influential supporters (with Internet access) of their activities and campaigns. New media are especially valuable as a low-cost way of soliciting funds from international supporters. Since TAC's support base is, however, also made up of members that do not have access to new media, they still have to rely on traditional means of communication, as will be discussed in the next section.

The possibility of integrating different media forms

The APF: The fact that the largest part of APF's constituency is the poor and without access to new media, necessitates that they use new media in combination with more traditional forms of communication. McKinley (Rolls and October, 2004) draws attention to just how diverse these forms of communication may be:

> The Internet is mainly used to inform other organisations and people of our existence and mission. We also supply T-shirts and caps etc. to communicate our mission. This is especially when we have protest marches. I think every medium has its benefits. We use email to reach comrades who have access to computers. The Internet is basically used to post general information to the broader public. In doing this we inform and educate the broader public of our goals. We interact with other organisations through the Internet. (…) (U)nequal access (to ICTs— HW) is just a perpetuation of existing inequalities in our society. We should use that to free our people from poverty—not to disempower them more.

He points to the combination aspect of their mobilisation strategy, through which different modes of communication amplify the others (Rolls & October, 2004):

> I think every medium has its benefits. We use email to reach comrades who have access to computers. The Internet is basically used to post general information

to the broader public. In doing this we inform and educate the broader public of our goals. We interact with other organisations through the Internet.

This multi-directional flow of communication is reiterated by Themba Mbhele, general secretary of the APF (Rolls & October, 2004):

> Most of our comrades do not have access to computers or cell phones. Specific comrades in the community are contacted through cellular phones by head office and from there the message is sent to all in the community. We are putting up more offices in the townships which bring the organisation closer to the people. Everybody is thus well-informed regardless of computer access.

In the light of the APF's constituency, therefore, email and the Internet alone are not considered viable media to mobilise activists on a large scale.

TAC: In spite of the fact that TAC has used new media successfully to reach parts of its constituency, the bulk of its mobilisation efforts focuses on more traditional media like pamphlets, word of mouth, phone calls and house-to-house visits (Ahmed and Swart, 2003). There is, however, a fair amount of synergy between traditional communication methods, using the mainstream media and new media technologies. The National Executive Secretary of TAC, Ruka Cornelius, explains (Ahmed and Swart, 2003):

> Emails get sent to provincial offices, who contact branches, who contact districts, who distribute posters and pamphlets at train stations and taxi ranks. We go to churches on foot—the message is more simplified usually—also go to NGOs, or fax all of them.

TAC's communication strategy can therefore be seen as an integration of media forms, of which new media plays an important part.

The possibility of interactivity and use of databases

The APF: As mentioned above, the APF's website contains a list of press releases about protest action, the reasons for such action, and the movement's position on certain developments. The clearest example of how the APF website attempts to serve as a forum for interactivity is a section titled 'Debate and discussion' where comment from site visitors is invited. The heading to this section reads:

> This section is a forum for free and open discussion and debate on organising and related matters. If you feel strongly about it send in your opinion for

publication. All views and ideas are welcome as long as they make sense to you, the writer.

Although this invitation articulates the potential of the website to stimulate interactivity, its success is dubious, since it contains articles by only two writers, of which the APF organiser, Trevor Ngwane, is one.

TAC: Hyperlinks are provided on TAC's website to South African AIDS organisations and activist groups as well as to reports and documents. In this way, TAC uses its website to complement information that might, due to space and other concerns, not readily be found in the mainstream commercial media. It also provides the opportunity for users to jump to related sites that might be of interest to them, such as information on treatment literacy (educating people to use antiretrovirals correctly) and contact details for public health facilities offering antiretroviral treatment.

TAC's use of email lists has been mentioned above. This is an example of how new media can be used to facilitate interactivity between a movement and its supporters, locally and globally. On its website TAC also provides an email address to which enquiries can be sent and telephone numbers of contact persons within the organisation.

Conclusion

The above examples show that the advantages that new media provide for social activists in 'developed' countries also apply to a developing country like South Africa. However, the severe infrastructural limitations and general levels of poverty demand that social movements find creative ways of using what connectivity they do have in combination with more traditional forms of communication. In the case of both the APF and TAC, new media extend the range of communication tools available, and are used in conjunction with other forms of communication to extend existing communication networks rather than radically altering them.

When examining the role that new media may play in the work done by social movements, it is therefore important not only to look at the quantitative aspects of new media use (e.g. The connectivity levels), but to use a culturalistic approach to assess in what ways the use of new media in these contexts is related to broader social, economic and political power relations. It remains vital that new media be studied in its social context, with attention to detail and the lived experience of its users, instead of approaching them in isolation.

CHAPTER SUMMARY

- This chapter provided an overview of the potential of new media technologies, especially the Internet and email, for the promotion of social activism.
- The two South African movements relied on in this chapter were the Treatment Action Campaign (TAC), a movement that works for greater access to anti-retroviral drugs for people living with HIV/AIDS in South Africa, and the Anti-Privatisation Forum (APF), an activist movement opposing the privatisation of public resources, especially basic services like housing, electricity and water.
- This chapter sought to explain, through a comparison of the successful use of new media by these two South African social movements, the advantages that new media can bring to activists working in a development context.

Tutorial questions

The two groups studied in this research show evidence of being highly selective in their choice of Internet options for communicating with group members as opposed to communicating with the wider community.

1. What lessons do the case studies reported here provide as to the importance of:

- using new technologies when they are available?
- developing a communicative plan for using the Internet that is tailored to the needs of the group?
- taking care that the communication channels used match the capacity of the audience to access the information provided?

2. Why did the two groups decide to use the Internet and how effective were they in tailoring their use of the Internet to the needs of their members? Could they have made better use of the Internet and, if so, how?

Recommended reading

Lesame, N.C. (ed.), 2005, *New Media—Technology and Policy in Developing Countries,* Van Schaik, Pretoria, pp. 120–41.

McCaughey, M. & Ayers. M.D., 2003, *Cyberactivism—Online Activism in Theory and Practice,* Routledge, New York.

Van de Donk, W., Loader, B.D., Nixon, P.G., Rucht, D., 2004, *Cyberprotest—New Media, Citizens and Social Movements,* Routledge, London.

Websites

Treatment Action Campaign: www.tac.org.za
Anti-Privatisation Forum: www.apf.org.za
Bridges: www.bridges.org
Panos: www.panos.org.uk

Note

1   Information contained in this case study was mostly obtained through personal interviews with mem-
    bers of the respective social movements. Full details available in Ahmed and Swart (2003) and Rolls and
    October (2004).

References

Ahmed, S. & Swart, C., 2003, *Report on the use of ICTs by the Treatment Action
    Campaign*, transcriptions of interviews conducted with TAC staff members and
    volunteers, 29–30 September. In possession of author.
Agre, P.E., 2002, 'Real-Time Politics: The Internet and the Political Process', *The
    Information Society*, 18, 31, pp. 311–31.
APF, 2004, Anti-Privatisation Forum Website. www.apf.org.za
Bennett, W.L., 2003, 'The Internet and Global Activism', in Couldry, N. & Curran, J.
    Contesting Media Power: Alternative Media in a Networked World, edited by Couldry,
    N.; Curran, J. Rowman & Littlefield.
Brants, K., 2002, 'Politics is E-verywhere', *Communications* 27 (2002), pp. 171–88.
Bray, J., 1998, 'Web Wars: NGOs, Companies and Governments in an
    Internet-connected World', *Greener Management International*, 98 (24),
    Winter, 115–30.
Chadwick, A., 2005, 'The Internet, Political Mobilization and Organizational
    Hybridity: "Deanspace", MoveOn.org and the 2004 US Presidential Campaign',
    paper presented to the panel 'The Internet and Political Mobilization', Political
    Studies Association of the United Kingdom Annual Conference, University of
    Leeds, 5–7 April.
Deibert, R.J., 2000, 'International Plug 'n Play? Citizen Activism, the Internet, and
    Global Public Policy', *International Studies Perspectives*, (2000) 1:255–72.
Etta, F.E. & Parvyn-Wamahiu, S. (eds), 2003, Information and Communication
    Technologies for Development in Africa—Volume 2: The experience with
    community telecentres, Ottawa & Dakar: International Development Research
    Centre (IDRC) & Council for the Development of Social Science Research in
    Africa (Codesria).

Ferdinand, P., 2000, 'The Internet, Democracy and Democratization', *Democratization* 7(1):1-17.

Gillwald, A., 2005, Introduction, in: Gillwald, A. (ed.) *Towards an African e-index: Household and individual ICT access and usage across 10 African countries,* ResearchICTAfrica.net. Johannesburg

Jacobs, S., 2004, *Public Sphere, Power and Democratic Politics: Media and Policy Debates in Post-Apartheid South Africa,* unpublished PhD dissertation, Birkbeck College, University of London.

Kellner, D., 2002, 'New Media and New Literacies: Reconstructing Education for the New Millennium' in Lievrouw, L., and Livingstone, S. (ed) *The Handbook of New Media,* London, SAGE Publications.

Lesame, Z., 2005a., 'Bridging the Digital Divide in South Africa and Selected African Countries', in: Lesame, N.C. (ed.) *New Media—Technology and Policy in Developing Countries,* pp. 1–16, Van Schaik, Pretoria.

Lesame, Z., 2005b, 'Bridging the Digital Divide in South Africa', in: Lesame, N.C. (ed.) *New Media—Technology and Policy in Developing Countries,* pp. 17–29 Van Schaik, Pretoria.

Lie, R., 2005, 'Community Development and the Internet', in Lesame, N.C. (ed.), *New Media—Technology and Policy in Developing Countries,* pp. 120–41, Van Schaik, Pretoria.

McCaughey, M. & Ayers, M.D., 2003, *Cyberactivism—Online Activism in Theory and Practice,* Routledge, New York.

McKinley, D., 2004, 'The Rise of Social Movements in South Africa', *Debate* 10, May, pp. 17–21.

Nyamnjoh, F.B., 1999, 'Africa and the information superhighway: The need for mitigated euphoria', *Ecquid Novi* 20 (1): 31–49.

Papacharissi, Z., 1999, 'The Virtual Sphere: The Internet as a Public Sphere', paper presented at the Annual Convention of the Association for Education in Journalism and Mass Communication (AEJMC), August, available online at AEJMC Archives, www.aej.org

Robins, S., 2004, '"Long Live Zackie, Long Live": Aids Activism, Science and Citizenship after Apartheid', *Journal of Southern African Studies* 30(3), pp. 651–72.

Rolls, C. & October, A., 2004, *Report on the use of ICTs by the Anti-Privatisation Forum,* transcriptions of interviews conducted with APF staff members and volunteers, November. In possession of author.

TAC, Treatment Action Campaign website, www.tac.org.za

Van de Donk, W., Loader, B.D., Nixon, P.G. & Rucht, D., 2004, *Cyberprotest—New Media, Citizens and Social Movements,* Routledge, London.

Wasserman, H., 2006a, 'Is a new world wide web possible? An explorative comparison of the use of ICTs by two South African social movements'. Forthcoming in *African Studies Review.*

Wasserman, H., 2006b, 'New Media in a New Democracy: An exploration of the potential of the Internet for civil society groups in South Africa', forthcoming in Sarikakis, K. & Thussu, D., *Ideologies of the Internet*, Hampton Press, Creskill, NJ.

Wasserman, H., 2005a, 'Renaissance and Resistance: Using ICTs for Social Change in South Africa', *African Studies* 64(2), pp. 177–99.

Wasserman, H., 2005b, 'Connecting African Activism with Global Networks: ICTs and South African social movements', *Africa Development* 30 (1&2), pp. 129–48.

Wasserman, H. & De Beer, A.S., 2004, 'E-governance and e-publicanism: preliminary perspectives on the role of the Internet in South African democratic processes', *Communicatio* 20(1): 64-89.

Wright, S., 2004, 'Informing, Communicating and ICTs in Contemporary Anti-capitalist Movements', in: Van de Donk, W., Loader, B.D., Nixon, P.G., & Rucht, D., 2004, *Cyberprotest—New Media, Citizens and Social Movements*, pp. 77–93, Routledge, London.

GUNN ENLI AND
TRINE SYVERTSEN
(PaP Research Group)[1]

Participation, Play and Socialising in New Media Environments

9

CHAPTER OVERVIEW

This chapter discusses new media user patterns, and specifically the trend whereby audiences are invited to respond to television programs and channels. The chapter demonstrates how the media industry through email, the Web and SMS creates opportunities for audiences to be more active. These efforts can be explained with reference to the media's need to sustain their position in the face of increased competition from new media. The chapter presents the results of a survey investigating the extent to which the audiences use the new response facilities and their motivations for doing so. This is in turn related to three key terms in media theory/sociology: participation, play and socialising.

Key terms

participation
play
personalisation
individualism
socialising

Issues

- How do people use new media to respond to television programs and producers?
- How can new media use be understood in the light of traditional media theory?
- What are the basic motivations for people to participate in media activities?

Introduction

The advent of digital technology and the convergence between media, markets and services have been predicted to lead to major changes in communication patterns. So far this millennium, convergence has not manifested itself as a coming together of all media into a super-medium or über-box (Fagerjord, 2002). What we are seeing instead is a process of diversification where traditional media remain distinct, but where companies move into each other's markets and create services based on the combination of platforms. These moves fit well with two key trends in media production and consumption, those of *media personalisation* and *user involvement in production*. The first of these trends has characterised media developments for decades—gradually more and more technological appliances have been designed to allow individuals to personalise their content (from the remote control, to the Walkman, to MP3 players and electronic program guides). The trend of audience involvement is more recent, but since 2000 much of the focus and strategic energy in press and broadcasting have concerned how to design formats that may elicit responses from readers and viewers.

Both traditional and new communication channels are used for audience response. Traditionally, viewers and listeners have been able to communicate with broadcasters through letters and telephone calls, forms of communication that have been extended to fax and email. As the World Wide Web and Internet developed in the 1990s, broadcasters set up response facilities on their new and emerging websites (Fagerjord, 2003; Rasmussen, 2002; Siapera, 2004). Websites are frequently used by media companies as a way of 'community-building'; the purpose is to make the public feel part of a privileged and integrated community and identify more strongly with the program (Syvertsen, 2005). The possibility to send short text and image messages through mobile phone is the newest form of activity. In a number of programs the public is urged to vote, offer opinions or chat with other guests or the host using SMS and MMS. Viewers may function as co-producers by, for example, selecting music videos in jukebox formats or initiating dialogues in chat-formats (Enli, 2005; Beyer et al., 2006). Some global mega-formats, most notably *Big Brother* and *Pop Idol,* integrate all the above platforms. Through a variety of response channels, audiences determine who should leave and who should stay, and may also interact with producers, participants and each other (Jones, 2003; Colombo, 2004).

The aim of this chapter is to discuss the trend towards cross-platform activity with a particular emphasis on television-related formats. We begin by placing the trend towards audience involvement in the context of increased individualism in society. Then we present the result of a Norwegian survey based on more than 1200 respondents indicating the extent to which audiences use the available feedback opportunities and their motivations for doing so. This is in turn related to three key concepts in media theory/sociology: participation, play and socialising. The concept of *participation* is crucial within democratic theory and is related to the idea of people taking part in discussions in the public sphere (Pateman, 1970; Habermas, 1989). In media studies, the development of new formats has revitalised the debate over whether mainstream media may function as arenas for civic participation (Livingstone & Lunt, 1994; Syvertsen, 2001). The term *play* belongs, academically speaking, to the field of pedagogy and studies of performance and ritual, but has more recently been taken up by new media and game studies (Aarseth, 2001; Tronstad, 2004). The term play illuminates that media activities are not just a matter of rational deliberation on public matters, but also a means of entertainment and an exciting way to spend leisure time. The third term *socialising* illuminates yet another aspect of media activity. Related to media, socialising describes activities where viewers come into contact with others and exchange everyday small talk through mediated networks (Hjarvard, 2003).

Think about it

- Will audience participation in the media promote participatory democracy?
- Do the new feedback opportunities make the media more democratic?

Audience involvement: Understanding the trend

The emerging trends towards media personalisation and participation may be related to general developments in society. One key feature of modern society is individualism, whereby traditional collective institutions, such as religion and family, are losing authority and are in part being replaced by individual freedom and choice. It is not adequate, however, to see this as a development towards increased isolation and atomisation of individuals. As Bauman (2000) argues, modernity implies a paradox because the individual's increasing freedom and autonomy produces an even stronger dependency on society. Personal choices are not made in solitude, but rather in dialogue with the society.

In an increasingly complex society, the development of new media technologies might function as a response to the individual's need for control and communication. For example, the mobile phone is described by Rasmussen (2002) as one of the new media technologies that may enable people to engage in what

see Lury, Chapter 18; Nightingale Chapters 2 and 17

Theory link

Giddens (1991) terms 'the reflexive monitoring of daily life'. In this light, the media industry is not so much causing as trying to respond to and exploit the trend towards individualism. As Sonia Livingstone argues, 'The implicit assumption that the media are cause rather than a consequence of social change is too technologically deterministic' (1999, p. 160).

The move towards media personalisation and audience involvement may partly be seen as a defensive move on the part of the media industry, as media institutions have also lost some of their traditional authority. Confidence polls indicate that journalists are far down on the list of professions considered the trustworthiest, and the loss of allegiance is seen in shifting reader and viewer patterns. Reader patterns for newspapers in the postwar era were far more stable than today (and in many countries followed party-political loyalties), and compared with the present day, public broadcasters had stable and solid support. With decreasing loyalties and more shifting individual preferences, media have to compete more aggressively for viewers' time and affection. Syvertsen and Ytreberg (2006) and Sundet (2006) both point to the media's need to build stronger ties with the audience—and particularly younger viewers—as a key reason why media corporations develop interactive solutions. For new generations—familiar with digital media—it seems natural to have influence over media content. Increased audience activity is seen as 'an excellent way to woo an increasingly "promiscuous" audience' (Jones, 2003, p. 419). The theory is that if viewers get an opportunity to influence, they will feel more ownership of the product and increase their loyalty to programs and companies (Prebensen, 2005, p. 67).

This loyalty is in turn seen as necessary to secure the media's financial base. Both licence-fee funded and commercial channels are worried that traditional sources of revenue are endangered. Formats involving audience activity may offer good value for money; they constitute an inexpensive way to fill broadcast time and a good way of exploiting cross-media ownership. In small television markets formats based on audience involvement may by themselves make good economic sense. As Enli (2005, p. 120) argues, low availability of viewers creates a situation where 'it may be financially preferable to base income on direct payment from audiences rather than trying to sell audiences to advertisers'.

Think about it

- What are the editorial implications of increased audience activities in the media?
- Will audience contributions improve quality in the media content?

Participation in cross-platform activities

We turn now to a case study of audience activity on Norwegian television. Norway is a small and wealthy country (pop. 4.6 million), where audience activities have proliferated in recent years. In order to map to what degree audiences actually use the opportunities provided, a survey was carried out, based on more than 1200 respondents. The purpose of the survey was to get reliable data on the public's use of television in combination with other media, to investigate what activities they prefer, to explore their motivations, and to speculate, more tentatively, on similarities and differences between users of different platforms.[2] In the study our interest lies not only in the overall level of activity, as this is bound to change as opportunities proliferate, but also in the relative differences between various activities.

Our first issue concerns the overall use of the feedback opportunities, which appear to be relatively high. In 2004, 22 per cent of the sample population had somehow communicated with a television station during the previous twelve months: either through sending and SMS/MMS, through the Internet, or through letters and phone calls. The distribution of the various activities is laid out in Table 9.1:

Table 9.1 The uses of cross-platform activities connected with television. Respondents could give more than one answer. (N=1232)

Type of activity	Per cent of population
Have sent MMS/SMS to TV channel while watching television program (within last 12 months)	13
Have visited website in order to communicate with TV program (within last 12 months)	6
Have sent letter, email or phoned in order to communicate with TV program (within last 12 months)	5
Have done at least one of the activities	22

The possibility to send SMS and MMS messages while communicating with television programs is the newest form of activity and also the most widespread. As indicated above, there are opportunities for offering opinions in many different formats: news, features, sports and entertainment. The opportunities are particularly ample in programs for young people, and there are also a range of so-called SMS-TV formats based entirely upon audience messages. In Norway since 2000, there has been a rapid development of such formats, and SMS-TV now constitutes more than half the transmission time on some of the smaller channels (Karlsen et al., 2006). Table 9.1 shows that as early as 2004, as many as 13 per cent of the population confirmed that they had sent an SMS/MMS to a television station simultaneously while watching a program. Every third of these respondents claimed to have sent more than five such messages within the previous twelve months. To the degree that a typical heavy user can be identified it seems to be a young person living outside the capital—but responding to television programs is in no sense something that is exclusively used by young people.[3]

The second most frequent activity is to respond to a television program through the program's website. As noted the establishment of websites with feedback opportunities in connection with television programs has become more common in recent years. The sites commonly provide extra material, and possibilities to sign up for services such as newsletters or useful hints. Websites also constitute an arena where viewers are invited to ask questions, discuss issues, chat or offer comments after the regular broadcast is over (Syvertsen, 2006). In the above survey, 6 per cent of the population reported that they had visited a website in order to communicate with a television program over the past twelve months. This is less frequent than responding through mobile telephone messages and those who had visited websites had also done it fewer times than those who had sent SMS/MMS. The survey thus confirms claims from Norwegian broadcasters that it is more difficult to direct viewers from television to web than from television to mobile phone (Ytreberg, 2006). The user profile is nevertheless similar to those who have sent SMS/MMS: The typical user seems to be a young person living outside the capital, but there are also older users.

Responding to television programs is not an entirely new phenomenon, and traditional response facilities such as letter writing and telephoning continue to exist. Children's programs frequently have competitions where audiences may respond through a variety of feedback channels, including letters and emails. Phone-ins, which became commonplace in the 1970s, remain in use both in radio and television. Email strongly extends the capacity of television producers to receive response from the audience and include these in programming. In the survey, 5 per cent of the respondents reported that they had contacted a television program through phone, email or letter in the past twelve months. Responding by phone is the most common (44 per cent), followed by sending emails (36 per cent) and writing letters (18 per cent). These are also media for young people, but here age matters to a lesser degree than for the other feedback opportunities. Email is clearly the preferred medium for young adults (20–39 years old), whereas the young (nine to nineteen) and old (over sixty) are overrepresented among those who had sent a letter. There is a slight tendency that more highly educated people living in central areas use these feedback opportunities, but here our case study does not give precise answers.

The survey shows little overlap between different activities. While 22 per cent of the population had used at least one type of response facility, only 3 per cent had used more than two and less than 1 per cent had used all three. So far, people clearly stick to one main mode of communication, and the newest mode, SMS, is already the most popular. This is interesting in the light of the thresholds for different activities. Three types of threshold are relevant: the economic threshold (the cost of the service), the technological threshold (what equipment do you need), and the articulation threshold (does the activity require speaking, writing or only pushing buttons?). Although SMS is more expensive than letter writing or phoning, it seems clear that the low technology threshold combined with a low articulation threshold makes this type of response facility attractive to many people. The ease by which the mobile phone can be used as a response facility while watching a program further helps to explain why it has the potential to become much more popular than other communication channels.

Media activity as participation, play and socialising

The case study shows that many people readily get involved in communication with television. In 2004, 22 per cent of the Norwegian population indicated that they had responded to television programs in the previous twelve months. This figure is probably growing as more feedback opportunities become available and the threshold of participation is lowered. We turn now to the question of what motivates audience members and for what purpose they choose to get involved. For each feedback channel—SMS/MMS, website, or phone/mail—respondents where asked about what had motivated them to make contact. The distribution of the answers is laid out in Table 9.2.

Table 9.2 The motivations of cross-platform users. Respondents could give more than one answer. (N=1232)

Motivation: Why did you respond to the television program?	Per cent of population
To express an opinion or advocate an argument	6
To take part in competition or play games	12
To chat with hosts or guests	2
Other motivations	6
Total of cross-platform users	22

Entertainment-related activities such as taking part in competitions, voting for contestants or playing games are clearly most popular. Among those who had sent a text/image message, a large majority had done it to take part in an entertainment-related activity, and also among those who had visited a website, entertainment-related activities were the most common. Only among those who had phoned or sent a letter or email, a majority claimed to have done it in order to express an opinion. At the time when the survey was carried out, few people had used the opportunities for chatting with hosts or guests in television programs. It is interesting that as many as 6 per cent gave other/unspecified reasons for responding to television programs. Responding to television programs through external platforms is not an established activity, and predefined categories may not really fit.[4]

Below, the discussion of audience motivation is related to three key concepts in media theory/sociology, those of participation, play and socialising. To what degree may the new media activities be seen as an extension of previous possibilities for involvement, enjoyment and communication with others?

Participation

Theory link

see Lax, Chapter 12; Carpentier, Chapter 13

Media participation may be understood in a wide sense as any activity that involves individuals in any form of communication with media, including playful activities with no clear societal purpose. In a more limited sense, media participation may be understood as civic participation, i.e. Activities that are more specifically related to social and political issues such as taking part in discussions, offering opinions and investing in certain policy outcomes. Historically, to involve people in social and political issues have been an important ideological tenet both in public television and so-called media democratisation movements. The 1970s was a period of intense discussion about media democratisation; throughout the decade 'public-access movements' campaigned for more participatory media structure where the public would not only be consumers but also producers of messages (Berrigan, 1977; Barbrook, 1985, see also Enzensberger, 1979 and Brecht, 1979).

New information and communication technologies have led many writers to renew their hopes about the potential of the media to involve people in social and political issues. '[W]e are at a critical juncture,' wrote Lana F. Rakow (1999), claiming that 'The convergence of technologies—telephone and computers in particular—is producing a moment in the history of communication technologies that provides the opportunity to change the terms of debate and the outcomes' (Rakow, 1999, p. 77, see also Dahlberg, 1998, 2004 and Coleman, 1999). Others have been more critical of the idea that the new media of communication—the Internet, multimedia and computer-mediated communication (CMC)—can be used to encourage active political citizenship. Daminan Tambini (1999, pp. 305–6) argues that 'barriers to participation' is not the most important reason why people remain passive or uninvolved and that it is not sufficient to focus on easier access. Tambini draws on political and election research to argue that the motivation for participating is more complex; it is often not about rational debate and decision-making but more about having a good time: 'e.g. The social enjoyment, role and identity that result from taking part in civic action rather than its policy outcome'. He argues:

> It is likely that many of those who participate in civic networks do so not because they seek to invest in an individual or collective good, but simply for amusement or to learn how to use the new medium. These forms of political participation are therefore likely to be unstable in the long term [...] (Tambini, 1999, p. 324).

The typical pattern of participation is 'obsessive use followed by boredom and neglect' (p. 324). Further that 'citizens may simply not be interested in taking part, particularly once the initial novelty of the 'virtual world' has faded' (p. 324). The phenomenon novelty fatigue might explain why media companies are in constant search for ways of implementing new return channels and combinations of platforms.

When we examine the motivations of the people in our case study, we find that 6 per cent of respondents had done it in order to express an opinion. Clearly, however, other forms of motivation, and particularly participating in competitions, are more prominent.

Play

This brings us to our second term, play; another crucial term in a discussion of the potential gratifications of media activity. Above we have indicated that social and political involvement is only one of several potential and actual motivations for media participation. While it is difficult to map precisely the reasons why people participate, it is clear that entertainment-oriented motivations are more prominent than social and political (civic) motivation: in the case study, 'taking part in competitions' is the most frequent answer to the question of why people had communicated with television. Twelve per cent of the respondents indicated that they had communicated with television in order to take part in a competition, play games or vote in an entertainment program.

Studying responses to television as a form of play illuminates that media activity is not just a matter of rational deliberation on traditional public matters; it is also a means of entertainment, risk-taking, competition and a way to spend leisure time. Following Huizinga (1955, p. 28), play can be defined as voluntary, non-committal activities standing outside ordinary life. Play differs from everyday life, and also from civic participation, by being 'not serious', an intermezzo, and an interlude in daily life (Huizinga, 1955). One key response of the television industry, faced with increased competition from new leisure activities such as computer games, has been to develop services that celebrate audience involvement and investment. This is done in part by linking television and computer games, for example in the form of console games played on the TV screen and game-elements as add-ons to television programs (Marshall, 2004). Further, it is done in the form of new television formats designed around game-like features, such as competitions and other forms of participatory television.

As noted, reality TV is among the genres which most heavily have used digital platforms to establish playful relations with the audience. Among the international television formats that most successfully have incorporated communication with the audience are *Big Brother* and *Pop Idol*. In these formats, the audience becomes involved in the game and may influence the outcome by voting for their favourite contestants. The activity of determining a narrative by voting bears similarity to how a game player influences the development of the game by solving different puzzles and assignments. Thus, the act of voting in relation to competition and reality formats might be understood as an extension of the play activities available to the individual.

The main attraction of play is that it offers a zone where other rules apply than in everyday life (Caillois, 1979). Play needs to be free and not obligatory, because otherwise it would lose its attractive and joyous quality as diversion. Play proceeds within its own proper boundaries of time and space according to fixed rules and in an orderly manner (Caillois, 1979, pp. 8–10). Play activities are exciting because the outcome is uncertain; the course cannot be determined, nor the result attained beforehand. Excitement and unpredictability are two key elements of television contests, and these elements are indeed crucial to understand why people partake and are actually willing to spend money to have their vote count. In this light, it may be seen as a form of reductionism to be concerned only with the media's potential for involving people in social and political issues; excitement, joy and diversion are also valid purposes that may enrich people's lives.

Socialising

Expressing opinions or voting in contests may bring fulfilment and excitement, and an interest in repeating the communication. Nevertheless, people involved in research and development in the television and gaming industry are concerned that, in the long run, participants will demand a more individual response in order to continue communication. The idea that inclusion in a community will be a key to success in the future is a central concern within the media industries and such communities are certainly regarded as new opportunities for broadcasters to connect with their audiences and to offer attractive media-related activities.

In spite of the future optimism for socialising, mediated socialising is so far a fairly marginal phenomenon in broadcast media: in our case study, the third most important motivation for communicating with television is chatting with hosts and other guests. Of the respondents, 2 per cent had chatted with hosts and guests. The typical users of this type of activity are young people; almost all are nine to nineteen years old and live outside the capital. Also among those visiting websites, chatting is the third most important. The fact that young people are the most active users of socialising activities might strengthen the hypothesis of a future market potential.

Related to media, the term socialising means coming in contact with others and exchanging everyday small talk through mediated networks. In these activities, being together and communication is the most important aspect (Hjarvard, 2003). The social functions of the media have been discussed as parasocial interaction because of one-sided interpersonal involvement of a media user with a program character (Horton & Wohl, 1956). In formats offering two-way communication, this relation is taken a step further; the social aspect of broadcasting is no longer just implicit in the programming, but also developed into an actual invitation to personal response. Sociable aspects of media use and the inclusive effect of liveness, which is extensively included in cross-media formats, has the potential to create a communicative sociability, linking the private individual to the larger collective of an audience. The desire to partake in mediated communication can be explained by the reduced importance of traditional relations and increased individualism in post-modern societies. Mediated communication might therefore compensate for isolation, and represent a needed connection between individuals and the society.

Conclusion

In this chapter we have discussed the trend whereby the media increasingly invite responses and contributions from audiences. We have explained this trend with reference to the media's need to sustain their position in the light of increased competition and increasingly shifting and disloyal audiences. The chapter then presented the result of a Norwegian survey based on more than 1200 respondents, indicating the extent to which audiences use the available feedback opportunities. The survey showed that sending SMS/MMS to television rapidly is becoming more popular than responding through a website or through traditional means such as phone or mail. The survey also showed that games and entertainment, especially voting in competitions and entertainment programs, were clearly the most popular activities. Expressing an opinion is less frequently cited as a motivation for communicating with television, while chatting with hosts and guests so far is rather infrequent.

We then related the survey results to three key concepts in media theory/ sociology: participation, play and socialising. We discussed whether taking part in activities designed by the media could be seen as an extension of previous possibilities for involvement, enjoyment and communication with others? It seems clear that the new response facilities extend the possibilities for feedback and entertainment-related activities—these facilities are simply making television more enjoyable for many people. Through the possibilities for getting involved in media communities, it is also evident that audience members may enlarge their networks and enrich their lives.

The question of whether these activities are extending the possibilities for social and political involvement is more complicated. Whereas theories of representative democracy concentrate on whether the formal methods of periodic elections are in place, participatory democratic theorists have urged that more opportunities must be provided for participation by the ordinary citizen beyond the simple act of voting (Birch, 2001). In the often-cited work, *Participation and Democratic Theory*, Carol Pateman (1970) argues strongly that participation on a political level requires social training; participation requires skills that may be obtained on other arenas. In this light, the increased possibilities for participating in media-related activities may have psychological and educational effects through providing skills and experiences with democratic praxis. Importantly, though, the audience activities are developed on the media's terms; feedback opportunities are developed according to institutional, editorial and economical considerations rather than societal con- siderations of media participation as an empowering tool. This implies that the activities initiated by the media are increasingly media centric. Indeed, Syvertsen (2004) argues that while media professionals historically have perceived their role to be that of stimulating people to get more involved in society, today's activities are more geared towards getting people to play an active role in the media. Thus, the media becomes, through its new audience activities, both the vehicle to stimulate audience activity, the arena where the activity it is played out, and the business sector to profit from it financially.

CHAPTER SUMMARY

- This chapter has examined the burgeoning trend of audiences to respond to television programs and channels, demonstrating how the media industry through email, the Web and SMS creates opportunities for the audience to be more active.
- It has been argued that these efforts can be explained with reference to the media's need to sustain their commercial position in the face of increased competition from new media.
- The chapter presents the results of a survey investigating the extent to which audiences use new interactive modes, and their motivations for doing so. Not surprisingly, the desire for enhanced individual entertainment figures more highly than broader social and political goals.
- Three key terms in media theory/sociology have been used to account for these audience activities: participation, play and socialising.

Tutorial questions

1. Why do Enli and Syvertsen argue that analysing the role that play performs in media engagement is so important? What does the study of media play add to traditional media theory?
2. What types of play are associated with cross-platform delivery of television programs?
3. How might the 'playfulness' of cross-platform media activities contribute to young people feeling more strongly connected to society as a whole, and why is it argued that this is important for the future of the democratic process?

Recommended reading

Bauman, Z., 2000, *Liquid Modernity,* Polity Press, Cambridge.

Colombo, F. (ed.), 2004, *TV and Interactivity in Europe: Mythologies, Theoretical Perspectives, Real Experiences,* V & P Strumenti, Milano.

Syvertsen, T., 2004, 'Citizens, Audiences, Customers and Players—a conceptual discussion of the relationship between broadcasters and their publics', in *European Journal of Cultural Studies,* Vol.7 (3), pp. 363–80.

Websites

Games studies: www.gamestudies.org
Participation and play in converging media: http://imweb.uio.no/pap/index.php/
    ?page_id=8

Notes

1   This article is based partly on empirical evidence gathered under the auspices of the research group
    Participation and play in converging media (PaP). The group, which is based at the Department of
    Media and Communication at the University of Oslo, brings together researchers on broadcasting and
    new media, focusing, among other things, on how regulatory frameworks, industry structure and poli-
    cies frame the production and use of multi-platform media hybrids (see project outline at http://im-
    web.uio.no/pap/).

2   The study was conducted during week 36 and 37, 2004, carried out by TNS Gallup, and 1234 re-
    spondents age nine and older were interviewed using telephone.

3   When we divide into subgroups the number of people in each category gets too small to provide firm
    answers, thus we can only speculate about certain tendencies.

4   A particularly high proportion of those who said they had visited a website in order to communicate
    with a television program claimed to have done it for other than the predefined reasons.

5   Research interview with Director General in *Telitas Interactive Production*, Finn H. Andreassen (14 June,
    2005).

References

Aarseth, E., 2001, *Computer Games Studies, Year One*, in *Game Studies, The International
    Journal of Computer Game Research 1, no. 1*, available from http://www.
    gamestudies.org/0101/editorial.html

Barbrook, R., 1985, 'Community Radio in Britain', in The Radical Science Collective
    (eds), *Making Waves: The politics of Communication*, Free Association Books, London.

Bauman, Z., 2000, *Liquid Modernity*, Polity Press, Cambridge.

Berrigan, F.J. (ed.), 1977, *Access: Some Western Models of Community Media*, UNESCO,
    Paris.

Beyer, Y., Enli, G., Maasø, A., & Ytreberg, E., 2006, 'Small talk makes a big difference:
    Recent developments in interactive, SMS-based television', paper presented
    to the SCMS 2005 conference, London, article version under publication in
    Television and New Media.

Birch, A., 2001, *Concepts And Theories Of Modern Democracy* (2nd edn), Routledge,
    London.

Brecht, B., 1979, 'Radio as a Means of Communication', in *Screen* 20, 1, first published
    1932.

Caillois, R., 1979, *Man, Play and Games,* translated by Meyer Barash, Schocken Books, New York.

Coleman, S., 1999, 'The New Media and Democratic Politics', *New Media & Society*, Vol. 1:1; pp. 67–74, Sage Publications, London.

Colombo, F. (ed.), 2004, *TV and Interactivity in Europe: Mythologies, Theoretical Perspectives, Real Experiences,* V & P Strumenti, Milano.

Dahlberg, L., 2004, 'Net—Public Sphere Research: Beyond the First Phase', in *Javnost—The public,* Vol. 11, 2004:1.

Dahlberg, L., 1998, 'Cyberspace and the Public Sphere: Exploring the Democratic Potential of the Net' in *Convergence,* Vol. 4:1, pp. 70–84.

Enli, G., 2005, 'Fenomenet SMS-TV. Institusjonelle strategier og semiprivate interaksjon', in *Norsk medietidsskrift.*

Enzensberger, H. M., 1979, 'Constituents of a Theory of the Media', in Enzenberger, *The Conciousness Industry,* Seabury, New York.

Fagerjord, A., 2003, 'Rhetorical Convergence: Earlier Media Influence on Web Media Form', unpublished PhD dissertation, Faculty of Arts, University of Oslo.

Fagerjord, A., 2002, 'Reading-View(s)ing the über-box: A critical view on a popular prediction', in Eskelinen. M. & Koskimaa, R. (eds) *Cybertext Yearbook 2001,* p. 99–110, publications of the Research Centre for Contemporary Culture, Jyvaskyla.

Giddens, A., 1991, *Modernity and Self-Identity,* Polity Press, Cambridge.

Habermas, J., 1989 [1981], *The Transformation of the Public Sphere: An Inquiry into a Category of Bourgeois Society,* Polity Press, Cambridge.

Hjarvard, S., 2003, *Det Selskabelige Samfund: Essays om medier mellom mennesker,* Forlaget Samfundslitteratur, København.

Horton, D. & Wohl., R., 1956, 'Mass Communication and Para-Social Interaction: Observation on Intimacy on a Distance', in Gumper, G. & Catchcart, R. (eds), *InterMedia,* 1979, Oxford University Press, New York.

Huizinga, J., 1955, *Homo Ludens. A Study of the Play-Element in Culture,* Beacon Press, Boston.

Jones, J. M., 2003, 'Show Your Real Face: A Fan Study of the UK Big Brother Transmissions (2000, 2001, 2002), investigating the boundaries between notions of consumers and producers of factual television', in *New Media & Society,* Vol. 5 (3): 400–421.

Karlsen, F., Sundet, V.S., Syvertsen T. & E. Ytreberg, 2006, 'Media Participation: Opportunities and How They Are Used', paper presented at ESF SCSS Exploratory Workshop, 1–3 September 2006, Oslo, Norway.

Livingstone, S., 1999, 'New Media, New Audiences', in *New Media & Society,* 1(1), 59–66.

Livingstone, S. & Lunt P., 1994, *Talk on Television, Audience Participation and Public Debate,* Routledge, London and New York.

Marshall, D. P., 2004, *New Media Cultures: Cultural Studies in Practice,* Arnold, London.

Pateman, C., 1970, *Participation and Democratic Theory,* Cambridge University Press, Cambridge.

Prebensen, I., 2005, 'Interaktivitet' og publikumsdeltakelse I NRK Fjernsynet, hovedoppgave i medievitenskap, Institutt for medier og kommunikasjon, Universitetet i Oslo.

Rakow, L. F., 1999, 'The Public at the Table: From Public Access to Public Participation', *New Media & Society,* Vol. 1:1, pp. 74–82, Sage Publications, London.

Rasmussen, T., 2002, *Nettmedier: Journalistikk og medier på Internett,* Fagbokforlaget, Bergen.

Siapera, E., 2004, 'From Couch Potatoes to Cybernauts? The Expanding Notion of the Audience on TV Channels` Websites', in *New Media & Society,* Vol. 6(2), pp. 155–72.

Sundet, V. S., 2006, 'Multi-platform formats and audience participation in press and television: Perceptions of benefits, successful formats and business models', paper presented at Cost A20 Conference, Delphi 26–28.

Syvertsen, T., 2006, 'Television and Multi-Platform Media Hybrids: Corporate Strategies and Regulatory Dilemmas' in Marcinkowski, F., Meier, W.A. and Trappel, J. (eds) *Media and Democracy: Experience from Europe.* Bern, Stutgart, Wien: Haupt Verlag.

Syvertsen, T., 2005, *Television and multi-platform media hybrids: Corporate strategies and regulatory dilemmas,* paper for the 17th Nordic Conference on Media and Communication Research, Aalborg, 11–14 August 2005.

Syvertsen, T., 2004, 'Citizens, Audiences, Customers and Players—A Conceptual Discussion of the Relationship Between Broadcasters and Their Publics', in *European Journal of Cultural Studies,* Vol. 7 (3), pp. 363–80.

Syvertsen, T., 2001, 'Ordinary people in extraordinary circumstances: A study of participants in television dating games', *Media, Culture & Society,* Vol. 23, No. 3, 319–37.

Syvertsen, T. & Ytreberg, E., 2006, 'Participation and play in converging media: Institutional perspectives and text-user relations', *Nordicom Review* 27(1): 107–11.

Tambini, D., 1999, 'New Media and Democracy' in *New Media & Society,* Vol. 1:3; 305–29.

Tronstad, R., 2004, *Interpretation, Performance, Play & Seduction: Textual Adventures in Tubmud,* PhD dissertation, Faculty of Arts, Department of Media and Communication, University of Oslo.

Ytreberg, E., 2006, 'Plattformkombinering som en utfordring for beslutningstakere i norsk medieindustri', Under publication in Anja Bechmann Pedersen and Steen K. Rasmussen (eds) *Cross-media i medieorganisasjoner'.*

ELAINE LALLY

Creativity, Collaboration and New Media Innovation in a Community Context

10

CHAPTER OVERVIEW

The socially innovative effects of new technologies emerge from how they are taken up by their users within specific contexts. In the case of technologies that mediate communication and interaction, the technologies themselves are shaped by the network of relationships of those people. In recent years, new information and communications technologies have provided many new tools for social networking and creative collaboration, making it possible for people to work together to produce new forms of collaborative media, sometimes across physical and cultural distances that were previously unbridgeable.

This chapter explores the potential for personal and collective transformation through creative collaboration in new media forms. Conceptually, the chapter focuses on the notions of *creativity* and of *collaboration*, to demonstrate how these processes together result in *social and cultural transformation*.

Creativity, and hence innovation, often builds most productively on the shards and fragments of different understandings, experiences and expertise. The chapter describes how creative collaboration, as a process of shared making, is not just about collaboration between people, but also between the patterns and symbols they create, and how these are mediated by new information and communications technologies.

Key terms

creativity
collaboration
social and cultural
   transformation
social networking

Issues

- What types of social groupings are best able to take advantage of the networking possibilities offered by the Web?
- What is it about the World Wide Web that has caused the renewal of interest in creativity?
- Is it possible for creativity to 'add value' across the economy and have broader socially transformative effects?

Theory link

see McGuigan, Chapter 1; Goggin and Newell, Chapter 6; Kivikuru, Chapter 7; Lax, Chapter 12; Burton and Van der Hoven, Chapter 14

Introduction

At the end of the twentieth century it was commonly said that we were living in an 'information society' or 'information age'. Since then we have seen this terminology morph into talk of the 'knowledge economy' or 'knowledge society'. Yet these ways of describing the contemporary world already seem tired and old-fashioned. Who remembers the 'information superhighway' these days?

In his book *A Whole New Mind*, Daniel Pink suggests that a fundamental shift is now taking place. The 'Information Age', he says, is giving way to what he has called the 'Conceptual Age':

> The last few decades have belonged to a certain kind of person with a certain kind of mind—computer programmers who could crack code, lawyers who could craft contracts, MBAs who could crunch numbers. But the keys to the kingdom are changing hands. The future belongs to a very different kind of person with a very different kind of mind—creators and empathizers, pattern recognizers and meaning makers. These people—artists, inventors, designers, storytellers, caregivers, consolers, big picture thinkers—will now reap society's richest rewards and share its greatest joys. …We are moving from an economy and a society built on the logical, linear, computer-like capabilities of the Information Age to an economy and a society built on the inventive, empathic, big-picture capabilities of what's rising in its place, the Conceptual Age (Pink, 2005, pp. 1–2).

Think about it

- Is Pink correct in identifying a fundamental social reorientation?
- If so, what is the role of new information and communications technologies in making this happen?
- Are these different ways of describing the world tracking real shifts in the way contemporary society is organised?
- Or are they just conceptual fashions that come and go in what seems like an ever-quickening cycle?
- Or maybe they are both: could they be part of our never-ending quest to both make sense of and construct our world?

One thing is certain. Pink is right in observing that there is more interest in 'creativity' than ever before. Business leaders and governments are all increasingly keen to find out how to cultivate creativity. One of the most influential promoters of creativity is the economist Richard Florida, who argues that it is a driving force underlying social and economic development. Under contemporary global conditions of transformation, flux and uncertainty, he sees 'the rise of human creativity as the key factor in our economy and society' (Florida, 2003, p. 4).

One indicator of the new level of recognition and appreciation for 'creatives' (creatively trained professionals) is widespread international growth in the 'creative industries' (Cunningham, 2006). The creative industries are defined differently in different parts of the world but generally include such activities as advertising, architecture, the art and antique markets, crafts, design, designer fashion, film and video, graphic design, interactive leisure software, jewellery, music, the performing arts, photography, publishing, software and computer games, television and radio.

In Australia, as in the rest of the industrialised world, the creative industries are among the fastest growing industry sectors. They contribute approximately $25 billion to the Australian economy per annum, with the most dynamic areas, such as digital media content, growing at twice the rate of the overall economy (NOIE, 2003, p. 12). It is increasingly argued, too, that creativity can 'add value' across the economy, through creative inputs into service industries such as finance, health, government and tourism (Hartley, 2005, p. 2).

The UK Ministry for Culture, Media and Sport defines the creative industries as 'those industries which have their origin in individual creativity, skill and talent and which have a potential for wealth and job creation through the generation and exploitation of intellectual property' (DCMS, 1998). As this definition makes clear, the creative-industries model recognises the capacity for 'individual creativity, skill and talent' to create social and economic value as it is applied, incorporated into products, and distributed. The emphasis is decidedly on the creation of *economic* value, however. What we will explore in this chapter is the potential of this new level of acknowledgement and appreciation for creative activity to have broader, socially transformative effects.

Community development through creativity

While the 'creatives' who work in the creative industries apply their talent and training across a broad range of areas, the form of creativity that springs most readily to mind is that of art and artists. In many communities, art-based community programs play an important role in community building:

Arts and other cultural activities can enhance the environment, educate, enchant and excite us. They can reflect and shape our sense of community identity. They involve local people in community development, build community pride and social cohesion. Creative practice provides opportunities for personal development and can stimulate economic activity' (Queensland Government, 2005, p. 9).

The relevance of the arts has emerged as critical in considerations of social and cultural capital, participatory citizenship, quality of life and sustainable development as well as economic prosperity (Mills and Brown, 2004). It is argued that the arts can contribute to broader social, environmental and economic development goals (Hawkes, 2001; Throsby, 2001).

Art can be a potent source for social and cultural transformation because it is a powerful medium for expressing complex ideas. Coupled with the power and representational flexibility of new information and communications technologies, new media art can provide us with new modes of individual and collective expression, of which we have only just begun to explore the potential.

The most influential model of community-based arts practice is that of Community Cultural Development (CCD). With its emphasis on art as an instrument for the creation and affirmation of community, CCD has indeed been defined as 'community action, which is motivated by social justice and political needs, and uses the arts' (Feral Arts, 1999, p. 15). CCD became prominent during the 1980s and 1990s as an antidote to the perceived elitism of the existing arts sector: 'the principles of "participation" and "access" ran counter to the dominant funding objective of "excellence" and "nation"' (Hawkins, 1993, p. 63).

Something of a separation between community-based arts and other areas of contemporary arts practice persisted until very recently. There are now signs of this breaking down, in a trend, which might be an aspect of the shift that Pink identifies as the move to the Conceptual Age. Productive engagement with community is now increasingly on the agendas of galleries and other cultural organisations. In 2005 the Australia Council for the Arts dissolved Community Cultural Development as a separate funding category, replacing it with an injunction to all its funding areas to develop 'community partnerships'.

In the Conceptual Age, it seems that creativity is rapidly becoming democratised. Anyone can be creative; we all have talents and have a right to explore them. The somewhat welfare-oriented tone of CCD is giving way to an increasing sense of the mainstreaming of creative potential and exploration. Professional artists working with communities are working with local culture from its base as a resource or asset, not from a remedial starting point (Burnham et al., 2004, p. 25).

These changes parallel Hartley's observation that the source of cultural value is shifting from cultural 'elites' (producers, critics, academics) to cultural consumers (audiences, readers, fans). Long-standing assumptions about the distinction between and relationship between producers and consumers are breaking down (Hartley, 2004).

More generally, as Negus and Pickering point out, creative activity is not just about designing and manufacturing artworks or commodities, but is about making collective meaning, and communicating our shared experience: 'creativity is a process which brings experience into meaning and significance, and helps it attain communicative value' (2004, p. vii). Through creative activity, available cultural resources are combined and recombined in novel ways, so that they tell us something we haven't heard before, or had only dimly recognised. Cultural resources include all kinds of material and immaterial resources, whose affective impact is achieved because they are both familiar and unfamiliar at the same time (Negus & Pickering, 2004).

[handwritten margin note: is bug bears creative activity]

New media

In recent years, new media technologies have given us unprecedented flexibility to combine and recombine elements of all kinds of traditional media. Not much more than ten years ago this capacity was sufficiently new that the term 'multimedia' was used to describe its novelty. It's rare to hear that term these days—it seems that all media are multimedia.

In the extensive debates currently circulating about creativity—from Florida's creative class to the creative industries, from art in community development to creative inputs to high tech industries—one thing that seems to be missing is the sense that all creativity is about imaginatively engaging with a *medium*. New media technologies, then, are interesting and important to us because of the new imaginative and representational possibilities they open up for creative exploration.

As Brenda Laurel said in her 1993 book *Computers as Theatre*: 'think of the computer, not as a tool, but as a medium' (1993, p. 126).

Indeed, back in 1984, in the same year that the idea of the Internet was dimly foreshadowed in the 'cyberspace' of William Gibson's novel *Neuromancer*, computer pioneer Alan Kay asserted that the computer was the first 'metamedium':

> The protean nature of the computer is such that it can act like a machine or like a language to be shaped and exploited. It is a medium that can dynamically simulate the details of any other medium, including media that cannot exist physically. It is not a tool, although it can act like many tools. It is the first metamedium,

and as such it has degrees of freedom for representation and expression never before encountered and as yet barely investigated (Kay, 1984, p. 52).

The intervening two decades or so since Kay wrote these words have seen a proliferation of digital modes of representation and interfaces for manipulating digital content. We now have many technologically inter-related meta-media that give us powerful tools for expressing ourselves and for exploring ideas creatively.

Literacy with these new modes of representation can only become more important as the mediating new technologies become more and more ubiquitous. Digital content creation is a key area of literacy that positions new media users and creators 'not merely as consumers but also as citizens' (Livingstone, 2004, p. 11). And, it can surely be argued, as creators.

A key aspect of the social power of these media—and crucial to their capacity to underpin socially transformative activity—is that they don't just allow us to communicate with each other, but that they are also platforms for collaboration:

> All of our thinking tools, from language to logic, involve an acquired skill at constructing mental models and communicating them. And the power of these mental models is that they give the whole species a platform for thinking and expressing ourselves more effectively, for communicating and collaborating and building the next higher level of symbolic thought (Gassée, 1990, p. 225).

Collaboration has indeed been defined as a process of shared creation: 'two or more individuals with complementary skills interacting to create a shared understanding that none had previously possessed or could have come to on their own' (Shrage, 1990, p. 40).

Creative community

Let's focus now on a particular part of the creative collaborative new media landscape, that of community-based new media arts for cultural development.

Community-based arts, particularly in the mode known as community cultural development (CCD), have been in use since the 1970s as forms of community action and the development of a shared sense of identity and group belonging.

CCD works by engaging community members in participatory art-making that is often issue-focussed (Burnham et al., 2004, p. 11). The process allows a group 'to explore and strengthen their sense of identity, sense of place and capacity to shape and enact their own future' (Queensland Government, 2005, p. 8). CCD is characterised by a process- rather than outcome-orientation. Because projects are often problem-focused, the role of the professional arts worker is that of cultural broker, rather than the producer of an artwork. The creative skills called on are those of facilitating the group to creatively collaborate in exploring the complexities and contradictions inherent in an issue:

> A project might develop in response to culturally-based conflicts experienced by a marginal group in a particular place or community. The approach requires development of an understanding of the overall dynamic of the situation. It calls for developing relationships with a broad range of stakeholders, often with conflicting ideologies and differing agendas (Feral Arts, 1999, p. 43).

In the rest of this chapter, these issues are brought together and fleshed out via a discussion of the work of a new media-based community cultural development organisation working in the Greater Western Sydney region in New South Wales, Australia.

ICE

Information and Cultural Exchange (ICE; see http://ice.org.au) is a community-based arts organisation working across the Greater Western Sydney region.

Its diverse programs bring together community cultural development, new media, and a grassroots focus on culturally diverse communities, youth, and artists. It has developed strong networks across the Western Sydney region, and cross-sector partnerships with a range of organisations, including migrant and community agencies, artists, state, federal and local government, businesses, private sponsors, charities and foundations.

Its CCD, professional development and arts programs involve hundreds of individuals, artists and communities annually, producing high quality digital arts and technology training programs and products with Western Sydney artists, groups and communities:

> ICE works creatively with Western Sydney's diverse communities at the convergence of arts, culture information and technology. ... ICE is an innovation hub where arts, culture and creative technology converge in unique programs for communities and artists to develop professional skills and creative thinking (see http://ice.org.au/about/intro).

SWITCH

SWITCH is ICE's media arts lab, with state-of-the-art software and hardware for digital video, audio, animation and design. It provides a space for artists to create new work, and a facility where artists and media professionals can work with emerging artists and communities to create hybrid work and undertake alternative forms of training.

> SWITCH is grounded in the idea of giving artists and communities a stronger hold on collectively and individually expressing themselves with technology. We work with people who might be on the 'outside' of those things, to support them to create animation, installations, video art, music, or even radio and television productions (Nahlous & Hoh, 2006).

SWITCH provides an infrastructure dedicated to developing alternative media projects with communities, particularly newer migrant and refugee communities who lack local access to 'mass' media forms in their own languages. Through SWITCH, ICE has supported the development of film festivals, incubated a television production house, 'Somali TV', and a Sudanese radio program, 'Voice of the Nile'. ICE's training programs develop a skills base, and SWITCH provides an infrastructure that assists artists and communities to create their own media work.

ICE explicitly locates the art activity it supports within the context of a contemporary urban culture that is saturated with media. For ICE, 'new media art' is not just about using digital media to create art, but about creating art that bears a strong relationship to mass media forms, especially the rapidly developing media forms supported by the Internet and mobile platforms. Because of this emphasis, ICE has been particularly successful in working with young people, especially those from emerging communities (such as refugees and newly arrived migrants), and with groups that have had difficulties bridging the 'digital divide', such as Indigenous youth and people of non-English-speaking background.

SWITCH projects often 'deconstruct the distinctions between high and low culture, working with professional artists and vernacular communities alike' (Nahlous and Hoh, 2006). For example, at the prestigious Sydney Writers' Festival in 2005, ICE staged 'Hip Hop Projections', an event incorporating spoken word, live music, sound, animation and experimental video. The event was the culmination of a music-writing program for young unemployed people:

> Hip hop met video art and the international literary world in a three-way collision, pushing the validity of the MC/spoken word aspect of hip hop culture as 'writing', but also challenging the very idea of 'writing' as a cloistered, elitist practice … Young people with important things to say approach popular music as a medium for desire—the constructive, transgressive energies that create new worlds (Nahlous and Hoh, 2006).

Darkness over Paradise

In August 2006, after three years of collaboration, ICE and the Association of Sierra Leonean Journalists in Exile launched 'Darkness over Paradise' (http://darkness overparadise.squarespace.com), a 60-minute documentary about the experiences of journalists during the civil war in Sierra Leone, based on primary footage all shot under hazardous conditions.

The Sierra Leonean group, all media professionals in their homeland, had smuggled hundreds of hours of VHS footage out of Sierra Leone. ICE facilitated a process that prioritised collaboration, exchange and training. The journalists worked alongside professional Australian-based arts workers, media professionals, editors and documentary film-makers, learning digital video skills in the process. The Sierra Leoneans had previously only used analogue video. This documentary, and the process of creating it, has the potential to effect social change on a range of levels: by providing alternative discourses about Sierra Leone; by enabling self-expression and communication for individuals; by increasing awareness at a local, regional and global level; and by providing professional development pathways for its participants. It would have been quicker to take the footage and hand it over to a professional director and editor, but this would not have resulted in the unfolding of a process that could lead to greater autonomy for the people involved.

Originate

ICE's Originate program brings together all the organisation's program areas in a hands-on development program involving emerging digital artists and arts workers from small and emerging migrant and refugee communities. Participants undertake accredited training in CCD processes and arts project management, as well as professional development in their specialist digital art-forms. The project culminates in assistance for the participants to put the skills they have developed into action, with mentorships and formal placements to work on developing community-based projects within their own communities. The program aims to build substantive capacity within diverse communities to develop creative digital community development projects.

Several new projects and entities were spun off from the first intake of twenty-five Originate participants in 2005. Squeaky Wheel, a production house formed by participants, is working towards producing a regular program showcasing arts activity for TV Sydney, the local community-access television station. In 2006 a second Originate intake targeted Australian Indigenous and Pacific Islander artists and community workers.

Digital storytelling

Burgess uses the term 'vernacular creativity' to describe the kind of grassroots, socially innovative activities facilitated by organisations like ICE. Vernacular creativity can be defined as 'creative practices that arise from highly particular and non-elite social contexts and communicative conventions' (Burgess, 2006).

An emerging genre of digital content arising in this and similar contexts is that of 'digital storytelling'. The rapid rise in popularity of sites like MySpace and YouTube, where anyone can create and share digital content in 'bite-sized' chunks, demonstrates that there is untapped demand and potentially unlimited audience interest in vernacular content forms.

Digital storytelling

is based on everyday communicative practices—telling personal stories, collecting, and sharing personal images—but remixed with the textual idioms of television and film; and transformed into publicly accessible culture through the use of digital tools for production and distribution. Through this process of remediation, it transforms everyday experience into shared public culture (Burgess, 2006, p. 210).

good explaination

While the large Internet-based social networking communities demonstrate the scale of the potential impact of these developments, locality-specific organisations like ICE are exploring the potential of digital storytelling for place-based community building and cultural development.

In Queensland, for example, the 'Sharing Stories' project uses collaborative activities to engage both artistic practitioners and the community in investigating and documenting the public history of the Kelvin Grove Urban Village, a newly developed master-planned inner city community. A real sense of community can't be manufactured by any simple process but must be researched and nurtured organically. A research history program was devised to capture the social heritage of Kelvin Grove and deliver it back to the evolving local community in ways that are accessible and allow their audiences to be part of the Village's ongoing history. The project has encompassed many community-based workshops and events, two books, and an online Web-based archive including oral history, digital storytelling, personal stories and accounts, photographs and artwork (Klaebe, 2006, p. 2). Digital storytelling has been used to generate materials that are 'relevant to each person within the community in some way so that they see themselves as part of the fabric of the area and have a sense of ownership and belonging' (Klaebe, 2006, p. 2).

Remembering Minto

In stark contrast to the Kelvin Grove 'Sharing Stories' project, which aims to build a sense of belonging to a community under formation, ICE's 'Remembering Minto' project uses digital storytelling to help to preserve a sense of community under conditions in which the 'real' community is actively being destroyed.

Minto, on the south-western outskirts of Sydney, is a community living through enormous change, with whole areas being redeveloped, including a public housing estate that has stood since the 1970s. Parts of the estate have already been demolished. Over the next ten years, the entire estate will be cleared and the public housing residents all relocated. Streets and open spaces will be reconfigured, and the publicly owned land sold off for private development.

The Remembering Minto project was initiated by a group of local public housing residents, in response to these changes. It is a partnership between the Remembering Minto Group, a group formed by the residents, ICE and the NSW Department of Housing. Remembering Minto will produce a book and online archive of stories for ex-residents and residents of Minto. The project was launched with a planning consultation involving many residents who both laughed and cried as they shared their stories. The program for the project includes a Storytelling Festival to be held as part of the 2006 Sydney Writers' Festival. The local Technical and Further Education College (TAFE) is also a partner in the initiative, providing training in digital recording and radio, and in graphic design and digital arts.

The project aims to work with past and present residents to 'Remember Minto' through storytelling, including recording reflections from residents and local groups, and photographs of residents, families and landscape. The process 'will enable them to collect, collate and reinterpret the stories of their lives and the life of their place' (ICE, 2006, p. 13).

Storytelling is an ancient form of creativity and communication. Digital technologies and literacies seem to be coming into their own as a new medium for capturing and retelling powerful narratives, through collaborative processes of creative expression:

> digital storytelling can be understood not only as a media form but also as a field of cultural practice: a dynamic site of relations between textual arrangements and symbolic conventions, technologies for production and conventions for their use; and collaborative social interaction that takes place in local and specific contexts. Digital storytelling as a 'movement' is explicitly designed to amplify the ordinary voice. It aims not only to remediate vernacular creativity

but also to legitimate it as a relatively autonomous and worthwhile contribution to public culture (Burgess, 2006, p. 207).

Conclusion

In the late twentieth century ... we are witnessing a breakthrough in how people can express complex ideas. ... I believe that this new capability will have a profound influence on humanity over a long period of time and will be the thing that's remembered many years from now (Sussman, interviewed in Crevier, 1993, pp. 330–1).

Sussman is describing here what he believed would be remembered as the most important influence of Artificial Intelligence research in the latter half of the twentieth century. Well before the rise of the Internet brought with it previously unimagined possibilities for communication and information sharing in social networks, Sussman was describing how computer programming languages have given us powerful new methods of describing complex algorithmic processes.

In this chapter, we have explored the potential of collaborative creative activity through digital media for expressing complex ideas, sharing experience and facilitating social transformation. If, as Kay suggested in the words quoted above, digital technologies have given us a qualitatively more powerful medium—a metamedium—than has previously been available, then the most interesting and profoundly significant long-term effects of this are perhaps along the lines that Sussman envisaged.

As Shrage points out, 'creativity often builds on the shards and fragments of different understandings. ... we don't just collaborate with people; we also collaborate with the patterns and symbols people create' (Shrage, 1990, p. 41). The 'new' in new media has therefore perhaps shifted from the newness of the technologies themselves, to an exciting sense that they allow us to do new things. New media give us a new playground for creating and sharing our ideas, our view of the world, and our unique experiences.

Our real 'new medium' is perhaps, then, in the social networks these technologies allow us to form. Indeed, it has been recently suggested (in the context of the field of community cultural development) that we might call such 'networks of networks'—where we create, collaborate and communicate—an 'internet':

It goes without saying that such deep experience can create a lasting collegial atmosphere, and can vastly improve cross-disciplinary collaborations. In effect, it can create whole new webs of networks organised around a shared topic or problem. In fact, the field itself might even be called an 'internet', yielding valuable new platforms and interdisciplinary tools for creating, synthesizing and integrating knowledge (Burnham et al., 2004, p. 29).

CHAPTER SUMMARY

- The chapter has argued that new information and communications technologies (ICTs) provide many new tools for social networking and creative collaboration, making it possible for people to work together to produce new forms of collaborative media.
- The chapter explored the potential for personal and collective transformation through creative collaboration in new media forms. It focused on the notions of creativity and of collaboration, to demonstrate how these processes together result in social and cultural transformation.
- Case studies of new media-based community cultural development organisations, through a model of community-based arts practice, or Community Cultural Development (CCD), was used to describe creative collaboration as mediated by ICTs.

Tutorial questions

- In what ways is it argued that creativity is an important component of community development and what role does art play in this process?
- Why is it argued that digital content creation is a key area of media literacy and that it has the capacity to position new media users and creators as citizens, as much as consumers?
- What is meant by 'digital storytelling' and what role can it play in successful community development?

Recommended reading

Gassée, J. L., with Rheingold, H., 1990, 'The Evolution of Thinking Tools', in Laurel, B. (ed.) *The Art of Human-Computer Interface Design*, Addison-Wesley, Reading, Mass., pp. 225–27.

Hawkins, G., 1993, *From Nimbin to Mardi Gras: Constructing Community Arts*, Allen and Unwin, Sydney.

Pink, D., 2005, *A Whole New Mind: Moving from the Information Age to the Conceptual Age*, Allen & Unwin, Crows Nest.

Websites

Australia Council for the Arts: www.ozco.gov.au
Darkness over Paradise: www.darknessoverparadise.squarespace.com
ICE: www.ice.org.au/

References

Burgess, J., 2006, 'Hearing Ordinary Voices: Cultural Studies, Vernacular Creativity and Digital Storytelling', *Continuum: Journal of Media and Cultural Studies*, 20(2): 201–14.

Burnham, L.F., Durland, S. & Ewell, M.G., 2004, *The CAN Report: The State of the Field of Community Cultural Development: Something New Emerges*, Saxapahaw NC: Art in the Public Interest, available online at http://www.canreport.org

Cunningham, S., 2006, Platform Papers 9, *What Price a Creative Economy?* Currency House, July.

Crevier, D., 1993, *AI: The Tumultuous History of the Search for Artificial Intelligence*, Basic Books, New York.

Department of Culture, Media and Sport (DCMS), 1998: Creative Industries Mapping Document, UK, see http://www.culture.gov.uk

Feral Arts, 1999, Symposium: 'They Shoot Ferals Don't They? Debates in Community Cultural Development', http://www.feralarts.com.au (accessed 29 April 2005).

Florida, R., 2003, *The Rise of the Creative Class: And How It's Transforming Work, Leisure, Community and Everyday Life*, Basic Books, New York.

Gassée, J. L., with Rheingold, H., 1990, 'The Evolution of Thinking Tools', in Laurel, B. (ed.) *The Art of Human-Computer Interface Design*, pp. 225–27, Addison-Wesley, Reading, Mass.

Hartley, J., 2004, 'The "Value Chain of Meaning" and the New Economy', *International Journal of Cultural Studies*, 7(1), pp. 129–41.

Hartley, J., (ed.), 2005, *Creative Industries*, Blackwell, Oxford UK.

Hawkes, J., 2001, *The Fourth Pillar of Sustainability: Culture's Essential Role in Public Planning*, Cultural Development Network (Vic) and Common Ground Publishing.

Hawkins, G., 1993, *From Nimbin to Mardi Gras: Constructing Community Arts*, Allen & Unwin, Sydney.

ICE (Information and Cultural Exchange), 2006, 22nd Annual Report: January to December 2005, see http://www.ice.org.au

Kay, A., 1984, 'Computer Software', *Scientific American*, September, 52ff.

Klaebe, H., 2006, 'Sharing stories: collaboration, creativity and copyright', presented at Speculation and Innovation: Applying Practice-led Research in the Creative Industries, April 2005, Brisbane, Queensland University of Technology.

Laurel, B., 1993, *Computers as Theatre*, Addison-Wesley, Boston.

Livingstone, S., 2004, 'Media Literacy and the Challenge of New Information and Communication Technologies', *Communication Review*, 7, pp. 3–14.

Mills, D. & Brown, P., 2004, *Art and Wellbeing*, Australia Council for the Arts, Strawberry Hills, NSW.

Nahlous, L. & Hoh, B., 'Learning to Love New Media Arts', *In Videotage: New Media Arts, Dislocating its Privilege,* Hong Kong Arts Development Council, 2006.

National Office for the Information Economy 2003, 'The Current State of Play', NOIE, Canberra, http://www.noie.gov.au/projects/framework/Progress/csop.htm

Negus, K. & Pickering, M., 2004, *Creativity, Communication and Cultural Value*, Sage, London.

Pink, D., 2005, *A Whole New Mind: Moving from the Information Age to the Conceptual Age,* Allen & Unwin, Crows Nest.

Queensland Government, 2005, *The Art of Renewal: A Guide to Thinking Culturally about Strengthening Communities,* Arts Queensland & Department of Housing, Brisbane.

Shrage, M., 1990, *Shared Minds,* Random House, New York.

Throsby, D., 2001, *Economics and Culture*, Cambridge University Press, Cambridge.

JACQUI EWART,
SUSAN FORDE,
KERRIE FOXWELL
AND MICHAEL
MEADOWS

11

Community Media and the Public Sphere in Australia

Key terms

first sector (commercial) media
second sector (government-
    funded) media
third sector (community) media

Issues

- What is the status of Australia's community broadcasting sector?
- What is the role of community broadcasting in your community?
- How is community broadcasting different from first (commercial) and second sector (government-funded) broadcasters?

CHAPTER OVERVIEW

This chapter looks briefly at the emergence of community broadcasting in Australia before examining in detail the significant contribution the sector makes to the Australian community. Whereas the commercial media sector is driven by the need to make a profit, those who work or volunteer for community broadcasting are inspired by a different set of motives. Australia has one of the most unique and diverse community broadcasting environments in the world. In this chapter we will introduce you to the sector and explore some of the ways that community broadcasting is challenging and redefining the traditional roles of media. As well, we will look at some of the recent sector research, in particular a project in which we have examined the unique relationships between community broadcasters and their audiences.

Third sector/community media Community media is funded by subscriptions and grants and run mainly by volunteers. It is a medium that offers 'a clear alternative' to the mainstream. While many independent media producers offer perspectives that differ little from the mainstream, there are other elements that distinguish them such as intent, focus, size etc. We see the community media sector as a cultural resource that facilitates cultural citizenship in ways that differentiate it from other media.

Introduction

It is something of a paradox that the concentration of ownership and the homogenisation of news that now characterises the global media environment have enabled the emergence and subsequent burgeoning of Australia's community broadcasting sector. Community broadcasting in Australia has flourished under difficult conditions, particularly lack of funding, so its success is testament to the contribution and passion of those who work in the sector in paid or voluntary capacities, and their audiences. Community broadcasters play an important role here in providing alternative content, approaches, views and opinions, and in making available spaces where people can speak for and about themselves in ways that empower them.

In this chapter, we briefly review the development and status of Australia's community broadcasting sector before examining recent research findings. In particular, we look at the key outcomes of a national study into community broadcasting audiences, which explored why people tune into community radio and television. While this information is important for community broadcasters, it is just as important for you—journalism students and potential journalists. Many of you will begin your careers in community media and some of you might make community broadcasting a long-term choice. While our research focuses on Australia, we believe it has relevance to community media internationally.

Activity 11.1

Choose a community radio or television station in an area or town near you.

Discuss the station's format and identify the different audiences of the station.

What implications does community broadcasting have for democracy?

How would you like community broadcasting to operate?

see
Nightingale,
Chapter 2;
Carpentier,
Chapter 13

Theory link

Community broadcasting in Australia: An overview

The *Broadcasting Services Act 1992* defines community broadcasting services as non-profit and provided for 'community purposes'. They must be made available free to members of the public and able to be received by 'commonly available equipment' (*Broadcasting Services Act 1992*). As we explain later in this chapter, this means the stations are not only operated for the community, but also in a sense owned by the community.

The Australian Communications and Media Authority (ACMA) lists around 350 community broadcasters (including seventy-seven specialist remote Indigenous community broadcasters) and thirty active aspirant stations working towards a full licence in 2005. In comparison, there are 255 commercial licenses. In around forty communities in Australia, community radio is the *only* broadcast service (Meadows, Forde, Ewart and Foxwell, 2006). Community radio stations can be found in metropolitan, regional, rural and isolated parts of Australia.

Community broadcasting was established in Australia in the 1970s and, within less than ten years from its inception, four distinct types of radio stations existed. The first of these was what we might call educational radio, where universities set up stations to broadcast educational material (Moran, 1995, p. 151). Stations that focused on providing classical music and ethnic language programming came next (Forde, Meadows and Foxwell, 2002a, p. 10). Towards the end of the 1970s, stations whose mandate was to support the politically marginalised were set up, many initially located on university campuses and run by students. The rapid growth of the sector has continued and, more recently, some parts of the sector have expanded into online environments.

There are also six community television stations in Australia, four located in capital cities and two in regional areas. Today, Australia's community broadcast sector attracts diverse audiences and stations encompass a wide range of formats including fine music, information-based programming, religious, youth, Indigenous, ethnic language and generalist.

Think about it

What positive values are added to the experience of media in Australia by community media?

The research

In 2002, the first comprehensive study of community radio in Australia revealed that the sector had become a significant community cultural resource (Forde, Meadows and Foxwell, 2002a). It had emerged as a series of local public spheres or a community public sphere—place and space for local level public discussion and debate for those whose voices were typically marginalised or non-existent in mainstream media (Forde, Foxwell and Meadows, 2002b, 2003). Another significant finding was the enormous contribution volunteers make to community radio. More than 25,000 people undertake an estimated $145 million a year of unpaid labour (Forde et al., 2002a). Still, little was known about the number of people tuning in or the kinds of expectations those audiences might have of community radio and television.

In 2004 a national survey of community broadcasting audiences in Australia revealed its importance to Australians, regardless of where they lived (McNair Ingenuity survey, 2004). The data indicated that one in four Australians had listened to community radio in the week prior to the survey, with that figure almost doubling for listeners in the previous month. The survey found that 685,000 people (aged fifteen and over) listened exclusively to community radio in a typical week. In addition, the survey confirmed the importance of community radio as a source of local information and news for those living outside metropolitan areas (Forde, Meadows and Foxwell, 2002a).

Our current research, started in 2005, addresses audience expectations of community broadcasting. That study explores the views, feelings and attitudes of audiences towards community media in urban, regional and remote Australia. We have gathered data from listeners to twenty-four community radio stations, five community television stations, eleven ethnic language programs and from fourteen Indigenous communities (Meadows, Forde, Ewart and Foxwell, 2005; Ewart, Meadows, Forde and Foxwell, 2005). In speaking to third sector media audiences, some important themes have emerged.

1   Community radio and television challenges the audience–producer barriers found in traditional forms of media and, in doing so, reworks those relationships in innovative and unique ways.
2   Australia's community broadcasters have created a series of community public spheres where groups, usually marginalised by traditional media, find new ways of having their voices heard.
3   The sector provides important background on local issues, and often experiments with innovative ways of presenting that information.

4   The sector creates a sense of community for audiences, often expressed as an invisible but strong connectivity between what are sometimes disparate individuals and groups. It underpins and strengthens existing cultural networks, especially among Australia's ethnic and Indigenous communities.

Community broadcasting and the new media technologies environment

While the growth of the Internet and the audience's increasing use of online information has an impact on community broadcasting (as it does with all other media sectors), key findings from our project indicate the aspects audiences most value about community broadcasting cannot be provided in an online environment. One of the common themes emerging from the data is that audiences relish the 'ordinary' tone of community broadcasting presenters—they love knowing that the voice they are hearing on the radio is 'one of us'—a non-professional.

Secondly, listeners value the immediacy of local content. News about what is happening in small country towns, or in specific geographic locations around major cities, will not be found on the Internet—audiences need access to grassroots sources, such as local informants in order to discover true local information.

Furthermore, the fact that the majority of community broadcasting occurs in regional areas reinforces the minimal impact that the Internet has so far had on traditional community broadcasting formats. While Australia has one of the highest Internet adoption rates in the world with 84 per cent of the population having some sort of access to the Internet (van Vuuren, 2005, p. 57), only 56 per cent of Australian households have access to the Internet at home (ABS, 2005). Even fewer regional households use the Internet regularly—in fact, 30 per cent of regional Australians have never accessed the Internet, anywhere at any time (Downie et al., 2005, p. 8). These figures suggest that, while the Internet is growing and impacting on traditional media outlets, the very local and grassroots nature of community radio is the reason why people tune in. It is true that some community radio stations have started to offer audio streaming and can be tuned into online. An excellent example of this is the youth program *Cafe Rhapsody* delivered in Mandarin on Brisbane's 4EB. Listeners use an online service to chat to each other about the content of the program while it is being aired. Program presenters monitor the comments of listeners and are able to respond immediately, altering program content to suit the audience. At the moment this is more a complementary aspect of community radio than a model that will usurp community broadcasting's traditional methods and role.

Audience–producer relationships

Community broadcasting is successfully challenging the traditional producer–audience barriers that exist in mainstream media, and fulfilling their obligations under the *Broadcasting Services Act 1992* to a service to their various communities of interest (*Broadcasting Services Act 1992*). The audience members we have spoken to over the past eighteen months have consistently praised the level and extent of access they have to stations. For many of them, access to their local radio station creates a sense that they, and other members of the public, own them. Significantly, this relationship does not exist between them and any other types of media outlets. One focus group participant explained how being able to access program presenters and station workers easily and quickly contributed to the sense that the community 'owned' the station:

> It's for us, about us, and like I said if you want to ring up and put a request on, if they're doing a theme and it's a request for a birthday, they'll happily put it in and do it (ROX FM, Roxby Downs focus group, 2005).

This level of access means that members of the community have unique opportunities to participate in program production—something that traditional forms of media have more difficulty delivering. The division between audiences and content producers are less clear in community radio because it relies on volunteers to produce programs and often to help with station operations. Although volunteering is a requirement of the license, the ways in which different stations interpret this and put it into practice seems to vary according to the nature of the relationships between various communities and their local stations. One focus group participant outlined the benefits of this close alliance:

> Because the presenters are coming from … the communities about which they are talking, [which] they work within, it's not like listening to a show where it's a journalist covering a topic of the week. Because they themselves are working in that particular area, they know the people, if they don't know it themselves they've rung up … [like] the food show; they know all the chefs and have them out. So you actually do get a better quality of information to a degree (RRR focus group, 2005).

Another listener felt he was able to talk to the station presenters because they were from the community and they were 'ordinary people':

> The people [station presenters] are just so down to earth, they are just like us here. They're not like presenters who think they're that little bit better [they

don't say]: 'I'm a presenter and you know, you're just nothing' (Bendigo focus group, 2005).

Members of the audience sometimes produce programs or supply information, contribute to discussion and debate, or provide feedback. Importantly, this means audiences have more input into and control over the final product and in the process move from audiences to active publics. One listener explained:

> Well there are a variety of programmes and a lot of, the presenters as they're known, do, do requests and you know, there's a great calling of people out there who are very lonely, that seem to have the need to know that somebody knows that they're there by phoning in to ask for requests or just to speak to the announcers, the presenters, or whoever's on the phones as the case may be. Some of the presenters have so many phone calls that they do have somebody answering the phone (2QBN focus group, 2005).

By facilitating this degree of interactivity, community radio is not only challenging the traditional relationships that exist between media producers and audiences, but also it is actively reworking them, creating spaces where these relationships are renegotiated in unique and powerful ways. One focus group participant summed it up like this:

> But I think they [local musicians] really support Radio Adelaide because they have been given the support here as either young or more successful artists. [They know] that this is, you know, one of the only places you can go to get any sort of [support]. It's not just supported [it's] in a sense being, being recognised. I've found that to be one of the really good things about the team here. You can ring up and find out, it is an information resource. It's a resource as well as a radio station. It is a resource to many of our members anyway (Radio Adelaide community group Orsen, South Australian Music Industry Association).

The focus is often on the relationships between the content producers and the communities they serve. This critical relationship was explained by one focus group participant:

> And the fact is that if you just go in there, you're, we're welcomed. You just walk into the station and there's not one person I know, even when Tina or whoever's been there… you know when they're under stress and stuff, there's not once they haven't made you feel welcome (ROX FM Roxby Downs focus group, 2005).

And another said:

> Yes, it's almost a family to family, you switch on Sonshine like that, oh isn't that, that Arthur and Heather [who] just had little Daniel and you feel like part of their family. You get to know these people as people, not just a voice on the radio station (6SON Perth 2005).

Another important point to emerge from the research is the willingness of audience members to provide feedback, but cogently they were less critical of presenter's errors. Many focus group participants said they enjoyed the unpolished presentation style many program announcers adopted, believing that it humanised presenters and made them seem friendlier. This was in direct contrast to what many listeners saw as the polished presentation on commercial radio, which many felt distanced them from those presenters.

Think about it

What are the similarities and differences between audience-producer materials and relationships available online and those available through community media?

The public sphere

Australia's community broadcasters and their publics have created a unique space and place within which groups usually marginalised by traditional media find new ways of speaking and having their voices heard. This 'community public sphere' should be seen as a discrete formation that develops in a unique context as the product of contestation with the mainstream public sphere. In Australia, community media provide an alternative to mainstream media, and an antidote to both the dominance of mainstream news media by elites and institutions and to the 'good news is no news' problem, thus creating and facilitating an alternative public sphere (Forde, Foxwell and Meadows, 2002b; Rodriguez, 2001). One focus group participant put it this way:

> Essentially community radio is to have somewhere where people can express a different view on things. What we hear in major media, you can't believe, and the news is slanted and the limited ownership of the media is scary. It

is absolutely essential that we hear all different voices and views. Community radio is a good way of righting the balance (Radio NAG focus group, 2005).

Another way of understanding this is by thinking about community broadcasting as sites through which cultural empowerment occurs and personal identity enhanced. By providing sites where people can participate on a personal and local level in the development of understanding and cultural literacies, community broadcasting also helps communities and individuals work through the issues they face. In the Torres Strait, this is particularly evident where geographically dispersed communities/islands use their local community radio station to address local issues:

> It's a program … where the peak bodies appear. The TSOI or the ICC can get information across or people may wish to bring issues up and leadership can come out and respond to [those issues] and it's a program that, because everyone listens to it, they refer to it [the radio station] as the regional public meeting (Torres Strait Focus group, 2005).

Community radio and, in particular, ethnic language programs, provides listeners with a sense of belonging to a specific part of the community in Australia, while also reminding them of their traditional homelands:

> You get to listen to the radio and you feel at home listening to your own language. This community is very isolated from other Tongan communities in Australia. Without the radio program we would feel very cut off. There is no Tongan food or music here [in Adelaide] and so the radio program gives us a sense of home (5EBI Tongan language focus group).

For many listeners to ethnic language programs on community radio, the stations perform a vital role, connecting disparate sections of particular ethnic communities. In some cases these were sections of communities that would never have willingly made contact with each other, if it were not for the radio programs. Indeed, focus group participants have acknowledged the crucial role played by local language programs in bringing together multicultural and sometimes antagonistic elements of ethnic communities (Macedonian Focus Group, 2006; Sudanese Focus Group, 2006; Turkish Focus Group, 2006).

Theory link

see Nightingale, Chapter 2; Carpentier, Chapter 13

News and information

Despite the existence of the three different media sectors, Australia has a relatively limited media environment in terms of ownership and availability of local news and information. In the past two decades or so, Australians have increasingly sought information from alternative outlets and networks. This appears to be due, as

McCallum (2005, p. 297) suggests, to the lack of engagement by mainstream media with 'the multiple narratives that exist in local talk'. Mainstream media often fail to engage with the issues at the local level where everyday conversation occurs (McCallum, 2005, p. 293), so community radio is well placed to tap into this conversational mode.

Dwyer, Chapter 15

Theory link

In 2002, Forde et al. found that a lack of funding made it difficult for many community radio stations to produce regular local news bulletins (Forde et al., 2003). While many audience members identify the important contribution community broadcasting makes to local news, and many listeners reported they would like even more local content on community radio—content about local cultural events, local people, news events and so on—the provision of such information is often a resource-intensive activity for the station involved and essentially beyond their means.

Forde et al. (2003, p. 245) revealed that original news and current affairs programs were produced by one-fifth of Australia's community radio stations. Of the news and current affairs produced by community radio stations in Australia 'three-quarters of the news and current affairs is specifically relevant to the local community' (Forde et al., 2003, p. 245). Our recent field work indicated that community radio audiences define news differently from the generally accepted format. For community media audiences, news exists within specific programs (e.g. sporting news in sports programs; arts news in cultural programs etc.) and does not always take the form of a 'news bulletin'. It seems from this that their definitions of news are not ruled by typical news values. Instead, they define 'news' as information that is useful and on which they can act. This was highlighted by the following comment:

> The local news component on Radio Nag comes through the programs, because most programs have news and information in them and they tell you what is happening locally. It is about local stuff that is happening here that you hear in each of the programs. It is in-depth information and a wide source of information about the community (Radio NAG Yeppoon focus group participant).

Program formats on community radio enable more in-depth exploration of issues and this is valued highly by those using the stations to get information. A community group member explained:

> Most of what mainstream media does is too simplistic and community radio gives us the opportunity to explain things in more detail. Community radio lets you get more of the message across because you have more time and more control as well. You are more likely to do live stuff on community radio than on commercial media and that means less chance of your stuff being edited. It can be more real with community radio (4ZZZ community group interview, The Big Issue, Brisbane).

Community radio places less emphasis on news values such as conflict as one community group representative explained:

> Community radio will allow you to talk, you know, will be interested, not only just when there are bad news stories, but also when there are good news stories. If there's not a crisis or something happening right at that moment that they [mainstream media] deem to be media worthy, it's much harder to get them to pick up and run a story (Friends of the Earth, Melbourne).

Because community radio's impassioned volunteer workforce uses an alternate range of sources and provides access to groups who are unable to access mainstream news media, it challenges both traditional news sourcing practices and traditional definitions of news values (Rodriguez, 2001).

Connecting communities and building community networks

Community radio in Australia is playing a pivotal role in bringing like-minded, and disparate, individuals and groups together. Participants in the focus groups we have held throughout Australia suggest that merely by listening to community radio made them feel they were part of a community. For those who were new to a region, town or suburb, the role of community radio in making them feel 'at home' was particularly important. One Melbourne listener explained:

> For me, I think it comes back to what I was saying before, it [the radio station] just gave me a connection into this community, I guess. I've made the decision that this is where I want to live now and I have lived all over the country and this is now where I'll stay and put my roots down if you like. And the start of that decision … had a lot, well not to do completely with Triple R, but had a lot to do with that. It sort of gave me that connection (RRR focus group, 2005).

Another Melbourne audience member explained that community radio had given him a 'sense of belonging to a community', while another described it as being part of 'a big family'. During our fieldwork this was a theme we heard repeatedly. One focus group participant explained what community radio meant to her in this way:

> It is something that actually brings the community together, whereas a lot of the stuff in the world today seems to be isolating us. You know, you can get all the information you need, sitting at home in front of your computer, and that sort of thing. Whereas, this is something that actually gives you a reason to get out

and into your community, and [it is] a community that is open and accepting of you (RRR, 2005).

As well as providing a space in which minority groups can have a say, community radio performs or, at least, has the potential to perform an educative role, exposing some listeners to people and groups with whom they previously had little contact and in the process, shattering stereotypical ideas. One focus group member explained it this way:

> When I first moved up here, and I don't know how to say this without sounding awful, but when I first moved, I'd tune in and there would be like people with disabilities, like speech disabilities on the radio and that really impressed me. I just thought, 'Oh this radio … ' Yeah, and I'd listen to that and they were great. I couldn't believe it. I thought they can do all this and say all this (Bendigo focus group).

see Goggin and Newell, Chapter 6

Theory link

Many participants in our audience research reported that community radio provided them with essential information about community activities. At 6RPH, Perth's radio for the print handicapped, one focus group member who was visually impaired explained that the radio station's role in providing information about community events and activities was essential because he would not otherwise get access to that information. The radio's role in publicising this information increased the opportunity for him to participate in the community. This was important in decreasing his sense of isolation and widening his personal contacts.

Community broadcasting also strengthens existing cultural networks. Examples of this are most prevalent in, but are not limited to, Australia's Indigenous communities and ethnic language groups. For Indigenous communities, community radio has a dual role—as a first level of service for local audiences and as a cultural bridge between Indigenous and non-Indigenous audiences. This was acknowledged by an inquiry into Australian broadcasting in 2000 by the Productivity Commission and reinforced by this listener:

> … It provides places like Palm (Island), Woorabinda, the Cape and other Indigenous communities, particularly the Indigenous population in the mainstream, with a voice, a balance, projecting our stories, our culture, our language the way we want to hear it but giving it to the wider audience too, people who live in the mainstream, people who don't often come in contact with Indigenous people (4K1G listener, 2005).

For another member of an Indigenous community radio station audience, the service provided her with a sense of pride in her Aboriginality and she believed the station played a role in extending that sense of pride to the rest of the community.

[The station helps you] to keep in touch with everybody around the country: the families in Townsville, the families in Cairns, the countrymen over in Darwin and Perth—Indigenous radio just opens the door. Some of the stuff they do is to advertise tombstone openings, cultural events and that's what the radio does. It gives us that benefit (Townsville focus group, 2005).

There is evidence from other focus groups that this multiple role of local radio is not confined to the Indigenous sector alone. A Tongan language focus group in Adelaide described how its weekly program on community radio connected it with other islander communities, and how community announcements broadcast in English helped to expose their culture to the broader Adelaide community facilitating networking between and within the arts and music communities.

Conclusion

Community radio is helping to empower communities by enabling them to tell the stories that are meaningful to them within the context of their everyday lives. Despite, or perhaps because of, limited media ownership and the decline in provision of local news and information, community broadcasting is providing an important alternative, or at least, a complementary media service, for a variety of publics, and this is perhaps its greatest strength.

CHAPTER SUMMARY

- In this chapter we have offered an overview of recent research into community broadcasting, revealing the varied role and importance of this sector of Australian broadcasting.
- We have discussed some of the key themes to emerge from our latest research, expressed through the voices of audience members, to highlight the significant contribution community broadcasting is making to the Australian society and culture.

Tutorial questions

- Are there any media outlets in your community that let you contribute material or ideas?
- How do these media outlets facilitate that process?
- Is the role played by community media in your town or city similar to or different from the roles described in this chapter and how?

Recommended reading

Meadows, M., Forde, S., Ewart, J. & Foxwell, K., 2006, 'The Untapped Potential of
Participation: New Methods for Evaluating Audiences in the Community Media
Sector', *Australian Studies in Journalism* (in press).

Meadows, M., Forde, S., Ewart, J., & Foxwell. K., 2005, 'A Perfect Match? Qualitative
Research and the Community Media Sector', *3CMedia*, 1(1): www.cbonline.org.
au/3cmedia/3c_issue1/index.shtm.

Moran, A., 1995, 'Multiplying Minorities: The Case of Community Radio', in Craik,
J., Bailey, J. & Moran, A. (eds) *Public Voices, Private Interests: Australia's Media Policy*,
Allen & Unwin, St Leonards.

Rodriguez, C., 2001, *Fissures in the Mediascape: An International Study of Citizens' Media*,
Hampton Press, Creskill, NJ.

Website

Australia's Community Broadcasting Association: www.cbonline.org.au/

References

ABS (Australian Bureau of Statistics), 2005, *Household Use of Information Technology*,
Category Number 8146.0, ABS, December, Canberra http://www.abs.gov.au/

Broadcasting Services Act (1992) Section 15: Community Broadcasting, see www.austlii.
edu.au/au/legis/cth/consol_act/bsa1992214/s15.html, accessed on 8 May 2006.

Downie, C. & Macintosh, A., 2005, 'New Media or More of the Same? The Cross-
media Ownership Debate', *The Australia Institute,* May 2006, available at: http://
www.tai.org.au/documents/downloads/WP86.pdf

Ewart, J., Meadows, M., Forde, S. & Foxwell. K., 2005, 'Media Matters: Ways to Link
Community Radio and Community Newspapers', *Australian Journalism Review*,
27(2), pp. 87–104.

Forde, S., Foxwell, K., & Meadows, M., 2003, 'Through the Lens of the Local: Public
Arena Journalism in the Australian Community Broadcasting Sector', *Journalism*,
4(3), pp. 317–42.

Forde, S., Foxwell, K. & Meadows, M. 2002a, *Culture, Commitment, Community: The
Australian Community Radio Sector,* Griffith University, Brisbane.

Forde, S., Foxwell, K. & Meadows, M., 2002b, 'Creating a Community Public Sphere:
Community Radio as a Cultural Resource', *Media International Australia*, 103, pp.
56–67.

Harcup, T., 2003, '"The Unspoken—Said": The Journalism of Alternative Media',
Journalism, 4(3), pp. 356–76.

McCallum, K., 2005, 'Local talk as a construction of public opinion on Indigenous issues in Australia', unpublished thesis, University of Canberra, Australia.

McNair Ingenuity, 2004, Audience research data: www.cbonline.org.au/index.cfm?pageId=44,133,2,0. Accessed 20 March 2007.

Meadows, M., Forde, S., Ewart, J. & Foxwell, K., 2006, 'The Untapped Potential of Participation: New Methods for Evaluating Audiences in the Community Media Sector', *Australian Studies in Journalism*, in press.

Moran, A., 1995, 'Multiplying Minorities: The Case of Community Radio', in Craik, J., Bailey, J. & Moran, A. (eds) *Public Voices, Private Interests: Australia's Media Policy*, Allen & Unwin, St Leonards.

Rodriguez, C., 2001, *Fissures in the Mediascape: An International Study of Citizens' Media*, Hampton Press, Creskill, NJ.

Van Vuuren, K., 2005, 'Community Media in Transition: Emerging Frameworks for their Regulation, Practice and Theory', *Australian Journal of Communication*, 32(2): 57–70.

Note: This research is made possible with financial and in-kind support from the Community Broadcasting Association of Australia (CBAA), the Community Broadcasting Foundation (CBF), and the Department of Communication, Information Technology and the Arts (DCITA). Other industry advisers include representatives from the National Ethnic and Multicultural Broadcasting Council (NEMBC), the Indigenous Remote Communications Association (IRCA), the Australian Indigenous Communication Association (AICA), and Radio for the Print Handicapped (RPH). The qualitative audience research project is being jointly funded (with DCITA) through a Linkage Grant from the Australian Research Council.

Part Two Summary

This section provides an important collection of case studies that explore the differences in the communications environments both between and within developed and developing nations. In a developed nation like Australia the media worlds people live in are radically different depending on where they happen to live—but differences of culture, values and physical and mental ability can be just as disadvantageous as geographical isolation or a dispersed community. These differences affect which media people find accessible, and how they choose to use media to improve their worlds, to redress inequalities and to ensure their group members are better served by the media.

Taken together these chapters therefore provide an invaluable account of how users and audiences for new media are imagined by media industries and governments, and the extent to which such imaginings fall short of the needs of real people. Real people need opportunities to play with new media, to produce media content for a wider audience than their own close circle of friends, and to use media as a way of establishing their identity within a community, and sometimes beyond it. Indigenous and ethnic communities need opportunities to develop resources of community information and knowledge that will allow them to maintain communal memories about their histories and experiences. Being enabled to participate in and to contribute to public discussion of cultures, values and beliefs is an important way this can occur.

- What are the communication and media rights that local groups and communities are trying to secure? Make a list of those mentioned in each of the chapters in this section.
- How is it suggested that governments and media industries need to reconsider the ways they imagine the user/audiences for new media? What action is it argued should be taken to achieve this?

$\rightarrow$

QUESTIONS

- Why is it important that community access to traditional media production be maintained and what role could it play in the new media world?

Recommended reading

Anderson, B., 1983, *Imagined Communities: Reflections on the Origin and Spread of Nationalism,* Verso, London.

Goggin, G. (ed.), 2004, *Virtual Nation: The Internet in Australia,* University of New South Wales Press, Sydney.

Rodriguez, C., 2001, *Fissures in the Mediascape: An International Study of Citizen's Media,* Hampton Press, Cresskill, NJ.

Shrage, M., 1990, *Shared Minds,* Random House, New York.

von Lewinski, S., 2003, *Indigenous Heritage and Intellectual Property: Genetic Resources, Traditional Knowledge and Folklore,* Aspen Publishers, London.

PART THREE

Access

Part 3 takes up issues of access and participation, questioning the extent to which the changes outlined in Part 1 permeate the social fabric of global culture, and in doing so explores discourses that may shape how the media activism described in Part 2 is able to find expression. In this Part we show that the capacity to take advantage of new media opportunities varies markedly within and between nations; demonstrating that what is at stake in arguments about access and participation in the developed world varies dramatically from what is at stake in the developing world.

The development of digital technologies, including private communications infrastructures that operate globally, has been driven by capitalist investment in developed nations where most, but not all, sectors of society have sufficient disposable income to pay for Internet access. But there remain some social sectors for whom access is denied, and the future of the media world facing these sectors is taken up by Stephen Lax (Chapter 12) who outlines the social and cultural ramifications of the commercial imperative driving the implementation of new media, in the context of an historical analysis of discourses of 'the information society'. The media worlds of the welfare dependent, who queue at local libraries for free access to ageing computers with slow Internet speeds, is worlds apart from the high-speed access increasingly being designed only for business and the extremely wealthy in the West. Lax warns of a future media world of extreme inequality, where access is beyond the dream of many. He asks us to think about who will do the 'dirty work' in such a world if government policies are not implemented to ensure that the basic learning and ICT skills are widely available.

Nico Carpentier (Chapter 13) undertakes a systematic first principles critique of some key terminological debates, laying bare their taken-for-granted ideological meanings. Carpentier suggests that in recent years the term 'participation' has been stripped of its political connotations. Yet this has occurred as another term and has slipped *into* the communications media debate—the term 'interactivity'. As Celia Lury (Chapter 18) argues, interactivity and interaction are not the same thing. Interactivity is a responsive activity—as for example when we 'interact' with a computer program but not to the extent of actually being able to step outside the terms for engagement defined by the program's software. Interaction, by contrast, means that both parties have opportunity to change the terms on which the negotiation is based. One example of where interaction occurs online is in the Wikipedia community, but even here interaction occurs around content, not at the level of code. Most of the Internet's interactivity is at the level of content, rather than code. Even social networking is oriented to the interaction with content rather than code. Carpentier draws our attention to this limitation and the way it is drawn into the use of the term 'participation'. He suggests that for the Internet to be a truly participatory medium, the political connotations of the term 'participation' need to be reappropriated.

The problem of preparation for access to Information and Communication Technologies (ICTs) is investigated in Simon Burton and Anton Van der Hoven's (Chapter 14) case study of the introduction of a telecentre in Bhamshela, South Africa. Burton and Van der Hoven trace the mixed outcomes generated by a South African government policy designed to introduce ICTs into small, rural South African communities. Their chapter shows that good policy intentions are not sufficient to ensure success at the level of community engagement, where the local population often is inadequately prepared for the introduction of such an initiative. Their chapter provides an important addition to the global media picture because, as they point out, whether a policy venture fails or succeeds, it may nevertheless have a symbolic meaning for the local community that, if followed up appropriately, can be beneficial in the longer term. They caution, however, that one of the main threats to such a longer term future is linked to the rhetoric generated by technological determinism that may lead governments to imagine that installing computers in local centres is sufficient. They argue, instead, for the importance of community development initiatives to assist local communities to include ICTs in their imagining of their own future media worlds.

Tim Dwyer (Chapter 15) argues that 'diversity' has several distinct meanings in media policy discourses. In Australia (as in many other nations) media diversity and media pluralism are used to describe both the architecture of service provision in terms of their licensing categories and institutional structures, and the range of available formats and content genres. Often diversity is discussed only in terms of ownership and control of media outlets: historically the presumption has been in some policy circles that diversity of ownership will ensure diversity of content and commentary. Cultural diversity, on the other hand, is considered a matter of ethnicity, religion and (limited) cosmopolitanism and tends to get separated off from broader structural questions of media diversity. Dwyer argues that this separation is artificial and a barrier to the development of inclusive media policy, because it fails to recognise: firstly, that content is common to both these debates; and secondly, that diversity of content is fundamentally an 'access and participation' issue. For ordinary people, content relevant to their everyday interests and affiliations is what makes access worth having. Creating a media system that allows concentrated ownership affects access through the constraints placed on diversity. The challenge for governments and their agencies is to attempt to balance the inevitable contradictions and tensions between global flows of people, products and services and images, and the desire to maintain local cultures, traditions and institutions.

While Dwyer's argument favours increased community representation and participation in media policy development, Derek Wilding's (Chapter 16) case study provides a close examination of what 'public participation' can mean when the community is defined as 'consumers', and their participation sought in a system based on industry 'co-regulation' or, as it is more widely known, 'self-regulation'. Industry self-regulation is beneficial for media operators because policy is seen as mostly 'advisory' and 'light-touch'; where compliance with policy is a matter of goodwill. In the development of such policy, the parties to the deliberation are government, industry and consumer representatives. Wilding's case study focuses on the establishment of an alliance of policy actors who together develop a code of practice addressing the fairness of mobile phone contracts; his 'insider' account details the way policy development 'participation' was managed by both government authorities, consumer advocacy groups and the telecommunications industry. He demonstrates that the basis on which consumer participation occurs is highly constrained and, even in this limited form, strongly resisted by industry. Wilding's analysis includes a useful analysis of the strengths, weaknesses and limitations of media self-regulation.

The choice of the term 'consumer' as the basis on which an industry forum is constructed means that the interests of society's most vulnerable sectors (e.g. children, the aged and the welfare dependent) may be overlooked or mis-represented. It is for this reason that the issue of access needs to be considered alongside participation, and the reason why the politics of participation is so important if the emerging media world is to be broadly inclusive.

STEPHEN LAX

'Access Denied': Arguments about Equality and Access to New Media in the Information Society

12

CHAPTER OVERVIEW

One of the claims about new information and communications technologies (ICTs) is that they can help to bring about a fairer, more equal society. Studies of technology suggest that assumptions about their impact are often unfulfilled. Nevertheless, arguments about a new information society have again elevated the importance of technology as a social force. Here we will examine the ways in which public policy making is bound up with assumptions about the kind of society we live in and the role of technology within it.

Key terms

poverty and inequality
information society
meritocracy
technological determinism

Issues

- Can new media technologies create a more equal society?
- Is the increase in information creating a new kind of society?
- What is the role of governments?

Introduction

There can be no doubt that the world exists in a state of staggering inequality. The United Nations reports some sobering statistics: the world's richest 500 individuals have a combined income greater than that of the poorest 416 million; the 2.5 billion people living on less than $2 a day account for 5 per cent of global income while the richest 10 per cent account for 54 per cent. Within individual countries, whether rich or poor, similar inequalities persist; inequality in both the USA and the UK is significantly greater than in Albania or Ethiopia (UNDP, 2005, pp. 4, 55).

Not surprisingly, these general material inequalities are reflected in levels of access to technologies. While in Sweden and the UK in 2004, for example, there were more mobile phones than people, in Mozambique just 3.7 per cent of the population had one; in North America, 62 per cent of people had Internet access compared with 2.6 per cent in Africa (ITU, 2005). The World Summit on the Information Society (WSIS), convened under the auspices of the United Nations, noted at its first meeting in 2003 that:

> The benefits of the information technology revolution are today unevenly distributed between the developed and developing countries and within societies. We are fully committed to turning this digital divide into a digital opportunity for all, particularly for those who risk being left behind and being further marginalized.
>
> The rapid progress of these technologies opens completely new opportunities to attain higher levels of development. The capacity of these technologies to reduce many traditional obstacles, especially those of time and distance, for the first time in history makes it possible to use the potential of these technologies for the benefit of millions of people in all corners of the world. (WSIS, 2003, p. 2)

In many countries governments seek to overcome this division by providing access to, for example, Internet-connected computers in public libraries.

Theory link

see Carpentier, Chapter 13; Wasserman, Chapter 8

Think about it

Should ICTs be considered a basic skill, alongside numeracy and literacy? What are the criteria by which we should decree an area of human activity an essential or 'basic' skill? Are there any other skills which should similarly be regarded as essential? How about driving? Are those who can't drive socially disadvantaged any less than those who can't do ICT?

While it is hard to imagine anyone arguing against opening up ICT access to all, the suggestion that a more equitable exposure to new communications technologies will lead to a reduction in inequalities more generally depends on a number of assumptions, firstly about an understanding of the term 'equality' and secondly about the role of technology in society. At an instinctive level, we may feel we know what an egalitarian society would look like, but in fact we probably know better what an *unequal* society looks like. Gross disparities in material wealth and possessions have been documented above; further, most would acknowledge the unequal nature of the barriers to *acquiring* wealth faced between those born into the poorest families in even the wealthiest nations and those growing up in families that are readily able to afford to pay for the best schools and healthcare. The intractability of social position is underscored by research revealing static or even reducing levels of social mobility. For example, Blanden and Gibbons's (2006) study of UK adults found that those who had grown up in poor families in the 1980s were *more* likely to remain poor themselves in later life in comparison with children growing up ten years earlier. In other words, levels of **poverty** were increasingly persistent across generations. Equivalent studies in the USA also find low or reducing levels of intergenerational mobility (Corak, 2004; Hertz, 2006). Thus we have the compound inequalities of the absolute differences in material wealth and the obstacles, evidently increasing, which prevent those at the bottom easing their way out of poverty and closing the gap with the better off.

Poverty and inequality Poverty can be absolute or relative. How thresholds of poverty are defined is contentious—what are basic minimum living standards? Relative poverty is defined in terms of inequalities: the poor in a wealthy country are likely to be better off than the poor in a developing country.

The digital divide

There are two possible objectives in tackling these aspects of **inequality**: *equality of outcome* or *equality of opportunity*. The former approach seeks to ensure, through social policies targeted at both disadvantaged *and* advantaged groups, that levels of inequality between rich and poor are reduced; the latter meanwhile is more concerned with targeting the poorest in society through highly focused policies to support them in getting on the first rung of the social ladder, to set a basic minimum level of entitlement that therefore doesn't directly affect those already free from social deprivation. The outcome-focused approach tends to be associated with currently unfashionable, interventionist politics (based on redistribution of wealth through tax and welfare policies) while the equality of opportunity approach is popular with liberal (or neoliberal) politicians who favour governments playing merely an enabling role that seeks to impact minimally on the free market. While this characterisation is necessarily crude, its significance lies in the approach to new media technologies taken by governments and non-governmental organisations across the globe. Policy makers argue that we are in danger of developing, or deepening, a 'digital divide', a schism between those who are able to access and make use of new media technologies and those who, for a variety of reasons, cannot. Governments are increasingly migrating everyday services such as tax returns to the World Wide Web and conducting online consultations as part of the policy making process. Further, campaigning and political organisations outside government are using the Web to publicise and debate civic and political issues. The Internet is extensively used too for commercial transactions with all kinds of goods and services being traded. It is thus feared that those who do not have access to these communications technologies risk being marginalised, having restricted choice as consumers and also being left out of an important part of the democratic process (Lax, 2004).

In most industrialised nations, therefore, initiatives have taken place to secure public access to ICTs through public provision of Internet-connected computers. Examples include national projects, such as 'Networking the Nation' in Australia, in which rural communities were given funding to establish public access points, or the installation of 'the People's Network' of Internet-connected computers in the UK's public libraries. These are supplemented by countless smaller-scale projects in which public terminals are placed in schools or community centres and so in such places few people can be said to be completely 'disconnected' in the sense of having no *material* access to the Internet. For non-industrialised nations, as we saw earlier in the WSIS declaration, similar goals are defined for universal access through public provision of Internet terminals.

However, there is no guarantee that this provision will lead to more equitable use of the networks. The ways in which people use the Internet, and indeed whether they do so at all, are far more complex than simply a question of access to the technology itself. For example, countless market research studies show that in advanced countries like the USA and the UK, household access to the Internet via home computer is reaching a plateau of around 60 per cent—while computers and the cost of Internet access itself have both become cheaper, more than one in three households remain without Internet access (ITU, 2005; Ofcom, 2006, p. 157). Evidence about the ways in which public Internet terminals are used is variable.

Hardy and Johansen (2003) studied users of public terminals placed in libraries in Victoria, Australia, and concluded that users tended to be drawn more from lower-income groups or the unemployed than in the population at large, although the educational background of users was much higher than typical. Simpson et al. (2004) and Strover et al. (2004), in their respective Australian and US studies, both concluded that in many cases community provision of Internet terminals was characterised by a lack of clarity as to their purpose. The notion of 'access' is nebulous—is access about increasing the total number of users, or increasing usage among a particular social group? Such questions affect the choice of location for Internet terminals, and in the absence of an answer it is difficult to interpret, in terms of success or failure, the consequent usage.

Think about it

Leadbeater reckons our children will work with their brains, not with their hands. Can all manual labour be replaced with machines? If not, whose kids will do the dirty work?

Beyond questions about who actually uses these public terminals, evidence about the wider social consequences of Internet usage is variable. Studies of Internet users' political engagement suggests that those who are politically active online (for instance emailing representatives, taking part in consultations or political organisations) are generally the same people who were active in the absence of the Internet—the evidence that a new political engagement is engendered by access to the Internet is insubstantial (Gibson et al., 2004). Another area where the use of the Internet was anticipated to result in social gain was in education, in particular lifelong learning for adults. The UK government's view has been consistently positive about the effects of ICTs on educational provision—the education secretary has declared, 'sometimes people can't access the learning they need because courses simply don't fit around their daily lives. New technologies open up huge opportunities to give people access to the learning they want in a way that suits their needs' (Morris, 2002). While this may be an almost universal position among policy makers, again evidence suggests that ICTs in public places make almost no difference to the take up of educational provision in later life. Family, geography and other social factors are much more important and patterns of 'lifelong learning' in the new technological era are almost unchanged from the 'non-technological' past (Selwyn et al., 2006).

An information society

So how do we begin to explain the enthusiasm with which new technologies like the Internet are proposed as furthering the cause of equality and fulfilment of individuals? The explanation lies in a particular view of a new technological society. Influential thinkers have been prominent in the past few decades in describing far-reaching social changes, in part wrought by new technologies, heralding a new stage of social evolution following the agricultural and industrial phases (Toffler, 1980). While there is no coherent account of this new era, it is generally labelled the **information society**. This notion identifies information (and knowledge) as the central feature of society: your place in that society is bound up with your relationship with information, your access to it and what you do with it (May, 2002).

GLOSSARY

Information society   A society where access to and manipulation of information becomes the key determinant of one's place in society.

Industrial society   A society where position depends on social relations under capitalism.

Agrarian society   A society where position depends on feudal relations such as land ownership.

The information society idea can be traced back to Daniel Bell. He began writing in the late 1960s of the 'post-industrial society', one in which the reliance on manufacturing as the main source of wealth was being replaced by the service industries. These depend far more for their success on access to information rather than the raw materials of industrial manufacturing. For Bell this heralded a new kind of social order, with shifts in the balances of wealth and power. These transformations would be every bit as important as the change from an **agrarian society** to an **industrial society** in the seventeenth and eighteenth centuries, in which the absolute rule of feudal landlord (the aristocracy, who assumed power solely by birth) was replaced with the rise of a capitalist class (where power was conferred by monetary wealth) and its own form of rule (parliamentary democracy). In the 'post-industrial society', power no longer depends upon access to wealth and physical labour, but instead on access to knowledge and the skills to select and manipulate that knowledge (mental labour).

It becomes clear that the 'old' industrial order is passing and that a 'new society' is indeed in the making. To speak rashly: if the dominant figures of the past hundred years have been the entrepreneur, the businessman, and the industrial executive, the 'new men' are the scientists, the mathematicians, the economists, and the engineers of the new computer technology. And the dominant institutions of the new society—in the sense that they will provide the most creative challenges and enlist the richest talents—will be the intellectual institutions. The leadership of the new society will rest, not with businessmen or corporations as we know them (for a good deal of production will have been routinized), but with the research corporation, the industrial laboratories, the experimental stations, and the universities (Bell, 1970, p. 394).

The 'post-industrial society' became translated during the 1980s and 1990s into the 'information society', a term which Bell himself also came to use, though it should be noted that Bell's explanation of modern society was not as exclamatory as many of the more recent 'information society' advocates. While the notion of 'post-industrial' society is clear and precise in that it implies a break with the previous industrial society, the term 'information society' is more vague, and this is part of the problem in dealing with it.

However vague we may find the idea, and Webster (2005) points out clearly the lack of precision in most attempts at definition, it has nevertheless captured the hearts and minds of political leaders and advisers. Shortly before becoming the UK's Chancellor of the Exchequer, Gordon Brown wrote about equality in the 'fast-changing information-based economy dominated by the importance of knowledge'. He continued, 'the defining characteristic of economy is less an individual's ability to gain access to capital and far more his or her ability to gain access to knowledge and to use it creatively' (Brown, 1996). Here was a new kind of economy that offered a new kind of politics, the 'Third Way'. Keenly adopted by US President Clinton and the UK Prime Minister Tony Blair, it was articulated by Antony Giddens as a rejection of both 'old left', social democratic politics and the neoliberalism of the 'new right' (Giddens, 1998). In fact, Third Way ideas embrace much of the neoliberal economic agenda (Callinicos, 2001). A fascinating insight is given by Charles Leadbeater, a former adviser to the Blair Government and member of the think tank Demos, which was highly influential on UK government thinking in the late 1990s. Indeed, Leadbeater's book, *Living on Thin Air* (2000), carried an endorsement by Prime Minister Tony Blair on the front cover: '…an extraordinarily interesting thinker. His book raises critical questions for Britain's future'. Two passages give a flavour of the ideas:

Most of us earn our livings providing service, judgement, information and analysis, whether in a telephone call centre, a lawyer's office, a government department or a scientific laboratory. We are all in the thin-air business. That should allow our economies, in principle at least, to become more humane; they should be organized around people and the knowledge capital they produce. Our children will not have to toil in dark factories, descend into pits or suffocate in mills, to hew raw materials and turn them into manufactured products. They will make their livings through their creativity, ingenuity, and imagination (p. ix).

An economy which becomes more knowledge-intensive has the potential to become more inclusive and meritocratic. Everyone with an education can have a go. … In an economy which trades know-how and ideas, everyone seems to have a chance to make it, working from a garage, their kitchen or their bedroom. Twenty-five-year-old drop-outs can create best-selling computer games; a nerd fresh out of college can create the Internet's best browser; a boy with no formal education can become Europe's most precocious fashion designer (Leadbeater, 2000, p. 33).

A knowledge economy

This new knowledge economy then is one which is overhauling social institutions, and in the process, becoming more equal, 'in principle at least'. It is a seductive argument. Leadbeater outlines how he himself deliberated long and hard before deciding to become a 'portfolio worker', but having made the leap is now reaping the rewards. No longer having to work for an organisation where 'some ambitious manager points the spotlight at you', he can organise his life around his family and earn his living 'by finding people who will pay me to do things I am interested in' (2000, p. 2). While acknowledging that he is helped by having a good degree and a list of useful contacts through his earlier career as a journalist, for Leadbeater this simply helps make his argument: there are no barriers to this kind of life provided a good education is available to all.

Again we see the importance of new technology to the claims made about the new economy. When wealth is derived from manipulating and trading information, access to technology becomes vital.

Activity 12.1

Think of some more examples of 'thin air' kinds of employment. Try and envisage what living in a society that relies only on these categories of work would actually be like. Will any other workers be required? What will those people be doing? Develop a short description of such a society.

Whereas in an industrial society 'access to technology' (in the form of factories and machinery) could equally be argued as key to wealth, access was also required to raw materials (including labour) and markets—and access here meant physical transportation of goods. In an industrial society, then, this kind of access was inevitably privileged and uneven. But the technologies of the new economy are different. Leadbeater chastens those who are pessimistic:

> Yet this ought to be an age of excitement and optimism. Consider, first, the breathtaking possibilities of technology. By 2007, the hard disk in the average television set top box should have enough memory to store all the songs ever recorded. By 2010, it should be able to take every film. Telecommunications bandwidth is doubling every 12 months. The capacity of fibre to transmit information has increased by a factor of 16,000 in less than five years; it will soon carry everything we can say, write, compose, play, record, film, draw, paint or design. The entire contents of the US Library of Congress could be passed through an optical switch in less than three seconds (Leadbeater, 2004, p. 30).

Not only is this an impressive list of technological achievements, for the new economy the point is that these are relatively cheap and therefore accessible technologies. Leadbeater's college drop-outs can be on a similar footing with long-established corporate giants when it comes to creating some best-selling software. It was no surprise when the **meritocracy** that Leadbeater alluded to in 2000 became a topic of earnest debate in Third Way economies. In the lead-up to the 2001 general election, Tony Blair declared that the UK would become a truly meritocratic society, a natural consequence of the emergence from industrial society into an information society. The contrast with old industrial societies seemed clear. Inequalities and unfairness are endemic to industrial society, where prosperity resulted from ownership of large capital assets. These assets were often acquired not through any mechanism that rewarded skill, capability or effort, but more often were inherited through accident of birth, however poorly suited the recipient might be to the role. Now, thanks to the accessibility of the tools of the information economy, the new ICTs, it would be possible to open up its wealth-creating potential to all. This logic underpins the policy objective of providing public access to ICTs for those who do not have access elsewhere.

Meritocracy   A meritocracy is a social order in which each individual acquires social status on the basis of merit: skill, ability and effort, rather than gender or class. Superficially a fairer society, the notion is in reality hypothetical due to complexities of defining merit and tends to cement social position, consigning 'non-elite' members of society to unfulfilling manual labour.

A meritocratic society?

The same logic of a meritocratic society explains the changing role of education in many industrialised nations. In the UK, information and communications technology has been placed at the centre of educational policy, not merely as a tool for learning but as a subject in its own right as one of the only three subjects (alongside maths and English) required to be taught to all throughout compulsory schooling. Amid much publicity in 1997, a National Grid for Learning was established and plans put in place to connect all schools to the Internet—the importance of ICT was in no doubt (Lax, 2001). The government could claim that it had set in place the basis of an egalitarian society—one in which all would have access not only to the technologies of the information society but also to the basic skills needed to exploit them. Having established a level playing field, whatever anyone chose to do with those skills and technologies was their own choosing. If they applied their skills successfully, then they deserved whatever reward came their way; should they be unsuccessful, then really they could not complain. In Leadbeater's words, 'everyone with an education can have a go'. Michael Young, who coined the term in 1958 in *The Rise of the Meritocracy 1870–2033*, was concerned that the point of his satire had been missed: the meritocracy would be a divided society. When those at the top were able to believe (wrongly) they had truly acquired their status on their own merits, then equally those beneath them deserved their lot and certainly no sympathy nor, logically, any assistance (Young, 2001). Yet here we can see why a belief in the possibility of meritocracy means that calls for equality are in terms of opportunity rather than outcome. If one believes in the possibilities of an information society, then the role of government is limited to providing equality of opportunity, and that is delivered by equalising access to technology and the requisite basic skills. One can readily extend the argument to accept the logic of 'laptop welfare' where, rather than cash benefits, welfare provision might be more valuably conferred by giving the poor incentives to buy laptop computers; such schemes were proposed in 1995 by US Senate leader Newt Gingrich and in 1999 by UK Chancellor Gordon Brown.

The foregoing has suggested that to believe we live in an information society can imply that the conditions exist in which a true meritocracy can be achieved. In such circumstances, governments can justify intervening only minimally in the workings of society, ensuring that there is a basic provision of access to ICTs and skills. As the entry costs to ICTs are so low, equality is achieved as everyone has the same *opportunity* to acquire wealth. But such beliefs are readily challenged on two grounds: firstly on the singling out of technology as the main driver in this social change; and secondly on interpreting general shifts in economies from manufacturing to service industries as signifying more fundamental social changes.

The first objection focuses on the assumption that the technologies of communication (such as those listed by Leadbeater) are themselves independent entities in this process of social change. In other words, the technologies merely exist, evolving according to some internal logic of technical change. This view, labelled **technological determinism**, sees technology as autonomous, largely outside of social forces, but nevertheless having far-reaching social consequences. This claim seems intuitively true; in some instances it is even enshrined in dictums such as 'Moore's Law' (which states that computer processing power doubles every eighteen months). No doubt computers and networks will get faster and generally more capable, and this can seem like some natural process. However, it doesn't require much investigation to see that technological change is most certainly impacted upon by social forces. Economic forces selectively impel some technologies forward, such as ICTs today, just as different economic needs were crucial to developing and establishing other technologies such as radio communication 100 years ago, and the prime funders of scientific and technical research are governments and large industrial enterprises. Thus instead of seeing the technologies of the information society as somehow *naturally* progressing along the particular trajectory they currently follow, we should recognise that this path is socially shaped. The progress of a particular technology and its consequences are reflections of the society from which they emerge as much as any inherent capabilities of the technology.

see McGuigan, Chapter 1; Goggin and Newell, Chapter 6; Kivikuru, Chapter 7; Burton and Van der Hoven, Chapter 14

Theory link

Technological determinism A belief that technology develops independently of society and in so doing is the central cause of consequent social 'impacts'. Widely challenged, nevertheless the idea is found in many historical accounts of social change and lies behind countless predictions of future social trends.

The second problem with the claims about the information society is that it is assumed that the changes that have undeniably taken place over the past few decades, in particular the increase in the quantity and speed of information in its many guises, imply fundamentally new social forms. For example, the new information workers identified by Leadbeater above include those in 'a telephone call centre, a lawyer's office, a government department or a scientific laboratory': all are lumped together in the 'thin air' business. Meanwhile, the factory worker, the weaver and the miner are all from a past age. Leadbeater believes that the divisions of old, between manual worker and manager, are swept away in the new age of information. Yet working conditions in today's call centres share far more with twentieth-century factories or nineteenth-century weaving sheds than a lawyer's office or government department (Poynter & Miranda, 2000). That a call centre worker should see herself as aligned with lawyers and scientists in an information economy is readily dismissed.

More fundamentally, we have seen already that despite the growth of service industries over several decades, traditional inequalities persist doggedly. Whether we study social mobility, participation in political activity or the take-up of educational opportunities, we find no convincing evidence of novel trends that might suggest some social transformation. The alternative conclusion is that we are simply witnessing a particular phase of the continuing social order known as capitalism. Webster makes the connections explicit. He suggests that, rather than today's society requiring redefinition, it is enough to look at the historical nature of capitalist society to explain the present. For if we look at what characterises capitalism, we see a number of tendencies: access to goods and services being dependent on ability to pay; private rather than public provision; market criteria (profitability) as the dominant factors in deciding whether something is available; wage labour as the norm in the workplace (Webster, 2000). There is little here that does not apply when we include the growth of information availability and the growth of information work. For example, the growth in the numbers employed in the service industries or information work has not substantially (if at all) altered the relationship between employer and employee. The increasing numbers entering (or staying in) education is part of a long-term trend of professionalisation of work roles rather than a feature just of the past few years (and it is significant that many of these professionals, teachers and doctors for instance, now find themselves in conditions of less professional autonomy and more subject to metric and prescriptive practices historically associated with manual workers). Hence it is quite possible to explain today's information-rich age as fully part of a continuing but ever-transforming capitalist system.

Think about it

- The information society debate obviously keys into a discussion of globalisation. Although globalisation is a big area, we haven't had time to consider it here, but it is worth thinking a little about the connection between the two.
- When the telephone was introduced over 100 years ago, the telephone companies issued advice and instructions in its usage (e.g. how to speak into the microphone: 'distinctly and directly'). The idea seems laughable now. Is it just a matter of time then before everyone can use the Internet without giving it a moment's thought?

Conclusion

If we are to seek a society that is more equal, in which more people not only have greater *opportunities* to improve their own lives and those around them, but also are actually able to *achieve* those objectives, then we cannot rely simply on the provision of access to technology. Technology here is a distraction. Despite the ubiquitous presence (in industrialised nations) of ICTs and the information they process, there is no reason to see this as changing our understanding of society. Instead, as has been debated (and fought over) for decades or even centuries, the route to equality and fairness requires us to look more fundamentally at the ways in which society is divided, and to seek to overcome the assumptions and activities that give rise to those divisions.

CHAPTER SUMMARY

- This chapter has described how communications technologies are claimed to deliver social change.
- In particular we have seen that public provision of Internet access is seen as a public policy goal.
- It has explained that such policies are based on assumptions about the role of technology in society and about the kind of society in which technologies develop.
- We have explored issues such as the information society and technological determinism.

Tutorial questions

- Can access to new media technologies create a more equal society?
- Which characteristics were argued in this chapter to be indicative of a new kind of society and economy?
- How can the notions of an 'information society' and a 'meritocratic society' work together to justify limited government intervention in the provision of access to ICTs and skills?

Recommended reading

MacKenzie, D. & Wajcman, J. (eds), 1999, *The Social Shaping of Technology,* 2nd edn, Open University Press, Buckingham.

Warschauer, M., 2004, *Technology and Social Inclusion: Rethinking the Digital Divide,* MIT Press, Cambridge, Massachusetts.

Webster, F. (ed.), 2004, *The Information Society Reader,* Routledge, London.

Williams, R., 1990 [1974], *Television: Technology and Cultural Form,* Routledge, London.

Winston, B., 1998, *Media Technology and Society,* Routledge, London.

Websites

Digital Divide: see www.benton.org and www.digitaldividenetwork.org

European Union's Information Society Portal: www.europa.eu.int/information_society/text_en.htm

Wikipedia: www//en.wikipedia.org/wiki/Technological_determinism

World Summit on the Information Society (WSIS): www.itu.int/wsis/index.html

References

Bell, D., 1970, 'Notes on the Post-industrial Society' in Olsen, M. (ed.), *Power in Societies,* Collier Macmillan, London.

Blanden, J. & Gibbons S., 2006, *The Persistence of Poverty Across Generations: A View from Two British Cohorts,* Policy Press, Bristol.

Brown, G., 1996, 'In the Real World', *Guardian*, 2 August, p. 13.

Callinicos, A., 2001, *Against the Third Way,* Polity, Cambridge.

Corak, M. (ed.), 2004, *Generational Income Mobility in North America and Europe,* Cambridge University Press, Cambridge.

Gibson, R., Römmele, A. & Ward, S., 2004, *Electronic Democracy: Mobilisation, Organisation and Participation via New ICTs,* Routledge, London.

Giddens, A., 1998, *The Third Way: The Renewal of Social Democracy,* Polity, Cambridge.

Hardy, G. & Johansen, G., 2003, 'Characteristics and Choices of Public Access Internet Users in Victorian Public Libraries', *Online Information Review* 27(5), pp. 344–58.

Hertz, T., 2006, *Understanding Mobility in America,* Center for American Progress, Washington.

ITU, 2005, *ICT Statistics*, available at www.itu.int/ITU-D/ict/statistics/ (accessed 30 November 2005).

Lax, S., 2004, 'The Internet and Democracy' in Gauntlett, D. & Horsley, R. (eds) *Web Studies* (2nd edn), Arnold, London.

Lax, S., 2001, 'Information, Education and Inequality. Is New Technology the Solution?' in Lax, S. (ed.) *Access Denied in the Information Age,* Palgrave, Basingstoke.

Leadbeater, C., 2004, 'Globalisation: Now the Good News.' *New Statesman* 1 July, pp. 29–31.

Leadbeater, C., 2000, *Living on Thin Air: the New Economy,* Penguin, London.

May, C., 2002, *The Information Society: A Sceptical View,* Polity, Cambridge.

Morris, E., 2002, 'Estelle Morris welcomes report on learning with new technology,' press notice 0161, Department for Education and Skills.

Ofcom, 2006, *The Communications Market 2006,* Office of Communications, London.

Poynter, G. & de Miranda, A., 2000, 'Inequality, Work and Technology in the Services Sector' in Wyatt, S., Henwood, F., Miller, N. & Senker, P. (eds), *Technology and Inequality: Questioning the Information Society,* Routledge, London.

Selwyn N., Gorard, S. & Furlong, J., 2006, *Adult Learning in the Digital Age: Information Technology and the Learning Society,* Routledge, Abingdon.

Simpson, L., Daws, L. & Pini, B., 2004, 'Public Internet Access Revisited', *Telecommunications Policy,* 28(3–4), pp. 323–37.

Strover, S., Chapman, G. & Waters, J., 2004, 'Beyond Community Networking and CTCs: Access, Development, and Public Policy,' *Telecommunications Policy* 28(7–8), pp. 465–85.

Toffler, A., 1980, *The Third Wave,* Collins, London.

UNDP, 2005, *Human Development Report 2005,* UNDP, New York.

Webster, F., 2005, 'The Information Society Revisited' in Lievrouw, L. & Livingstone, S. (eds) *The Handbook of New Media: Social Shaping and Consequences of ICTs,* Sage, London.

Webster, F., 2000, 'Information, Capitalism and Uncertainty', *Information, Communication & Society* 3(1) 69–90.

WSIS, 2003, *Declaration of Principles,* WSIS, Geneva.

Young, M., 2001, 'Down with Meritocracy', *Guardian,* 29 June.

13

Participation, Access and Interaction: Changing Perspectives

Key terms

participation
interactivity
interaction
access

Issues

- How have the meanings of the terms 'participation', 'access' and 'interactivity' changed in the past decades, and particularly with the introduction of a new generation of media?
- Why have these changes occurred?

CHAPTER OVERVIEW

In recent years, 'participation' has become intertwined with the concepts 'access' and 'interaction', both of which in the past were connotations associated with 'participation' though neither of these 'new' terms fully accounts for the meanings covered by 'participation'. As a result, the use of the term in media theory is changing. This chapter traces these changes, with emphasis on the ways they reflect the impact of a new generation of ICTs. The argument usually used to justify the changed usage is that because we have *access* to the new worlds of ICT, people find themselves in a constant state of *interaction* and *participation*. This chapter argues that, in this context, the term 'participation' becomes equivalent to being online and surfing the Web or participating in online chat. When this happens, earlier usage of the term 'participation' to denote active engagement in a politically relevant discourse is lost and, more importantly, the possibility of critical reflection on the expansion of digital media and the World Wide Web is compromised.

Introduction

The word 'participation' has changed its meaning over time and its progressive redefinition has had clear **ideological** consequences. Although it is tempting to see such redefinitions as neutral events or as accidents of history, they are not neutral. In the case of 'participation', the strongly emancipatory and potentially critical implications of this concept—that dealt with power imbalances—have been erased from its meaning. This kind of **semantic reductionism** makes it more difficult to distinguish between the different levels and intensities of people's participation in new and old media. And, importantly, it helps obscure the sometimes unacceptable imbalances in contemporary power structures, both in media environments and in society in general. In other words, the conflation of interaction and participation makes it more difficult to see that citizens' political activities, and their efforts to secure social and cultural capital in the new media world, are not confined to the realm of traditional politics, but extend into our cultural and media spheres.

Ideology   Louis Althusser defines ideology as the system of ideas and meanings that arise as a consequence of the cultural practices and representations by which people imagine the conditions of their life. The resulting meanings are always socially constructed, since no meanings are natural or inherent to a process, object or event.

Semantic reductionism   Semantic reductionism is used here to refer to the way contemporary word usage may result in a significant loss of complexity in the meaning of a given term.

GLOSSARY

By re-analysing old and new media theories and the relationships they create between participation and the two other key concepts, access and interaction, an analytical model is developed that positions these three concepts in relation to each other. This repositioning shows the gaps and fissures in the meanings of all three concepts that often remained unaddressed. Moreover it allows revalidation of the more radical power-related aspects of participation without disregarding the fluid nature of all three.

Access and participation in traditional media theory

In the past scholars have tried to stop 'participation' from being diluted in meaning by using dichotomies like 'real' versus 'fake' or 'authentic' versus 'pseudo' to show why they believed a particular change in usage was unhelpful. In the field of political participation for example, Verba (1961, pp. 220–1) points to an awareness as early as the 1960s of the existence of 'pseudo-participation', in which the emphasis is not on creating a situation in which participation is possible, but on creating the *feeling* that participation is *possible*. An alternative concept, used by Strauss (1998, p. 18) among others, is 'manipulative participation'. Other scholars developed complex constructions of hierarchically ordered and multi-layered systems. A seminal example is found in Pateman's (1970) book *Participation and Democratic Theory*. The two definitions of participation that she introduces are 'partial' and 'full participation'. Partial participation is defined as: 'a process in which two or more parties influence each other in the making of decisions but the final power to decide rests with one party only' (Pateman, 1970, p. 70), while full participation is seen as 'a process where each individual member of a decision-making body has equal power to determine the outcome of decisions' (Pateman, 1970, p. 71).

Activity 13.1

Think of examples of where you have experienced 'full' and 'partial' participation in reaching decisions about matters that affect you and others. Look for examples from the realms of the political, the social, the cultural and the media. Look at all parties involved and chart their restrictions and capacities. Write an explanation of how you believe you can tell the difference between 'full' and 'partial' participation.

Communication as a human right

The right to communicate was originally proposed in 1969 by the French civil servant, Jean d'Arcy. A more contemporary definition can be found in Hamelink and Hoffman (2004, p. 3): 'those rights—codified in international and regional human rights instruments—that pertain to standards of performance with regard to the provision of information and the functioning of communication processes in society'.

In the 1970s, the UNESCO debates on the New World Information and Communication Order (NWICO) and the related discussions on *communication rights* proved especially important for defining the role of participation in the media system (MacBride, 1980). These documents, along with the report of the 1977 Belgrade meeting as transcript of this discussion, attempted to better define the concepts **access**, **participation** and **self-management**.

Definitions from the MacBride Report

Access is defined from a reception perspective, as 'the use of media for public service. It may be defined in terms of the opportunities available to the public to choose varied and relevant programs and to have a means of feedback to transmit its reactions and demands to production organisations' (in Servaes, 1999, p. 85). Not all authors agree with this emphasis on media reception and use. Lewis (1993, p. 12), for example, has defined access from a community media production perspective as 'the processes that permit users to provide relatively open and unedited *input* to the mass media'.

Participation is defined as follows: 'participation implies a higher level of public involvement in communication systems. It includes the involvement of the public in the production process and also in the management and planning of communication systems. Participation may be no more than representation and consultation of the public in decision-making' (from Servaes, 1999, p. 85).

Self-management is the most advanced form of participation. In this case, 'the public exercises the power of decision-making within communication enterprises and is also fully involved in the formulation of communication policies and plans' (from Servaes, 1999, p. 85).

GLOSSARY

Think about it

Is there reason for concern that the meaning of the term 'participation' appears to have lost some of its most important connotations?

Within the field of *community and alternative media*, Lewis described participatory media as the 'antibodies' of 'conventional media' (Lewis, 1993, p. 15), in that they correct the distortions and bias of mainstream media that would otherwise remain unchallenged. Servaes, a writer who is comfortable using terms like 'genuine' and 'authentic participation', believes that the 'real' form of participation has to be seen as participation '[that] directly addresses power and its distribution in society. It touches the very core of power relationships' (Servaes, 1999, p. 198). It is obvious in these definitions how crucial *power* is to the definition of participation. White emphasises a similar point, commenting that 'it appears that power and control are pivotal subconcepts which contribute to both understanding the diversity of expectations and anticipated outcomes of people's participation' (1994, p. 17).

Community radio AMARC-Europe (1994, p. 4) defines community radio as 'a non-profit station, currently broadcasting, which offers a service to the community in which it is located, or to which it broadcasts, while promoting the participation of this community in the radio'.

Access in new media theory

The arrival of yet another generation of 'new' media has drastically changed the nature of the debate about human rights and communication. One of the major differences has been the reduced emphasis on the responsibility media organisations are expected to bear in relation to their service to the public. Ordinary users, but also civil society organisations, are often assumed to have been empowered by new media because they can avoid the mediating intervention of the 'old' media organisations, and are able to publish material (almost) directly on the Web, and to establish their own communicative networks. These more active forms of participation by the public in media production have impacted on definitions of access and participation in a fundamental way. Although the key notion of participation has not vanished completely from the theoretical scene, its symbolic reach has been restricted and some of its previous meanings are now shared with the concepts *access* and *interaction*.

The importance of access, structurally, has increased with the techno-utopian assumption that everyone will have access to all information at all times (Negroponte, 1995). The critical backlash resulting from such claims has focused on the very real lack of access for particular social groups and communities. The situation where some people have access but others are excluded both from access and the cultural, social and economic benefits that result is described as 'the digital divide'. The digital divide is considered to be a problem because in general it is believed that access should be equally available to all, and because those who are unable to access the new media are also likely to be less economically productive—they are denied the economic, social and cultural benefits that flow from participation in the information society. As argued elsewhere (Carpentier, 2003) the core of the digital divide discourse is based on the articulation of three elements:

1 Recognition of the importance of access to online computers.
2 Recognition that use results in increased levels of information, knowledge, communication or other types of socially valued benefits.
3 Recognition that access and use are in turn so vital that the absence of access and the resulting 'digibetism' (or computer illiteracy) will eventually create a divided society of haves and have-nots.

In particular, unequal access to online computer technology plays a crucial role because it functions as a nodal point of the digital divide discourse. Access is central to debates about the information society, as is illustrated by the enormous amount of research documenting socio-demographically based differences in ICT access (see, for instance, the websites of the Worldbank's Global-ICT taskforce (http://www.worldbank.org/) and the US Department of Commerce (http://www.commerce.gov/). It is important to recognise, however, that this approach to the articulation of the discourse of the digital divide, with *access* as its nodal point, excludes a series of other important meanings. Here, three different excluded fields can be distinguished: skills, content and participation.

The first critique of these discursively exclusionary practices is based on the multi-dimensional character of (Internet) access and the diverse skills needed for effective engagement with the Internet. Steyaert (2002) for instance argues that 'physical access' (stressing the materiality of access) should be complemented with the different necessary skills required for the interaction with ICT. Steyaert distinguishes three types of skill associated with access: *instrumental, structural and strategic skills* that can be identified in user practices. As Silverstone (1999, p. 252) remarked on the domestication of ICT: 'The more recent history of home computing indicates that individuals in the household construct and affirm their own identities through their appropriation of the machine via processes of acceptance, resistance, and negotiation. What individuals do, and how they do it, depends on both cultural and material resources.' So physical access is only the first step. Learning how to use the computer, learning what (meaningful things) you can do online, and co-opting access into your sense of identity and capacity to make a difference in the world are equally important aspects of access.

Secondly, specifically content-oriented approaches to discussions of access focus on 'missing content', from a user perspective. This approach recognises that not enough content is available for certain social groups, who are then effectively systematically excluded from access. The Children's Partnership (2000), for instance, points to the absence of content of interest to people (living in the USA) with an underclass background, with low levels of literacy in English and with interests in local politics and local culture. They argue that, 'underserved Americans are [those] seeking the following content on the Internet: practical information focusing on local community; information at a basic literacy level; material in multiple languages; information on ethnic and cultural interests; interfaces and content accessible to people with disabilities; easier searching; and coaches to guide them.'

Thirdly, a critique aimed at a more *political* explanation of the digital divide explicitly highlights the disappearance of political connotations from 'participation'. Gandy's article entitled 'The real digital divide: citizens versus consumers', is an example. In this work, Gandy sees 'the new media as widening the distinction between the citizen and the consumer' (Gandy, 2002, p. 448). His citizens/consumers distinction refers to a 'consumer' and a 'civic model' of network activity, and he claims that the balance between both models will eventually determine the role of the Internet in post-industrial democracy. Gandy's main concern is that the 'new economy' will tip the balance towards consumerism, making the civic model redundant. This would foreclose the potential of the new media to deliver an expansion of democracy (see also Barber, 1998; Kellner, 1999). These kinds of analyses show that some of the assumptions inherent in discussions of the digital divide and in particular the concern with access are not totally uncritically accepted, and that openings could be created that would allow participation to regain its earlier meanings.

Adding 'interaction' and 'interactivity' to the debate

In the context of new media, the term **interaction** and its derived concept, **interactivity**, have come to play a significant role in the discourse on participation. In Rheingold's (1993) summary of the social impact of new media, for instance, ideas about the importance of supporting citizen activity in politics and power, of ensuring opportunities for increased interaction with diverse others, and the development of a new vocabulary and form of communication, feature prominently in the discussion of 'interaction'.

Interaction 'The exchange and negotiation of meaning between two or more participants located with social contexts' (O'Sullivan, 1994, p. 154).

Interactivity The *process* whereby interaction occurs.

Just like the concept 'participation', interaction and interactivity also have highly fluid meanings, leaving them often undefined or underdefined (McMillan, 2002, p. 164; Rafaeli, 1988, p. 110). Manovich (2001, p. 55) for example problematises the newness and broadness of the concept interactivity. He firstly argues that it can be found at work in many older cultural forms and media technologies. Secondly, he refers to the 'myth of interactivity', claiming that its meaning becomes tautological when it is used in relation to computer-based media: 'Modern HCI [or Human-Computer Interaction] is by definition interactive. [...] Therefore, to call computer media 'interactive' is meaningless—it simply means stating the most basic facts about computers.' He also points to the danger of reducing interaction to physical interaction between a user and a media object, at the expense of the psychological dimensions of interaction: 'the psychological processes of filling-in, hypothesis formation, recall, and identification, which are required for us to comprehend any text or image at all, are mistakenly identified with an objectively existing structure of interactive links' (Manovich, 2001, p. 57). In other words, interactivity is not just a matter of usage, but importantly includes cognitive and emotional processes as well.

In order to deal with this fluidity and diversity, many authors have reverted to categorising systems that distinguish between different forms of interaction (see Jensen, 1999). A first group has introduced a distinction between two broad types of interaction: person-to-person interaction and person-to-machine interaction (Carey, 1989; Hoffman et al., 1996; Lee, 2000), while others have identified three levels of interaction. Szuprowicz's (1995) distinction between user-to-user, user-to-documents and user-to-system is one of the more commonly used threefold categorisation systems.

Both the person-to-person (or user-to-user interaction) and user-to-documents interactions are hardly new, as these processes have been analysed in a diversity of academic fields such as communication studies, sociology, literary theory and cultural studies. However, user-to-system interaction is central to the new media, as it focuses on the human–computer relationship. Originally interaction was used in this tradition to describe the more user-friendly interfaces that transcended the perceived limitations of batch processing. Later human–computer interaction (HCI) research focused 'analogous to reception studies […] on the user-technology interaction, rather than the technology per se. It deals with usage of technology, or, to speak in discourse lingua, the pragmatics of technology' (Persson et al., 2000).

This focus allows us to return to the concept of interactivity, and Jensen's (1999, p. 17) definition of interactivity as 'a measure of a media's potential ability to let a user exert an influence on the content and/or form of the mediated communication.' In this definition interactivity is seen as the characteristic of specific media technologies (or systems) that incorporate the possibility of user-content and user-user interaction through the interaction between user and technology.

Some authors have attempted to bring some of the key characteristics of participation—namely power—back into the discussion of interaction and inter-activity. McMillan's (2002) important contribution to this debate is that she very explicitly links interactivity with questions of control and power. One of the important arguments here is that the relationship between the user and their 'extension' remains externally defined and can hardly be questioned. In order to theorise this reduction Penny (1995) proposes the word '**interpassivity**', echoing the above-discussed hierarchical systems that distinguish between 'real' and 'false' interaction. Rokeby (1995, p. 148) argues that interactivity is about 'encounter rather than control'. Later he continues: 'interactive media have the power to [...] expand the reach of our actions and decisions. We trade subjectivity [...] for the illusion of control; our control may appear absolute, but the domain of that control is externally defined. We are engaged, but exercise no power over the filtering language of interaction embedded in the interface' (1995, p. 154).

However valuable these attempts are, they are unable to affect the agenda of the mainstream approach to interaction. As power is not semantically articulated that strongly with interaction and interactivity, both concepts lack the analytical strength to thoroughly deal with questions of power. This does not imply that the concepts interaction and interactivity can no longer be used, but it does imply that we need to untangle the Gordian knot that traps both interaction and participation. The key to this problem is exactly the notion of balanced power, or of co-decision making, which is strongly present in the history of the concept of participation, and to a much lesser degree in the concepts of interaction and interactivity, where mainly the 'mere' exchange of meaning is at stake.

Interpassivity The 'Pavlovian interactivity of stimulus and response' (Penny, 1995, p. 54).

Editor's comment Lury (Chapter 18) is also critical of the implication of equality of status between the parties to an interaction (or the power balance) when the terms 'interaction' and 'interactivity' are used. She notes that when consumers 'interact' with brand websites, they do so in ignorance of information the brand does not wish to disclose.

Participation in new media theory

meanings of participation linked to consumer power seem under ncept has managed to maintain a presence in a number of academic ecially in alternative and community media, even though neither lds offers a dominant model for new media participation. In both ctices and the academic literature on their practices have sought to ipation (Carpentier et al., 2003) by stressing the possibility of non-nals co-deciding on issues ranging from actual programming to the ion's general policies and ownership. More importantly perhaps, the theoretical reflections on electronic democracy and new media have offered, at least at first sight, a safe haven for 'participation'. These elaborations partially continue the earlier work from participatory theorists like Barber who earlier focused on 'interactive video communications' (Barber, 1984, p. 289) but whose more recent work is about the World Wide Web:

> The World Wide Web was, in its conception and compared to traditional broadcast media, a remarkably promising means for point-to-point lateral communication among citizens and for genuine interactivity (users not merely passively receiving information, but *participating* in retrieving and creating it) (Barber, 1998, p. 81, my emphasis).

Similar analyses point to the potentially beneficial increase in information, which challenges the 'existing political hierarchy's monopoly on powerful communications media' (Rheingold, 1993, p. 14), the strengthening of social capital and civil society, and the opening up of a new **public sphere**, or a 'global electronic agora' (Castells, 2001, p. 138).

Public sphere　'By the "public sphere" we mean first of all a realm of our social life in which something approaching public opinion can be formed. Access is guaranteed to all citizens. A portion of the public sphere comes into being in every conversation in which private individuals assemble to form a public body' (Habermas, 1984, p. 49).

When this discussion is framed in the quest for more **direct and/or deliberative democracy**, the notions of power and decision-making make an especially remarkable comeback. Budge (1996, p. 1) for instance defends the move towards more direct democracy, where 'public policy can be discussed and voted upon by everyone linked in an interactive communications net'. But here the safe haven turns out to be more treacherous than expected. When such attempts to deepen democracy are contrasted with representative democracy, the entire project becomes (rightfully) vulnerable to the critique of '*technopopulism*' (Coleman & Gøtze, 2001, p. 5) and risks yet another form of discreditation. Coleman and Gøtze, for example, seek a new balance between representation and participation and manage to avoid the more dubious interpretations by explicitly referring to the OECD's (2001) three-stage model, which distinguishes information distribution and consultation from active participation. Quite similar to Pateman's work (1970), the OECD defines participation as 'a relation based on partnership with government, in which citizens actively engage in the decision- and policy-making process. It acknowledges a role for citizens in proposing policy options and shaping the policy dialogue—although the responsibility for the final decision on policy formulation rests with government' (OECD, 2001, p. 16).

GLOSSARY

Direct democracy A system where every citizen votes on every piece of legislation that comes before the parliament. The more extreme versions of direct democracy stress the repressive nature of representative democracies, and argue that representative democracy (party political democratic systems) should be replaced by the self-rule of the oppressed classes.

Deliberative democracy Jon Elster (1998, p 1) defines deliberation as 'decision-making by discussion among free and equal citizens,' which is not necessarily contradictory to a representative democracy. The argument here is that policy making, legislative debate and decision-making should be more open to input from citizens.

In this context, however, 'participation' is articulated with politics in its more traditional and narrow meaning. New media are seen as instrumental for increasing civil participation in two party politics, rather than as allowing 'participation' in a wider range of political interventions around issues like gender, race and ethnicity, age, child care, health and education, particularly when articulated through local situational politics. This restricted articulation thus confines participation to politics and inherently disconnects it from the media sphere, where only the other two concepts—access and interaction—maintain their relevance. This seriously hampers the application of participation beyond politics (in the sense of party politics), and its articulation as an emancipatory toolkit supporting pleas for more equal power balances between audiences, users and non-professionals on the one hand and the professionals from both content producing organisations (CPOs) and in technology-producing organisations (TPOs) on the other.

The Access, Interaction and Participation (AIP) Model

The following model (see Table 13.1) presents an approach that integrates the different theoretical positions on access, interaction and participation discussed in this chapter. The core structure is the distinction between production and reception. The first level deals with access in its traditional meaning, where the reductive meaning of access (as access to technology) finds its place. The other forms of access (as access to organisations and to content) are included on the second level, covering the different forms of access. The third level focuses on interaction in its different forms. Here a distinction is again made between forms of interaction: namely user-to-technology interaction, user-to-content interaction,

Table 13.1 Access, interaction and participation

Production	Reception
Level 1: ACCESS	
Access to media technology	
Possession of equipment to engage in communication, to produce content and have it published/broadcast	Possession of equipment to engage in communication and to receive relevant content
Level 2: ACCESS	
Access to the content considered relevant	
	Ability (and skills) to receive content
Access to the content- and technology-producing organisation (CPO & TPO)	
Opportunity to have the produced content published/broadcast	Providing feedback
Level 3: INTERACTION	
User-to-media technology interaction	
Ability (and skills) to use equipment to produce content	Ability (and skills) to use equipment to receive content
User-to-content interaction	
Creating content	Ability (and skills) to interpret content
User-to-user (and user-to-media professional) interaction	
Creating content	
User-to-content- or technology-producing organisation interaction (CPO & TPO)	
	Discussing content and form (feedback)
Level 4: PARTICIPATION	
Participation in the produced Content	
Co-deciding on content	Evaluating the content
Participation in the content producing organisation (CPO)	
Co-deciding on policy	
Participation in the technology producing organisation (TPO)	
Co-deciding on technology	

and user-to-user (including media professionals and organisations) interaction. The inclusion of these first three levels emphasises the specificity of participation, in particular its intimate relationship with power and the process of 'co-deciding', both at the level of the organised production of content and of technology. The fourth level demonstrates how, in the context of the World Wide Web, opportunities for participation at the level of reception are minimal. Users are able to engage in co-decision making in regard to the production of content, but excluded from opportunities for co-decision making as regards the activities of the companies and organisations that are active in the World Wide Web.

Activity 13.2

Analyse on what level and to which degree at least three of the following facilitates access, interaction and participation, using the analytical model:

a   Video Nation (http://www.bbc.co.uk/videonation/)
b   One World Radio (http://radio.oneworld.net/)
c   YouTube (http://www.youtube.com/)
d   CurrentTV (http://www.current.tv/)
e   Indymedia (http://www.indymedia.org.au/)
f   the A-Infos Radio Project (http://www.radio4all.net).
Which of these websites offers the widest range of participatory activities?

Conclusion

The arrival of the current generation of new media has resulted in a number of changes in the definitions used to refer to the terms access, participation and interaction. All are signifiers that have had a long history in communication and social sciences. Although participation has not completely disappeared from media analyses and practices, it has lost its primary role. The contrast with the other two signifiers—access and interaction—is marked. Access, interaction and interactivity have become buzzwords in the wonderful world of ICT, happily floating around (meaning everything and nothing, but still being very new).

This chapter contains a strong plea to restore to the term 'participation' its capacity to refer to political empowerment by disentangling it from access and inter-action. Although access, interaction (and interactivity) currently have a conceptual 'surplus-value', they are embedded in sophisticated models (see for instance Jensen's (1999) three-dimensional 'cube of interactivity') and therefore remain important for theorising the relationship between people and media. This chapter, however, has sought to rescue 'participation' for its capacity to direct attention—more than interaction or interactivity can ever do—to the power/knowledge relations (Foucault, 1977) that still decisively characterise traditional and new media.

Because of the emphasis on access, interaction and interactivity another fundamental division in society tends to be normalised. It is a division between those who structurally control the interface, the media organisations and the content, and those who can only gain access to it and interact with it, those whose actions are constrained by the framework that has been created by the first group. In order to theorise and analyse the differences between the 'control-haves' and 'control-have-nots', the possible forms of resistance and the blurring of the boundaries between control and non-control (within a structural power imbalance), the concept of participation remains a necessary third component for any conceptual evaluation of traditional and new media.

CHAPTER SUMMARY

- This chapter has argued that 'participation' needs to be understood and (re)used beyond politics, as part of a toolkit to analyse the power relationships between all actors involved in the digital media landscape.
- At the moment 'participation' has been displaced by emphasis on 'access' and 'interaction' in talk about new media, and analysis of the new media is the weaker for it. The demoting of 'participation' means that the politics of the World Wide Web is largely unquestioned, and its potential impact on democratic practices unexplored.
- In response to this exclusion, and as an attempt at redress it, the developed AIP-model offers a visual representation of the need to bridge both societal and political (power) divisions. When put to use it shows the gaps and fissures that remain often unaddressed in dealing with the traditional and new media.
- By reintroducing the term 'participation' into new media studies, the study of embedded power imbalances will again be normalised in the analysis of the media.

Tutorial questions

- What did the term 'participation' encompass in its earlier usages?
- What are the similarities and differences between 'participation' and 'access'?
- What are the similarities and differences between 'participation' and 'interaction'?
- What might be the consequences if the political meanings associated with the term 'participation' are lost?

Recommended reading

Manovich, L., 2001, *The Language of New Media*, MIT Press, Cambridge.
Pateman, C., 1970, *Participation and Democratic Theory*, Cambridge University Press, Cambridge.
White, S., 1994, *Participatory Communication: Working for Change and Development*, Sage, Beverly Hills.

Websites

A-Infos Radio Project: www.radio4all.net
CurrentTV: www.current.tv
Indymedia: www.indymedia.org.au
One World Radio: www.radio.oneworld.net
US Department of Commerce: www.commerce.gov/
Video Nation: www.bbc.co.uk/videonation
YouTube: www.youtube.com

References

AMARC-Europe, 1994, 'One Europe—Many Voices: Democracy and access to communication', conference report AMARC-Europe Pan-European conference of community radio broadcasters, Ljubljana, Slovenia, 15–18 September 1994, AMARC, Sheffield.
Barber, B., 1998, *A Place for Us: How to Make Society Civil and Democracy Strong*, Hill and Wang, New York.
Barber, B., 1984, *Strong Democracy. Participatory Politics for a New Age*, University of California Press, Berkeley.
Budge, I., 1996, *The Challenge of Direct Democracy*, Polity, Cambridge.
Carey, J., 1989, 'Interactive Media', in *International Encyclopaedia of Communications*, Oxford University Press, New York.
Carpentier, N., 2003, 'Access and Participation in the Discourse of the Digital Divide: The European Perspective at/on the WSIS', in Servaes, J. (ed.) *The European Information Society: A Reality Check*, Intellect, Bristol, UK and Portland, USA.
Carpentier, N., Lie, R., & Servaes, J., 2003, 'Community Media—Muting the Democratic Media Discourse?', *Continuum*, Vol. 17, No. 1, pp. 51–68.
Castells, M., 2001, *The Internet Galaxy: Reflections on the Internet, Business, and Society*, Oxford University Press, Oxford.
Children's Partnership, 2000, *Online Content for Low-Income and Underserved Americans: An Issue Brief*, Los Angeles/Washington, Children's Partnership, http://www.childrenspartnership.org

Coleman, S. & Gøtze, J., 2001, *Bowling Together: Online Public Engagement in Policy Deliberation*, The Hansard Society, London.

Elster, J., 1998, 'Introduction' in Elster, J. (ed.), *Deliberative Democracy*, Cambridge University Press, Cambridge.

Foucault, M., 1978, *History of Sexuality, Part 1: An Introduction*, Pantheon, New York.

Gandy, O., 2002, 'The Real Digital Divide: Citizens Versus Consumers', in Lievrouw, L. & Livingstone, S. (eds) *The Handbook of the New Media: The Social Shaping and Consequences of ICTs*, Sage, London.

Habermas, J., 1984, 'The Public Sphere: An Encyclopaedia Article (1964)', *New German Critique* (Autumn), pp. 49–55.

Hamelink, C. J., & Hoffman, J., 2004, *Assessing the Status Quo on Communication Rights*, Preliminary Report, University of Amsterdam, Amsterdam.

Hoffman, D., Novak, T., & Schlosser, A., 1996, 'The Evolution of the Digital Divide: How Gaps in Internet Access May Impact Electronic Commerce', *Journal of Computer Mediated Communication*, Vol. 5, No. 3.

Jensen, J., 1999, 'The Concept of "Interactivity" in Digital Television', in Beute, B., Dorman, C., Jensen, J.F., Olesen, H. & Rose, M. (eds) *White Paper on Interactive TV. IM Publications No. 4*, Intermedia, Aarhus, Denmark.

Kellner, D., 1999, 'Technologies, Welfare State, and Prospects for Democratisation' in Calabrese, A. & Burgelman, J. (eds), *Communication, Citizenship and Social Policy*, Rowman/Littlefield, Lanham.

Lee, J. S., 2000, 'Interactivity: A New Approach', paper presented at the 2000 Convention of the Association for Education in Journalism and Mass Communication, Phoenix, Arizona.

Lewis, P., 1993, 'Alternative Media in a Contemporary Social and Theoretical Context', in Lewis, P. (ed.) *Alternative Media: Linking Global and Local*, UNESCO, Paris.

MacBride, S., 1980, *Many Voices, One World: Report by the International Commission for the Study of Communication Problems*, UNESCO & Kogan Page, Paris and London.

Manovich, L., 2001, *The Language of New Media*, MITPress, Cambridge.

McMillan, S., 2002, 'Exploring Models of Interactivity from Multiple Research Traditions: Users, Documents and Systems', in: Lievrouw, L. & Livingstone, S. (eds) *The Handbook of the New Media: The Social Shaping and Consequences of ICTs*, Sage, London.

National Telecommunications and Information Administration (NTIA), 1999, 'Falling Through the Net: Defining the Digital Divide', NTIA, Washington, downloaded on 7 September 2006 from http://www.ntia.doc.gov/ntiahome/fttn99/

Negroponte, N., 1995, *Being Digital*, Knopf, New York.

OECD, 2001, *Citizens as Partners: Information, Consultation and Public Participation in Policy-Making*, OECD, PUMA.

O'Sullivan, T., 1994, 'Interaction/Social Interaction' in O'Sullivan, T., Hartley, J., Saunders, D., Montgomery, M. & Fiske, J. (eds), *Key Concepts in Communication and Cultural Studies*, Routledge, London and New York.

Pateman, C., 1970, *Participation and Democratic Theory*, Cambridge University Press, Cambridge.

Penny, S., 1995, 'Consumer Culture and the Technological Imperative', in Penny, S. (ed.), *Critical Issues in Electronic Media,* State University of New York Press, New York.

Persson, P., Höök, K. & Simsarian, K., 2000, 'Human–Computer Interaction versus Reception Studies: Objectives, Methods and Ontologies', paper presented at NorFA Research Seminar Reception: Film, TV, Digital Culture, Department of Cinema Studies, Stockholm University 4–7 June.

Rafaeli, S., 1988, 'Interactivity: From New Media to Communication', in Hawkins, R.P. & Wiemann, J.M. (eds), *Advancing Communication Science: Merging Mass & Interpersonal Processes*, Sage, Newbury Park, CA.

Rheingold, H., 1993, *The Virtual Community: Homesteading on the Electronic Frontier*, Addison-Wesley, Reading.

Rokeby, D., 1995, 'Transforming Mirrors: Subjectivity and Control in Interactive Media', in Penny, S. (ed.), *Critical Issues in Electronic Media,* State University of New York Press, New York.

Servaes, J., 1999, *Communication for Development: One World, Multiple Cultures*, Cresskill, Hampton Press, New Jersey.

Silverstone, R., 1999, 'Domesticating ICTs', in Dutton, W. (ed.) *Society on the Line: Information Politics in the Digital Age,* Oxford University Press. Oxford.

Steyaert, J., 2002, 'Inequality and the Digital Divide: Myths and Realities', in Hick, S. & McNutt, J. (eds) *Advocacy, Activism, and the Internet: Community Organization and Social Policy*, Lyceum Press, New York.

Strauss, G., 1998, 'An Overview', in Heller, F., Pusic, E., Strauss, G. & Wilpert, B. (eds), *Organizational Participation: Myth and Reality*, Oxford University Press, New York.

Szuprowicz, B., 1995, *Multimedia Networking*, McGraw-Hill, New York.

Verba, S., 1961, *Small Groups and Political Behaviour*, Princeton University Press, Princeton.

White, S., 1994, *Participatory Communication: Working for Change and Development*, Sage, Beverly Hills.

Acknowledgment: The author would like to acknowledge the support of the Flemish Community (Policy Research Centres Program—Programma Steunpunten voor Beleidsrelevant Onderzoek) in the preparation of this chapter. This text contains the views of the author and not the views of the Flemish Community. The Flemish Community cannot be held accountable for the potential use of the communicated views and data.

Universal Access in South Africa: Broadening Communication or Building Infrastructure?

SIMON BURTON AND ANTON VAN DER HOVEN

14

CHAPTER OVERVIEW

Although the new media have, since their inception and initial dissemination, been intertwined with ideologies of progress and development, it is increasingly recognised that the social context at large and the imperatives of local everyday life are important, even crucial, factors in the uptake of information technologies. As a result, the determinism often underpinning the more celebratory accounts of the new media needs now to be qualified by the recognition that social factors always make the social integration of new technologies open-ended, provisional and peculiarly vulnerable to unintended consequences (Silverstone, 2005, p. 5). The following discussion of information and communication technologies (ICTs) in the South Africa situation will show that this is as true in the context of a developing country as it is in the so-called first world (Silverstone, 2005).

Key terms

ICTs
universal access
telecentres
participation
domestication
affordances
everyday life

Issues

- If you had the task of developing a communications infrastructure for a whole nation, how central would the concept of 'universal access' be for your planning?
- What dangers might 'technological determinism' pose for the uptake of new technologies?
- How would you go about balancing the difference between introducing digital technologies and expanding traditional media services?

Communication in the 'new' South Africa

'A whole new world of opportunities and information'

SAFM Media Programme, 10 September, 2006, On 'The Extension of ICTs to Rural Areas'
Albi Modise, Spokesperson, South African Department of Communications

The transition from a white-ruled apartheid state to the fully fledged democracy of the 'new' South Africa, led by the iconic figure of Nelson Mandela, has been hailed as one of the miracles of the late twentieth century, not only because it was, to a remarkable degree, achieved peacefully, but also because the contesting parties were able to agree to a new constitution that is one of the most progressive in the world.

One of the key characteristics of the South African transition has been its 'bottom up' character. This has its origins in the mass movement nature of resistance to apartheid that was lead by the Congress of South African Trade Unions (COSATU) and the United Democratic Front (an umbrella organisation made up of a wide range of community and sector-specific organisations) who, in conjunction with the externally based liberation movement, the African National Congress, brought the new South Africa into existence in 1994. Some twelve years down the line South Africa remains a society with many tensions: it is deeply divided along somewhat revised class lines, but is firmly committed to the maintenance and strengthening of its democratic institutions. The discourses of mass participation, poverty alleviation, empowerment and rural upliftment have remained central since 1994 and permeate not only government discourse but also that of the opposition parties, not to mention the contributions of COSATU affiliates and other trade unions, civic organisations and more conventional left-wing groupings such as the globally connected Anti-Privatisation Forum.

These political dynamics are also visible in the development of the media in South Africa. Here we have witnessed a change from a tightly controlled state broadcast system supplemented by a small but frequently harassed alternative press to a far more open terrain characterised by a commitment to public broadcasting and a diverse, increasingly black-empowered private industry. However, it also needs to be pointed out that the emerging **neo-liberal** ethos has not been kind to the media in South Africa. A gradual shift to market-dominated, stakeholder-driven policy and a less than adequately skilled bureaucracy manifestly struggling to implement communications policy, have all but overwhelmed the ideological motivations that shaped both the pre-liberation media landscape and the post-liberation commitment to a new **participatory media regime**.

Within this context Information and Communications Technologies (ICTs) have emerged as a particularly important aspect of South African communications policy since here, as elsewhere in the developing world, the state has seen digital technologies, and the diverse range of communication possibilities (such as e-government and e-commerce) as key factors in democratising public communication and harnessing it for development purposes. As Van Audenhove writes,

> Put rather simply, South Africa's political leaders share the vision that ICT's can help to overcome some of the legacies of apartheid. Especially in the area of services, ICT's are identified as facilitators in the restructuring of sectors and as the means of delivering services not readily available, through tele-education, tele-health, tele-government etc. This vision is based on a central belief in the possibilities of ICT's for social change (1999, p. 47).

The mobilisation of ICTs for development and redressing past injustices has centred on the idea of **universal service** and the practical problems associated with broadening connectivity to all areas of South Africa. The Telecommunications Act of 1996 provided for the creation of the Universal Service Agency (USA) whose task it would be to establish a **telecentre** movement in South Africa that would develop universal access as a first step towards universal service.

see Dwyer, Chapter 3; Lax, Chapter 12

Theory link

Neo-liberalism The rival of doctrines of the 'free market' in the United States in the late 1970s, and a social and economic theory that argues that completely free and open markets are the best way of ordering society. Thus it is a return to a once discredited liberalism in political economics, the nineteenth-century espousal of *laissez faire* economics for free trade in an international division of labour, and minimal state intervention within the nation. For governments in the West, from the 1940s through to the 1970s, it was the conventional wisdom that capitalism had to be managed by the state, and that rewards needed to be equalised through welfare entitlements in order to maintain social cohesion (see McGuigan, 2005, p. 230).

Participatory media regime A set of formal and informal rules that regulate the operation of the media system.

Universal service Access to ICTs within all individual dwellings. It implies a level of resources and infrastructure not usually present in the developing world; universal access is access to shared facilities and thus requires that users must leave their homes if they wish to make use of the ICTs.

GLOSSARY

Funding for the telecentre movement is provided by statutory transfers from private telecommunications operators. While it became clear that there were major shortcomings in the framework of telecentre rollout, the USA nevertheless began setting up pilot telecentres and at last count was instrumental (along with a range of partners, donor agencies included) in developing sixty-five centres with varying degrees of success throughout South Africa (Benjamin 2001, p. 32). These evolving state initiatives have now hybridised telecenters into digital villages, multi-purpose community centres and e-learning centres (Lesame, 2005, pp. 25–6), but questions remain as to how adequate to the task they will be.

Paradoxically, the participatory model has made it even more difficult for the state to implement its programmes. In order to enfranchise the formerly disenfranchised there has been a huge thrust to changing the civil service and state bureaucracy from its previous control by conservative white **Afrikaners** to the newly-enfranchised black majority. But frequently these new employees do not have the same levels of skill or experience as those they have replaced. The result is a double bind: those who are most willing to deliver often do not have the capacity to do so. As James (2001) has argued in respect of telecentres, lack of resources, both human and material, has plagued the implementation of an effective ICT policy.

Afrikaners   The white, Afrikaans-speaking ethnic group who ruled South Africa from 1948 until 1994.

Among other things, James points out that:

- Policy has not been supported with the resources necessary for proper implementation, and the USA, in particular, has encountered serious problems with collecting funds from both operators and the Treasury (2001, p. 87).
- The USA has suffered from a serious lack of capacity and 'far from sufficient attention has been paid to the lack of institutional capacity' (2001, p. 87); in addition, a weak and ineffective regulator has not been able to fulfil functions 'essential to the successful realisation of policy objectives' (2001, p. 88).
- These difficulties have been caused by serious human resource skills constraints; in South Africa, the understanding of ICT's and of the procedures of policy making and implementation are 'extremely low', and the lack of human resources in ICTs in government is partially explained by the high remuneration offered in the private sector (2001, p. 89).

- Information and research on the working of the telecommunications sector is not readily available in the public domain, nor are certain areas well understood (for example, the use of ICTs, especially by disadvantaged groups), and this lack of good data to establish benchmarks makes effective monitoring extremely difficult (2001, p. 89); indeed, a pilot scheme was broadened into a full rollout program without the necessary budget or management skills in place (2001, p. 79).

These are, indeed, all serious difficulties that will require honest attention and substantial resourcing if the state is serious in its commitment to extending access to ICTs as a viable medium for social development in the 'new' South Africa.

The view that 'external' issues such as access, funding, and proper management are the key to the successful mobilisation of ICTs in South Africa is certainly the dominant one. Albi Modise, spokesperson for the Department of Communication and quoted as an epigraph to this section of the chapter, sees rural South Africa as poised on the threshold of 'a whole world of opportunities and information' now that ICTs are being deployed. Perhaps more surprisingly, this is also the dominant view among researchers in South Africa. N.C. Lesame, the editor of a recent South African publication, *New Media: Technology and Policy in Developing Countries*, argues that '[o]nly when most people have access to ICT's will the digital divide be reduced, if not bridged' (Lesame, 2005, p. 12), while, in the same volume, Mmusi, drawing conclusions in 'Telecentres and their Potential for Rural Community Development,' writes that '[t]he USA in South Africa should improve its rollout of telecentres and should train telecentre managers in technical and financial management skills. This will help avoid telecentre closure and ensure that managers learn the business management strategies necessary to sustain these centres' (Mmusi, 2005, p. 173).

Benjamin, on the other hand, is one of a far smaller group who are more sceptical of current government policy. Writing in 2001 he comments that the USA, because it has been too narrowly focused on providing ICT technology, has 'unintentionally ... created dependency and stifled local adaptation and ownership' and that 'top down planning is very unlikely to achieve bottom up development' (2001, p. 37). The research described below is sympathetic to Benjamin's view, although we question precisely what is meant by terms such as 'local adaptation' and 'bottom up development'. Are these simply terms pointing to the need for closer consultation with the communities involved, or do they suggest that we need to change our epistemological approach to the question of ICT usage, from one that assumes that technologies guarantee their 'proper' use to one that regards them as 'symbolic objects .... [that are] .... constituted in and through everyday practices of both production and consumption' as Silverstone has argued (Silverstone, 2005, p. 4).

Think about it

- Do you think it's better to establish telecentres and hope that people will be able to understand how they will benefit local communities, or to wait until local communities ask for this type of media infrastructure?
- In what ways might a communications technology centre be a better infrastructure investment than a radio or television centre or even a newspaper office?

Case study

The telecentre at Bhamshela

Bhamshela is a small urban node about 90 kilometres east of Pietermaritzburg, South Africa, in an area called Ozwathini. It comprises a few shops, a school, and a couple of government buildings that service a scattered rural population (approx. 20,000) in what used to be the non-independent **homeland** of Kwa-Zulu. Along with many similar rural settlements, there is little formal employment in Bhamshela, few NGOs and it bears the scars of political conflict in the late 1980s and early 1990s.

The telecentre established in Bhamshela was owned by two community groups, the Bhamshela Arts and Culture Group and the Open Window Network (a Cape Town-based NGO with a chapter in Bhamshela). The centre was launched in 1998 but closed in late 2001 owing to the disconnection of the phone lines by Telkom, the product of unpaid bills and unresolved management issues. Despite its closure, surveys categorised the Bhamshela telecentre as 'successful' and, up until mid 2001 it was regarded as such by the centre's management staff themselves (Benjamin and Stavrou, 2000; Espitia, 2001). It is currently waiting relocation to a newly constructed

. . . ⟩

GLOSSARY

Homeland A geographical area designated by the previous white-minority rulers as an area for settlement by black ethnic groups. Homelands were intended to be independent but some groups, including the Zulus, rejected this self-rule as tokenism. Homelands make up a total of 13 per cent of the land in South Africa.

Telecentre In South Africa, a telecentre is a facility offering communication services such as email and Internet services, but also basic telephony, typing, photocopying and faxing.

Multi-Purpose Community Centre (see below) to be managed by the Government Communication and Information Service.

The difficulties faced by this telecentre (many of which are endemic to the telecentre phenomenon in South Africa, as identified in the *Telecentre 2000* and *Community ICT Survey*), included the following:

- The computing and Internet services offered at the centre were under-utilised and not regarded as relevant by the general population of the area; phoning, faxing and photocopying became the main activities.
- Insufficient attention was paid to the 'natural allies' of the centre, such as learners and business people and, notwithstanding discussion of a resource centre and library, little effort was made to integrate the centre's services with other local initiatives.
- The services at the centre were expensive, given the high unemployment in the area; this meant that telephone revenue was the mainstay of the centre.
- Training of centre staff (which was conducted by the USA) was inadequate, and staff turnover contributed to a lack of skills (particularly as far as computers were concerned).
- No planning for technical problems and their solution was ever undertaken, resulting in long periods when key technologies were unavailable (for example, the printer and the fax machine).
- No serious monitoring or evaluation of the impact of the centre was ever undertaken.

In effect, the Bhamshela telecentre functioned as a phone shop—with idle computers, few linkages to the local community and without a clear sense of its information role in the community itself, let alone more broadly. According to Benjamin (2001, p. 33), problems of this nature would account for the failure of about half of the telecentres surveyed in late 2000.

Subsequent research on the Bhamshela telecentre, including interviews with the centre's two managers as well as a number of structured attempts to gauge community understandings of the role the centre could and did play, has shown that:

- The discursive gap between the dominant ICT rhetoric that sees telecentres as the first step in developing a working 'information society' and the consciousness of ordinary community members, including the youth, is extremely wide. The view that computers could act as a panacea for marginalisation and under development was largely unsupported by the reality of the centre's activities.
- The initial interest and enthusiasm of the local Arts and Culture Group, which had been a key factor in the establishment of the centre, soon dissipated

$\longrightarrow$

into factionalism as part-time employment at the telecentre was given to some community members and not to others. Indeed, what initially promised to empower the community by increasing the resources available to it turned into disempowerment, as the general functioning of a number of existing civil organisations went into general decline when the promises of training in computers and general administration failed to materialise.

- Their dedication and resourcefulness notwithstanding, the centre's two managers showed little progress towards fulfilling the 'infomediary' role so often imagined in the literature, and regarded as an essential aspect of ICT use in a development context (Heeks, 1999).

- It thus became apparent that the telecentre, while certainly making life easier for many community members (by providing telephones that could be used in emergencies and to contact relatives, a fax machine that could be used to send CVs to potential employers and, less frequently, word-processing for community notices), had no real impact on the existing social infrastructure and circulation of authoritative information. In the day-to-day lives of Bhamshela residents, traditional (tribal) community leaders continued to be regarded as the most trustworthy and relevant sources of information.

It should be clear that these latter points suggest that there are problems of a different order from those usually discussed, when policy concerning telecentres in a development context is drawn up, or reasons for its failure canvassed. The usual approach focuses on access and infrastructure, training and capacity, all instances of what Stavrou calls 'externalities' (2001, p. 5). This research suggests that such an approach is unlikely to reach the heart of the matter. As Gillwald has suggested, 'behind many of the policies and implementation strategies in South Africa has been ... **technological fetishism**' and that, 'laudable as [the government's] intentions are, millions of rands have been spent fruitlessly on getting technology into telecentres, multi-purpose community centres and the like, without any attempt to contextualize their usage' (2001, p. 180). Indeed, focusing more clearly on the dynamics of contextualisation rather than on external contingencies is likely to take us a lot further towards understanding the failure of the telecentre at Bhamshela.

Theory link

see McGuigan, Chapter 1; Goggin and Newell, Chapter 6; Wasserman, Chapter 8; Lax, Chapter 12

Technological fetishism An almost supernatural belief in the power of technology to change the world. It is a more extreme version of 'technological determinism'.

Discussion and analysis

In order to understand the events at Bhamshela we need to get beyond description of external factors and, as Gillwald suggests, focus more closely on the context in which the technology has been introduced. But how are we to understand a context that is made up of a combination of a rural community and the machines that embody some of the latest computer technologies?

Media determinism

A useful first step will be to briefly rehearse the long-standing media debate between the media determinists and the anti-determinists. The strong determinist position argues that provision of a technology (in this case, computers) is sufficient for its appropriate use: introduce a technology and it will 'naturally' lead to its productive use. This view is implicit in the USA policy discussed above that has been designed around the view that one simply has to make the technology as widely available as possible and that it will be appropriately used. If this policy fails then it is because of external factors, from poor access to poor maintenance, to poor training. If these problems can be overcome, then development will follow and South Africa will find itself a fully-fledged participant in the information age.

The opposing anti-determinist position locates appropriate media use not in the technology itself but exclusively in the goals of the people who use them. Raymond Williams, for example, writes that 'all technologies have been developed and improved to help with known human practices or with foreseen and desired practices ... A technology, when it is achieved, can be seen as a general human property, an extension of a general human capacity'(Williams, 1974, p. 129). In this view, technology plays a secondary role in social development, facilitating practices that are already 'known' or 'foreseen'. In other words, the strong anti-determinist position conceptualises human beings as free, rational subjects who are largely unshaped by their cultural context and come, pre-equipped as it were, with a universal set of known capacities with which technology can assist them. Stavrou has just such a view of people when he writes that the provision of computers in under-developed communities will provide 'contextually relevant, easily accessible and affordable information [that] should reduce uncertainty'; conversely, 'groups who do not have access to information ... [experience] a dramatic increase in the transaction cost component of any economic activity and a drastic decrease in their ability to exercise their social and political rights' (Stavrou, 2001, p. 6). This is, he concludes, because 'information is central to the solution of any society's economic and social problems, and as such should be regarded as a factor of production' (op. cit.). The difficulty with this position is that it asks us to understand the events at Bhamshela as instances either of idleness or backwardness—the residents of Bhamshela lacked the will to make the telecentre work and/or are insufficiently rational in their approach to it. Such a view will not take us very far: rather than constructively addressing the problem it merely reiterates it, but this time by condescendingly regarding the potential users as incompetent.

Neither of these positions is useful in understanding the difficulties faced when attempting to extend universal access to communities that are deeply marked by custom and tradition, poverty and low levels of education. What is needed is a more nuanced way of analysing the relationship between human subjects and technologies. In particular we will look at two concepts, *affordances* and *everyday life*, which will allow us to negotiate a more useful path between the potential possibilities that a technology can provide (such as access to jobs, individual and community development, etc.) and the actual uses to which the technology is put. In so doing we may be able to come to a better understanding of why it is that technologies do not get taken up in under-developed communities, despite the fact that they could prove extremely useful.

Affordances

The term *affordances* was initially introduced by the theorist of perception, J.J. Gibson (1979) in order to designate the possibilities of action that an object or environment offers. It has subsequently been developed by Hutchby (2001) in his efforts to explore the relationship between forms of technology and structures of social interaction. Beginning by arguing against the view that a technology has no intrinsic properties, and becomes 'useful' only when humans make it so, Hutchby suggests that technologies do have intrinsic capacities (or affordances), which are a determining factor in their use but are also always only realised in particular contexts (2001, p. 26):

> Technologies do not impose themselves on society, mechanistically altering the pattern of human relations and social structures. Neither does human agency encounter technologies as blank states. Technologies do not make humans; but humans make what they do of technologies in the interface between the organized practices of human conversation and the technology's array of communicative affordances (2001, p. 26).

On the one hand this points to the fact that technologies do have determining properties; they are not free potentialities whose use is wholly secondary to the subject interacting with them. On the other hand, the mere presence of a technology does not guarantee the uses to which it will be put. Some of these uses may coincide with those envisaged by the manufacturer, but others may not. In the case of new ICTs at a telecentre, the affordances are partially functional and partially symbolic. The computer cannot, for example, be used as a bicycle, but it can be used as a status symbol, a signifier of modernity, for a particular community and this even if it doesn't work. Research at Bhamshela shows that the majority of 'users' are not able to say exactly what the computers (particularly the Internet) can do for them (see also Wilson, 2001). Indeed, most people in the community don't even know what information it is that they lack. Thus we find that at Bhamshela, where there is currently no electricity, the computers are nevertheless being used for 'training'—or perhaps even just a reason to meet socially.

Nevertheless, the telecentre in Bhamshela does offer the community a set of *symbolic affordances* beyond the functional use of the centre for phoning, faxing and printing. These could include affordances for: politically motivated individuals to further their interests; new collectivities to form; new circuits of information (networks) to be created; increased job opportunities; access to donor funding; insertion into a status hierarchy; and, possibly, new vision of hope.

Symbolic affordances are important because they offer social or ideological rather than direct practical value.

It is difficult to predetermine these affordances without understanding the particular community into which the technology has been placed. In addition, novice users would probably require a period of exploration or 'play' in which they might discover which of the technology's functions and capacities are relevant to them, before one could start developing independent notions of productive use.

This poses an enormous challenge to communication researchers and policy makers because it means that they must go beyond the normal practice of determining and codifying 'best practice'. Interaction with communities and in-depth qualitative research into information need as they are perceived by those on the ground is equally necessary.

Everyday life

Affordances are not, however, primarily the constructions of individual users; they emerge within and are shaped by particular forms of life. As Rubinstein (2001, p. 139) argues, it is primarily collective practices that enable things such as opportunities. While the concept of everyday life is more often associated with modern urban living than with rural village communities, nevertheless it is useful in this context. *Everyday life* is a term used to describe the ordinary processes of communal life and includes the forming and maintenance of daily routines, including family relationships, cultural practices and the organisation of the spaces in which people make daily sense of their lives (Lister et al., 2003, p. 220). Typically, engagement with the media takes place in this sphere of the everyday and, as the concept of affordances has already made clear, it is not possible to decide beforehand to what extent everyday life is transformed or constrained by the media that enter it.

Forms of life The way a people live, which, according to the philosopher Wittgenstein who first used the term, has a profound affect on the way they understand the world.

In the South African context it is clear that traditional social structures play an important role in the circulation of information, particularly in the rural areas. Parallel work conducted at another site (the Multi-Purpose Community Centre at Mbazwana) indicates clearly that information needs cannot be separated from the general way in which the community is organised and, in particular, the importance of traditional authority in structuring and mediating knowledge. Members of the Bhamshela community are neither rational actors making calculations that will reduce uncertainty nor are they, to put it more colloquially, savvy, independent knowledge surfers able to 'play' the knowledge economy.

Conclusion

The South African government has recently shifted its emphasis away from the establishment of telecentres to the creation of Multi-Purpose Community Centres (MPCCs). In addition to housing a telecentre facility, these bigger centres will incorporate other government services—related to health, safety and security, welfare social grants and identity documentation—to local communities. It is envisaged that by 2014, every one of the 274 existing municipalities will have an MPCC. This partial shift in emphasis, from providing a communication infrastructure to delivering services, is likely to raise new policy questions and practical difficulties, especially regarding capacity and coordination across government departments. For this reason, questions concerning infrastructure and the 'externalities' of training and management and security are likely to continue to dominate the policy arena.

It is unlikely, therefore, that there will be much serious engagement with the nature and needs of the potential users of such facilities. But the question of universal access will not go away; indeed this new approach will only serve to raise further questions about the kinds of information that people, like those living in Bhamshela, will find useful. The work of Leach (2001) and Menou (2003) indicates that it is only through lengthy processes of face-to-face interaction that potential users are able to begin to grasp the opportunities or envisaged affordances associated with higher levels of information. What the Bhamshela case study shows is that the provision of a communication infrastructure does not guarantee appropriate use; on the contrary, such uses have to be developed in a complex negotiation in which the technologies themselves are inserted into the everyday life of the people who are going to use them.

This chapter has examined the attempts the South African government has made to establish telecentres as part of its strategy to provide universal access to ICTs to all levels of South African society. This has included:

- introducing the South African context;
- explaining the strategic action proposed to provide universal access to ICTs in South Africa—the telecentre strategy;
- presenting a case study of what happened to one such centre at Bhamshela In the Kwa-Zulu homeland;
- analysing the case study and presenting an argument as to why providing access without appropriate preparation and skilling of the local populations may be a recipe for failure.

CHAPTER SUMMARY

Tutorial questions

- This chapter has been about the provision and use of ICTs in rural South Africa, but it has made general points about the social use of technology and its application to urban areas as well. What are the social features which shape the acceptance and use of ICTs (a) in the city (b) among students?
- ICTs can only be fully understood when they are seen as part of the everyday life of those who use them. Consider the uses that people in your community make of the following technologies, paying particular attention to how they adapt them to the imperatives of their everyday lives: mobiles, MP3 players; digital cameras.

Recommended reading

Chaney, D., 2002, *Cultural Change and Everyday Life,* Palgrave, Basingstoke.

Dant, T., 2005, *Materiality and Society,* Open University Press, Maidenhead, Berkshire.

Horwitz, R.B., 2001, *Communication and Democratic Reform in South Africa,* Cambridge University Press, Cambridge.

Websites

International Development Research Centre, *Telecentres, Access and Development:* www.idrc.ca/en/ev-88200-201-1-DO_TOPIC.html

Multi-purpose Community Centres: www.southafrica.info/public_services/citizens/services_gov/mpcc.htm

References

Benjamin, P., 2001, 'Telecentres in South Africa', *The Journal of Development Communication* 12 (2).

Benjamin, P. & Stavrou, I., 2000, *Telecentre 2000 Synthesis Report,* paper presented at the Telecentre Learning Workshop in 2001, Johannesburg, convened by the International Development Research Centre (IDRC).

Espitia, D., 2001, *Community ICT Survey,* paper presented at the Telecentre Learning Workshop in 2001, Johannesburg, convened by the International Development Research Centre (IDRC).

Gibson, J.J., 1979, *The Ecological Approach to Visual Perception,* Houghton Mifflin, Boston.

Gillwald, A., 2001, 'Building Castells in the Ether', in Muller, J., Cloete, N. & Badat, S. (eds), 2001, *Challenges to Globalisation: South African Debates with Manuel Castells,* Maskew Miller Longman, Cape Town.

Heeks, R., 1999, Information and Communication Technologies, Poverty and Development, Institute for Development Policy and Management, University of Manchester, available at http://idpm.man.ac.uk/idpm/diwpf5.htm

Hutchby, I., 2001, *Conversation and Technology: From the Telephone to the Internet,* Polity, Cambridge.

James, T. (ed.), 2001, *An Information Policy Handbook for Southern Africa,* International Development Research Centre, Ottawa.

Leach, A. 2001. 'The Best Thing is Communicating Verbally: NGO Information Provision in Rural KwaZulu-Natal', in Stilwell, C., Leach, A. & Burton, S., *Knowledge, Information and Development: An African Perspective,* University of Natal, School of Human and Social Studies, Pietermaritzburg.

Lesame, N.C. (ed.), 2005, *New Media: Technology and Policy in Developing Countries,* Van Schaik, Pretoria.

Lister, M., Dovey, J., Giddings, S., Grant, I. & Kelly, K., 2003, *New Media: A Critical Introduction,* Routledge, London.

McGuigan, J., 2005, 'Neoliberalism, Culture and Policy', *International Journal of Cultural Policy,* Vol. 11, No. 3.

Menou, M., 2003, 'Telecentres', in Feather, J. & Sturges, P. (eds) *International Encyclopedia of Information and Library Science,* Routledge, London.

Mmusi, S.O., 2005, 'Telecentres and their Potential for Rural Community Development', in Lesame, 2005, pp. 155–75.

Rubinstein, D., 2001, *Culture, Structure and Agency: Toward a Truly Multidimensional Society,* Sage, London.

Silverstone, R. (ed.), 2005, *Media, Technology and Everyday Life in Europe: From Information to Communication,* Ashgate, Aldershot.

Stavrou, I., 2001, 'Information for Underdeveloped Communities,' paper presented at the IDRC Telecentre Learning Workshop, Johannesburg.

Van Audenhove, 1999, 'South Africa's Information Society Policy: An Overview', in *Communicatio* 25(1 & 2), UNISA Press.

Williams, R., 1974, *Television, Technology and Culture,* Fontana, London.

Wilson, M., 2001, 'Information and Communication Technology, Development and the Production of "Information Poverty"', unpublished M.Phil Thesis, Oxford University.

TIM DWYER

15

Dimensions in Media Diversity

Key terms

internal pluralism
external pluralism
structural diversity
cultural diversity

Issues

- What does 'diversity' mean in the context of media policy?
- How is 'internal' diversity different from 'structural' diversity?
- Does more content choice in new media necessarily equate to greater diversity?
- Why is 'diversity' a desirable media policy objective in democracies?

CHAPTER OVERVIEW

This chapter explores the different meanings of *diversity* that recur in media policy debates. In these debates particular vested policy interests are often talking at cross-purposes, and not comparing similar media categories. It is argued that the concepts that underpin these different categories of 'diversity' have different contributions to make in pluralistic democratic media systems. Although new media platforms can be an important source of content output for audiences, they may not necessarily lead to the provision of more diversified content. Often, for example, news and opinions that are first disseminated in a traditional media platform such as a newspaper, or on broadcast television or radio, will simply then be remediated via an online outlet owned by the first platform.

Introduction

In media policy debates the term *diversity* is invoked for a variety of reasons, and these can have quite different meanings (Nightingale and Dwyer, 2005, pp. 109–29; Hitchens, 2006, p. 9). As a rationale for media ownership regulation, the desirability of diversity in ownership stems from fears of a media dominated by one or a few powerful voices (Gibbons, 1998, p. 205), an over-representation of certain political viewpoints, or the dissemination of news reflecting the self-interest of owners (Doyle, 2002, p.. 13). However, in broader media policy debate the definition of diversity is dependent on varied, and at times competing, policy objectives. As well as the notion of a variety of views and opinion, particularly in relation to news and current affairs content, *diversity* has also been defined as:

- an inclusive representation of a culturally diverse Australia
- the development of a strong national, regional or local identity in an increasingly internationalised media
- a strong representation of regional and local issues to regional and local communities
- a range of viewpoints within media formats and genres
- a range of media platforms and output that delivers content relevant for a diverse range of interests.

But how can we better understand these different dimensions of diversity in the context of particular national media systems? Hallin and Mancini (2004), in a comparative analysis of the relations between media and political systems, draw an important distinction between 'external pluralism' and 'internal pluralism'. For the purposes of our discussion in this chapter, their use of the concept of pluralism closely corresponds to the term 'diversity'. They provide an account of the two ways in which media systems 'handle diversity of political loyalties and orientations'. They argue:

> *External pluralism* can be defined as pluralism achieved at the level of the media system as a whole, through the existence of a range of media outlets or organizations reflecting the points of view of different groups or tendencies in society ... The contrary term, *internal pluralism*, is defined as pluralism, achieved within each individual media outlet or organization. The term is actually used in two different ways in the media studies literature. We will generally use it to refer to cases where media organizations both avoid institutional ties to political groups and attempt to maintain neutrality and 'balance' in their content ... Internal pluralism is also sometimes used to refer to media organizations—

usually broadcasting organizations—that formally represent a variety of political forces within the structure and content of a single organization (2004, pp. 29–30).

Hallin and Mancini's broader argument concerns the connections that exist between the political and media systems in Europe and North America. Their distinction between external and internal pluralism leads them to conclude that media systems characterised by external pluralism will 'have a high level of **political parallelism**'. Conversely, in systems characterised by internal pluralism there tends to be a 'low level of political parallelism'.

GLOSSARY

Political parallelism The extent to which the structure of the media system parallels the political party system. It can be seen to operate in a number of ways including through:

- *Media content*: the extent to which the different media represent distinct political orientations in their news and current affairs reporting, and sometimes also in their entertainment content.
- *Organisational connections*: between media and political parties or other kinds of organisations, including trade unions, cooperatives, churches.
- *Media personnel:* the tendency for people working in the media industries to be active in political life—including the tendency for the career paths of journalists and other media personnel to be shaped by their political affiliations.
- *Media audiences:* the partisanship of the people who will read and watch media depending on its political orientation.
- *Journalistic role orientations and practices:* for example, more or less of a 'publicist' or provider of 'balanced' or 'neutral' information, or alternatively, a commentary and analysis approach (Hallin and Mancini, 2004, pp. 27–8).

Of course, these are ideal models for understanding different nations' media systems and the way they overlap with political arrangements, and most nation states will have a mixture of these characteristics. But this modeling allows them to observe both similarities and differences between various nation states, even where they are ostensibly similar. For example, Australia, the United States and Britain share many features in common in their political and media systems, yet differences in political institutions and cultures, commercial media institutions, and traditions in journalism lead to actual divergences. All three operate within what Hallin and Mancini describe as a 'North Atlantic' or 'Liberal Model'; however, the interaction of the state and the market, and journalistic traditions, all have a variable influence on the extent of insulation of media from political control (2004, p. 75). Responses by governments to questions of diversity in their media systems are ultimately conditioned by their specific histories.

Media diversities

In Australia, the policy rationales for 'cultural diversity' used by the commercial television sector are important because this is still the most widely used media form; and therefore, arguably, the most broadly influential in terms of offering engagement with the general community. In the Australian content standard, a regulatory instrument for fostering local production, cultural diversity in commercial television broadcasting is to be achieved by:

- promoting the role of broadcasting as developing and reflecting:
    - a sense of Australian identity
    - a sense of Australian character
    - a sense of Australia's cultural diversity
- supporting the community's continued access to TV programs produced under Australian creative control.

Editor's comment   See the *Broadcasting Services (Australian Content) Standard 2005*, cl. 4. This objective is based on s 3(e) of the *Broadcasting Services Act 1992*: to promote the role of broadcasting services in developing and reflecting a sense of Australian identity, character and cultural diversity. For the full text of the Australian content standard see: http://www.acma.gov.au.

This policy rationale for achieving cultural diversity in Australian commercial television is one that is, in many senses, the antithesis of how many people would understand the term 'cultural diversity'; attempting to define an overarching Australian 'identity' or 'character' is difficult, and possibly counter-productive, in a culturally diverse society (Nightingale and Dwyer, 2005). The narrowness of this conception of cultural diversity is emphasised by proliferating multi-channel television and new media generally in multicultural societies. Georgina Born suggests that this reality of social and cultural difference 'poses challenges to the media on a scale to which they have only begun to respond, challenges compounded both by contemporary commercial restructuring and by digital technologies' (Born, 2006). Further, she argues it is the media's responsibility in an 'age of diversity', indeed, in 'communicative democracies' to offer:

… a rich array of communicative channels for the self-representation, parti-cipation and expressive narrativisation of minority and marginalized groups, addressed both to and among those groups and to the majority (p.119).

Cultural diversity can also have different meanings in other media (Productivity Commission, 2000; Lewis, 2002). For example, O'Regan has argued that Australia's internationalising national film industry in the late 1990s was inevitably bound up with multiculturalism, cultural diversity debates and the politics of self-definition through the kinds of projects that were produced—often determined by the sources of available investment finance (O'Regan, 2001).

Under the content standard, media diversity can be distilled to mean:

- promoting locally produced content
- limiting dominance of US programming
- providing a mix of Australian and US programming.

This understanding of the term 'cultural diversity', within the context of main-stream commercial television policy, emerged as part of the suite of policies to foster a local content industry in the face of a very real threat of displacement by much cheaper US programming fare from the 1960s. It was policy directed at reducing the growing substitution of Australian-made programs with US programs, for cultural, economic and industry (that is, employment) reasons.

There are two main mechanisms in the standard:

- an annual transmission quota—55% of all programming broadcast between 6 am and 12 midnight; the transmission quota encompasses all first release and repeat Australian programs broadcast during this time period; and
- sub-quotas for Australian (adult) drama, children's programs (including children's drama) and documentary programs.

For subscription broadcasters, Part 7 of the *Broadcasting Services Act* imposes a mandatory expenditure requirement that obliges licensees to spend 10 per cent of drama budgets on eligible new Australian drama. This regulation follows the terminology of the Australian content standard, and has been subject to several general and specific genre reviews for the adult drama, children's drama and documentary sub-quotas. The logic of these mechanisms is to provide diversity (*from* the already heavy diet of US programming) by requiring broadcasters to schedule a minimum amount of those programs that are considered particularly vulnerable to replacement by cheaper imports. The adult drama, children's drama and documentary sub-quotas also contain a first release requirement to ensure audiences have access to recently produced Australian programs. Diversity in the standard, then, is 'chiefly assured by the requirement for certain levels of adult and children's drama and documentary programs' (ABA, 2002). Of course, this does not help us a great deal in relation to the question of how diversity will be represented and promoted in borderless new media worlds, which governments and regulatory agencies are only beginning to grapple with. Yet we need to bear in mind that diverse media ownership and content is a critical goal for sustaining our democracies.

Conflating content choice with diversity of viewpoints

As I have mentioned already, debates over changes to media ownership laws often reflects differing understandings of what we mean by 'diversity' in media policy discourses. In fact, the use of the term 'diversity' has tended to conflate often competing definitions and has, on occasion, rendered the concept of diversity to mean little more than a multitude of content on proliferating media platforms.

For example, some sections of the Australian film and television production industry have argued for mechanisms to increase content diversity as a trade-off for more relaxed media ownership regulation (Curtis, 2005, p. 7). But, as Wilding has argued, in this formulation 'diversity' is recast as meaning simply 'Australian made' (2005, p. 1).

In a media system that is so dominated by US content few would argue against the need for mechanisms that promote a diversity of cultural content in Australian media, to ensure better representation of Australia's cultural diversity; or which promote Australian production generally to maintain a distinctive cultural voice in the face of increasing globalisation. However, this is a different policy objective from the promotion of diversity in news, views and opinion through a plurality of ownership and control of the more influential media forms.

Indeed the production industry lobby has argued that in the context of increasing concentration of media ownership the only way to ensure diversity and plurality of television programming is to introduce an independent production quota for all free-to-air television services. In response, Wilding makes the point that:

> It is highly questionable whether legislation which leads to larger media companies will necessarily result in better representation of Australian drama, or that the cross-media rules need to be abandoned in order to achieve that result. All that can be guaranteed is such legislation will lead to a further concentration of ownership (2005, p. 1).

Structural diversity versus content choice

Media diversity is also defined as a by-product of available industry segments. For example, broadcasting policy in Australia assumes that structural regulation ensures a plurality of sources through the separation of the various sectors involved in broadcasting:

- commercial
- national public broadcasting
- subscription
- community
- narrowcasting.

This structural diversity is enshrined as objectives in subsections 3(a) and (c) of the *Broadcasting Services Act 1992*: 'to promote the availability to audiences throughout Australia of a diverse range of radio and television services offering entertainment, education and information', and, 'to encourage diversity in control of the more influential broadcasting services'.

Changes in relation to how such structural diversity is configured also give rise to questions about the future role of specific sectors. For example, we can pose the question: what would a lessening of diversity in the commercial sector mean for the future role of 'community media'?

Plurality of owners equals diversity of viewpoints?

Recognising structural diversity as a distinct policy objective does not, however, solve the difficulty in identifying a direct correlation between the means (plurality of ownership) and the ends (diversity of opinion). For example, it is common for different, independently owned, radio or free-to-air television licensees to broadcast the same material via networking or syndication arrangements. And media organisations under shared control may well have separate newsgathering operations with separate and distinct editorial policies (Jackson, 1999, p. 5; Pritchard, 2001), though it is an open question whether, in practice, such artificial divisions allow an actual separation of corporate viewpoints. Again, we need to be able to distinguish between, for example, music formats on the one hand, and news or current affairs programming on the other. It is the latter which plays an important role in sustaining our democracies.

It is sometimes argued that greater program diversity may also emerge from large media organisations with the resources to develop different types of programming for different audiences (Albon and Papandrea, 1998, p. 64; Doyle, 2002, p. 13). For instance, you may find if there is a single owner of multiple radio stations within the same market, that owner may be more likely to program content for minority (or at least differing) tastes than if the radio stations were separately owned (Brenner, 1996, p. 1007).

But countries with relatively small markets such as Australia do face a dilemma in developing public policy that encourages ownership diversity. A small population base means there is unlikely to be a large number of players in the media industry, and those that do exist seek to consolidate and expand their businesses to increase domestic market share and to remain competitive in an increasingly globalised media market. Politicians keen to keep favour with the major media players are under continuing pressure from proprietors to relax ownership restrictions (Chadwick, 1995).

In a development of historical import, in 2006 the Howard conservative government in Australia repealed cross and foreign ownership restrictions that had been in place since 1987. This signalled a new era of media concentration and further reduction of diversity in opinions.

In Australia, many, although not all, of the major media organisations supported the removal of the long-standing laws limiting concentration of media ownership

(Senate, 2006). The few larger corporations opposing the reforms, including News Corporation, did so on the basis that the proposed changes were *insufficiently* deregulatory, and thus unable to deliver the radical changes that would permit them to acquire *any* media assets they wished. On the other hand, smaller independent media groups were able to distinguish between their own commercial gain, and a wider public interest served through access to diverse news and information resources.

In their submission to the 2006 Senate Inquiry into media ownership reform the lobby group Independent Regional Radio (IRR) saw the proposed amendments that were passed by the parliament as fundamentally flawed, arguing that the provisions relating to regional media should be deleted. Focusing on the impact of the proposed changes in regional areas IRR opposed relaxation of cross-media ownership restrictions in regional markets on the grounds that:

- no public benefit can be demonstrated by the government
- removing the restrictions will reduce the existing diversity of both ownership and content wherever mergers occur
- removing cross-media restrictions would almost certainly enable one media group to dominate and exploit a market without the possibility of competition by another group on equal terms
- power would be conferred on a single media proprietor with multiple influential media outlets to set the news and current affairs agenda within its market and to influence public opinion, especially on matters of local interest and issues of concern (IRR, Senate submission, 2006).

After a short and carefully stage-managed consultation process, a 'one size fits all' deregulatory framework that limits ownership to '2 out of 3' categories of traditional media of radio, TV and newspapers was passed by a Senate controlled by the Howard Government in 2006. This new rule was coupled with numerical limits of a minimum of four separate media ownership groups per market in regional areas, and five in metropolitan areas; implicitly conceding that there would be adverse political, economic and cultural affects from concentrated ownership.

Despite the indirect connection between ownership and content, there has been long-standing international support for the proposition that plurality in ownership is more likely to promote diversity of opinion than other, non-structural approaches to regulation. In other words, structural limits on the number of media outlets owned by one proprietor has been regarded as a precondition for achieving a diverse range of viewpoints in Australia and a range of other democratic nations, including the UK and the USA (Dwyer et al., 2006). It has also been assumed that concentrated ownership confers power on owners to influence governments: this can be in relation to either their media or non-media assets.

In the context of the Australian media ownership reforms it is significant that both the UK and USA prohibit unfettered print–broadcast cross ownership. But there has been significant liberalisation and consolidation within single media sectors in both these countries. In a sense this is fairly predictable. As Bettig and Hall argue, 'media concentration is an ongoing trend that follows the predominant tendency with capitalism toward centralisation of economic power in the hands of oligopolies' (2003, p. 16).

In the lead-up to the historic repeal of Australia's media ownership laws, the Media Entertainment and Arts Alliance (MEAA) teamed up with the online investigative journalism outlet *Crikey* to survey working journalists on critical issues likely to affect them. Premised on an understanding that a useful litmus test of the likely impacts of media ownership deregulation was to ask the profession itself for their views, their findings included:

- 82 per cent believed the changes to the media laws will have a negative impact on the integrity of reporting
- 85 per cent said the changes will reduce diversity
- 87 per cent were opposed to the removal of cross-media laws
- 74 per cent were opposed to the removal of foreign ownership restrictions
- 53 per cent said they were unable to be critical of the media organisation they work for
- 38 per cent said they had been instructed to comply with the commercial position of the company they work for
- 32 per cent in print media (34 per cent in TV and radio) felt obliged to take into account the political views of their proprietor
- 63 per cent believe Australian media companies/owners have too much influence in deciding how Australians vote
- 71 per cent said media companies/owners have too much influence in determining the political agenda (MEAA/*Crikey*, 2006).

Does structural diversity matter?

It is unclear whether diversity in media ownership actually resonates as an important public policy issue within the wider community. While diversity in ownership is subject to ongoing debate in political and academic circles, there is relatively little research, in Australia at least, as to whether concentration in media ownership matters to the wider community, or indeed whether the wider community perceives a strong correlation between ownership concentration and lack of diversity. The ABA's 2001 report, *Sources of News and Current Affairs*, while not examining community attitudes to ownership concentration, did, however, attempt to collate community views on the accuracy, objectiveness and relevance of the news and current affairs that people use. The findings included that:

- Australian audiences believe that the business interests of media organisations are the greatest source of influence on what they read, hear or see in news and current affairs.
- Sensationalised reporting is of most concern in relation to news and current affairs, followed by intrusive reporting, with biased content and inaccurate reporting ranked third and fourth.
- Three-quarters of Australian audiences believe the media covers local news and current affairs less adequately than they could and attribute inadequate coverage of local events and issues to a general lack of community and media interest in local matters (ABA, 2001, p. 378).

The first point suggests that Australian audiences are at some level concerned about the ownership of Australian media, at least to the extent to which the proprietors' commercial interests may influence news and current affairs content. It may have been interesting if the study had asked whether those people who perceived a less than adequate commitment to local events and issues saw any correlation between consolidations of media ownership and a reduction of local news and current affairs production. This question may have had particular relevance for people in regional areas affected by increased media ownership concentration over the past twenty years. In *Content, Consolidation and Clout: How will regional Australia be affected by media ownership changes?* the authors found that, at least in respect of regional media, issues of media ownership *per se* are less important to the wider community than the quality of journalism and the relationship between local media outlets and local power elites (Dwyer et al., 2006).

There is no doubt that the rise of the Internet is changing how news and current affairs information is accessed. Yet that access needs to be considered in light of the evidence in relation to ownership of the most frequently accessed new online media. The major incumbent media operators (in broadcast and print) are also the owners of the most-frequented websites and portals. As Sparks notes, 'offline media across the spectrum from print to broadcasting have strong online presences' (Sparks, 2004, p. 310). Similarly, opinion polling in Australia shows that of the 25 per cent of people who regularly use the Internet to obtain news and current affairs, around 90 per cent of them rely on websites controlled by or associated with traditional media sources (Downie and Macintosh, 2006, p. 9).

It is reasonable to conclude that news and information delivered by free-to-air TV, radio and newspapers are still the most popular sources, and therefore justifying continued ownership restrictions. The evidence clearly suggests that the removal of these rules will further concentrate cross-media ownership, reducing the diversity of sources of information to audiences.

Multiculturalism, cultural diversity and commercial TV

David Carter has argued that 'as a policy, multiculturalism is based on the *recognition* that the nation is in fact a "multicultural" or ethnically diverse society … rather than seeing the migrant as "a problem"' to be managed, ethnic, cultural and linguistic diversity should be understood as a *positive* addition to Australian society' (2006, p. 333). Carter argues that in Australian society and in other societies there are conflicting forces, some 'tending towards diversity', others tending towards 'shared' experiences (p. 351). This is certainly a useful way of considering our mediascapes too.

Sociologist Ulrich Beck has powerfully argued that the world is now irrevocably cosmopolitan in a number of ways. In contrast to what he calls nation states' 'territorial prison theory of identity, society and politics' he suggests it is possible to distinguish five 'interconnected constitutive principles of the *cosmopolitan outlook*':

1. *The experience of crisis in world society*: the awareness of interdependence and the resulting 'civilisational community of fate' induced by global risks and crises, which overcomes the boundaries between internal and external, us and them, the national and the international.
2. *The recognition of cosmopolitan differences* and the resulting *cosmopolitan conflict character*, and the (limited) curiosity concerning differences of culture and identity.
3. *Cosmopolitan empathy and perspective-taking* and virtual interchangeability of situations (as both an opportunity and a threat).
4. *The impossibility of living in a world society* without borders and the resulting compulsion to redraw old boundaries and rebuild old walls.
5. *The mélange principle*: the principle that local, national, ethnic, religious and cosmopolitan cultures and traditions interpenetrate, interconnect and intermingle—cosmopolitanism without provincialism is empty, provincialism without cosmopolitanism is blind (Beck, 2006, p. 7).

Beck argues that we can understand these principles at both a philosophical–normative level and in their practical everyday manifestations. In other words, he suggests the 'cosmopolitan outlook' is a reflexive outlook, where the state must find a way to reorder and redefine their interests 'among the ruins of former certainties in whatever way makes continued coexistence possible' (p. 8). In fact, a number of researchers have found evidence of a broad dissemination of this general cosmopolitanism: more and more people are conscious of living in an age of global flows, where local, regional, national and global influences interpenetrate (Tomlinson, 1999; Szerszynski and Urry, 2002; Beck, 2006).

In terms of national media policy and multiculturalism, if Australia's multicultural public broadcaster, the Special Broadcasting Service (SBS), is the most visible emblem of multicultural policy, then any reference to multiculturalism in the commercial broadcasting sector, is at best, obscured.

The Australian commercial television industry, through its Code of Practice and associated Advisory Notes (*Cultural Diversity* and *Portrayal of Aboriginal and Torres Strait Islanders*), recognises the promotion of Australian cultural diversity as one of its aims. First introduced in August 1994, these aspirational (non-binding) notes appended to the Code are intended to encourage best practice. The Note on Cultural Diversity explains its purpose as:

> To help and encourage reporters and program producers to produce programs which treat all people with equal respect, regardless of their national, ethnic or linguistic background. It also suggests ways to avoid promoting or provoking prejudice, stereotyping or unwarranted generalisation. As such, it will also be of assistance to programmers, program promotion producers and program classifiers (Code of Practice).

Theory link

see Wilding,
Chapter 16

The multicultural aim of the Code of Practice, then, is to avoid giving offence, and by default, rather than explicitly, to encode multiculturalism as a mainstream value—but this is an implicit encoding.

Since the 1990s, a number of empirical studies have been undertaken in Australia into the lack of participation of people of culturally and linguistically diverse backgrounds on commercial television, and consequentially, into commercial broadcasting's contribution to 'an impoverished representation of Australia's cultural diversity' (May, 2001; Jakubowicz, 1994; Bell, 1993; ABA, 1993; CLC, 1992; Coupe, 1992).

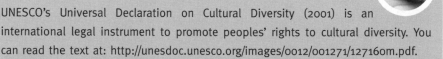

Activity 15.1

Theory link

see Salazar,
Chapter 5

UNESCO's Universal Declaration on Cultural Diversity (2001) is an international legal instrument to promote peoples' rights to cultural diversity. You can read the text at: http://unesdoc.unesco.org/images/0012/001271/127160m.pdf.

Which articles from the Declaration, and objectives from the action plan accompanying the document, do you think are relevant to promoting diversity on commercial television?

Of course Australia's policy framework for cultural diversity in the Code of Practice and associated Advisory Notes is embedded within the overall political economics of commercial television in a mature global marketplace. Papandrea has outlined the process in these terms:

> Although popular with audiences, the relatively higher cost of domestic drama renders it less appealing to stations than high-rating imported substitutes. Relative to lower rating imports, however, the high popularity of domestic drama is sufficient to outweigh the program cost disadvantage. Nonetheless, the commissioning of domestic drama represents a much higher risk to stations than the purchase of imported substitutes whose market appeal has already been tested in overseas markets. Thus, while broadcasters have an incentive to schedule domestic drama after it has proven its audience appeal, the high initial risk of commissioning the drama is a disincentive to a high level of production. Consequently, without the regulatory requirements, it is likely that the level of domestic drama production would decline below the regulated levels (Panpandrea, 1997).

Into this dynamic mix, policies for local content diversity are attempting to trade off several complex interacting factors including station profitability, industry employment, cultural objectives and audience taste. A key concern in the future is how a right to intervene in cultural markets will be sustained in the face of cultural, politico-economic and technological pressures that are occurring on an unprecedented international scale. Increasingly, the national debate for media regulation is conducted within a wider global context of the increasing prominence of international economic organisations, corporations, and free trade agreements (Canclini, 2001).

In the Australian context, the combination of structural diversity of the media and the absence of multicultural responsibilities for commercial broadcasters creates lack of tolerance for both Australian production and for local and community programming. In a self-perpetuating cycle multicultural values and beliefs do not appear more widely on peoples' screens because specifically 'cultural' values and beliefs seldom reach a level of saturation that can compete with the Anglo-American media mainstream. At the same time, the development of commercial broadcasting as consumerist broadcasting appears to be responsible for the current drift of older audiences to public sector (national) broadcasters (ABC and SBS) and to subscription services, and for redefining the aged (over fifty-fives) in the mass audience as potentially a 'special needs' category.

A similar process of exclusion operates with multicultural audiences, and presumably even more strongly for aged culturally and linguistically diverse and

Indigenous audiences. The inclusion of young people from ethnically diverse backgrounds in reality TV programs like *Big Brother* and *Australian Idol*, as an example of recognition by the commercial sector of the multicultural diversity of young Australians (Roscoe, 2004), is on terms strictly defined and controlled by the broadcasting, production and sponsoring companies, and even of the international format suppliers (Nightingale and Dwyer, 2006).

The audience development power and priorities of commercial broadcasters actively shape a sense of the Australian cultural imaginary that appears to allow few Australians, of whatever origin, to recognise themselves in its programming, as demonstrated by the *Living Diversity* report. And despite their ability to critically use new media technologies many 'younger Australians of culturally diverse backgrounds still feel an incomplete acceptance by mainstream society' (see Ang et al., 2002 and 2006).

As the commercial entertainment media focus more narrowly on advertiser-defined audiences, the public broadcasters inherit a role as providers of entertainment for the increasing array of minority audiences. Under these conditions the role of commercial broadcasting in the global knowledge economy becomes even more critical.

Conclusion

Discussions of media diversity inevitably occur within a wider context of the political and media systems of a nation. This means that differences in political institutions and cultures, commercial media institutions, and traditions in journalism will all play a part in how notions of 'diversity' are embedded, and ultimately represented, in media systems. There will be contradictions and tensions between on the one hand, global flows of people, products and services and images, and on the other hand, the desire by governments and their agencies to preserve or maintain local cultures, traditions and institutions. The prevalence of a cosmopolitan disposition, in large measure the result of media representations, is expanded through extensive mobility (not just corporeally but also imaginatively and virtually), consumption practices, curiosity about other places, and in general, heightened knowledges and semiotic skills for interpreting cultural difference.

In this context the Australian media is characterised by an ecology that promotes limited cultural diversity mainly by way of the public national broadcasting and the community sectors. The availability of diverse formats and genres over a range of old and new media platforms will continue to be an important part of this equation. But, in future years, as the pressures continue for concentrating ownership into fewer hands, our legislators and regulatory agencies will need to explore new means of promoting the objective of making multination Australia available to all citizens. Pluralist societies constituted by a range of culturally and linguistically diverse social groups should by definition have democratic mechanisms available to them to express their diversity across traditional and new media platforms.

CHAPTER SUMMARY

- In this chapter we have examined the multiple dimensions of the notion of 'media diversity'.
- We have discussed how media policy regulation for 'cultural diversity' has very specific meanings and impacts.
- We have discussed how 'structural diversity' shapes the diversity of content that is available to audiences.
- In his chapter we have seen the contradictory tendencies of multiculturalism in commercial media.
- We have seen how in a self-perpetuating cycle commercial media avoids multi-cultural values and reproduces the Anglo–American mainstream.

Tutorial questions

- Which different meanings can 'diversity' take on in the context of media policy debates?
- Do we need 'structural' diversity as well as 'content' diversity?
- Since discussion of media diversity occur in the context of nation states, what kinds of contradictions and tensions does this create?

Recommended reading

Bettig, R. & Hall, J., 2003, *Big Media, Big Money: Cultural Texts and Political Economics,* Rowman & Littlefield, Lanham, Boulder, NY, and Oxford.

Carter, D., 2006, *Dispossession, Dreams and Diversity: Issues in Australian Studies,* Pearson Longman, Sydney.

Hallin, D.C. & Mancini, P., 2004, *Comparing Media Systems: Three Models of Media and Politics,* Cambridge University Press, Cambridge, UK.

Websites

Australian Communications and Media Authority: www.acma.gov.au

Federation of Ethnic Communities' Councils of Australia: www.fecca.org.au

Office of Communications: www.ofcom.gov.uk

The Special Broadcasting Service: http://www20.sbs.com.au/sbs_front/index.html

Universal Declaration on Cultural Diversity (2001): http://unesdoc.unesco.org/
images/0012/001271/127160m.pdf

References

ABA (Australian Broadcasting Authority), 2002, *Regulatory Impact Statement Broadcasting Services Act 1992, Broadcasting Services (Australian Content) Standard Variation 2002 (No. 1).* December, Sydney, 15.

ABA (Australian Broadcasting Authority), 2001, *Sources of News and Current Affairs,* A research report conducted by Bond University for the Australian Broadcasting Authority, May.

ABA (Australian Broadcasting Authority), 1993, *The People we See on TV: Cultural Diversity on Television,* Monograph No.3, ABA, Sydney.

Albon, R. & Papandrea, F., 1998, *Media Regulation in Australia and the Public Interest,* Institute of Public Affairs, Canberra, November, 64.

Ang, I. et al., 2002, *Living Diversity: Australia's Multicultural Future,* Special Broadcasting Services Corporation, Sydney.

Ang, I. et al., 2006, *Connecting Diversity: Paradoxes of Multicultural Australia,* Special Broadcasting Services Corporation, Sydney.

Beck, U., 2006, *The Cosmopolitan Vision,* Polity Press, Cambridge, UK.

Bell, P., 1993, *Multicultural Australia in the Media: A Report to the Office of Multicultural Affairs,* AGPS, Canberra.

Bettig, R & Hall, J., 2003, *Big Media, Big Money: Cultural Texts and Political Economics,* Rowman & Littlefield, Lanham, Boulder, NY, and Oxford.

Born, G., 2006, 'Digitising Democracy', in Lloyd, J. & Seaton, J (eds), *What Can Be Done? Making the Media and Politics Better,* The Political Quarterly Special Issue, Blackwells Publishing, London.

Brenner, D., 1996, 'Ownership and Content Regulation in Merging and Emerging Media' 45 *DePaul L Rev* 1009, 1017.

Canclini, N.G. (2001) 'Multicultural Policies and Integration via the Market' in *Consumers and Citizens: Globalisation and Multicultural Conflicts,* tr. George Yudice, University of Minnesota Press, Minneapolis and London.

Carter, D., 2006, *Dispossession, Dreams and Diversity: Issues in Australian Studies,* Pearson Longman, 332–55, Sydney.

Chadwick, P., 1995, 'Same Faces in Control of Media' 3(7) *Telecommunications Law and Policy Review* 70.

CLC (Communication Law Centre), 1992, *The Representation of Non-English Speaking Background People on Australian Drama,* University of NSW, Sydney.

Coupe, B. et al., 1992, *Next Door Neighbours*, Office of Multicultural Affairs, Department of the Prime Minister and Cabinet, AGPS, Canberra.

Curtis, S., 2005, 'Offsetting Cross-media Ownership and Media Concentration: Examining the "Canadian model"' 24(2) *Communications Law Bulletin* 7.

Doyle, G., 2002, *Media Ownership*, Sage Publications, London.

Downie, C. & Macintosh, A., 2006, 'New Media or More of the Same? The Cross-media Ownership Debate', The Australia Institute, http://www.tai.org.au

Dwyer, T., Wilding, D., Wilson, H. & Curtis, S., 2006, *Content, Consolidation and Clout: How will Regional Australia be Affected by Media Ownership Changes?,* Communications Law Centre, Melbourne.

Gibbons, T., 1998, *Regulating the Media* (2nd edn), Sweet & Maxwell, London.

Hallin, D.C. & Mancini, P., 2004, *Comparing Media Systems: Three Models of Media and Politics,* Cambridge University Press, Cambridge, UK.

Hitchens, L., 2006, *Broadcasting Pluralism and Diversity: A Comparative Study of Policy and Regulation,* Hart Publishing, Oxford, UK, and Portland, USA.

Independent Regional Radio, 2006, Submission to Senate inquiry into Media Ownership package, 'Silk Purse or Sow's Ear?', September.

Jackson, P., 1999, *Convergence and the Cross-Media Rules*, Research Note 20, Parliamentary Library, 5.

Jakubowicz, A., 1994, (ed.) *Racism, Ethnicity and the Media*, Allen & Unwin, Sydney.

Lewis, K., 2002, 'Deliberating on Diversity: Australia's Print Media Inquiry and the Productivity Commission's Inquiry into Broadcasting' 29(3) *Australian Journal of Communication* 31, 33.

May, H., 2001, 'Cultural Diversity and Australian Commercial Television Drama: Policy, Industry and Recent Research Contexts' 19(2), *Prometheus* 161–70.

Media Entertainment and Arts Alliance/*Crikey*, 2006, Survey by Roy Morgan Polling.

Nightingale, V. & Dwyer, T., 2006, 'The Audience Politics of "Enhanced" TV Formats', *International Journal of Media and Cultural Politics,* Intellect, UK.

Nightingale, V. & Dwyer, T., 2005, 'Community Attitudes and Changing Audiences: Integrating Australia's Multicultural Diversity in Media Policy' 32(3) *Australian Journal of Communication* 109–29.

O'Regan, T., 2001, '"Knowing the Processes but Not the Outcomes": Australian Cinema Faces the Millennium', in Bennett, D. & Carter, D. (eds) *Culture in Australia: Policies, Publics and Programs,* Cambridge University Press.

Papandrea, F., 1997, *Cultural Regulation of Australian Television Programs*, Bureau of Transport and Communications Economics, AGPS, Canberra.

Pritchard, D., 2001, 'A Tale of Three Cities: "Diverse and Antagonistic" Information in Situations of Local Newspaper/Broadcast Cross-ownership' 54 *Fed Comm L J*.

Productivity Commission, 2000, *Broadcasting*, Report No. 11, Ausinfo, Canberra, March, 314.

Roscoe, J., 2004, 'Reality Television: A Site of Diversity?' *Australian Mosaic* (Media in a Pluralistic Society), Issue 5, pp. 29–30.

Senate Standing Committee on Environment, Communications, Information Technology and the Arts, 2006, *Report on Broadcasting Services Amendment (Media Ownership) Bill 2006 and related legislation*, October, Parliament of Australia, Canberra.

Sparks, C. (ed.), 2004, *Toward a Political Economy of Culture: Capitalism and Communications in the 21st Century,* Roman & Littlefield, Maryland.

Szerszynski, B. & Urry, J., 2002, 'Cultures of Cosmopolitanism' *Sociological Review*, 50(4).

Tomlinson, J., 1999, *Globalisation and Culture,* Polity Press, Cambridge, UK.

Wilding, D., 2005, 'The New Diversity', *Media Ownership Update, Communications Update*, June, Communications Law Centre, 168.

DEREK WILDING

On Fair Terms: Public Participation in Communications Regulation in Australia

16

CHAPTER OVERVIEW

The object of this chapter is to explore one aspect of how communications regulation works in practice—how rules are made—and to reflect on the different approaches to regulation. The focus will be on the opportunities for public participation in and engagement with industry self-regulation. Students should be able to reflect on whether the public interest (in its many forms) is effectively served by contemporary approaches to regulation.

Key terms

communications regulation
self-regulation
consumer participation

Issues

- How has industry-based self-regulation changed the ways in which laws and regulations apply in the communications sector?
- How can consumer representatives and members of the public contribute to the development of communications regulation?
- Is the system effective?

Introduction

Advances in technology offer new products and services for consumers of new and old media. But the availability of media and communications services is very much controlled by regulation, not all of which is consistent and effective. Some new technologies—such as digital television or video content on mobile phones—present challenges that take years to resolve.

In this chapter we will look at the ways in which laws and regulations relating to media and communications services are made and the opportunities for the public and especially for consumers to participate in rule-making. To do so, we first need to understand the legal framework within which communications regulation operates.

Legal framework

Some of the reasons for government regulation of broadcasting, telecommunications and the Internet are broadly similar—for example, to prevent multiple use of the same frequencies in the radio communications spectrum, to prevent the distribution of offensive material, or to prohibit undesirable practices such as phone-tapping or spamming. Importantly, most aspects of communications regulation occur within the federal sphere, rather than via state and territory legislation. This is because, in Australia, the federal government has an express power under the Australian Constitution to legislate in relation to these services.[1]

However, broadcasting (meaning television and radio) and telecommunications are regulated by different Acts of Parliament. The *Broadcasting Services Act 1992* is the major act that applies to television and radio. The *Telecommunications Act 1997* is the major act that applies to telecommunications services. The Internet is regulated by different sources, including the *Interactive Gambling Act 2001* and the *Spam Act 2004*, as well as by both the *Telecommunications Act* and the *Broadcasting Services Act*.

The *Broadcasting Services Act* and the *Telecommunications Act* are structured in broadly the same way. In both systems, there are rules that have varying degrees of authority and enforcement behind them. In one sense, these specific rules are a secondary matter: if an aspiring supplier wishes to provide a broadcasting or telecommunications service, they must qualify on other grounds before considering these requirements. Firstly, the person will be a licensee or a service provider within the meaning of the relevant Act. Secondly, certain rules will attach to the use of the licence or the person's conduct as a recognised service provider. Finally, there are obligations that come with the entitlement to operate a business—if the supplier breaches the obligations, they may be subject to enforcement procedures and penalties.

Categories of communications service

The categories of service used in Australia are as set out in Table 16.1. These categories are important because there are different obligations that attach to them, with more obligations placed on telecommunications carriers and on commercial television and radio broadcasters than on suppliers of other categories of services. Some of these categories (telecommunications service providers and narrowcasting television and radio services) do not require individual licences and are instead provided under a 'class licence' system: providing the supplier complies with certain general rules, they will be free to set up a business without obtaining an individual service licence from the regulator. (They might, however, need a technical licence to operate a transmitter if they intend to use the radiofrequency spectrum.)

This decision to allow certain services to operate without an individual licence can be seen as part of a move away from prescriptive regulations and towards a system in which suppliers have more responsibility for contributing to the regulation of their industry. This approach includes the use of codes of practice that are developed by industry groups (usually in consultation with the regulator) and self-reporting on compliance with some of the broadcasting and telecommunications rules. Nevertheless, licensing does provide a legal mechanism for rules to be imposed on the providers of these services. Licence conditions can require that a provider actively does something (for example, the licence condition that requires Telstra to provide pensioner discounts) or actively avoids doing something (such as the requirement that community broadcasters must not engage in commercial activities).

Table 16.1 Categories of broadcasting, telecommunications and Internet services

Broadcasting[2]	
Category of Service	**Explanation**
National broadcasting service	The ABC and SBS
Commercial broadcasting service	Free-to-air television and commercial radio
Subscription broadcasting service	Pay TV providers such as Foxtel
Community broadcasting service	Community television and community radio
Subscription narrowcasting service and open narrowcasting service	Services of limited appeal or available to relatively small numbers of people
International broadcasting service	Broadcasts services from within Australia to overseas locations →

Telecommunications	
Category of Service	**Explanation**
Telecommunications carrier	Carriers own and operate infrastructure such as copper lines or fibre optic cables, or mobile phone networks
Service provider	Service providers use the infrastructure of carriers to provide services direct to the public[3]
Internet	
Category of Service	**Explanation**
Internet Service Provider	An ISP supplies an Internet carriage service to the public
Internet Content Host	An ICH hosts Internet content (i.e. stored content) in Australia for access using an Internet carriage service
Content Service Provider	A content service provider uses a carriage service to supply a content service to the public

While the use of 'light touch' regulation has been a trend of communications regulation since the *Broadcasting Services Act* was passed in 1992, it is true that there is still a great deal of prescription, some of which is the subject of dispute and debate within the industry.

Think about it

One of the difficulties that arises is in establishing rules that are appropriate to suit the problem. This regulatory challenge can be expressed as follows:

- *if* we accept the proposition that Acts of Parliament should create certain obligations for providers of broadcasting services and telecommunications services;
- *but* that it is not practicable for parliament to set all the rules for every conceivable situation;
- *then* how do we design a system that allows new rules to be imposed by sources other than parliament and how do we make sure that the system itself is effective?

It is in response to this regulatory challenge that systems of industry self-regulation have emerged.

Self-regulation in communications and media

The distinction is often made between 'command and control' regulation and industry-based self-regulation. The former category is concerned primarily with 'black letter law'—relatively strict rules set out in legislation, coupled with an ability and willingness on the part of the regulator to monitor compliance with the law and to enforce it. In contrast, self-regulation is 'light touch' regulation in which rules are formulated at least partly by industry participants and are embodied in instruments (usually codes of practice) that industry has some responsibility for maintaining, updating and enforcing.[4]

Although there is considerable theoretical speculation on the meaning and effect of self-regulation, in practice 'pure' self-regulation is likely to be unenforceable; that is, the regulator does not have a role in formulating or enforcing the rules. This means that in Australia, although there are examples of this kind of regulation (for example, the Direct Marketing Code of Practice, the Australian Press Council's Statement of Principles, and the Disability Guideline produced by the Australian Communications Industry Forum), most of the regulation that we refer to as 'self-regulation' is in fact a form of co-regulation. Co-regulation is often characterised by the participation of the regulator in formulating, along with the formal registration of the code by the regulator. In the first instance, industry participants will usually take the enforcement role and will respond to complaints, but these codes all have some capacity for the regulator to intervene in cases of serious or ongoing code breaches. Examples of self-regulatory instruments that are all co-regulatory in nature are listed in Table 16.2.

Communications regulation has been the site of such debate since at least the early 1990s when the *Broadcasting Services Act* introduced a more far-reaching approach to self-regulation. Arguments in favour of self-regulation include the following:

Table 16.2 Examples of self-regulation

Issue	Instrument	Effect
Preventing unfair terms in telecommunications contracts	Consumer Contracts Industry Code developed by ACIF and registered with ACMA under Part 6 of the *Telecommunications Act*	Certain terms will be unfair and are not permitted in consumer contracts (including contracts with small businesses)
Preventing access by minors to pornography on the Internet	Internet Industry Codes of Practice developed by the Internet Industry Association and registered with ACMA under Schedule 5 to the *Broadcasting Services Act*	Internet Content Hosts are required to establish mechanisms for verifying the age of consumers who seek to access content rated R 18+
Ratings to be given to television programs	Commercial Television Code of Practice developed by Free TV Australia and registered with ACMA under Part 9 of the *Broadcasting Services Act*	All programs except news and some sports programs must be classified according to their content; restrictions are imposed on the time of day when these programs may be broadcast

- It avoids the inappropriate use of high-end enforcement options for relatively minor infringements—that is, it solves the 'sledgehammer to crack a walnut' phenomenon noted by Ayres and Braithwaite (1992, p. 52).
- It is less costly for government to administer.
- It enables those with detailed knowledge of a fast-changing industry to participate directly in rule making, helping to offset obsolescence.[5]

However self-regulation has also been subject to much criticism. Many of these criticisms are based around the perceived ineffectiveness of self-regulation, with critics questioning the motivations for self-regulation. Margot Priest (1997–98, p. 269) explains that self-regulation enables certain matters to be moved 'off the books' of government, while at the same time allowing government to point to some activity in relation to that matter. A further criticism is noted by Hamilton who, in a review of self-regulation in the insurance industry in 1995, speculated that the industry was 'perhaps primarily interested in protecting itself from legislative intervention rather than committing itself to an effective self-regulatory regime' (p. 363).

In Australia, consumer groups have argued that consumer interests are undervalued and that industry groups have been more successful in influencing the content of codes of practice.[6] In addition, regulators have been seen as slow to move in enforcing codes of practice when breaches occur. The Commercial Radio Inquiry of 2000 (the 'cash for comment' inquiry), revealed what the regulator described as:

> a systemic failure to ensure the effective operation of self-regulation particularly in relation to current affairs programs including a lack of staff awareness of the Codes and of their implications (ABA, 2000, Finding 2, p. 4).

However, much of the criticism in relation to this issue was directed at the self-regulatory system itself and the inadequate enforcement powers provided to the regulator in regard to both codes of practice and the licence conditions that it placed on the broadcaster.

One response to complaints about the effectiveness and motivations of self-regulation is that its potential is in fact only enlivened when there is a committed government regulator with effective regulatory tools operating in the background to the self-regulatory system. Ayres and Braithwaite describe such an agency by using the term 'benign big gun'. Gunningham and Rees (1997, pp. 402–3) propose independent third-party oversight as an additional measure of accountability and effectiveness. Both Ayres and Braithwaite and Gunningham and Rees incorporate consumer representatives into these effective systems of self-regulation. Ayres and Braithwaite explain that a 'tripartite' system of regulation involving industry, consumers and government helps to guard against convenient allegiances and regulatory capture that act against the public interest (p. 77). Gunningham and Rees cite the conclusions of a Canadian critic in relation to the effectiveness of voluntary codes:

> Meaningful involvement by consumer and other public interest groups is often what sets apart the successful codes from those which have received less support from government and the general public … it is difficult to imagine a situation where a voluntary arrangement could succeed without meaningful community, consumer and/or other third party involvement (Gunningham and Rees, 1997 p. 403 citing Webb and Morrison, 1996).

Activity 16.1

The former broadcasting regulator of the 1980s, the Australian Broadcasting Tribunal, was one of a small set of regulators identified by Ayres and Braithwaite (1992) as having far-reaching enforcement powers: by revoking a company's licence,

$\rightarrow$

the regulator could effectively put the company out of business. But the regulator itself (and its successor, the Australian Broadcasting Authority) identified some major limitations of a system that did not feature any 'mid-range' powers.

- What were the problems with broadcasting enforcement powers that the ABT identified in the late 1980s and the ABA noted a decade later? Are those criticisms still valid today?
- How would the changes to broadcasting powers outlined by the Department of Communications, Information Technology and the Arts (2006) change this situation?

Consumer consultation in self-regulation—the community 'portals'

Importantly, self-regulation has the potential to offer a greater role to consumer involvement than direct regulation. Both the *Telecommunications Act* and the *Broadcasting Services Act* require some participation or consultation with consumer representatives. This is an obligation that is placed on the regulator, the Australian Communications and Media Authority (ACMA), at the point of registering a new code. ACMA may only register a code if:

- in the case of telecommunications codes, ACMA is satisfied that at least one body or association that represents the interests of consumers has been consulted about the development of the code;
- in the case of broadcasting codes, ACMA is satisfied that members of the public have been given an adequate opportunity to comment on the code;
- in the case of Internet content codes, ACMA is satisfied that the body or association that developed the code 'invited members of the public to make submissions about a draft of the code and gave consideration to any submissions that were received from members of the public'.[7]

The difference between the *Telecommunications Act* on the one hand and the *Broadcasting Services Act* (regulating both broadcasting and Internet content) on the other, is significant: the *Telecommunications Act* effectively enshrines the role of representative associations, whereas the *Broadcasting Services Act* requires only consultation with members of the public. This difference explains the enhanced role of consumer groups in the drafting of telecommunications consumer protection codes in conjunction with industry representatives. It was in this context, through the Australian Communications Industry Forum (ACIF), that the Consumer Contracts Industry Code (listed in Table 16.2) was developed.

It is important to recognise that this model of self-regulation, despite criticism in relation to compliance and enforcement, demonstrates a more sophisticated engagement with consumers and a more sustained approach to community consultation. Nevertheless, experience in the telecommunications sector demonstrates that developing a code of practice can be a lengthy process, as industry participants, in some cases in conjunction with consumer groups or community representatives, cooperate to identify and describe the problem, draft a set of regulations, release that draft for public consultation, then revise the draft code to take account of feedback from other suppliers, consumer organisations, regulators and members of the public.

When the code is finalised by the committee, it must then go through a series of quality checks to ensure that it complies with established drafting standards (including the requirements of the Office of Regulation Review) and that it passes the community consultation tests described above, (as set out in a Certificate of Mandatory Consultation required by ACMA prior to registration). It may then be registered with the regulator—in this case, ACMA.

In order to understand how an issue makes it onto the self-regulation agenda such as this, we will look at how the Consumer Contracts code was developed.

Case Study

Consumer Contracts Industry Code

Background

In the late 1990s, consumer groups began lobbying the telecommunications regulator, the Australian Communications Authority (the ACA), to take action over unfair contract terms in consumer contracts for fixed-line (home) phone services, mobile phone services and Internet services. Some of these terms are set out in Table 16.3.

Table 16.3 Examples of unfair contract terms

Contract Term	Effect
Hidden charges—several contracts by leading suppliers included fees that were described but not quantified in either a summary of the contract (i.e. a brochure given to the consumer) or the full contract (usually available on the supplier's website)	Suppliers could nominate an administrative fee or other fee at any time during the contract and could impose new fees unknown to the consumer at the time of entering the contract

→

Reconnection fees and monthly fees were payable in all circumstances following disconnection of the customer by the supplier	These fees applied even in circumstances where the customer was disconnected as a result of supplier error
Supplier's right to unilateral variation of the contract	The supplier could introduce new terms, including increases in charges, at any time; however, the customer was not permitted to exit the contract without paying an early termination fee
Automatic extension of fixed-term contract	A customer was deemed to accept a variation or extension to a fixed-term contract (e.g. an extension for a further fixed term of 12 months or 24 months) if they did not respond within 14 days of a letter from a supplier notifying the customer of the intention to extend or vary

Consumer groups working in the telecommunications sector lobbied to have this matter placed on the agenda of the ACA and the telecommunications industry self-regulatory body, the ACIF (now called the Communications Alliance). A study of unfair practices in telecommunications sales and the various sources of law and regulation was conducted by one of the consumer groups. The report concluded that additional regulation was required and, as a result, in 2002 ACIF created a voluntary industry guideline. In 2003 one of the consumer groups conducted two audits of compliance with this guideline and found that there was widespread failure to comply. On the basis of this work, the ACA requested that ACIF develop a mandatory code of practice that would be registered with, and ultimately enforceable by, the ACA.[8]

In a parallel effort, other consumer groups, including the community legal centres, highlighted a need to amend state fair trading legislation or for the federal *Trade Practices Act 1974* to address the issue of unfair terms across all industries.[9]

The ACIF committee is formed

ACIF duly called for nominations to a working committee to develop the code. The committee was comprised of representatives from four suppliers (Telstra, Optus, Vodafone and Hutchison) and four consumer groups (Consumers' Telecommunications Network, Communications Law Centre, Small Enterprise Telecommunications Centre, and the Country Women's Association of Australia), along with participants from the ACA, the Australian Competition and Consumer

Commission, and the Telecommunications Industry Ombudsman. The committee had an independent chair and was supported by ACIF's manager of consumer codes.

Over twenty-five meetings took place in Sydney over the period May 2004 to January 2005. Most of these were full-day meetings held at ACIF's office, with telephone links to other locations when required. These meetings were intensive. Some were collegial, some were confrontational; all were time-consuming. Often, there was considerable work to be done outside meetings, in formulating ideas, drafting clauses and consulting with colleagues (in the case of supplier representatives) and other consumer organisations (in the case of consumer representatives).

Drafting the code

The committee did not start from scratch. It had a template for codes that required certain items to be included and it had the voluntary guidelines on the same subject, which, by that time, had been in operation for almost two years. It also had research and audit work conducted by one of the consumer organisations. Despite these resources, it took many hours of painstaking negotiation and drafting to turn a list of principles into a set of code provisions. While in-principle agreement was reached early in the process on the inclusion of some matters, considerable time was taken to fine-tune the choice of words with which to express those ideas in the code.

Gradually over the months that the committee met, the list of outstanding matters (essentially, those in dispute) was reduced until there were a handful of critical issues unresolved. At this point, a mediation session was called in an attempt to find new approaches to the problems or new ways of finding common points of interest. Although the mediation session itself did not provide the answers to the problems, it did serve to pinpoint the differences between the two sides. Several additional sessions resulted in some compromises from both sides with the result that a draft code of practice was released for public comment. The code participants agreed to some adjustments to the draft code on the basis of comments received at this time, following which ACIF delivered the code to the ACA in May 2005.

Registration by the ACA and commencement of the code

After some further revisions, the ACA registered the code with a phased introduction period. While some provisions came into force immediately, others were delayed until January 2006, when the code became fully operational and enforceable—just over five years after the Communications Law Centre delivered its first report on unfair practices in telecommunications contracts to industry and regulators at the end of 2000. Examples of some of the new code provisions are set out in Table 16.4.

Table 16.4 Examples of Consumer Contracts Code provisions

Issue	Effect of contract term before the Consumer Contracts Code	Rule imposed under the Consumer Contracts Code
Reconnection fee payable for any disconnection	The consumer must pay a fee even if they have been disconnected as a result of the supplier's own error	It will be unfair to impose a fee for reconnection where disconnection results from supplier error or the supplier's failure to perform its own obligations under the contract
Exclusion of all liability by the supplier	Statements made by salespeople are excluded from liability; the supplier is not liable for any damage caused by products and services	The supplier can only exclude liability as permitted by law, e.g. under the *Trade Practices Act*; the supplier must not attempt to exclude liability in a way that misleads the consumer as to their rights at law
Indefinite suspension	Exclusive and unlimited right of the supplier to suspend services while still requiring the customer to pay service fees	Clauses permitting the supplier to indefinitely suspend a service will be unfair under the Code
Automatic renewal of contract	The supplier can automatically extend a fixed-term contract	The supplier must obtain the customer's express consent at a reasonable time prior to the expiry of a fixed-term contract
Unilateral variation of the terms of a fixed-term contract	The supplier may increase charges at any time; the consumer is not permitted to terminate a fixed-term contract without paying an early termination fee	If the increase has anything more than a neutral or minor detrimental effect on the consumer, the consumer may exit the contract without paying an early termination fee

Assessment of consumer participation

The case study above describes a sustained effort to develop new rules to address a problem that affects many consumers of communications services. This approach is not unique to the telecommunications sector, but it is a useful example of consumers playing an active role in formulating new rules for consumer protection. Its importance in decision making, however, needs to be placed in context.

Firstly, this model for consumer consultation is more akin to the process that Reddel and Woolcock (2004, p. 75) describe as 'citizen engagement' (meaning 'efforts to expand citizen participation into decision-making') rather than a more far-reaching process of 'participatory governance' (meaning 'active partnerships and collaboration between civil society, the private sector and governments'). The authors note that attempts at community engagement are sometimes based on restrictive, linear methods of consultation that are familiar to governments but have limited value. They warn that:

> Dangers exist in replicating previous consultative models, linked to rational and linear policy-making, thus reducing citizen engagement to a selection of 'menus' which ultimately reinforce centralised and passive models of decision-making (p. 85).

To a large extent, the selection of 'menus items' for telecommunications consumer codes were already well established by the time the committee members arrived at the table to draft the contracts code. However, there were also elements to this case that do not appear in any policy and procedure handbook and it would be a mistake to underestimate them. The need for ACIF to confirm that it was capable of producing a result on a prominent consumer issue was instrumental, for example, in the decision to fund weekly airfares and accommodation for one of the consumer representatives to travel from Atherton (in far north Queensland) to Sydney. The vulnerability of ACIF was a useful factor for consumer groups seeking to maintain pressure on industry for a result, with the prospect of media coverage sympathetic to consumer interests held in reserve as consumer representatives continued to provide media comment on the issue (against the protests of other participants).

Secondly, the case study described above is only one, subjective account of the process and as Boxelaar, Paine and Beilin (2006) observe, there may be multiple accounts of any such process in which the various actors construct their own interpretations of events and allocate meanings in retrospect. Importantly, the authors note that although actors provide such interpretations, both at the time at which they participate and in recounting their experience later, they are not free to invent at will the rules of participation or their own role in the process (pp. 115–16).

Boxelaar, Paine and Beilin note that participants who set out with the best intentions of being open and engaged, sometimes revert to established methods of interaction:

> … participation by stakeholders occurs within parameters set by government, as the linear approach it entails ensures that government remains the owner and driver of the development process. This is likely to lead to the kind of community engagement that assimilates community and other stakeholders into government regimes of practice (p. 120).[10]

They conclude:

> Agencies have to come to terms with the fact that their organisational structures, processes and practices are constitutive of the social organization of the change process, and hence critical to the success of the engagement and collaboration process more broadly. It is important to diagnose where the tension between prevailing tools and instruments of public administration compromise the construction of inclusive platforms for change that create a space for diverse participants to participate (p.124).

In contrast, other critics such as Christine Parker (2002) would emphasise the importance of responsiveness on the part of a corporation, rather than relying on the role of the regulator in fostering democratic processes. Parker also places less emphasis on direct participation of 'third parties' such as consumer representatives. In advocating the internalisation of stakeholder concerns and values, Parker foregrounds the role of employees and self-regulation professionals within the organisation to promote a degree of 'permeability' within an 'open corporation' (see Chapter 8).

Interestingly, it appears that this approach may be in the ascendancy within the communications sector, judging by the character of self-regulatory processes adopted in relation to Internet content regulation and proposed in relation to mobile content. These models mark a substantial lessening of representative consumer participation in self-regulation when compared to the consultative approaches adopted for the code work of ACIF or the Telephone Information Services Standards Council (TISSC). They can perhaps be seen to occupy the opposite point on the spectrum of participation to the systematic consultative model proposed by the Consumer Driven Communications project sponsored by the ACA in 2004.

Against this background, the participatory process used in the Consumer Contracts Code is a good example of both the benefits and limitations of this method of consumer consultation. The institutionalised nature of code formation in telecommunications in Australia meant that it took five years for the code to be in force, and required many months of demanding negotiation and drafting by committee. It is also important to remember the practical difficulties faced by consumers in accessing these forums. The initial audit of contract terms was only possible because one of the consumer groups had access to a volunteer law graduate for six months; similarly, the ACIF Committee member representing one of the other consumer groups contributed her time without remuneration from that organisation or from ACIF or from Department of Communications Information Technology and the Arts (DCITA).

Thirdly, there are certainly some compromised outcomes from both the supplier and consumer perspective in the content of the Consumer Contracts Code. ACIF's mode of consensus decision-making meant that several of the code rules were transformed from clear consumer objectives into more abstract principles with significant exemptions. Similarly, for suppliers, some important protections for business practices were ultimately clouded by qualifications grafted onto provisions that themselves constituted exemptions to first-order rules.

Conclusion

The development of the Consumer Contracts Code may have formed the apex of consumer engagement in communications regulation in Australia. Recent proposals for self-regulatory schemes dealing with mobile phone content suggest an attempt by some sections of the industry to retreat from the degree of consumer participation evident in the ACIF process. The terms of engagement for consumer representation and community participation appear to be shifting. While it is not a perfect model of consumer consultation, the ACIF committee structure as it operated in this case was probably the most influential source of consumer input so far in telecommunications regulation. Consumer groups saw a direct translation of their objectives into code rules, largely without the mediating influence of a regulator. Whether the level of compromise demanded by the system itself, and expressed in the content of the code outweighs the benefits of industry-sponsored and implemented rules, remains to be seen. But if this is to be replaced by a new model that winds back the existing levels of consumer participation and community consultation, opposition to self-regulation is likely to escalate while public confidence withers.

- This chapter presents a case study for the formulation of a new code of practice in the telecommunications industry, with an emphasis on the role of consumer organisations in developing the code rules.
- The chapter provides the context for the development of this code and sets out some of the arguments for and against industry self-regulation.

Tutorial questions

- Can consumer representatives and members of the public effectively contribute to the development of communications regulation?
- What are the strengths and weaknesses of a participatory process like the one used for the Consumer Contracts Code?
- What are some of the areas in media regulation where industry-based self-regulation is clearly not the best approach?

Recommended reading

Australian Communications Authority, 2004, *Consumer Driven Communications: Strategies for Better Representation*, ACA, Melbourne.

Ayres, I. & Braithwaite, J., 1992, Responsive *Regulation: Transcending the Deregulation Debate,* Oxford University Press, New York.

Black, J., 2002, 'Critical Reflections on Regulation', *Australian Journal of Legal Philosophy* 27, pp. 1–35.

Senate Select Committee on Information Technologies, 2000, *In the Public Interest: Monitoring Australia's Media,* April, Parliament of Australia, Canberra.

Websites

Australian Communications and Media Authority: www.acma.gov.au

Australian Communications Industry Forum (now called Communications Alliance): www.acif.org.au

Australian Competition and Consumer Commission: www.accc.gov.au

Communications Law Centre: www.comslaw.org.au

Consumers' Telecommunications Communications Network: www.ctn.org.au

Office of Communications: www.ofcom.gov.uk

Notes

1   This power is found in placidum 51(v) of the Constitution that relates to 'postal, telegraphic, telephonic and other like services'. For a discussion of this power, see Holly Raiche (2001).

2   In addition to the categories of service listed in the table, datacasting services are dealt with separately under Schedule 6 to the BSA. The national broadcasting services (the ABC and SBS) are exempted from most sections of the BSA and operate under their own acts of Parliament, the *Australian Broadcasting Corporation Act 1983* and the *Special Broadcasting Service Act 1991*.

3   If a carrier uses its own infrastructure to provide services to the public it will (with some exceptions) be both a carrier and a service provider.

4   For an outline of the 'command and control' approach and alternative approaches based on self-regulation, see for example Ayres and Braithwaite (1992) and Darren Sinclair (1997).

5   On the potential applications for self-regulation, see Ayres and Braithwaite (1992); Angus Corbett (2002); Margot Priest (1997–98); Darren Sinclair (1997); Neil Gunningham and Joseph Rees (1997); Robert Baldwin (2004). For a more far-reaching approach to self-regulation, based largely on internal corporate systems and a theory of corporate social responsibility, see Christine Parker (2002).

6   Attitudes to self-regulation are canvassed in the 2005 Senate Committee report, *A Lost Opportunity? Inquiry into the provisions of the Australian Communications and Media Authority Bill 2004 and related bills and matters* (pp. 76–84). The Productivity Commission reports into *Broadcasting* (2000, Chapter 13) and *Telecommunications Competition Regulation* (2001, Chapter 13) also document positions from a range of groups. See also the Senate inquiry reports, *In the Public Interest: Monitoring Australia's Media* (2000). For a sustained critique of deregulation and self-regulation, see Robert Britt Horwitz (1989).

7   *Telecommunications Act* section 117(1)(h)(i); *Broadcasting Service Act* section 123(4)(b)(iii); *Broadcasting Services Act* Schedule 5, clause 62(1)(e).

8   See the reports by the Communications Law Centre (2001, 2003a and 2003b).

9   For a review of the parallel operation of the Consumer Contracts Code and the provisions of the *Fair Trading Act 1999* (Vic.), see Robert Neely and Olivia Kwok (2006).

10   In making this point, the authors refer to the work of M. Dean (1996).

References

ABA (Australian Broadcasting Authority), 2000, *Commercial Radio Inquiry: Final Report of the Australian Broadcasting Authority,* August, Australian Broadcasting Authority, Sydney.

ACA (Australian Communications Authority), 2004, *Consumer Driven Communications: Strategies for Better Representation,* ACA, Melbourne.

ACIF (Australian Communications Industry Forum), 2005, *Industry Code—Consumer Contracts,* ACIF, Sydney.

Ayres, I., & Braithwaite, J., 1992, *Responsive Regulation: Transcending the Deregulation Debate,* Oxford University Press, New York.

Baldwin, R., 2004, 'The New Punitive Regulation', *Modern Law Review* 67.3 (May 2004), pp. 351–83.

Boxelaar, L., Paine, M. & Beilin, R., 2006, 'Community Engagement and Public Administration: Of Silos, Overlays and Technologies of Government', *Australian Journal of Public Administration* 65.1 (March 2006), pp. 113–26.

Communications Law Centre, 2003a, *Report on Fair Terms in Telecommunications Consumer Contracts 2003,* Communications Law Centre, Sydney.

Communications Law Centre, 2003b, *Telecommunications Consumer Contracts: Compliance with the ACIF Consumer Contracts Industry Guideline,* Communications Law Centre, Sydney.

Communications Law Centre, 2001, *Unfair Practices and Telecommunications Consumers,* Communications Law Centre, Sydney.

Corbett, A., 2002, 'The (Self) Regulation of Law: A Synergistic Model of Tort Law and Regulation', *UNSW Law Journal* 25.3, pp. 616–650.

Dean, M., 1996, 'Putting the Technological into Government', *History of Human Sciences* 9.3, pp. 47–68, cited in Boxelaar, L., Paine, M., and Beilin, R., (2006), p. 121.

Department of Communications, Information Technology and the Arts (2006), *Meeting the Digital Challenge: Reforming Australia's media in the digital age*, March, DCITA, Canberra.

Department of Communications, Information Technology and the Arts 2005, *Proposed Reforms to the Broadcasting Powers of the Australian Communications and Media Authority—Issues Paper*, November, DCITA, Canberra.

Gunningham, N. & Rees, J., 1997, 'Industry Self-Regulation: An Institutional Perspective', *Law and Policy* 19.4 October, pp. 363–414.

Hamilton, J., 1995, 'The Duty of Disclosure in Insurance Law—The Effectiveness of Self-regulation', *Australian Business Law Review* 23.5 October, pp. 359–67.

Hitchens, L., 2004, 'Commercial Broadcasting—Preserving the Public Interest', *Federal Law Review* 32.1, pp. 79–106.

Horwitz, R.B., 1989, *The Irony of Regulatory Reform: The deregulation of American Telecommunications*, Oxford University Press, New York.

Neely, R. & Kwok, O., 2006, 'Unfair Terms in Consumer Contracts—The New Benchmark', *Communications Law Bulletin* 24.4, pp. 19–22.

Parker, C., 2002, *The Open Corporation: Effective Self-regulation and Democracy,* Cambridge University Press, New York.

Priest, M., 1997–98, 'The Privatisation of Regulation: Five Models of Self-Regulation', *Ottawa Law Review* 29.2, pp. 233–302.

Productivity Commission, 2000, *Broadcasting*, Report No.11, AusInfo, Canberra.

Raiche, H., 2001, 'The Communications Power: The Real Threat to States' Rights?'
    Communications Law Bulletin, 20.1, pp. 14–19.

Ramsay, I., 2005, *Reform of the Broadcasting Regulator's Enforcement Powers,* Australian
    Communications and Media Authority, Sydney.

Reddel, T. & Woolcock, G., 2004, 'From Consultation to Participatory Governance? A
    Critical Review of Citizenship Engagement Strategies in Queensland', *Australian
    Journal of Public Administration* 63.3 September, pp. 75–87.

Senate Environment, Communications, Information Technology and the Arts
    References Committee, 2005, *A Lost Opportunity? Inquiry into the provisions of the
    Australian Communications and Media Authority Bill 2004 and related bills and matters,*
    March, Commonwealth of Australia, Canberra.

Sinclair, D., 1997, 'Self-Regulation Versus Command and Control? Beyond False
    Dichotomies', *Law and Policy* 19.4 October, pp. 530–59.

Webb, K. & Morrison, A., 1996, 'The Legal Aspects of Voluntary Codes', draft paper
    presented to the *Voluntary Codes Symposium*, Office of Consumer Affairs, Industry
    Canada and Regulatory Affairs, Treasury Board, Ottawa, 12–13 September, cited
    in Gunningham and Rees (1997).

Part Three Summary

In this Part we have offered several complementary perspectives on the question of 'access' in new media worlds. It was shown that fundamental issues of social inequality underpin the terms of people's access to new media, and ICTs more generally.

Similarly, the term 'participation' has been shown to mean a great deal more than simply interaction or interactivity. In fact, access, interaction and participation are all signifiers that have had a long history in communication and social sciences. But while participation has not completely disappeared from media analyses and practices, it has lost its primary role. It was argued that for the term to continue to have value, there is a need for a restoration of notions of power into our analyses of access and participation in traditional and new media.

The South African government's shift in emphasis away from the establishment of telecentres to the creation of Multi-Purpose Community Centres (MPCC's) is a renewed social policy strategy to engage with those with particular needs. In MPCCs, communications services are provided with other government services—related to health, safety and security, welfare social grants and identity documentation—to local communities. This partial shift in emphasis, from providing a communication infrastructure to delivering social services, will undoubtedly raise new policy questions and practical difficulties, especially regarding capacity and coordination across government departments; questions concerning infrastructure, training, management and security to name some of the main ones.

Discussions of policies for achieving media diversity inevitably occur within a wider context of the political and media systems of a nation. The discussion of these diversities pointed to contradictions and tensions between, on the one hand, global flows of people, products and services and images and, on the other hand, the desire by governments and their agencies to preserve local cultures, traditions and institutions. This is the context for policies for diverse media provision in democracies.

'Co-regulation', as a form of self-regulation may have reached a high-water mark in consumer engagement in communications regulation in Australia with the development of the ACIF Consumer Contracts Code. Yet the terms of engagement for consumer representation and community participation appear to be shifting again, towards even more self-regulatory models. The role of consumer groups in the process of regulation may be significantly reduced in such a scenario.

QUESTIONS

- What are the social conditions required, in addition to simply the provision of ICTs, before people will be in a position to benefit from such access?
- How will the term 'participation' need to be rejuvenated to remain useful in evaluating new media technologies and systems?
- What are the main underlying contradictions and tensions to be managed by nation states wishing to develop policies for media diversity?
- Which features characterised the model for consumer engagement in communications regulation?

Recommended reading

Black, J., 2002, 'Critical Reflections on Regulation', *Australian Journal of Legal Philosophy* 27, pp. 1–35.

Hallin, D.C. & Mancini, P., 2004, *Comparing Media Systems: Three Models of Media and Politics,* Cambridge University Press, Cambridge.

Horwitz, R.B., 2001, *Communication and Democratic Reform in South Africa,* Cambridge University Press, Cambridge.

Manovich, L., 2001, *The Language of New Media*, MIT Press, Cambridge.

Pateman, C., 1970, *Participation and Democratic Theory*, Cambridge University Press, Cambridge.

Webster, F. (ed.), 2004, *The Information Society Reader,* Routledge, London.

PART FOUR

Participation

This is the final and shortest section of this book. It draws together and extends discussion of key themes that emerge and are explored in depth earlier. Those themes include social networking, commercialisation of the World Wide Web, and its mediatisation and corporatisation. The chapters here also address several of the key motivations for participation in new media cultures—motives like longing or desire (search), need and its perversion (greed), and social control expressed through the convergence of Web moralities.

The expression of these motives takes on a special significance in the context of the new media and the history of the Internet, and in this section these motives are represented through three developments in new media culture: innovations in search and the emergence of social networking; the emergence of brand as a new communications medium through which value is returned to commodities and return on investments is assured, and the contested domain of Net morality where commercial imperatives run up against older human needs for communal and individual expression.

In Chapter 17, Virginia Nightingale suggests that the new *search* paradigms that characterise Web 2.0, or the *semantic* web, provide a key to understanding the appeal of social networking. She argues that it is not just 'mobile privatisation' (Jim McGuigan, Chapter 1) that makes new media attractive, but the psycho-social attachment users develop to Web culture, and to the types of online engagements it makes possible. Search connects powerfully with the humanness of Web users and with the very human desires its potential 'knowability' promises to satisfy. It's easy to imagine that, if searched the right way, the world online is ready to deliver answers to life's secret and unfulfilled longings. The longing inherent in search is a powerful motivator for participating in life online and for social networking. New search developments are commonly used to describe the diversification of Web platforms (Web 1.0; Web 2.0, Web 3.0 etc.) that essentially reference shifting modes of participation practised in the World Wide Web. Social networking offers users the capacity to access and benefit from the Web's collective intelligence, and in the process sets up expectations against which real world social interactions are evaluated.

Celia Lury (Chapter 18), by contrast, draws attention to the ways that money, and more recently 'brands', mediate our communications with others. Lury points out that money emerged very early in human history as a medium of commerce and communication. As a communication medium, money speaks a very specific language—one where quality and values are always measurable, and therefore comparable. Still it has taken thousands of years for monetary value to seep into aspects of life now being commercialised online. In this context, Lury argues that brand is a way of reintroducing the concept of quality into debates about value and worth, by linking products and commodities with attractive lifestyles and prosperity. For this reason, brand has today become a new medium of communication. Lury's chapter helps us to recognise that beyond the digital 'machinery' of new media, there is a different social technology at work. As she reminds us, money is a medium that frames our achievements, identities and personal commitments. Money provides access to, and opportunities for engaging with, the world. In a similar way, the brand mediates our engagements with the world of objects and products, and also frames identity and a sense of belonging. But it assists the progressive rendering of all life into the money system.

Think about it

The linking of brand and identity raises an interesting question about the role brands play in contemporary culture. Mediation works in two directions. Brands may be useful in reconciling money and quality, but:

→

- When we integrate these ideas into our frames of identity and belonging, are we not also putting a monetary value on ourselves?
- What is the difference in quality between a Porsche identity and a Honda identity?
- Is branding making it more likely that we will value each other by the brands we choose and the communications services we subscribe to, even the 'coolness' of our capitalism (McGuigan, Chapter 1)?

Money, as Graham Murdock (Chapter 19) shows, works as a powerful motive force in attracting some people to life online. This has led to a particular controversy in Second Life (SL), an online world that has its own currency. The controversy has arisen because some 'residents' of SL have been able to capitalise on innovations and properties developed in SL by selling them in the real world. Through eBay, the Linden has acquired an exchange rate with the US dollar. The real world profiteering from SL property has caused some soul-searching about the nature of SL and the values that underpin it. Murdock uses this transformation of SL as an exemplar on which to base a discussion of the three moral economies we usually regard as interlinked: commerce, public goods and gifts.

In this final chapter, Murdock points to the contradictions that emerge in Web culture when, as discussed by Nightingale in Chapter 2, the World Wide Web is both corporatised and mediatised. In this context, gifting is usurped by commerce and users locked into systems of reciprocity dictated by contracts and agreements that seem to multiply more rapidly than online users. The inherent reciprocity of gift-giving is transformed into legal obligation, and in that form fights against the initial philosophy of sharing that made the World Wide Web such a radical departure from the traditional media.

- Returning to the issue of motives—it may sometimes seem that greed and control are coming to dominate life online. What implications might this have for the survival of interest and curiosity, the search for the reciprocity, sharing and communalism in emerging media worlds?

QUESTIONS

Emergence, Search and Social Networking

17

CHAPTER OVERVIEW

'The brain of a bee looks puny, but it may hold the secrets that will change the world' (Macey, 2006). The theory of evolution has provided metaphors that inform theories of *artificial emergence*, or self-organising systems design. The resulting emergent systems are deployed in many of today's most popular Web services—like YouTube and MySpace. Most importantly emergent systems inform new approaches to search, designed to harness the power of collective intelligence. But the use of evolutionary motifs cannot disguise the fact that the Internet is not a natural phenomenon but a complex, chaotic, human artefact. Using it changes the way people relate to each other and to the world around them. This chapter examines the shift to the social networking and networked individualism of Web-interactivity, and considers the social implications of the shift away from the social formations they are replacing.

Key terms

emergence
search
social networking
collective intelligence
social formations

Issues

- Why are insect and fungus metaphors so often used to describe the World Wide Web?
- Why has Google become so powerful, and does it matter?
- Is there life online without search?
- Are mass Web entertainments like MySpace and YouTube signposts to the future of the Internet?

Introduction

> When I imagine the shape that will hover over the first half of the twenty-
> first century, what comes to mind is not the coiled embrace of the genome,
> or the etched latticework of the silicon chip. It is instead the pulsing red and
> green pixels of Mitch Resnick's slime mold simulation, moving erratically across
> the screen at first, then slowly coalescing into larger forms. The shape of those
> clusters—with their lifelike irregularity, and their absent pacemakers—is the
> shape that will define the coming decades. I see them on the screen, growing
> and dividing, and I think: That way lies the future (Johnson, 2001, p. 23).

Human activity in cyberspace is sometimes likened to the activity of insects or
moulds and fungi. The metaphors are pervasive: the 'Web' situates us in the insect
world before we even realise we've entered a habitat. Once there, we discover
that the spider has scuttled off and the Web has been occupied by ant colonies or
worker bees, and when climatic conditions are right, the spore of sludge mould
(Johnson, 2001) suddenly blooms and oozes across the virtual landscape. This is
because the simple intelligence of insects is the preferred model on which the
current development of artificial intelligence, and especially artificial emotional
intelligence, is based. In Johnson's work the metaphors are used to explain difficult
concepts and to predict the future shape and transient nature of cyber cultures. But
they also reveal a preference for *biological* explanation that reduces human agency to
a form of intuitive response to the prevailing conditions of cyberspace.

The frontispiece of Johnson's book reproduces two diagrams. The first is a
diagram of the human brain and the second a map of Hamburg, Germany, drawn in
1850 (Johnson, 2001, p. 8). The two images demonstrate a remarkable similarity in
shape: the brain and the city appear almost identical as though the human brain has
somehow, inexplicably, replicated itself in the city's plan or alternatively the citizens
of Hamburg have intuitively organised the city as a cerebellum. The images invite
the reader to assume that there is something in our nature motivating us to create
organisational structures that replicate the structure of the human brain. Another
surprising feature of the juxtaposition of the two images is that they suggest a rather
extraordinary variation on Kant's ideas about **transcendence**, which far exceeds the
primarily constructivist position presented in Johnson's book. The images suggest
an isographic identity—the city looks like the brain and vice versa—so a superficial
visual similarity between two images supposedly confirms a parallel between the
body as a living organism to create itself and the city as a living communities. The
same idea is repeated in Johnson's fascination with the images of slime mould,
which he sees as a representation of the life force at work in the World Wide Web.

It is instructive to consider the consequences of such an approach. If the
emergence of cyber culture is attributed ultimately to our genes or to a life force,

it is a small step to also thinking that its quality and nature space is 'natural'—that the provision or withdrawal of the conditions that feed the growth of the cyber 'sludge mould' is not the product of deliberative human action, but an inevitable outcome of evolution. There is a danger in the use of such analogies of presuming that cyberspace is **biologically determined**; and then failing to investigate the power structures that control and place limits on the expression of human agency in, and access to it.

Transcendence The process of transcendence, which can be traced from the philosophical writings of Immanuel Kant (1724–1804), has been called 'transcendental idealism'. George Herbert Mead (1863–1931) explained Kant's position like this: '[Kant's] doctrine has been called also transcendental idealism, because it implies that the ideas, the meaning of the world is to be accounted for not by the world itself as it presents itself immediately to our senses and thought, but by running those forms of thought, those ideas and meanings back to the nature that knows them' (George Herbert Mead, 1909, para 11).

Biological determinism Reyna (2002, p. 166) points out that this is a form of reductionism that seeks 'to explain a higher level of reality in terms of a lower one', as occurs when people imply that 'what happens at the level of the social and cultural is ultimately explained at the biological level by the genes'.

GLOSSARY

Evolutionary theories of technological innovation usefully remind us that the World Wide Web has been made by humans for human use (e.g. Ziman, 2000; Mokyr, 2002); that the imprint of our humanity, of human bodies and human minds, and of our evolutionary history, is inherent in the very nature of the World Wide Web and its ergonomics of engagement. But if the use of biological modelling fosters notions that the future of the Internet is beyond control by institutions of power and privilege, ethics and rationality, it deflects critical analysis from a proper concern with the power structures currently shaping the emergence of cyber culture. This occurs when insect and fungus metaphors shift from being models on which new software design is based, to being assumed explanations of human behaviour in cyber space.

A second level of critical analysis, equally deserving of analysis and research, is also 'naturalised' by biologically determinist explanation—the implications for human society and culture of the long-term use by humans of systems where artificial emergence is deployed. This concern currently finds expression in media stories of computer game addiction:

[handwritten note in left margin:] Similar feeling with social networking sites? ✳

'Gamers report they feel much calmer when they are playing and feel euphoric when they win. Playing the game sets up a series of patterns, habits and routines that are addictive in the same way drugs are' (quote from clinical psychologist, Jo Lamble, in Bachl, 2006).

[handwritten note in left margin:] V. true for 'bug bears'? ✳

These patterns are alleged to cause trouble when life online seems more attractive than real life, when online 'you can be somebody you're not ... you live a life you would like to lead' but 'you become out of touch with society altogether' (in Bachl, 2006). The 'out of touch' theme is also a feature of debates on the impact of ICTs for the future of democracy (Putnam, 2000; Coleman and Gøtze, 2001) and political participation. These concerns point to the importance of clarifying the implications of the deployment of self-organising (or *emergent*) systems in cyberspace and the impact they are having on cyber culture. So while Johnson underestimates the importance and power of the giant corporations of cyber culture, his work provides the basis for a critical evaluation of how emergent systems might be changing the organisation of ways humans organise their patterns of engagement with the world around them.

Questions

1   What, if anything, does slime mould demonstrate about emergent systems?
2   If slime mould offers a template for the future, what sort of future might it be?
3   What are the limitations of emergent systems for understanding cyber culture?

Links: Slime Mould

News: 'Slime mould solves maze puzzle.' Abbie Thomas (News in Science) reports on the experiment that showed that slime mould can 'solve' a maze puzzle. ‹http://www.abc.net.au/science/news/stories/s189608.htm›

Photos: This site provides photos of slime mould so you know what it is. ‹http://waynesword.palomar.edu/slime1.htm›

Movies: This site includes a series of QuickTime videos of slime mould in action. ‹http://cosmos.bot.kyoto-u.ac.jp/csm/movies.html›

Criticism: This site provides a mildly critical review of Mitch Resnick's book, *Turtles, Termites, and Traffic Jams: Explorations in Massively Parallel Microworlds* (1994). Resnick's work strongly influenced Johnson's book. ‹http://serendip.brynmawr.edu/complexity/course/emergence06/bookreviews/drosen.html›

Activity 17.1

Read the introduction to Steven Johnson's book *Emergence: The Connected Lives of Ants, Brains, Cities, and Software* (2001) and then check out the following links to information on slime mould. Johnson suggests that studies of the action of slime mould can explain emergent systems as models for human activity in cyberspace, and that it can also offer models for designing emergent systems of artificial intelligence that will change the way we organise our lives. The following links are a small sample of information available online about slime mould—but what do you think?

The next Web

Johnson has pointed out that the study of *self-organising systems* or 'morphogenesis' has informed a field of engineering that produces systems of '*artificial emergence*'. Some such systems are already a feature of everyday life in cyberspace. They are so widely used in online applications to guide and influence consumer choices that Johnson argues, 'In recent years our day-to-day life has become overrun with *artificial* emergence: systems built with a conscious understanding of what emergence is, systems designed to exploit those laws the same way our nuclear reactors exploit the laws of atomic physics' (Johnson, 2001, p. 21).

Much of the online human action we think of as 'interactivity' falls into the Web 2.0 category. Software, modelled on the interactive skills of its creators, enters into dialogue with human users and creates a site-based response environment where the software predicts the user's intentions based on current and past choice patterns. The better the software is at predicting the user's intention, the more satisfying the use of the site is felt to be. This type of software specialises in making better use of collective intelligence and user-generated content. The technology gurus talk about the ways this type of software is changing the nature of business practices online. In broad terms, Web 1.0 was about establishing websites and encouraging search (the Microsoft era); Web 2.0 discovered user-generated content and financed the cost of collecting it with advertising (the Google era); Web 3.0 will complement user-generated content with data-sharing options and finance these expensive services by linking the choices of individual users to the automatic generation of market research data. Chester (2006) sees huge problems in these developments:

Good for Media Ethics argument.

The most powerful communications system ever developed by humans is increasingly being put in the service of selling, commercialization and commodification. And it will lead to an inherently conservative and narcissistic political culture, in which the interests of the self and the consumption of products are the primary, most visible, media messages. And unless we begin to challenge it now, the emerging digital culture will seriously challenge our ability to effectively communicate, inform and organize (Chester, 2006, p. 2).

Chester's primary concern is not with Web 3.0 sites and services, but with the financing of their development and the liberties that are being taken with user freedoms by the alliances developed between advertising and the cyber culture giants (Google, Microsoft, Yahoo! etc.).

Think about it

What characteristics of the Internet and cyber culture make them so attractive to their users?

Emergent systems use 'an implicit "architecture of participation", a built-in ethic of cooperation, in which the service acts primarily as an intelligent broker, connecting the edges to each other and harnessing the power of the users themselves' (O'Reilly, 2005, p. 5). Organising a Web service based on an emergent system involves co-opting Internet users in the co-creation of content. In order for the emergent systems to be successful, users have to contribute information about themselves, lots of information ... The more information people disclose, the more the software is able to anticipate their preferences. For example, the more time spent using a voice recognition program, the more responsive and reliable the program should become. The more information and transactions a customer delivers to a brand or e-commerce site, the better the online service they should receive. So, emergent systems allow Internet sites to respond to past user actions by anticipating future interests or intentions, provided users keep feeding information into the system.

The importance of search

One area where the deployment of emergent systems is crucial is in search. When searching, users are continually providing information about what they are looking for. At the same time they provide collateral information about themselves: verification of identity (usernames, email addresses); their status as consumers (credit card details); and their geographic location (home addresses; selection of some search options). And needless to say, information about specific preferences of all kinds is also uploaded in the process: music and movie preferences; sexual preferences; ethnic and religious affiliations; pet and clothing preferences. Search is both:

- a catalyst for the release of valuable information from Internet users, and
- a means of generating additional information about users based on the analysis of click stream data.

The centrality of search in cyber culture is one of the reasons search engines like Google and Yahoo! have so quickly become giants of life online. In considering what makes the Internet compelling for humans, Battelle (2005) has suggested that search is motivated by two linked desires: *discovery* and *recovery*. Discovery refers to searching born of inchoate longing, a search for information 'we assume must be there', somewhere, because of the ubiquitous nature of the Internet. Recovery refers to the search for understanding or knowledge based on information we know 'is already available' on the Web (Battelle, 2005, p. 32). Both discovery and recovery remind us that 'desire' is the heart of human activity online.

However, emergent systems are not particularly sensitive to the psychodynamics of search to which human users are attracted. By its nature digitisation reduces human behaviour to patterns of on–off switching. When human action is reduced to on–off switching it loses connection to a 'way of life' and becomes instead a 'database of intentions' or the patterns that emerge from the click stream (Battelle, 2005). A 'database of intentions' may create the ephemeral and puzzling patterns of Internet traffic and networking that reinforce the supposed relevance of the insect world analogies, but it leaves little room to appreciate the sociability or the desires that can make cyberspace such a compelling place to spend time. More importantly it is unable to appreciate the emotional and psychological depth of human investment in the objects of search and even in the search process itself. Emergent systems, like Google's search algorithm, lack sensitivity to the human cost of investment in search (Battelle, 2005).

Google

As both a service and as an organisation, Google's initial growth occurred in response to grassroots demand for better search. As it has grown, and especially since its listing on the US stock exchange, Battelle notes that Google has had to formalise its responsiveness to the mass digital public in order to manage its responsibilities to new internal and external constituencies—its shareholders, its employees and its advertisers. Battelle argues that these new responsibilities have compromised Google's capacity to respond swiftly to problems experienced by search users, and he warns that sometimes users have more to lose than just search results from Google's expansion (Battelle, 2005, Chapter 6).

Activity 17.2

Read Chapter 7 of Battelle's (2005) book, *The Search: How Google and Its Rivals Rewrote the Rules of Business and Transformed Our Culture* (2005, pp. 153–72).

This is a case study of the impact of Google making a change to its search algorithm on an e-commerce business.

Questions

- What limitations does this case study suggest for the future of e-commerce businesses?
- What implications does this case study foreshadow for consumer freedoms and rights in cyberspace?

Battelle's investigation of Google and other online search companies shows the extent to which system users are dependent on the algorithms developed, on the management structures, and on the systems they set up for user feedback beyond the click stream. The click stream offers highly attractive data from an advertising industry perspective: the data is measurable, reliable and easy to analyse for additional information about consumers. In addition, the collateral information routinely provided by users can be mined using online data analysis as a form of consumer research (Ross and Nightingale, 2003, pp. 62–4). As a result, the advertising industry has been highly influential in securing the expansion of online search and in using its financial power to ensure that even the user-generated content available online is friendly to advertising. In the case of photo archiving sites, advertiser pressure has resulted in the introduction of continuous surveillance and censorship.

This extract from Reiter's Camera Phone Report illustrates the point.

The *WSJ* [Wall Street Journal] notes, 'My Space's ability to sell advertising, its primary source of income, depends in part on scouring the site for objectionable material. As part of that effort, My Space last year contacted other sites that help users post material online, most notably Photobucket, and asked them to launch cleanups of their own.'

Photobucket has 30 people working full time on monitoring images and will spend $1 million during the next year on the effort. The company can monitor more than half the images and wants to be able to check all of them (Reiter's Camera Phone Report, 17 May, 2006).

The specificity and usefulness of the sales and consumer information generated by *paid search services* and other online data analysis is used by marketers and advertisers to develop better and more cost effective media planning and campaign management. And click stream analysis has contributed to the evolution of new ways of understanding how people negotiate the choices available at a given website, the nature of a brand's appeal and the potential for brands to develop as media in their own right (Lury, 2004). The guiding hand of the advertising and e-commerce sectors has therefore been active in supporting the expansion of metasearch, the search for better search (Battelle, 2005, pp. 274–6).

see Lury, Chapter 18 on the brand as a medium.

Theory link

Varieties of search

The success of page rank search (the standard Google search service) has encouraged experimentation with additional ways of delivering search services (Battelle, 2005, Chapter 11). The new developments in search take existing approaches as their starting point and explore ways of generating richer search results in terms of usefulness to users. These approaches (Battelle, 2005, pp. 258–79) include:

1 *Ubiquity*: This type of search aims to improve search by ensuring that as much of the world's information as possible is available for searching. It is dependent on more and more people establishing websites and uploading 'more and more information into Web indexes'. The promise of ubiquity is alluring since if everything, everyone, and every data source in the world is searchable, then the possibility of finding the perfect answer to a question is greatly enhanced—at least as long as the list of results is not unmanageable.

2 *Personalisation* or 'local search' involves the use of a person's past search history (click stream) to generate more relevant search results for them, but also to predict what others who share a common characteristic with that person might find relevant. It is made possible by applying models of artificial emergence (mentioned above) to personal search histories, on the assumption that a

searcher's intent can be fairly accurately assessed on the basis of past searches and search outcomes.

3   The *semantic Web* (Battelle, 2005, pp. 263–76) (sometimes referred to as Web 3.0) involves finding ways to search information available online but that does not register in a Web-page-based search. Instead it is designed to locate semantic information: particular words, sounds, images or multimedia files. The most familiar form of semantic Web searching (or *metasearch*), and probably the easiest to understand and practise, is *tagging*, where existing files are tagged with semantic information, like keywords, which are searchable (see for example <www.Technorati.com>).

4   *Domain-specific search* aims to provide more complex and useful search for users interested in specialised fields of knowledge. Domain searching is a way of customising search results.

5   The *Web-time axis* aims to make it possible to recover every search ever carried out, by making it not a real-time but a recorded-time moment. In Battelle's words, currently 'the Web has no memory', but once it has a memory, once the Web itself has become a searchable data archive, the Web searches of every user will be re-searchable through time. This he suggests will be the impetus for more innovation and change in the nature of search.

In practice many popular search sites draw on a range of the above varieties of search and combine them with social networking options. Holohan (2006) recently described search services based on 'topic communities' and 'social search'. Clusty .com, an example of *topic community* search, is a form of domain-specific search in that it presents results as a cluster (or community) of topics, each referencing specific search domains. *Social search* builds social networking into the search process in ways that allow users access and share search results generated by other users. Yahoo!'s *del.icio.us* site is an example of **social bookmarking**. In this case the term, *social networking,* encompasses access, searching and, importantly, sharing.

The importance of social networking for the future of the World Wide Web is the topic of Henry Jenkins' (2006) exploration of convergence culture. For Jenkins, social networking, of the kind evident in studies of fandom, holds the key to the World Wide Web as a popular entertainment environment. Jenkins argues that fandom has provided models for the development of new popular culture forms for the World Wide Web because they established peer-to-peer sharing long before computing and the Internet delivered the World Wide Web.

And fans were quick to recognise the benefits the World Wide Web offered to search and share more effectively and efficiently. They also quickly adopted the Web as an environment for commercial transactions and for collectively pressuring

Theory link

see convergence discussion in Dwyer, Chapter 3

Social bookmarking   del.icio.us is a social bookmarking website, which means it is designed to allow you to store and share bookmarks on the Web, instead of inside your browser. This has several advantages.

First, you can get to your bookmarks from anywhere, no matter whether you're at home, at work, in a library, or on a friend's computer.

Second, you can share your bookmarks publicly, so your friends, co-workers, and other people can view them for reference, amusement, collaboration, or anything else. (Note that you can also mark bookmarks on del.icio.us as private—only viewable by you—if you like.)

Third, you can find other people on del.icio.us who have interesting bookmarks and add their links to your own collection. Everyone on del.icio.us chooses to save their bookmarks for a reason. You have access to the links that everyone wants to remember. You can see whether two people have chosen to remember a link, or whether it was useful enough for a thousand people to remember—which may help you find things that are useful for you, too (http://del.icio.us/about/; accessed 10 October 2006).

industry to take fan interests and demands seriously. Jenkins has argued (2003) that online investments of fandom operationalises and enacts *collective intelligence*, a term adopted from Pierre Lévy (1997).

Activity 17.3

Pierre Lévy defines collective intelligence as 'A form of universally distributed intelligence, constantly enhanced, coordinated in real time, and resulting in the effective mobilisation of skills' (Lévy, 1997, p. 13). He clarifies this definition by adding that, 'No one knows everything, everyone knows something, all knowledge resides in humanity. There is no transcendent store of knowledge and knowledge is simply the sum of what we know' (Lévy, 1997, pp. 13–14). Because the online search makes it easier to locate and apply all the little 'somethings' that everyone knows, Lévy argued that a new form of collective intelligence is emerging in cyberspace.

Compare Levy's definition of collective intelligence with Surowiecki's use of the same term, but based on the collective intelligence or 'wisdom' of crowds (Surowiecki, 2005, pp. xi-xxi).

Question

- What aspects of Levy's understanding of collective intelligence are missing from Surowiecki's account?

Jenkins no doubt overstates the significance of fandom, yet points to a very interesting sociological phenomenon—the migration of certain types of pre-existing communities-of-interest online. Fans are one example, but so are local family history societies, sporting clubs, stock market investment clubs, some church groups. These pre-existing communities of interest are local groups who benefit from the ease of contact and the access to data archives facilitated by the Web, and by sharing experiences, insights and importantly their personal collections of data. All provide compelling examples of how dependent the Internet is on its users to achieve any sort of *ubiquity* and *sociality*. What is not clear, however, is what impact the access to the global communities of interest has had on the local groups. Internet users transform previously semi-private communally-owned knowledge into globally searchable text, and at the same time generate new data about user action online. They play an important role in establishing and maintaining online archives of information relevant to their interests and in some cases have pushed the provision of public access to government archives. Through peer-to-peer sharing users push the traditional media industries towards new business models for the distribution of media products and new models for copyright ownership. What is often forgotten, however, is the fact that these communities are held together in the real and the virtual world by a passionate commitment to the objects of their search.

Networked individualism

The new culture on the Web is all about consumer creation; it's composed of things like the nearly 30 million blogs out there and the 70 million photos available on Flickr. With a click of the mouse, anyone can be a journalist, a photographer, or a DJ. The audience—that 1 billion-plus throng linked by the Web—itself is creating a new type of social media. That's leading to the creation of hundreds of promising Next Net businesses (Shonfeld, Malik and Copeland, 2006, accessed 10 October 2006)

Castells (2001, Chapter 4) chooses the term 'networked individualism' to describe the sociality of Web culture. He notes that this mode of affiliation is not new to Western culture, but has characterised the past 200 years of its transition to modernity. The shift from *ascribed* belonging to *affiliative* belonging, for example, was a major interest of early sociologists who sought to explain the shift from traditional communal organisation based on clans, tribes and class to urban individualism with its emphasis on identity formation through personal choice and individual expression. The World Wide Web intensifies the practice of individualism and replaces previously meaningful social formations (certain sorts of local clubs, teams, audiences, congregations) with networked individualism. The implications of the rise of the network and the concomitant reduction in the variety of human social formations is an interesting and perhaps perplexing outcome of the impact of emergent systems in Web culture. In much the same way that Mokyr (2002) has described how one outcome of the Industrial Revolution was the restructure and relocation of work (from extended family businesses based in the home, to managed workplaces situated in factories and offices), Castells points out that the significance of place is much reduced in the affiliative networks of Web culture. Where place was once the primary site of social contact and identity formation, the Internet now not only challenges but increasingly takes first place.

In Web culture, affiliation through networking is the means of access to affiliation-based communal experiences that previously were available only by belonging to a place-based community. As a result, the social groups where people invest in identity and belonging are as likely to be dispersed global entities (the '1 billion plus throng') as local groups. As a reaction to the pressures of contemporary working life, people increasingly seek to enjoy 'community' online, with people who share similar views or ideals, but this is an 'individualised relationship to society', a 'specific pattern of sociability, not a psychological attribute' (Castells, 2001, p. 128).

There is not to suggest that local community has been completely replaced by networked individualism. Other chapters in this book provide examples of the establishment of local groups as a result of Web access to data and resources.

And research about mobile communications, for example, reiterates the importance of the links users create between their real worlds and net communities (Ling, 2004). Ito has suggested that the 'pedestrianism' of mobile phone use links the person of the user to the places that the user frequents. This minimises, she suggests, the disconnection between Web-belonging and world-belonging; it grounds the mobile net more firmly in the lived environment of the user. However, even in this case, the user's local world becomes increasingly personalised—more family and home centred—as 'the virtual colonises more and more settings of everyday life' and the reasons for talking to strangers evaporate (Ito, 2006, p. 8).

So perhaps it's more accurate to argue that the Web extends the range and nature of the informal formations available for individual membership—formations

see Cook, Chapter 4; Lally, Chapter 10

Theory link

where membership and participation is voluntary. Networked individualism, the name Castells has given to this type of formation, avoids much of the political intrigue and real world responsibility of local and formal associations and clubs. However, it seems likely that the migration online of pre-existing communities-of-interest has cushioned the social impact of networked individualism. I suggest this because I began this chapter with a discussion of sludge moulds, ants and bees. Insect colonies suggest parallels with networked individualism. Ants and bees may have 'puny brains' but they get things done—they create termite mounds, make honey and hives, reproduce. They seem to resemble informal formations, like crowds, in their single-minded pursuit of an objective. And crowd behaviour has recently provided the rationale for Surowiecki's take on *collective intelligence* as 'the wisdom of crowds' where the 'waggle dance' of bees is described as a 'collectively brilliant solution to the colony's food problem' (Surowiecki, 2005).

In the last two years Yahoo! has bought Flickr and del.icio.us, News Limited has bought MySpace, Microsoft is developing its *Zune* platform and, in addition to developing its own sites to keep its users engaged, Google has now bought YouTube. But as Battelle has pointed out in relation to Google, these major takeovers lead of necessity to management styles that are slower to respond to the involvement of users as co-creators. Instead, the co-creation of content is routinised at most of these sites. User complaints and comments are also routinised. Site management and user service becomes a matter of 'crowd control'. And we are all the poorer for it.

Conclusion

In this chapter we have identified certain puzzling aspects of cyber culture today. Firstly, cyberspace creates an insatiable demand for information (Battelle, 2005). Second, like ants and worker bees, the inhabitants of cyberspace engage in endless unpaid labour, creating and uploading information (Johnson, 2001; Jenkins, 2006). Third, the seemingly inexplicable individual patterns of activity created by inhabitants of cyberspace and their activities assist the evolution of the cyber environment (O'Reilly, 2005; Lévy, 1997). And fourth, certain 'entrenched institutions' that have been made possible by and depend on the unpaid work of cyber culture's inhabitants, hold immense power to determine the terms on which people are permitted to participate in the culture those people have created (Battelle, 2005; Jenkins, 2006).

In order to sustain life online, emergent systems that promote user co-creation and that learn how to serve users by analysing their online activity, are playing a key role in the promotion of social networking. But social networking, though compelling, is a highly individualised form of sociality. Its power to render traditional people formations redundant raises important questions about the implications of a resultant disinvestment in more formalised aspects of communal life (like government, organisations, etc.). Finally, we noted early research results that suggest that the pedestrianism of the mobile net may play a role in minimising this disconnection, though at the same time intensifying the personalisation of the local.

This chapter has covered the following issues:

- The pitfalls of biological determinism as an approach to understanding cyber culture.
- The use of emergent systems in designing new software and services for cyber culture.
- The importance of search, and the emerging approaches to search.
- The implications of social networking and networked individualism.
- The ways networked individualism is replacing the use of other types of social formations, particularly informal formations.

CHAPTER SUMMARY

Tutorial questions

- Given that the Internet is dependent on user content, why are users expected to pay for access to the information they seek?
- Does Google's 2006 takeover of YouTube provide yet more evidence of the Internet being primarily a system for transforming the labour and interests of its users into exploitable products for e-commerce?

Recommended reading

Battelle, J., 2005, *The Search: How Google and Its Rivals Rewrote the Rules of Business and Transformed Our Culture*, The Penguin Group, Portfolio, USA.

Chester, J., 2006, 'The Google YouTube Tango', www.thenation.com/doc/20061030/chester, accessed 14/10/06.

Holohan, C., 2006, 'A Gaggle of Google Wannabees', *Business Week*, News Analysis, 10 October: www.businessweek.com/technology/content/oct2006/tc20061004_441574.htm/

Jenkins, H., 2006, *Convergence Culture: Where Old and New Media Collide,* New York University Press, New York and London.

Mead, G. H., 1909, *On the Influence of Darwin's Origin of Species*, unpublished manuscript (circa 1909?), 17 pages: spartan.ac.brocku.ca/~lward/Mead/Unpublished/Meadu06.html, accessed 10/10/2006.

O'Reilly, T., 2005, 'What is Web 2.0: Design Patterns and Business Models for the Next Generation of Software', published on O'Reilly, 09/30/2005. <http://www.oreillynet.com/lpt/a/6228>, accessed 12/10/06.

Websites

Google: www.google.com
O'Reilly, T: www.oreillynet.com

References

Bachl, M., 2006, 'Computers breed new addiction', *The Sun-Herald,* p. 42, 15 October.

Battelle, J., 2005, *The Search: How Google and Its Rivals Rewrote the Rules of Business and Transformed Our Culture,* The Penguin Group, USA.

Castells, M., 2001, *The Internet Galaxy: Reflections on the Internet, Business and Society,* Oxford University Press, Oxford and New York.

Chester, J., 2006, 'The Google YouTube Tango', www.thenation.com/doc/20061030/chester, accessed 14/10/06

Coleman, S. & Gøtze, J., 2001, *Bowling Together: Online Public Engagement In Policy Deliberation:* http://www.bowlingtogether.net/ (PDF format).

Holohan, C., 2006, 'A Gaggle of Google Wannabees', *Business Week,* News Analysis, 10 October: www.businessweek.com/technology/content/oct2006/tc20061004_441574.htm/

Ito, M., 2006, 'Introduction: Personal, Portable, Pedestrian', in Ito, M., Okabe, D. & Matsuda, M. (eds), *Personal, Portable Pedestrian: Mobile Phones in Japanese Life,* pp. 1–16, MIT Press, Cambridge, MA and London.

Jenkins, H., 2006, *Convergence Culture: Where Old and New Media Collide,* New York University Press, New York and London.

Jenkins, H., 2003, 'Interactive Audiences?', in Nightingale, V. & Ross, K. (eds), *Critical Readings: Media and Audiences,* Open University Press, McGraw Hill, Maidenhead, Berkshire, UK.

Johnson, S., 2001, *Emergence: The Connected Lives of Ants, Brains, Cities and Software,* Scribner, New York, London, Toronto, Sydney.

Lévy, P., 1997, *Collective Intelligence: Mankind's Emerging World in Cyberspace,* (trans.) R. Bonnono, pp. 13–19, Perseus Books, Cambridge, Mass.

Ling, R., 2004, *The Mobile Connection: The Cell Phone's Impact On Society*, Morgan Faufman, Elsevier, San Francisco.

Lury, C., 2004, *Brands: The Logos of the Global Economy*, Routledge, London and New York.

Macey, R., 2006, 'The Buzz in Science is What Makes a Bee so Smart', *The Sydney Morning Herald*, News Section, 17 October, 2006.

Mead, G. H., 1909, *On the Influence of Darwin's Origin of Species*, unpublished manuscript (circa 1909?), 17 pages: spartan.ac.brocku.ca/~lward/Mead/Unpublished/Meadu06.html, accessed 10/10/2006.

Mokyr, J., 2002, *The Gifts of Athena: Historical Origins of the Knowledge Economy*, Princeton University Press, Princeton and Oxford.

Putnam, R.D., 2000, *Bowling Alone*, Simon and Schuster, New York.

O'Reilly, T., 2005, What is Web 2.0: Design Patterns and Business Models for the Next Generation of Software, published on O'Reilly, 30 September: www.oreillynet.com/lpt/a/6228, accessed 12 October 2006.

Reiter's Camera Phone Report, 2006, http://www.cameraphonereport.com, 17 May.

Reyna, S.P., 2002, *Connections: Brain, Mind, and Culture in a Social Anthropology*, Routledge, London and New York.

Ross, K., & Nightingale, V., 2003, *Media and Audiences: New Perspectives*, Open University Press, McGraw Hill, Maidenhead, Berkshire, UK.

Shonfeld, E., Malik, O. & Copeland, M.V., 2006, *The Next Net 25*, published at CNN. Com

Surowiecki, J., 2005, *The Wisdom of Crowds: Why the Many Are Smarter Than the Few*, Abacus, London.

Ziman, J. (ed.), 2000, *Technological Innovation as an Evolutionary Practice*, Cambridge University Press, Cambridge and New York.

18 Just Do It: The Brand As New Media Object

Key terms

brand
medium
frame
image

Issues

- What role do brands play in organising how we think about the world—not only the ways we shop but the value we attach to the commodities we buy?
- In what ways can brands be described as 'new media objects'?
- Why do brands encourage interactivity—usually in the form of shopping and market research—and yet discourage interaction between customers and the company (especially when customers wish to question brand production ethics or product quality)?

CHAPTER OVERVIEW

The argument presented in this chapter will be that brands mediate the supply and demand of products and services through the organisation, coordination and integration of market information. The chapter therefore puts forward five reasons for arguing that brands resemble 'new media objects'.

- Brands are multi-layered: they involve a mode of production; a technical or physical support for their activities (a platform); and a set of conventions that articulate or give expression to that support or platform.
- Brands mediate between two spaces: the world of the producer or brand owner and the world of the consumer, where the brand is like an interface.
- Brands operate as an open-ended production loop, in that the brand is never a finished product (unlike the products it releases to the consumer market). Instead, the existence of the brand 'as a brand' is enough to alert the consumer to expect it to express itself periodically in a new or different form—as perhaps a new product range; a new advertising campaign; a new set of consumption options.
- Brands provide interactivity between two realms (production and consumption) but take absolute control of any interaction associated with the product. They appropriate information about their customers and integrate that information into planning for new products and new information campaigns.
- Their market position allows brands to control the time and place of their market interventions to take best advantage of the flows of the global economy.

As the Internet matures as a medium its role in supporting and elaborating this process becomes clearer. Cyberculture is emerging as an environment where commerce is organised through the online management of branded consumer communities.

> **Brand**   In this chapter, the terms 'the brand' or 'branding', are not meant to imply a single thing, or even a single set of processes. To assume that 'the brand' is a single thing would be to mistake the multiple and sometimes divergent layers of activity that have gone into producing the brand. The assumption here instead is that because the brand is a happening fact (Whitehead, 1978), there is a demand—a sociological imperative—for something else to happen yet.

A media theory of the economy

In a series of publications (Callon, 1998; Barry and Slater, 2002; Callon and Law, 2003), Michel Callon has addressed the operation of markets. It is of course economic theory that has traditionally been concerned with the economy and its major components, markets. But the anthropologist Callon's aim is to open up the market to multiple forms of knowledge, not simply the economic. What follows is an attempt to develop a *media* theory of the economy, that is, an account of how the economy is organised as if it were a medium. And the **brand** will be seen as an important driver in the organisation of the economy in this way. The argument will be that brands mediate the supply and demand of products and services through the organisation, coordination and integration of market information, and in doing so contribute to a change in the operation and culture of markets.

In classical economic theory, price is seen as the mechanism that is able to calibrate the market by coordinating supply and demand through the circulation of information. Put simply, in a market buyers oppose sellers, and the prices that resolve this conflict are the input but also, in a sense, the output or outcome of the agents' economic calculation (Callon, 1998). Another way of saying this is that price is a mechanism by which the equivalence—the substitutability—of goods is established in quantitative terms. In one of the most well known sociological discussions of price—*The Philosophy of Money* (1990 [1907]) by Georg Simmel— the role of money in privileging the quantitative as a mode of evaluation is understood in cultural terms. For Simmel, money is the representative of 'a cognitive tendency in modern science as a whole: the reduction of qualitative determinations to quantitative ones' (1990, p. 277). In short, money is responsible for the growth in significance of the category of quantity over that of quality. The quantitative tendency exemplified by money contributes, Simmel argues, to the loss of singularity and the acceptance of relativity, in which more and more things are not simply put in relation to one other, but are rendered comparable in value or made interchangeable.

Money, Simmel argues, underpins 'the tendency to dissolve quality into quantity, to remove the elements more and more from quality, to grant them only specific forms of motion and interpret everything that is specifically, individually and qualitatively determined as the more or less, the bigger or smaller, the wider or narrower, the more or less frequent' (1990, p. 278). This is what Simmel calls the 'merciless objectivity' (1990, p. 431) of money: 'money takes the place of the manifoldness of things and expresses all qualitative distinctions between them in the distinction of "how much"' (1990, p. 127). For Simmel, writing at the beginning of the twentieth century, money provides the conditions for the growth of calculative functions and the emergence of a blasé attitude in people, that is, to the growth of indifference toward qualitative distinctions between objects (and subjects).

Activity 18.1

1 Do you think Simmel was correct to argue that money reduces the quality of things to quantity, to more or less, to bigger or smaller?

2 Think of some examples where you believe the emphasis on quantity or price has led to a decline in quality or a neglect of values other than value for money, or where the loss of skills in terms of quality workmanship has resulted from an emphasis on 'good enough' production.

3 Can you think of examples where this is not the case—where the introduction of markets and money as the measure of value has improved the quality of production?

The brand is presented here as an alternative device for the calibration of the market; the suggestion is that the brand is not so much a *means*, as is argued of money by Simmel, but a *medium*. This claim can be broken down into a series of inter-linked points. The attributes of products able to function as elements of a mechanism of exchange in the case of the brand are multiplied, that is, price is only one of a number of attributes of the brand. The other attributes typically include the place (of purchasing a branded product or service, or entering into a brand experience), packaging, promotion and product qualities. In marketing discourse, these are known as the 'four Ps'. Like price, these product attributes are not fixed, but variable, and are able to act as multiple dimensions of judgment. Thus the brand—like price—is able to act as a mechanism for coordinating the activities of the market, of framing the exchange between producers and consumers, but this mechanism is comprised of multiple dimensions, not simply one, price. It is

see
Nightingale,
Chapter 2

Theory link

these multiple dimensions that provide the basis for the controlled reintroduction of quality into the means of exchange. That the brand acts as a medium in the coordination of markets is perhaps one of the most important reasons that Callon (2002) is able to describe the contemporary economy as an economy of qualities.

The writer Gertrude Stein seems to agree with Simmel when she writes, 'Whether you like it or whether you do not money is money and that is all there is about it' (1936, quoted in Zelizer, 1998, p. 59). But contemporary sociologist Zelizer argues that modern consumer society has turned 'the spending of money not only into a central economic practice, but *a dynamic, cultural and social activity*. … This is the irony: while the state and the law worked to obtain a single national currency, people actively created all sorts of monetary distinctions. Outside the world of printing and minting, people spent less energy on the adoption of different objects as currencies than on the creation of distinctions among the uses and meanings of existing currencies—that is, on earmarking' (1998, p. 59). In this perspective, money is not only a means but also a medium. And, so this chapter suggests, are brands; that is, they too are dynamic social and cultural activities, a way of making meaning. But, crucially, brands may be seen as a form of corporate earmarking: while not controlled by the state, brands are usually privately owned currencies. They are attempts by firms—not people in their everyday lives—to create their own worlds of distinction, and they have more power to introduce these mediums into our lives and so organise exchanges, not only economic transactions but also social and cultural interaction. Other examples of this tendency include electronically mediated forms of money being developed by banks, universities, transport companies, commercial firms, utilities and even Club Med (Zelizer, 1998, p. 65). In this way, brands can be seen to produce a media economy.

Activity 18.2

Brands online—some examples

Adam Ardvisson has suggested that:

> 'The brand … corresponds to the condition of a 'network culture' where the mediatisation of the social has progressed to the point that it is no longer meaningful to maintain a distinction between media and reality, where information is no longer something that represents reality, but something that provides an ambience in which reality can unfold' (Ardvisson, 2006, p. 126).

→

Visit each of the sites listed below and explore the sites as thoroughly as possible. Do not forget to visit the additional links they supply to their affiliated sites. Identify the range of products offered by each site and describe how the organisation of the site corresponds to a 'network culture'.

- Eddie Bauer Department Store: ‹http://eddiebauer.com›
- Porsche Design Group: ‹http://www.porsche-design.com/live/PORSCHE_DESIGN_ en.PorscheDesign›
- Friends Reunited: ‹http://friendsreunited.co.uk›

These sites have been chosen for the ways they demonstrate how the Internet is expanding the range of 'real world objects' that can be 'mediatised' and transformed into online commodities. The sites include a conventional department store that references the domestic lives of its users; a design group that explicitly prioritises 'quality' through workmanship, design and exclusiveness; and a social networking site that aims to reunite long-lost friends by making use of user-generated content.

- How would you describe the 'ambience' created by each of these sites?
- What real world objects have been 'mediatised' and transformed into online commodities by these sites?
- In what ways does each of these brands construct a relationship with its online community—what links between site users/customers are implied by the nature of the information available at the site?
- What objects, commodities or information flows are used to bind users to the sites?
- How does each of these brands address the issue of money?

The rest of this chapter seeks to explain how the brand may be seen as a medium, and with what implications, not just for the economy but also for culture more widely. In the approach that Callon adopts—sometimes called Actor Network Theory (or ANT)—technological devices or objects are seen as 'image instruments' or as 'media of translation' (Latour, 1987; Law, 1984). This chapter will make use of this approach in relation to the economy but intends to elaborate the notions of medium, frame and image. After all, the brand stands at the intersection of the diverse histories of computing, information technology and media as well as economics, marketing and design; as such, it may be described as a new media object (Manovich, 2001), an example of 'the "broadcast" distribution of commodities' (Rodowick, 1994).

Medium A casual glance at any dictionary draws attention to the multiple meanings of the word 'medium': as something in between or intermediate; a middle state or condition; a method or way of expressing something. The sense in which it is used in this chapter draws primarily on this last meaning. Just as money tells us how much a given commodity is worth, the brand tells us how much to value it. So, for example, vintage clothing stores trade primarily in second-hand goods with designer labels—a particular item may no longer command its original price, but the brand continues to communicate information about the cultural significance of the object.

In the new media environment, brands are able to actively engage their customers and potential customers using email newsletters, product promotions, online forums, games and competitions to push consumption. Brands are colonising the online environment and borrowing characteristic forms of online communication to achieve their ends.

The multi-layered character of the brand

A first way in which media theory is helpful in understanding branding is that it draws attention to the multi-layered character of the brand's ontological existence. Frederic Jameson describes a medium as consisting in a specific form of aesthetic production, a technology, and a social institution (1991, p. 67). Rosalind Krauss, in a discussion of fine art (1999), suggests that a medium involves a relationship between a technical or physical support and the recursive conventions with which a particular genre articulates or works on that support. Put simply, for Krauss, the medium is a dynamic support for practice. Lev Manovich describes a new media object in terms of an operating system, an interface, software applications or operations, and forms or commonly used conventions for recursively organising the new media object as a whole (2001, p. 11). And the brand or branding may similarly be seen to comprise a mode of production, a technical or physical support, and a set of conventions that articulate or work on that support. It too is a dynamic platform or support for practice.

Brands and communication media— two-way mirrors

Secondly, the notion of medium makes it possible to think of branding in terms of communication, and in particular of communication as the framing of temporal reciprocity across disunified or disparate spaces (Rodowick, 1994). This makes it possible to consider the brand in relation to the metaphors of **frame**, window and mirror as used in discussions of architecture, painting and cinema (see Deleuze and Guattari, 1994, pp. 186–99; and Manovich, 2001, pp. 95–103 for useful discussions). The most basic definition of the frame is 'a window that opens onto a larger space that is assumed to extend beyond the frame' (Manovich, 2001, p. 80), but it can also be described as that which 'separates two absolutely different spaces that somehow coexist' (Manovich, 2001, p. 95). As such, the frame organises two-way communication between different spaces—in the case of the brand, between the spaces of production and consumption. One of the key developments in the work of Deleuze (1986, 1989) and others on cinema is to consider the frame as itself dynamic: 'Frames or sections are not co-ordinates; they belong to compounds of sensations whose faces, interfaces, they constitute' (Deleuze and Guattari, 1994, p. 187). The suggestion here is that the brand organises the activities of the market as if it were an interface. As an interface, the brand is a frame that organises a two-way exchange of information between the inner and outer environments of the market, informing how consumers relate to producers and how producers relate to consumers, along the dimensions mentioned earlier—place, packaging, price and product qualities.

GLOSSARY

Frame   This term is used here to refer to the ways the brand is able to limit what is seen, like a window, and what is represented, like a mirror or a screen. The frame determines where we look and what we are likely to see. As a frame, the brand is much more active in communicating with its customers than was the screen in the era of broadcasting. Brands are active frames, like interfaces that present certain information and change what we are able to see in reaction to the button we click and the questions we ask.

The 'loop' as control structure for both media and brands

Central to the performativity of the brand as an interface are certain practices in marketing that function in an analogous way to programming techniques in both broadcasting and computing. The most significant example of these practices is the loop, a central control structure of many new media objects. This is then a third respect in which it may be helpful to consider the brand as a new media object. As

Manovich notes, 'Programming involves altering the flow of data through control structures, such as "if/then" and "repeat/while"; the loop is the most elementary of these control structures' (2001, p. xxxiii). From this perspective, the marketing practices developed in the advertising industry in the second half of the twentieth century—including the adoption of the four Ps—incorporate the activities of consumers in the processes and products of production and distribution. This incorporation—or looping—typically involves the marketer adopting the position of the consumer, that is, of imagining the consumer (Lury and Warde, 1996). However, as the practice of computer programming illustrates, the loop and the sequential progression are not necessarily mutually exclusive (Manovich, 2001). Just as a computer program progresses from start to end by executing a series of loops, so the marketing knowledge or information produced in the market research is used in a sequential process of product differentiation. As new products or services are developed, they themselves become marketing tools, generating further information, and so, the brand progresses or emerges in a series of loops. It is an open-ended object.

Interfaces for interactivity—but not interaction

Although the exchanges organised by the brand are dynamic and two-way, they are not direct, symmetrical or reversible. Or to put this another way, the brand as interface is a site—or diagram—of interactivity (not of interaction). The interface of the brand connects the producer and consumer and removes or separates them from each other; it 'is revealing of some relationships, but it keeps others very well hidden' (Pavitt, 2000, p. 175). From this point of view the brand may be seen as both promoting and inhibiting 'exchange' between producers and consumers, and informing this asymmetrical exchange through a range of performances of its own. In particular, it is important to bear in mind that the temporality that informs the communication of a brand is defined not by instantaneity, but by managing the temporal delay between receiving a request and responding to it (Rodowick, 1994). That is, the interface of a brand manages the 'response time' of interactivity, the interval in time between (qualitatively differentiated) products. These intervals may be organised—in the practices of brand positioning—to produce the relations between branded products (and branded places, packaging and promotion) as constancy or sameness, or as difference, as fashion, as novelty or as event.

In this way, the brand—whether its products are always the same like Coca-Cola or always changing like Nike—may be seen as an open, dynamic object. Yet while brands may be described as open this should not be taken to imply that this openness is either total or unregulated or that it contributes to freedom in any simple sense. Indeed, it does not even necessarily lead to more open competition between firms. On the one hand, brands may be distinguished from each other as more or less open; so, for example, Nike may be seen as slightly more open than Coca-Cola in the sense that it is organised so as to be more responsive to shifts in consumer use that are to do with lifestyle although it has been notoriously unresponsive to consumer criticism in relation to production practices. Paradoxically, its *openness* is one source of Nike's economic and cultural power as a brand: that is, responsiveness is one of the factors that has aided its domination of the sports apparel market, limiting the terms of entry for other firms.

In this sense, the 'openness' of brands is frequently more apparent than real in relation to many brands, including Nike. While brands have the potential to bring 'an understanding of the outside, of society, economy and customer, to the inside of the organisation and to make it the foundation for strategy and policy' (Drucker, quoted in Mitchell, 2001, p. 77), this potential is not often realised. In practice, the situation remains much as it did when marketing expert Theodor Levitt called for a marketing revolution in 1960:

> When it comes to the marketing concept today, a solid stone wall often seems to separate word and deed. In spite of the best intentions and energetic efforts of many highly able people, the effective implementation of the marketing concept has generally eluded them (quoted in Mitchell, 2001, p. 77).

The flow of brand culture

If the framing of the market by a brand is successful as is the case with Nike, the brand owner is able not simply to dominate a given market at a given moment in time, but to organise its spatial and temporal activities in the flows that characterise the global economy (Appadurai, 1996; Shields, 1997). And in this fourth respect too, the notion of the medium is helpful in the attempt to describe the role of the brand insofar as media have been widely understood in terms of flow, notably by Raymond Williams in his discussion of television (1974). Simmel had at the beginning of the twentieth century described the liquidity of money, drawing attention to the importance of the rhythm of its movements—of private saving, corporate investment, buying and selling, credit and debt—for the wider culture. As he puts it, 'Money is nothing but the vehicle for a movement in which everything else that is not in motion is completely extinguished' (1990, p. 511).

But Williams provides an elaboration of the notion of flow. In his account of the experience of watching television (1974), flow is a sequence or serial assembly of units characterised by speed, variability and the miscellaneous. In developing this account, Williams notes the historical decline of the use of intervals between programs in broadcasting. Or rather, he draws attention to a re-evaluation of the interval. In the early days of broadcasting on radio, for example, there would be intervals of complete silence between programs. But now, no longer dividing discrete programmes, no longer an interruption or silence, the interval is productive; as with the management of the response gap of interactivity, it is what makes a sequence of programs into a flow. Think here of the role of idents, that is the logos of broadcasting companies, which fill the previous gaps or silences, making possible multiple associations within and between programs. The true sequence or flow in broadcasting in such cases is now not the published sequence of program items, but a series of differently associated units, some larger and some smaller than the individual program. These associations are punctuated—or marked—by a logo. And in the case of branding, the use of a logo similarly enables the making of one link after another, and, in the process of making associations, makes brands— as hyperlinked objects—not only visible and identifiable, but also gives them a dynamic unity. In this respect, to draw a fifth parallel with media, brands may be seen as the effects of hyperlinking, the activity that forms the basis of interactive media (Manovich, 2001: 61).

Let me describe how this is organised in the practices of brand management. To begin with, in marketing practices, the logo—which may be a name (Nike), a graphic **image** (the Swoosh), or a slogan (Just Do It)—is able to secure the recognition of a brand through a process of repetition. That is, the insistent repetition of a logo in marketing means that when people are asked for examples of brands most of them are able to give a list of examples, displaying what marketers call 'brand awareness'. Marketers further argue, however, that 'awareness' must be supported, if a brand is successful, by a second aspect, 'image' (Keller, 1998). Brand image includes the associations that a consumer has of a brand. So, for example, for Nike, brand image is designed to include the desired associations of sports, determination and competitiveness. What marketers call 'image' is produced in the practices of brand positioning, which include product design, promotion and positioning products in the media as well as the management of the logo itself. In so far as they are successful, the logo comes to function as a specular or speculative device for magnifying one set of associations and then another. Through the management of brand image a brand owner may thus come to make and mark relations between a flow of products so as to produce a recognisable brand. Alternatively put, the brand is a device for the management of flow, providing some kind of security for the brand owner in highly dynamic, distributed markets.

Image This term, as used here, refers to the way brand logos operate like computer desktop icons or 'short cuts'. The brand represents itself by its logo. The logo in turn immediately brings to mind a reservoir of cultural knowledge about the brand that has been cultivated through the marketing of its previous products. Sometimes an imagined history is invented and 'sold' to audiences through an advertising campaign. This set of associations is then used to promote new products and to drive new sales.

Very often, the brand is able to be presented by its logo as having a personality or face, whether the logo is of a person or more abstract values. This process of personalisation is not so unusual in the economy; it has a long and complex history in the organisation of exchange. Simmel explains the significance of personalisation in relation to money as capital by suggesting that the significance of a sum of money, such as one million marks, is more than a mere aggregate of unconnected units. He argues that qualitative significance arises because an aggregate sum of money forms 'a comprehensive unit in the same way as the value of a living creature, acting as a unit, [and] differs from the sum total of its individual organs' (Simmel, 1990, p. 272). In other words, he suggests that capital as quantity, as units of land, of money is capable of being realised as quality in certain circumstances. Similarly, the point being made here is that a brand is capable of being related to in terms of both quantity (how much is it worth?) and quality (what does it mean?). Indeed, this second dimension is of vital importance in a brand's relation to consumers, since it is what underpins the affective relations between brands and consumers, which typically include—for a successful brand—some degree of trust, respect and loyalty but may also include playfulness, scepticism and dislike.

But it is also worth pointing out that consumers' relations with brands are often hard to put into words. They may operate at a subconscious level. Indeed, the reliance of marketing on the use of highly repetitive practices tends to mean that brands are not only so ubiquitous as to be obscene (Baudrillard, 1994) but might also be described as obsequious, at least in the sense in which the sociologist Bourdieu (1977) uses the term. As Bourdieu notes, the term obsequium was used by Spinoza to denote the 'constant will' produced by the conditioning through which 'the State fashions us for its own use and which enables it to survive'. Bourdieu adopts the term to designate the public testimonies of recognition that are set up in every group between individuals and the group. Here the term may be seen to apply to the 'constant will' called into being by the taken-for-granted ubiquity provided by brands in consumer societies.

As a medium of exchange the brand is not simply a matter of the communication of private individuals however: it is coordinated by organisations, including small- and medium-sized firms and multinational corporations as well as voluntary organisations, charities and public bodies. And at the same time that it is a social currency (Zelizer, 1998)—a way in which people bring meaning to various exchanges—it may be protected in law in the form of trademark as private property (see below). It is thus a kind of currency by fiat. Put more strongly, it is an example not only of the mediation of the economy and the marketisation of everyday life but also of the privatisation of the activities of the state, linked to the growing power of multilateral agencies such as the World Bank and the International Monetary Fund.

Editor's comment   The IMF has itself commissioned a series of promotional advertisements broadcast on CNN and other cross-national channels, perhaps the first stages of establishing itself as a brand.

In so far as a brand is protected as private property in the laws of trademark and passing off, it is not only potentially exploitable as the site of product innovation, but also as a means of corporate growth, both through brand extension, in diffusion lines and franchises, and regeneration as when companies such as Virgin are able to use the brand as a form of venture capital. Indeed, as an image instrument, the brand is an object by which capital may not only extract rent from (intellectual) property through for example licensing or merchandising arrangements, but also build monopolies, dominate markets and secure investments in the ownership of innovation (Strathern, 1999). Alternatively put, as John Berger says of the perspectival window in painting, the market frame of the brand is 'a safe let into the wall, a safe into which the visible has been deposited' (quoted in Manovich, 2001, p. 105).

Think about it

Mostly this chapter has talked about commodity branding, using Nike as the primary example. But in what ways might the brand power of digital media companies like Google and Microsoft add new dimensions to the promise and threat of their dominance of Web culture?

Conclusion

The argument put forward here is that the brand is an image instrument, and as such contributes to the mediatisation of the economy, that is, it contributes to the organisation of the contemporary economy as a medium. It is both a mechanism of relativity, as is price, and of relationality, as is jewellery (Simmel, 1990). In other words, the brand is both a means of establishing the relativity or the abstract equivalence of products in space and time and a medium of relationality, designed to support qualitative differentiation. On the one hand then, the brand subsumes the calculation of symbolic capital within the calculation of economic capital (to use the terms developed by Pierre Bourdieu (1984)). On the other, in the practices of branding the calculation of economic capital is not only quantitative, but is also qualitative.

Simmel notes that salt, cattle, tobacco and grain have all been simple means of exchange; their use typically being determined by individual or group interest. The use of jewellery as a medium of exchange, however, marks a new development for Simmel in so far as 'it indicates a relation between individuals: people adorn themselves for others' (1990, p. 176).

> Exchange, as the purest sociological occurrence, the most complete form of interaction, finds its appropriate representation in the material of jewellery, the significance of which for its owner is only indirect, namely as a relation to other people (1990, p. 177).

He notes that adornment is a social need for relationality, and that certain kinds of ornament are reserved for particular social positions; so, for example in medieval France, gold was not permitted below a certain rank. He goes on to suggest, however, that money is better able to serve as an absolute intermediary or means of exchange between products, although only, he says, if coinage is raised above its qualitative characteristics as a metal (such as gold).

An implication of the argument being put forward here is that branding contributes to what philosopher Brian Massumi calls a cultural condition of transitivity (2002). Let me expand on this a little. The condition of transitivity is one that is characterised by transition, that is, by being in movement. But, if you are familiar with what is meant by a transitive verb, you will know that this is a verb that requires an object. So, for example, 'to buy' is a transitive verb; we don't just buy, we buy something. By analogy, a condition of transitivity may be understood as a condition in which social agency—being and doing—is made to require or need an object. A transitive verb is incomplete without an object: in a condition of transitivity, we are always wanting. As has been described here, the brand is not total and complete but totalising and incomplete. It is this incompleteness—its openness, its ongoingness, its doingness—that defines the transitivity of brand power. The openness of the brand invites our participation and organises that participation in terms of interactivity. However, while it operates in terms of an injunction not that you should, but that you may (Barry, 2001), the invitation to participate is one which is increasingly difficult to refuse. Just Do It.

Beyond the level of inclusion through the act of purchase, there is another level of compulsory inclusiveness of subjects in the practices of branding. What is being referred to are the ways in which the incorporation of information about the everyday activities of subjects—which may be collected with or without their knowledge or permission—is an essential part of brand-making (Barry, 2001; Poster, 2001; Lyon, 2001). One example of this is the use of consumer profiling techniques in the collection of marketing data (Elmer, 2000). Here it is worth remembering the roots of many developments in computing (and indirectly the brand) in military and state surveillance, and the development of a vision of a 'mechanized circuit of detection, decision and response' (Manovich, 2001, p. 101). It is also important to note that compulsory inclusiveness at this level is designed to make the brand selective in its uptake, that is, to enforce exclusiveness at the other level, that of purchase.

Brands—among other complex objects—are what those of us living in the (post-) industrialised world have come to require in order to do many, if not most, things in everyday life. On the one hand it is important to recognise that this requirement is organised in terms of possibility not constraint; on the other, it should not be forgotten that because something is possible does not mean that it is desirable, or even sustainable. Possibilities may distend and distort as well as enable the many everyday activities that have conventionally been organised according to the every- day calculus of the probable (Heller, 1984); they may be anti-inventive as well as inventive (Barry, 2001). To sum up: brands are not simply a matter of *pouvoir* but also of *puissance* (Deleuze and Guattari, 1994: 174–191); they operate both as 'an instituted and reproducible relation of force, a selective concretization of potential' (the actual) and as potential, that is, as a scale of intensity or fullness of existence (the virtual) (Massumi, 2002, p. xvii). As such they add colour to the uniform colourlessness of money as described by Simmel, but they are no less merciless for that.

see
Nightingale,
Chapter 17

Theory link

CHAPTER SUMMARY

- This chapter challenges conventional assumptions about the media by examining the ways the brand can be considered to be a new media object.
- It has introduced the idea that media technologies can be social and cultural rather than electronic and digital, and it has argued that the brand serves the economy in much the same ways that media platforms serve the communication system.
- Increasingly brands are used to mediate the world and contribute to the ways it is represented because they are a way of reintroducing issues of 'quality' into a system otherwise dominated by quantitative measures of value or worth—a system where how many apples or watches or newspapers are sold for how much is considered more important than how good they are.
- Brands are capable of 'hyperlinking'—they are capable of acting like a desktop 'short cut' in the economy—if a new product is branded it automatically inherits, in the mind of the consumer, qualities previously associated with the brand and its products.
- The chapter also shows how closely money and media, the economy and the communication system, are intertwined. In order to fully appreciate the nature of the emerging media world it is important to recognise the diversity and complexity of mediation, the role brands currently play in the management of the economy, and that they are coming to play in the management of the information economy.

Tutorial questions

- What is the relationship between brands and money?
- In what ways is it argued in this chapter that brands 'drive the economy'?
- Would you describe Google as a brand? If so, what are its products?

Recommended reading

Ardvisson, A., 2006, *Brands: Meaning and Value in Media Culture*, Chapter 5, Routledge, London and New York.

Callon, M. (ed.), 1998, *The Laws of the Market*, Blackwell, Oxford.

Lury, C., 2004, *Brands: The Logos of the Global Economy*, Routledge, London and New York.

Lash, S. & Lury, C., 2007, *Global Culture Industry*, Polity, Cambridge.

Simmel, G., 1990, *The Philosophy of Money*, (ed.) D. Frisby, Routledge, London.

Websites

Eddie Bauer Department Store: http://eddiebauer.com

Friends Reunited: http://friendsreunited.co.uk

Porsche Design Group:
http://www.porsche-design.com/live/PORSCHE_DESIGN_en.PorscheDesign

References

Appadurai, A., 1996, *Modernity at Large*, University of Minnesota Press, Minneapolis.

Ardvisson, A., 2006, *Brands: Meaning and Value in Media Culture*, Chapter 5, Routledge, London and New York.

Barry, A., 2001, *Political Machines*, Athlone Press, London.

Barry, A. & Slater, D. (eds), 2002, Special Issue 'The Technological Economy', *Economy and Society*, Vol. 31, No. 2, May.

Baudrillard, J., 1994, *Simulacra and Simulation*, University of Michigan Press, Ann Arbor.

Bourdieu, P., 1984, *Distinction: A Social Critique of Taste,* Routledge and Kegan Paul, London.

Bourdieu, P., 1977, *Outline of a Theory of Practice,* Cambridge University Press, Cambridge.

Callon, M. (ed.), 1998, *The Laws of the Market*, Blackwell, Oxford.

Callon, M. & Law, J., 2003, 'Qualculation, Agency and Otherness', paper presented at 'Economics at Large' workshop, New York University, 14–15 November.

Callon, M., Meadel, C., & Rabeharisoa, V., 2002, 'The economy of qualities', *Economy and Society*, Vol. 31, No. 2, May, pp. 194–297.

Deleuze, G. & Guattari, F., 1994, *What is Philosophy?,* Columbia University Press, New York.

Elmer, G., 2000, 'The Politics of Profiling' in Rogers, R. (ed.) *Preferred Placement*, pp. 65–73, Jan van Eyck Akademie Editions, Amsterdam.

Heller, A., 1984 [1970], *Everyday Life,* Routledge and Kegan Paul, London.

Jameson, F., 1991, *Postmodernism, or, The Cultural Logic of Late Capitalism*, Verso, London.

Keller, K., 1998, *Strategic Brand Management*, Prentice-Hall, Saddle River, New Jersey.

Krauss, R., 1999, *'A Voyage on the North Sea': Art in the Age of the Post-medium Condition*, Thames and Hudson, London.

Latour, B., 1987, *Science In Action: How to Follow Scientists and Engineers Through Society,* Harvard University Press, Cambridge, Mass.

Law, J., 1984, *Organizing Modernity*, Blackwell, Oxford.

Lury, C., & Warde, A., 1996, 'Investments in the imaginary consumer: conjectures regarding power, knowledge and advertising', in Nava, M., Blake, A., MacRury,

I., & Richards, B. (eds), *Buy this Book: Studies in Advertising and Consumption*, Routledge, London, pp. 87–102.

Lyon, D., 2001, *Surveillance Society: Monitoring Everyday Life*, Open University Press, Milton Keynes, UK.

Manovich, L., 2001, *The Language of New Media*, MIT Press, Cambridge, MA.

Massumi, B., 2002, *Parables for the Virtual*, Duke University Press, Durham, NC.

Mitchell, A., 2001, *Right Side Up: Building Brands in the Age of the Organized Consumer*, HarperCollins Business, London.

Pavitt, J., 2000, (ed.) *Brand New*, V&A Publications, London.

Poster, M., 2001, *What's the Matter with the Internet?*, University of Minnesota Press, Minneapolis.

Rodowick, D.N., 1994, 'Audiovisual culture and interdisciplinary knowledge', *New Literary History*, Winter, Vol. 26, No. 1, 1995.

Shields, R., 1997, 'Flow', *Space and Culture*, 1: 1–5.

Simmel, G., 1990, *The Philosophy of Money*, (ed.) D. Frisby, Routledge, London.

Strathern, M., 1999, *Property, Substance and Effect: Anthropological Essays on Persons and Things*, Athlone Press, London.

Whitehead, A.N., 1978, *Process and Reality*, Free Press, New York.

Williams, R., 1974, *Television: Technology and Cultural Form*, Fontana/Collins, London.

Zelizer, V., 1998, 'The Proliferation of Social Currencies' in Callon, M. (ed.), *The Laws of the Markets*, pp. 58–68, Blackwell, Oxford.

Digital Technologies and Moral Economies

19

CHAPTER OVERVIEW

As soon as we begin to use digital communications technologies we are involved in webs of social relations that raise ethical questions about our responsibilities to our fellow users. Are we simply consumers of someone else's efforts or do we have an obligation to support the development of public facilities and to share our advice, knowledge and creativity in ways that other people can enjoy and benefit from? This chapter explores this question by examining the three moral economies that currently dominate the organisation of the Internet and asks if the future of the Web will be increasingly dominated by commercial activity or will a new digital commons, open to all and operating outside of the market, emerge.

Key terms

moral economy
commodities
public goods
gifts
digital commons

Issues

- How do the moral economies of commodities, public goods and gifts currently organise activity on the Internet?
- How is the situation changing?
- What are the prospects for a digital commons and how might it be organised?

Introduction—Second lives

A 39-year-old gay man living near Boston recently told a journalist that he spends anything from one to eight hours online, managing and socialising at Fire Island, a virtual space that he built 'as a homage to the cult gay hangout off New York's Long Island' and designed to provide a 'welcoming space for people' (Jeffries, 2006, p. 7). His online persona or avatar, Vito Desoto, is a resident of Second Life (SL), one of the largest and most rapidly expanding virtual environments on the Web. At the beginning of 2007 Second Life (http://secondlife.com) had an estimated 100,000 regular users, though in an average week more than three times that number log on. Most are just visiting but around 10 per cent stay and take up residence (Usborne, 2007, p. 15).

Second Life, launched by the Californian company, Linden Lab, in 2003, was intended from the outset as an engine of grassroots creativity. Residents are encouraged to design and build virtual objects out of the game's basic elements of matter known as 'primitives' (or 'prims'). Using the simple 3-D modelling, programming and texture mapping facilities provided, the website promises that 'you can create anything you can imagine [and] add behaviours to the objects you build … sculpt a butterfly, then write a short chunk of code that lets it follow you around as you walk' (Second Life, 2007).

Activity 19.1

Go to the Second Life website at http://secondlife.com to find out more about how it operates.

Second Life residents control the intellectual property rights to anything they create. Consequently, as the website points out, they 'can easily begin selling it to other residents' (op. cit.). This has generated a thriving internal economy with residents buying clothing and artefacts made by other residents, using the game's virtual currency, Linden dollars. In an average month an estimated 10 million objects are created and 230,000 are bought and sold (*The Economist,* 2006b, p. 99). The opportunities to build a business don't stop there. Second Life creations can also be bought on Internet auction sites for American dollars using the publicly posted exchange rate for Lindens. Some virtual creations become real-world products. In 2005 for example, Second Life resident, Kermitt Qirk, capitalised on the 'in-world' success of his invented game Tringo, a cross between bingo and the arcade game Tetris, by licensing the 'offline' rights to Game Boy Advance (Malaby, 2006). For many participants this 'self-interested trading behaviour … destroys the game's atmosphere, to the detriment of all' (Castronova, 2003, p. 19).

The big money in Second Life, however, is to be made in property. Linden Lab generates income by leasing virtual property to residents rather than selling advertising space. This has proved to be a shrewd move generating monthly revenues estimated at $1 million (*The Economist,* 2006b, p. 98). At the same time it has opened the way to land speculation within the game. In 2006 Ailin Graef, known within Second Life as Anshe Chung, became the first resident to accumulate US$1 million from dealing in virtual property. She makes an estimated $150,000 a year from her in-world real estate transactions. As in the 'offline' world some property is traded on the open market as residents compete to move into the most desirable beach home or penthouse apartment, but other homes are located within gated enclosures that vet potential purchasers.

Increasingly, participating in synthetic worlds is presented as a business opportunity for the budding entrepreneur as well as an arena for self expression, socialising and playful creativity. As the head of MindArk, developers of another popular online game, Project Entropia, put it , 'We want it to be a full second reality. We want you to make friends, make a business' (Hills, 2006, p. 11).

This drive to commercialise is not universally welcomed. A number of players see it as a betrayal of the original ideal of using personal creativity to contribute to the diversity of a shared collective environment that everyone can enjoy freely. Erecting barriers by building gated communities or reinforcing inequalities by encouraging more affluent participants to buy what they need runs counter to this ethos of openness and mutuality. This sense of betrayal is exacerbated by the cooptation and exploitation of real life companies intent on mobilising Second Life's grassroots creativity and sociability in the service of marketing. In 2006 Toyota became the first major car maker to enter SL, selling virtual versions of its Scion models. Its aim was to use transactions and talk within the game as a way of promoting the brand and to generate possible ideas for modifications by tracking how residents customised their cars.

Public cultural institutions too have seen Second Life as a way of breathing new life into their operations and have begun experimenting with using it to extend their reach and develop new relations with their publics. In 2006 the world's best known public broadcaster, the BBC, rented a tropical island in SL to stage its Big Weekend rock event in parallel with the regular broadcast over its main radio channel, Radio One, with an avatar of the DJ, Chris Moyles, as virtual host.

As these examples make clear, Second Life is the site of a continuing struggle between alternative conceptions of how best to use and develop its potential. This contest between the extension of commercialism on the one hand, and the revivification of public service and the promotion of free exchange on the other, is repeated across the Internet. It is rooted in moral economies offering very different ways of organising production, circulation and use, and the social relations these activities entail.

Moral economies

There are three kinds of goods in circulation in contemporary economies, commodities, public goods and gifts. Each is paid for in a particular way, invites particular forms of participation, supports particular kinds of social relationships, and circulates within a particular arena of action. These basic characteristics, shown in Table 19.1, taken together, make up the moral economy of that sector of economic activity.

Table 19.1 Competing moral economies

Goods	Commodities	Public Goods	Gifts
Payments	Prices	Taxes	Reciprocities
Identities	Consumers	Citizens	Communards[§]
Relations	Personal Possessions	Shared Use	Collaborative Creation
Arenas	Markets	Nations	Networks

§ Communard = member of a commune.

Commodities

Commodities are goods or services produced to be sold for a price. They are the building blocks of commercial activity and profit generation. We are encouraged to approach them as consumers searching the marketplace for the products that will best satisfy our personal needs or desires. Once we have decided what we want and paid for it, it is ours to keep. Unless we lend it or give it away no one else can have access to it or use it. Advertising reinforces this sense of personal ownership urging us to focus on the pleasures of possession and dissuading us from enquiring too closely into where the product has come from, how it was made and at what social and environmental costs. Buying a commodity then does not require us to enter into continuing social relations with producers or sellers or to take responsibility for anyone else's well-being.

Public goods

Public goods are defined in economics as goods or services that I can use without stopping you from using them at the same time or interfering with your enjoyment. Public broadcasting is a classic instance. It doesn't matter how many people watch a World Cup game or the athletics finals at the Olympics, everyone with the appropriate equipment can receive the same signal at the same quality at the same time. Other public cultural institutions are not so flexible. Their use is limited by physical capacity. In principle we can all go to see the paintings in the National Gallery in London, but in practice if too many people turn up at the same time each person's enjoyment will be curtailed. There is nothing more annoying than standing in front of a favourite work of art and being jostled by people pushing their way to the front of the crowd or having to listen to a tour guide loudly explaining its meaning.

In addition to this economic definition, however, the term 'public good' also carries two other meanings. In everyday language we identify public institutions as shared resources paid for collectively out of the public purse, either directly (as in the case of licence fees for public broadcasting) or indirectly, in the form of grants and subsidies from the overall pool of taxation. Beyond that, we also think of them as contributing to the general quality of public life as well as to our own personal enjoyment and development.

This extended conception of public goods invites us to think of ourselves not as consumers making personal choices in the marketplace but as citizens, members of a political and moral community, whose right to contribute fully to social life is accompanied by a responsibility to ensure that no one is denied the same entitlement. Although this ideal of citizenship has been internationalised and we now talk of 'global citizenship', in practice it is still nation states that guarantee its core rights. Being a citizen then has come to mean holding a passport issued by a particular nation state and paying taxes to support nationally public cultural institutions.

Gift economies

Gift economies are still widely regarded as characteristic of tribal societies. We see the anonymous marketplace of capitalist societies as 'leaving little room for a moral code based on gift-giving' (Godelier, 1999, p.107). We also think of gifts as tokens of friendship, love or respect, but the anthropological literature also reveals how they can be used as weapons in battles for status, advantage, and power (see Strathern, 1988; Bourdieu, 1990). Reputations depend on how much is given away rather than how much is accumulated, an idea inscribed in the names given to notables among the Kwakiutl Indians of the Northwest American coast; 'Always Giving

Blankets While Walking' or 'Whose Property is Eaten in Feasts' (Hyde, 2006, pp. 80–1). Faced with this conspicuous and very public generosity recipients may feel they are confronted with an obligation to reciprocate that they are unable to match but cannot evade.

The new gift economies developing on the Internet are more open ended and more widely informed by a spirit of generosity and mutuality rather than personal gain (see Shrift, 1997). They retain the core ethos of reciprocity, that a gift invites a response, but emphasise collaborative creation rather than individual enhancement. They invite people to participate as communards, a term I have borrowed from the Paris Commune when the people of the city set up their own collective institutions. The arena of action of today's communards is neither the market (as with commodities) nor the nation (as with public goods) but the network, the web of digital connections clustered around the central public space of the Internet, the World Wide Web, as it enters its second phase of development, Web.2.0.

Activity 19.2

1   Discuss the differences listed in Table 19.1 between commodities, public goods and gifts.
2   Using the terminology of Table 19.1, how would you classify the following cultural 'objects'?
    (a) Your local library.
    (b) Your neighbour's swimming pool.
    (c) The gymnasium attached to a high-rise apartment complex.
    (d) Your family tree.
3   In what ways and why are each of the above increasingly commercialising and restricting access?

Widening the net: Web 2.0

Web 2.0 refers both to technological innovations and new forms of use. Technologically it is built around the massive expansion in capacity generated by new broadband networks coupled with the increased flexibility and mobility of use delivered by more powerful laptop machines, wireless (wifi) hot spots, and Internet-enabled mobile phones. These innovations enable the Internet to handle even the bulkiest material, including films, television programs and three-dimensional environments. At the same time we are seeing a shift in the nature of the cultural material being created and exchanged on the Web, with the rapid rise of user-generated and directed content. Alongside creative environments like Second Life, we see the popularity of shared content sites like YouTube where anyone can post short film or video clips, the explosion of personal web logs, 'blogs', commenting on current events and issues, the rapid growth of grassroots citizen journalism, and the rise of popular recommendation sites offering first-hand advice on an ever expanding range of topics, from where to find the best restaurants in a city to how to get the most comfortable airline seats. It is here, in the new spaces opened up by Web 2.0, where the longstanding monopolies enjoyed by commercial corporations and cultural professionals are under challenge, that the contest between the competing moral economies underpinning Internet participation is being fought out most fiercely.

see Nightingale, Chapter 17

Theory link

Contested connections

The connectivity offered by digital communications technologies can be configured either vertically or horizontally. Until very recently public communications was dominated by vertical systems. Material was produced in centralised production sites (newspaper offices, television stations) and distributed to individuals at home or on the move. Audience members could talk back to producers by writing to the editor or voting in polls, but they were discouraged from communicating with each other. Feedback was designed to flow back up the same single vertical connection. In contrast the Internet was conceived as a decentralised, horizontal system, which allows every participant to originate material as well as to receive it, and to make their contributions available across the whole network. The resulting upsurge of popular creativity and peer-to-peer exchange on the Internet poses particular problems for commercial media organisations since it operates outside the economy of the market. As a consequence, companies are constantly looking for ways of limiting and managing the new gift economies and capitalising on their dynamism.

Corporate captures

Major media companies are currently pursuing three main strategies:

- takeover
- co-option
- pre-emption.

Faced with new competitors for consumers' time and allegiance the simplest option is to buy them. Social networking sites have been a particular target. Examples include: the take over of MySpace by Rupert Murdoch's News International; the acquisition of the iVillage network of women's sites by the US conglomerate NBC Universal; and the purchase of Friends Reunited by Britain's major commercial terrestrial broadcaster, ITV. The leading commercial Internet search companies have also been active, with Yahoo! buying the photo-sharing site Flickr and Google acquiring YouTube, the video posting site. All these companies are looking for ways of developing the sales potential of online communities without alienating the media-savvy and sceptical age group of sixteen- to twenty-four-year-olds, the key demographic segment for a wide range of consumer goods. As Kevin George of Unilever explained to a journalist; 'We need to be engaging with them, not banging them over the head with brandalism that pollutes their space' (*The Economist,* 2006a, p. 66). In pursuit of this goal Unilever signed a deal with Christine Dolce, who appears on MySpace as ForBiddeN, to promote their new male deodorant, Axe, by targeting the 900,000 'friends' linked to her site. The promotional interactive game she hosted attracted around 75,000 MySpace users.

These efforts to co-opt users are accompanied by a concerted push to limit their ability to generate their own material. Borrowing from and building on ideas and cultural artefacts already in public circulation is central to sustaining a creative society. At the same time, professionals working in the creative industries expect to make a living from their labour. A culture that is both dynamic and fair therefore requires rules that support and protect creators and innovators while guaranteeing that those who follow them 'remain as free as possible from the control of the past' (Lessig, 2004, p. xiv). Since the invention of printing made mechanised copying possible these competing claims have been managed by intellectual property (IP) laws that prevented the full-scale copying of works for commercial gain for a limited period but allowed for 'fair use'. The rise of the Internet, with its ever expanding facilities for reproducing, combining and distributing, has undermined this historic balance and, 'pushed by big media', prompted new regulations. The new IP regime has moved to close down popular creativity in two ways. Firstly it has extended the period covered by copyright. The USA, the source of much contemporary popular culture, provides a particularly clear example. Until 1978 the maximum copyright period was thirty-two years after which works passed into the public domain and could be freely reproduced and appropriated. The period now stands at ninety-five years. Secondly, the key distinction between republishing a work and building on and transforming it has been dismantled so that for the first time 'the ordinary ways in which individuals create and share culture [come] within the reach of the law' (Lessig op. cit., p. 8). As a result, critics argue, copyright 'has become too strong for its own good', stifling individual creativity and hampering the discovery and sharing of new ideas and forms of expression (Vaidhyanathan, 2006, p. 43).

One important response to these moves has been the development of Creative Commons agreements designed to strike a new balance between the extension of intellectual property lobbied for by major media companies and the piracy and the exploitation of creative labour pursued by some Internet users. Under the banner 'Share, reuse and remix-legally' the Creative Commons site (http://creative commons.org/) enables creators to move from the 'all rights reserved' regime of corporate copyright to a 'some rights reserved' arrangement that allows the re-use of their material for non commercial purposes. This principle of using private rights to create public goods has been adopted by the world's leading public broadcaster, the BBC, as the basis for their ambitious Creative Archive project (http://creativearchive.bbc.co.uk).

Think about it

Can you think of any disincentives that might be associated with people using 'creative commons' agreements?

Institutions without walls

As we noted earlier, the ability of public cultural institutions to make their holdings and expertise as widely available as possible has been limited historically by time and space constraints. Museums, libraries and university lecture halls are only open at certain times and can only be accessed by travelling to a particular location. The Internet has the potential to break down these barriers and allow public institutions to fulfil their core remit of securing universal access and advancing public understanding in more open and flexible ways.

Public broadcasting achieved universal coverage with the aid of extensive networks of ground-based transmitters and, later, cable networks and satellites, but still suffered from time limitations. Viewers could only watch transmissions in their scheduled slots. Video recording has enabled current programming to be time-shifted but access to program archives has remained dependent on what the organisation chose to issue commercially on video or DVD. The Internet, coupled with the digitalisation of program archives, has the potential to abolish these constraints. By making its past programming freely available to download for personal use the BBC's Creative Archive project aims to encourage users to become 'creative with content' (http://creativearchive.bbc.co.uk/archives/2005/03/the_rules_in_br_1.html). It permits viewers to use BBC material in their own creative and intellectual work on the condition that no productions are sold commercially, that contributors are properly credited, and that all secondary material is licensed for others to use on the same basis as the original. This scheme only applies to users within the UK however, tying it firmly to the historic link binding primary access of public goods to the nation state and its taxpayers. Other public institutions are taking a more internationalist approach.

In 1999, the provost of the Massachusetts Institute of Technology (MIT), one of the world's elite higher education institutions, asked staff to consider how they should position themselves in the emerging distance learning environment, which many universities were looking to as a useful source of additional income. They rejected the commercial option and opted instead to launch an Open Courseware initiative making their lecture notes and reading lists freely available over the Internet to students and self-learners around the world (see http://ocw.mit.edu/index.html). The principle idea behind this decision was simple. Since their intellectual work had been paid for largely out of public funds citizens should not have to pay again to access it. Public libraries, however, present tougher choices.

Digitalising major holdings makes access much more flexible but the costs are huge. In response, several of the world's largest collections, including those held by Harvard and Oxford universities and the New York Public Library, have become partners in Google's Book Search initiative (see http://books.google.com/intl/en/googlebooks/about.html). The results are technically impressive and have been warmly welcomed by some scholars (see Ree, 2007). But there is a catch. Google bears the costs of producing high quality, fully searchable, digital archives in return for the right to direct users to appropriate sales sites. Unlike the hard copy collection, users wanting to search digitalised books that are still covered by copyright can only secure a limited preview confined to a handful of pages or look at very brief snippets and be directed to a bookstore or library where a full copy can be obtained. This initiative is part of Google's wider strategy of using its advanced search technology to facilitate 'high-end' links. Its deal to provide click-through advertising connecting individual buyers and sellers on the non-US sites of the leading Internet auction site, eBay, is another example. Applying the same principle to public libraries, however, undermines the core principle of free universal access on which the moral economy of public goods rests.

Creative collaborations

The emerging digital gift economy was initially pioneered by the early computer 'hackers' who set out to challenge the domination of the operating systems being developed by commercial companies led by Microsoft. As Linus Torvalds, one of the movement's leading figures, put it, the primary 'ethical duty of hackers' is 'to share their expertise by writing free software and facilitating access to information and computing resources wherever possible' (Torvalds, 2001, p. vii). Contributors to what came to be known as the 'Open Source' movement set about developing computer programs by making the source codes they were using freely available for anyone to modify or change. This collaborative effort has produced computer programs that are more robust than their commercial equivalents. They include the basic operating system Linux, the Apache Web server, the Web browser Mozilla Firefox, and the office suite OpenOffice.org. The basic principle of posting something that anyone can add to, delete or alter was later generalised in the Wiki movement, whose best known product is Wikipedia, the world's most extensive encyclopedia, produced entirely by voluntary contributions (see http://www.wikipedia.org). It is a perfect example of the new moral economy of digital gifts. I write an entry on a subject I know well. I don't ask you to pay me but I do invite you to contribute to the common project by writing about a subject that you are expert in.

Think about it

What are the strengths and weaknesses of a gift economy?

Nor is it simply expertise that is exchanged. Experience, observation and comment also flow through the new horizontal circuits. Recent years have seen more and more people posting eyewitness accounts of current events. In some cases, such as the London underground bombings in July 2005, the grainy cell photo pictures taken by survivors are the only visual record we have of the aftermath of the attacks in the tunnels (see Allan, 2006, Chapter 8). Again, commercial interests have been quick to coopt this movement by buying up the rights to reproduce selected vernacular images. But citizen journalism is also taking on more durable forms. OhMyNews, originally launched in Korea but now with international coverage (see http://english.ohmynews.com), is a newspaper based almost entirely on stories posted by non-professionals and informed by a strong sense of the need to redress the silences and misrepresentations of the mainstream commercial media. As one contributor put it in a personal manifesto: 'The greatest beauty of citizen journalism is that the centre of power is in every citizen's hands' (Biriwasha, 2007). To this grassroots reporting we can add the proliferating range of Web logs ('blogs') commenting on current event and issues and the rich flow of home-produced art, fiction, music and film.

This upsurge of popular analysis and creativity is not without its problems however. It is often limited in scope, reproducing the mainstream media culture of sound bites and video clips. The commercial search engines that sift through the avalanche of available material respond to the number of hits on a site elevating popularity over significance. And, most important of all, substantial inequalities of access to the Internet remain, with large numbers of poor and elderly households permanently excluded from regular self-directed use. What then are the prospects for a digital commons?

Constructing the digital commons

The commons is made up of all those resources that are held in common and are essential to our collective well-being and shared future. Public parks are a good example. They are open to everyone and can be used in a variety of ways: for pleasure, for performances, for political demonstrations. At the same time, as the historical record shows all too clearly, access and use of communal resources has been continually threatened by commercial enclosure, by state regulation designed to manage popular expression and dissent, and by participants exploiting communal facilities for personal gain (see Murdock, 2001). The development of the Internet seems to be reproducing this familiar story. So where do we look for an alternative scenario?

One possibility is offered by the migration of Internet access from personal computers to digital television sets. Television's ubiquity and familiarity would help to alleviate current inequalities of access but it would not, in itself, address the fragmentation and dispersal of Internet content. Tackling this problem offers public broadcasting an unrivalled opportunity to develop a revivified public service ethos for the digital age. The material available behind the screen would become as important as what appeared on it. Watching a program would move from being a discrete event, bounded in time, to becoming a gateway to a range of resources generated by non-commercial sources, both public cultural institutions and popular creativity. In organising this new combination of digital public goods and gifts, public broadcasting has one major advantage, it is widely trusted. It is precisely because it finds itself caught between the drive for commercial enclosure and the political priorities of state and government, and struggles to keep both at arm's length, that it still commands public support, at least for the moment. This may not be the most secure basis on which to build a digital commons, but it offers a concrete opportunity that can be developed here and now by extending the multiple ways viewers and listeners are already being encouraged to talk back, engage in debate, create their own cultural products, and to pursue issues and programs through the multiple links offered on the institution's website (see Murdock, 2005).

Conclusion

As governments around the world shut down their analogue television transmissions and switch to digital systems there is a unique opportunity to develop a cultural commons that combines established and emerging practices. In the new media world now in the making, 'old' media may turn out to be the key to building a public culture that remains open to all, hospitable to diverse forms of creativity, and committed to facilitating encounters and conversations across borders in the search for new forms of understanding and mutuality.

- This chapter began with a case study of Second Life where inhabitants are currently divided about the benefits of the commercialisation of SL property and its sale on external markets for real world currencies. While this development intensifies the similarities between SL and the outside world, it also invites it to be valued (and devalued) by outside influences.
- A parallel is drawn between SL and the Internet, and the commercialisation of services originally developed within what can, in both cases, be described as having been initially a gift economy. The commoditisation of the gift economies of SL and the Internet is also challenging the nature of public culture and the value people attach to public goods.
- To offset the challenge to public culture, the idea of a creative commons has been proposed as a means of protecting people's rights to freely share each other's ideas in the service of creative action. The chapter argues that 'old' media may turn out to be the key to building a public culture for new media worlds.

CHAPTER SUMMARY

Tutorial questions

- In what ways does the new IP regime threaten the survival of popular creativity?
- What kind of resources should be available in a digital commons?
- Why might traditional or old media still play an important role in emerging media worlds?

Recommended reading

Godelier, M., 1999, *The Enigma of the Gift,* University of Chicago Press, Chicago.

Lessig, L., 2004, *Free Culture: How Big Media Uses Technology and the Law to Lock Down Culture and Control Creativity,* The Penguin Press, New York.

Murdock, G., 2005, 'Building the Digital Commons: Public Broadcasting in the Age of the Internet', in Ferrel Lowe, G. & Jauert. P. (eds), *Cultural Dilemmas in Public Service Broadcasting,* pp. 213–30, Nordicom, Goteborg University.

Murdock, G.& Golding, P., 2004, 'Dismantling the Digital Divide: Rethinking the Dynamics of Participation and Exclusion' in Calabrese, A. and Sparks, C. (eds), *Toward a Political Economy of Culture: Capitalism and Communication in the Twenty-First Century,* Rowman and Littlefield Publishers, Inc., Lanham.

Websites

BBC Creative Archive: www.creativearchive.bbc.co.uk

Creative Commons: www.creativecommons.org

Game Studies: www.gamestudies.org

Google Books: www.books.google.com/intl/en/googlebooks/about.html

OhMyNews: www.english.ohnynews.com

Second Life: www.secondlife.com

Wikipedia: www.wikipedia.org

References

Allan, S., 2006, *Online News: Journalism and the Internet,* Open University Press, Maidenhead, UK.

Biriwasha, M., 2007, 'On Being a Citizen Journalist' http://english.ohmynews.com/articleview_view.asp?article_class+8&no=3365, accessed 29 January 2007.

Bourdieu, P., 1990, *The Logic of Practice,* Polity Press, Cambridge.

Castronova, E., 2003, 'On Virtual Economies', *Game Studies,* Vol. 3, No. 2, December, p. 19 at http://www.gamestudies.org/0302/castronova/, accessed 10 November 2006.

Godelier, M., 1999, *The Enigma of the Gift,* University of Chicago Press, Chicago.

Hills, S., 2006, 'How Virtual Cash Earns Real Money', *Metro,* 3 May, p. 11.

Hyde, L., 2006 [1979], *The Gift: How the Creative Spirit Transforms the World,* Canongate, Edinburgh.

Jeffries, S., 2006, 'You Only Live Twice' *The Guardian,* 7 October, p. 27.

Lessig, L., 2004, *Free Culture: How Big Media Uses Technology and the Law to Lock Down Culture and Control Creativity,* The Penguin Press, New York.

Malaby, T., 2006, 'Parlaying Value: Capital in and Beyond Virtual Worlds', *Games and Culture,* Vol. 1, No. 2, April, pp. 141–62.

Murdock, G., 2005, 'Building the Digital Commons: Public Broadcasting in the Age of the Internet', in Ferrel Lowe, G. & Jauert. P. (eds), *Cultural Dilemmas in Public Service Broadcasting,* pp. 213–30, Nordicom, Goteborg University.

Murdock, G., 2001, 'Against Enclosure: Rethinking the Cultural Commons', in Morley, D. & Robins, K. (eds), *British Cultural Studies: Geography, Nationality and Identity,* pp. 443–60, Oxford University Press, Oxford.

Ree, J. (2007) 'The Library of Google', *Prospect,* Issue 131, February, pp. 32–5.

Second Life, 2007, 'Create Anything': http://secondlife.com.whatis/create.php, accessed 30 January 2007.

Shrift, A.D., 1997, 'Introduction: Why the Gift?', in Shrift, A.D. (ed.) *The Logic of the Gift: Towards an Ethic of Generosity,* pp. 1–22, Routledge, London.

Strathern, M., 1998, *The Gender of the Gift: Problems with Women and Problems with Society in Melanesia,* University of California Press, Berkeley.

The Economist, 2006a, 'ForBiddeN fruit', *The Economist,* 29 July, p. 66.

The Economist, 2006b, 'Living a Second Life', *The Economist,* 30 September, pp. 97–9.

Torvalds, L., 2001, 'Preface' to Himanen, P., *The Hacker Ethic and the Spirit of the Information Age,* pp. vii–xii, Vintage, London.

Usborne, S., 2007, 'Second Life: The A-Z Guide', *The Independent,* 26 January, pp. 14–15.

Vaidhyanathan, S., 2006, 'Copyright Jungle', *Columbia Journalism Review,* September/ October, pp. 42–8.

Part Four Summary

These chapters have explored directions currently being taken at the frontiers of life online that govern the quality of participation. Improvements in search technology are raising expectations about what information might be available online, when, to whom and in what form. The searchable-ness of the Web is one of its not-so-secret strengths, but this is matched by a quality of sharing with strangers and with significant changes to the groups an individual is likely to include in the 'knowable' community of their everyday life. At the same time, the World Wide Web increases the power of the money system to transform social relations into commodities—for example, increasingly even our casual acquaintances, friendships, prospective marital partners and our ancestors are being branded and monetised. The power of money, and its value system, has been magnified by the World Wide Web. The expansion of the money system, aided and abetted by the brand, is leading to a contraction of live encounters and a withdrawal of identity investment in our 'nearest and dearest'—perhaps because the World Wide Web is seen as a limitless source of access to replacements. For these reasons there is currently growing concern about the potential for the value system associated with commodities (money) to displace the moral economies based on public goods and gifting. These are the challenges faced by convergence and it is important that nations, communities and individuals examine seriously the ways the money system can be held in check so that everyone can enjoy the social and cultural excitement of the World Wide Web, the joy of limitless search, and the fascination and power of collective intelligence at work.

QUESTIONS

- Explain why Google's website search system is a Web 1.0 development while Yahoo!'s del.icio.us site is an example of a Web 2.0 development. What does this comparison demonstrate about the nature of social networking?
- Do you think there is any sense in which the personal website can be seen as a form of branding? What does your answer to this question tell you about the role of the brand as a new medium of communication?
- Consider the differences between commodities, public goods and gifts summarised in Table 19.1 (Murdock, Chapter 19). Why are these distinctions helpful in understanding current developments in the organisation of the World Wide Web?

Recommended reading

Callon, M. (ed.), 1998, *The Laws of the Markets*, Blackwell, Oxford.

Clark, A., 2003, *Natural-Born Cyborgs: Minds, Technologies And The Future Of Human Intelligence,* Oxford University Press, Oxford and New York.

Godelier, M., 1999, *The Enigma of the Gift,* University of Chicago Press, Chicago.

Lessig, L., 2004, *Free Culture: How Big Media Uses Technology and the Law to Lock Down Culture and Control Creativity,* The Penguin Press, New York.

Afterword

It is apt that the last chapter of this book should choose Second Life as its case study. Second Life is both an online world and a metaphor for the World Wide Web. The profiteering that SL is currently struggling to control echoes the discovery of cyberspace as a new frontier—an uninhabited country inviting colonisation (Hafner and Lyon, 1996). Like SL, the Internet started out as a cooperative venture, a game, a world of playful encounters. In a manner that uncannily resembles the commercial transformation of SL, the desire to find better and more efficient ways of communicating online allowed the pioneers of cyberspace to develop cultural capital. To continue to expand their cooperative and collaborative activities, they started selling access to their online services to raise new funding. The story of Google (Battelle, 2005) provides an excellent example of the transformation of Internet capital into real world capital, as does the success of MySpace and YouTube.

The World Wide Web started out as an environment with a moral economy based on sharing. But the scope and scale of the financial rewards achieved by some of its pioneers through the commercialisation of their initial in-kind investments in the World Wide Web (Google, Flickr, YouTube and MySpace are the stand-out examples) have led to a merging of old and new media industries. The success of early entrepreneurs like Sergey Brin and Larry Page, and the unimaginable wealth they so quickly accumulated, has attracted immigrants to cyberspace—new inhabitants, willing to pay vast sums of real world money for access to the online money flow. Initially the money flow was generated within the online community and with sensitivity to its customs and mores. The offline entrepreneurs, however, draw on a different business culture to inform the services they offer through their online properties.

For some new inhabitants—News Corporation provides an example—the World Wide Web was initially a culture shock. The expertise such firms bring to the management of their online properties was developed in an 'old' media environment. They moved in on the promise of financial returns rather than to promote the culture of sharing. This has contributed to the very interesting but ambiguous situation we see in cyberspace today—an uneasy fit between the economies of commodity, public goods and gifts.

Yet it is also clear from the arguments put forward in this book that the World Wide Web and the 'old' media are subject to a convergence process that is political, social and cultural as much as it is technological and economic. For this reason the authors have argued that now is an important time to reconsider the basis on which the commercialisation of online services is occurring. It is important now to look at access and participation, to understand better what is gained and what is lost in the shift to digital media, and by whom. It is important now to question who is served, and who is excluded from using the new media services and devices; and to do so in the context of ongoing debate about the social and cultural consequences of such changes.

We have seen that the constituencies of the groups currently engaging in media activism are extremely diverse. They act as independent groups formed on the basis of their shared interests, whether regional, cultural, physical or financial—or several of these (see Part 2). What media activism shows us is that the development of the Internet is not yet informed by a strong enough sense of the public good. And, moreover, while some national governments struggle to ensure at least the appearance of universal service and universal access, others—particularly in the developed nations—consider that the World Wide Web should be commercially developed. As a result, participation is patchy even in the wealthiest nations.

References

Battelle, J., 2005, *The Search: How Google and Its Rivals Rewrote the Rules of Business and Transformed Our Culture*, The Penguin Group, Portfolio.

Hafner, K. & Lyon, M., 1996, *Where Wizards Stay Up Late: The Origins of the Internet*, Simon & Schuster, New York.

Glossary

'Web 2.0' This should exhibit some basic characteristics. These include: 'Network as platform'—delivering (and allowing users to use) applications entirely through a Web browser; users own the data on the site and can exert control over the data; an architecture of participation and democracy that encourages users to add value to the application as they use it; a rich, interactive, user-friendly interface; and, some social networking aspects. Source: Wikipedia (Wikipedia is itself an example of Web 2.0. Although the online encyclopedia is criticised for inaccurate information, at the same time, as in this case, it can also provide the most up-to-date definitions based on 'collaborative' or 'collective intelligence').

Access is defined from a reception perspective, as 'the use of media for public service. It may be defined in terms of the opportunities available to the public to choose varied and relevant programs and to have a means of feedback to transmit its reactions and demands to production organisations' (in Servaes, 1999, p. 85). Not all authors agree with this emphasis on media reception and use. Lewis (1993, p. 12), for example, has defined access from a community media production perspective as 'the processes that permit users to provide relatively open and unedited *input* to the mass media'.

Accessibility The potential for a technology to be used by a wide range of users (ideally even *all* users), without barriers being placed in their way through discriminatory or exclusionary design or norms.

Afrikaners The white, Afrikaans-speaking ethnic group who ruled South Africa from 1948 until 1994.

Agrarian society A society where position depends on feudal relations such as land ownership.

Apartheid The formalised system of racial discrimination in South Africa put into place when the National Party came to power in 1948. South African society was segregated according to imposed racial categories. Only the minority 'white' section of the population was allowed to vote. The black majority was denied basic rights, and their economic exploitation by the white minority led to the crippling inequalities that continue today. Attempts to resist apartheid or overthrow the regime were met with violence, and many members of the liberation movements such as the African National Congress (ANC) or the

Pan-Africanist Congress (PAC) were harassed, tortured or incarcerated. Many leaders of these organisations, including Nelson Mandela (who later became the first president of democratic South Africa), were sent to the infamous Robben Island prison off the coast of Cape Town. A process of negotiations set in motion in 1990 led to the first democratic elections in 1994, when the ANC won control over the government.

Audience taste publics   A term that derives from Bourdieu's classic work *Distinction: A Social Critique of the Judgement of Taste*. Bennett et al., (1999), Ross and Nightingale, (2003) and McGuigan (2004) all variously apply the term to correlate 'taste' choices of cultural products and social and cultural capital, or hierarchies, which audiences bring to their media consumption.

Biological determinism   Reyna (2002, p. 166) points out that this is a form of reductionism that seeks 'to explain a higher level of reality in terms of a lower one', as occurs when people imply that 'what happens at the level of the social and cultural is ultimately explained at the biological level by the genes'.

Brand   Ardvisson (2006) proposes that brand refers to 'A context of consumption constructed by links between material objects, media discourses and life-world environments, and by accumulated consumer affect. This brand-space was furthermore open-ended and incomplete. It constituted a virtual promise or anticipation, to be actualised by the active involvement of consumers themselves. In their ongoing production of a common, consumers create the actual value of the brand: its share in meaningful experiences, its connection to social identities or forms of community: the practices that underpin measurable (and hence valuable) forms of attention' (Ardvisson, 2006, p. 95).

Brand   In this book, the terms 'the brand' or 'branding', are not meant to imply a single thing, or even a single set of processes. To assume that 'the brand' is a single thing would be to mistake the multiple and sometimes divergent layers of activity that have gone into producing the brand. The assumption here instead is that because the brand is a happening fact (Whitehead, 1978), there is a demand—a sociological imperative—for something else to happen yet.

Community radio   AMARC-Europe (1994, p. 4) defines a community radio as 'a non-profit station, currently broadcasting, which offers a service to the community in which it is located, or to which it broadcasts, while promoting the participation of this community in the radio'.

Convergence   A word that describes technological, industrial, cultural and social changes in the ways media circulates within our culture. Some common ideas referenced by the term include the flow of content across multiple media platforms, the cooperation between multiple media industries, the search for new structures of media financing that fall at the interstices between old and new media, and the migratory behaviour of media audiences who would go almost anywhere in search of the kind of entertainment experiences they want. Perhaps most broadly, media convergence refers to a situation in which multiple media systems coexist and where media content flows fluidly across them. Convergence is understood here as an ongoing process or series of intersections between different media systems, not a fixed relationship (from Jenkins, 2006, p. 282).

Deconstruction   The dismantling and reformulation of traditional business structures (Evans and Wurster, 2000, p. 39).

Deliberative democracy   Jon Elster (1998, p. 1) defines deliberation as 'decision-making by discussion among free and equal citizens,' which is not necessarily contradictory to a representative democracy. The argument here is that policy making, legislative debate and decision-making should be more open to input from citizens.

Digital Divide   The severe inequalities that mark access to new media technologies, and that often correlates with other societal divisions and reinforces them. The divide between those that are 'connected' and those that are 'disconnected' exists within countries, for instance between ethnic groups, classes or genders, but also on a global scale, between rich and poor countries. In the context of this book, for instance, there is a Digital Divide between countries in Africa and those in the 'developed' world (Europe, the USA, Japan), but also internally in South Africa between rich and poor citizens. (See Gillwald, 2005, p. 8; Lesame, 2005a, p. 3).

Direct democracy   A system where every citizen votes on every piece of legislation that comes before the parliament. The more extreme versions of direct democracy stress the repressive nature of representative democracies, and argue that representative democracy (party political democratic systems) should be replaced by the self-rule of the oppressed classes.

Disability   What society and culture makes of impairment; disability is shaped by power relations (like other categories such as gender, race, sex, class).

Disintermediation   Evans and Wurster distinguish between 'two basic forms of disintermediation':
- In its first (traditional) form, disintermediation occurs when a 'new competitor attacks the established intermediary by offering greater reach and less richness' (p. 70). The competitor 'typically offers a lower cost version of the product or service. This is a *different* value proposition and not necessarily a superior one. It does not destroy the established intermediary, but it does re-segment the market' (Evans and Wurster, op.cit., pp. 70–1).
- 'The second and more radical form occurs when technology allows for the richness/reach curve to be displaced, allowing new players to offer greater reach and greater richness simultaneously. This poses a far more direct threat to the established intermediary's business model. It threatens not just a re-segmentation of the business, but a total transformation' (ibid, p. 72).

Forms of life   The way a people live, which, according to the philosopher Wittgenstein who first used the term, has a profound affect on the way they understand the world.

Frame This term is used here to refer to the ways the brand is able to limit what is seen, like a window, and what is represented, like a mirror or a screen. The frame determines where we look and what we are likely to see. As a frame, the brand is much more active in communicating with its customers than was the screen in the era of broadcasting. Brands are active frames, like interfaces that present certain information and change what we are able to see in reaction to the button we click and the questions we ask.

Homeland A geographical area designated by the previous white-minority rulers as an area for settlement by black ethnic groups. Homelands were intended to be independent but some groups, including the Zulus, rejected this self-rule as tokenism. Homelands make up a total of 13 per cent of the land in South Africa.

Ideology Louis Althusser defines ideology as the system of ideas and meanings that arise as a consequence of the cultural practices and representations by which people imagine the conditions of their life. The resulting meanings are always socially constructed, since no meanings are natural or inherent to a process, object or event.

Image This term, as used here, refers to the way brand logos operate like computer desktop icons or 'short cuts'. The brand represents itself by its logo. The logo in turn immediately brings to mind a reservoir of cultural knowledge about the brand that has been cultivated through the marketing of its previous products. Sometimes an imagined history is invented and 'sold' to audiences through an advertising campaign. This set of associations is then used to promote new products and to drive new sales.

Impairment An injury, illness or condition that is held to cause or held likely to cause a long-term effect or limitation on appearance or function within the individual that differs from the norm.

Industrial society A society where position depends on social relations under capitalism.

Information and communication technologies (ICTs) The range of communications technologies associated with the distribution of information.

Information society A society where access to and manipulation of information becomes the key determinant of one's place in society.

Intellectual property rights (IPRs) Rights that arise from copyright laws that protect owners from the unauthorised use of their creative or 'intellectual property' works, for example, audiovisual content or other kinds of cultural products.

Interaction 'The exchange and negotiation of meaning between two or more participants located with social contexts' (O'Sullivan, 1994, p. 154).

Interactivity The *process* whereby interaction occurs.

Internet governance The development and application by governments, the private sector and civil society, in their respective roles, of shared principles, norms, rules, decision-making procedures and programs that shape the evolution and use of the Internet (Butt, 2005).

Interpassivity   The 'Pavlovian interactivity of stimulus and response' (Penny, 1995, p. 54).

IPTV   The distribution of video services over Internet Protocol networks (Ofcom, 2005–06).

Mediascapes   'Mediascapes ... provide ... large and complex repertoires of images, narratives, and ethnoscapes to viewers throughout the world, in which the world of commodities and the worlds of news and politics are profoundly mixed. What this means is that many audiences around the world experience the media themselves as a complicated and interconnected repertoire of print, celluloid, electronic screens, and billboards. The lines between the realistic and the fictional landscapes they see are blurred, so that the farther away these audiences are from the direct experiences of metropolitan life, the more likely they are to construct imagined worlds that are chimerical, aesthetic, even fantastic objects, particularly if assessed by the criteria of some other perspective, some other imagined world' (Appadurai, 1996, p. 35).

Medical model   The position that sees disability as a defect, handicap or health problem located in an individual.

Medium   A casual glance at any dictionary draws attention to the multiple meanings of the word 'medium': as something in between or intermediate; a middle state or condition; a method or way of expressing something. The sense in which it is used in this chapter draws primarily on this last meaning. Just as money tells us how much a given commodity is worth, the brand tells us how much to value it. So, for example, vintage clothing stores trade primarily in second-hand goods with designer labels—a particular item may no longer command its original price, but the brand continues to communicate information about the cultural significance of the object.

In the new media environment, brands are able to actively engage their customers and potential customers using email newsletters, product promotions, online forums, games and competitions to push consumption. Brands are colonising the online environment and borrowing characteristic forms of online communication to achieve their ends.

Meritocracy   A meritocracy is a social order in which each individual acquires social status on the basis of merit: skill, ability and effort, rather than gender or class. Superficially a fairer society, the notion is in reality hypothetical due to complexities of defining merit and tends to cement social position, consigning 'non-elite' members of society to unfulfilling manual labour.

Neo-liberalism   The rival of doctrines of the 'free market' in the United States in the late 1970s, and a social and economic theory that argues that completely free and open markets are the best way of ordering society. Thus it is a return to a once discredited liberalism in political economics, the nineteenth-century espousal of *laissez faire* economics for free trade in an international division of labour, and minimal state intervention within the nation. For governments in the West, from the 1940s through to the 1970s, it was the conventional wisdom that capitalism had to be managed by the state, and that rewards needed to be equalised through welfare entitlements in order to maintain social cohesion (see McGuigan, 2005, p. 230).

Network neutrality   The proposal by a coalition of private sector and public interest groups that no website's traffic should be privileged over any other site.

New media   The definition of what should be included under this term is often debated. In the context of this book, this term will refer mostly to the Internet, email and mobile (or cell) phones.

Next Generation Networks (NGNs)   NGN is partly a marketing term but it is also a concept used to describe the replacement of 'legacy' fixed copper wire distribution networks with a more diverse range of higher speed and capacity, mobile and 'nomadic', fibre, wireless and satellite networks. At the heart of the concept is the integration of existing separate voice and data networks into a simpler more flexible network using packet switch and Internet protocols. This will enable voice, text and visual messages to be carried on the same network and for each type of message to be responded to in any of these formats on that network.

Participation is defined as follows: 'participation implies a higher level of public involvement in communication systems. It includes the involvement of the public in the production process and also in the management and planning of communication systems. Participation may be no more than representation and consultation of the public in decision-making' (from Servaes, 1999, p. 85).

Participatory media regime   A set of formal and informal rules that regulate the operation of the media system.

Political parallelism   The extent to which the structure of the media system parallels the political party system. It can be seen to operate in a number of ways including through:
- *Media content*   the extent to which the different media reflect distinct political orientations in their news and current affairs reporting, and sometimes also in their entertainment content.
- *Organisational connections:* between media and political parties or other kinds of organisations, including trade unions, cooperatives, churches.
- *Media personnel:* the tendency for people working in the media industries to be active in political life—including the tendency for the career paths of journalists and other media personnel to be shaped by their political affiliations.
- *Media audiences:* the partisanship of the people who will read and watch media depending on its political orientation.
- *Journalistic role orientations and practices:* for example, more or less of a 'publicist' or provider of 'balanced' or 'neutral' information, or alternatively, a commentary and analysis approach (Hallin and Mancini, 2004, pp. 27–8).

Poverty and inequality   Poverty can be absolute or relative. How thresholds of poverty are defined is contentious—what are basic minimum living standards? Relative poverty is defined in terms of inequalities: the poor in a wealthy country are likely to be better off than the poor in a developing country.

Public sphere   'By the "public sphere" we mean first of all a realm of our social life in which something approaching public opinion can be formed. Access is guaranteed to all citizens. A portion of the public sphere comes into being in every conversation in which private individuals assemble to form a public body' (Habermas, 1984, p. 49).

RSS (or Really Simple Syndication) feeds   An easy way to be alerted when content that interests you appears on your favourite websites. Instead of visiting a particular website to browse for new articles and features, RSS automatically tells you when something new is posted online.

Self-management is the most advanced form of participation. In this case, 'the public exercises the power of decision-making within communication enterprises and is also fully involved in the formulation of communication policies and plans' (from Servaes, 1999, p. 85).

Semantic reductionism   Semantic reductionism is used here to refer to the way contemporary word usage may result in a significant loss of complexity in the meaning of a given.

Silo structures   This term refers to the separate broadcasting, telecommunications, publishing, and information technology industries that can be described as 'pre-convergence' and bound up with the previous industrial mass production organisations of the 'Fordist' period.

Social bookmarking   del.icio.us is a social bookmarking website, which means it is designed to allow you to store and share bookmarks on the Web, instead of inside your browser. This has several advantages.

First, you can get to your bookmarks from anywhere, no matter whether you're at home, at work, in a library, or on a friend's computer.

Second, you can share your bookmarks publicly, so your friends, co-workers, and other people can view them for reference, amusement, collaboration, or anything else. (Note that you can also mark bookmarks on del.icio.us as private—only viewable by you—if you like.)

Third, you can find other people on del.icio.us who have interesting bookmarks and add their links to your own collection. Everyone on del.icio.us chooses to save their bookmarks for a reason. You have access to the links that everyone wants to remember. You can see whether two people have chosen to remember a link, or whether it was useful enough for a thousand people to remember—which may help you find things that are useful for you, too (http://del.icio.us/about/; accessed 10 October 2006).

Social model   The position that sees disability as socially created through structures of oppression and exclusion; social model theorists draw a distinction between impairment (the bedrock biological or bodily condition) and disability (regarded as the social construction of impairment).

Social movements   These can be described in this context as groups of people representing the marginalised in society, such as the poor or the homeless, and who challenge state authority and the dominant socio- economic and political order by insisting on social change around specific issues. These groups aim to effect social transformation outside of formal political means. Social movements seek to change the current social or political order, rather than just attempting to improve conditions through short-term changes like the replacement of a political leader (Van de Donk et al., 2004, p. 3).

Technological determinism   A belief that technology develops independently of society and in so doing is the central cause of consequent social 'impacts'. Widely challenged, nevertheless the idea is found in many historical accounts of social change and lies behind countless predictions of future social trends.

Technological Determinism   The belief that media technologies possess certain inherent qualities that determine their influence in society. A more culturalistic perspective on the use of new media technologies would be to see them as part of social development and part of social and cultural practices (c.f. Lie, 2005, p. 123).

Technological fetishism   An almost supernatural belief in the power of technology to change the world. It is a more extreme version of 'technological determinism'.

Telecentre   In South Africa, a telecentre is a facility offering communication services such as email and Internet services, but also basic telephony, typing, photocopying and faxing.

Television Without Frontiers (TVWF) directive: For the full text, historical context, recent debates and amendments see http://www.euractiv.com/en/infosociety/twf-television-frontiers/article-117550

Third sector/community media   Community media is funded by subscriptions and grants and run mainly by volunteers. It is a medium that offers 'a clear alternative' to the mainstream. While many independent media producers offer perspectives that differ little from the mainstream, there are other elements that distinguish them such as intent, focus, size etc. We see the community media sector as a cultural resource that facilitates cultural citizenship in ways that differentiate it from other media.

Transcendence   The process of transcendence, which can be traced from the philosophical writings of Immanuel Kant (1724–1804), has been called 'transcendental idealism'. George Herbert Mead (1863–1931) explained Kant's position like this: '[Kant's] doctrine has been called also transcendental idealism, because it implies that the ideas, the meaning of the world is to be accounted for not by the world itself as it presents itself immediately to our senses and thought, but by running those forms of thought, those ideas and meanings back to the nature that knows them' (George Herbert Mead, 1909, para 11).

Transmedia storytelling   A transmedia story unfolds across multiple media platforms, with each new text making a distinctive and valuable contribution to the whole. In the ideal form of transmedia storytelling each medium does what it does best—so that a story might be introduced in a film, expanded through television, novels, and comics, and its world might be explored through game play or experienced as an amusement park attraction. Each franchise entry needs to be self-contained so you don't need to have seen the film to enjoy the game and vice versa. Any given product is a point of entry into the franchise as a whole. Reading across the media sustains a depth of experience that motivates more consumption. Redundancy burns up fan interest and causes franchises to fail (Jenkins, 2006, p. 96).

Universal Service Obligation (USO)   USO arrangements refer to the fundamental access and service provision regimes offered by networks that have traditionally been regulated by governments in developed countries. USO arrangements vary from country to country, but, in general, the current understanding of the term is that all users regardless of location can access quality voice service at an affordable price.

Universal service   Access to ICTs within all individual dwellings. It implies a level of resources and infrastructure not usually present in the developing world; universal access is access to shared facilities and thus requires that users must leave their homes if they wish to make use of the ICTs.

Voice over Internet Protocol or **VoIP**   This works by converting your voice into a digital signal (using Internet Protocol packets) that travels over the Internet via a broadband connection. Using specific software, VoIP converts the voice signal from the caller's telephone into a digital signal then converts it back at the other end to enable voice communication with anyone with a phone number. Typically, callers use the software on their computer, a handset connected to their broadband modem, or certain kinds of mobile (cell) handsets, to send and receive calls. VoIP offers several benefits including cost savings and nomadicity—or the ability to use the service in different locations.

Index